P9-AFQ-360

VOICES of WISDOM

Other books by Francine Klagsbrun

Married People: Staying Together in the Age of Divorce
Too Young To Die: Youth and Suicide
Free To Be . . . You and Me (Editor)
Freedom Now! The Story of the Abolitionists

Illustrated by Mark Podwal

JONATHAN DAVID PUBLISHERS, INC.
MIDDLE VILLAGE, NEW YORK 11379

Jewish ideals and ethics for everyday living

FRANCINE KLAGSBRUN

 Originally published in the United States by Pantheon Books, a division of Random House, Inc., New York, and simultaneously in Canada by Random House of Canada Limited, Toronto.

This edition published in 1986 by Jonathan David Publishers, Inc., Middle Village, New York 11379, by arrangement with Pantheon Books, a division of Random House, Inc.

1989 1988 1987 1986
10 9 8 7 6 5 4 3 2 1

ISBN 0-8246-0320-4

Since this copyright page cannot accommodate all permissions acknowledgments, they are to be found on the following pages.

LIBRARY OF CONGRESS CATALOGING IN PUBLICATION DATA
Klagsbrun, Francine.
Voices of Wisdom.

Bibliography: p.
Includes index.
1. Jewish way of life—Addresses, essays, lectures.
2. Ethics, Jewish—Addresses, essays, lectures.
I. Title.
BM723.K52 296.3'85 79-3314

Designed by Susan Mitchell

Manufactured in the United States of America

Grateful acknowledgment is made to the following publishers and authors for permission to use copyrighted material:

Bloch Publishing Company: "Thirteen Principles of the Faith." Reprinted by permission of Bloch Publishing Company from *The Authorized Daily Prayerbook*, revised edition, by Dr. Joseph H. Hertz. Copyright 1948 by Ruth Hecht. Copyright renewed 1975 by Ruth Hecht. Excerpts from *Jewish Medical Ethics* by Dr. Immanuel Jakobovits. Copyright 1959 and 1975 by Dr. Immanuel Jakobovits. Reprinted by permission of Bloch Publishing Company.

Cambridge University Press and Oxford University Press: Excerpts from the books of Ecclesiasticus, I Maccabees and II Maccabees in *The New English Bible*. Copyright © the Delegates of the Oxford University Press and the Syndics of the Cambridge University Press, 1961, 1970. Reprinted by permission.

Gerson D. Cohen: Excerpt from "The Blessing of Assimilation in Jewish History," commencement address at Hebrew Teachers College, June 1966.

Columbia University Press: Excerpts from *Fables of a Jewish Aesop*, translated by Moses Hadas. New York: Columbia University Press, 1967. By permission of the publisher.

Commentary: Excerpt from Richard L. Rubenstein in "The State of Jewish Belief," vol. 2, no. 42 (August 1966). Reprinted by permission of *Commentary* and Richard L. Rubenstein. All rights reserved.

Conservative Judaism: Excerpt from "The Other Half: Women in the Jewish Tradition" by Paula E. Hyman; excerpt from "Women's Liberation in the Talmudic Period" by Judith Hauptman, both in vol. 26, no. 4 (Summer 1972). Copyright © 1972 by the Rabbinical Assembly. Excerpt from "Abortion and Ethics" by David M. Feldman, vol. 29, no. 4 (Summer 1975). Copyright © 1975 the Rabbinical Assembly. Reprinted by permission of the Rabbinical Assembly.

Crown Publishers, Inc.: Excerpt from "I'm Lucky—I'm an Orphan" in *The Old Country* by Sholom Aleichem. Copyright © 1946, 1974 by Crown Publishers, Inc. Used by permission of Crown Publishers, Inc.

Doubleday & Company, Inc.: Excerpt from *A Bintel Brief* by Isaac Metzker. Translation and Introduction Copyright © 1971 by Isaac Metzker. Reprinted by permission of Doubleday & Co., Inc.

Farrar, Straus & Giroux, Inc.: Excerpts from *Love & Sex* by Robert Gordis. Copyright © 1978 by Robert Gordis. Excerpts from *The Insecurity of Freedom* by Abraham Joshua Heschel. Copyright © 1959, 1960, 1963, 1964, 1966 by Abraham Joshua Heschel. Excerpt from *A Passion for Truth* by Abraham Joshua Heschel. Copyright © 1973 by Sylvia Heschel as executrix of the estate of Abraham Joshua Heschel. Excerpt from "Reflections on Death" by Abraham Joshua Heschel. Copyright © 1973 by Sylvia Heschel as executrix of the estate of Abraham Joshua Heschel. This selection originally appeared in *Conservative Judaism*, vol. 28, no. 1 (Fall 1973). Excerpt from *Night* by Elie Wiesel. Reprinted with the permission of Hill and Wang (now a division of Farrar, Straus & Giroux, Inc.). Translated from the French by Stella Rodway. © Les Editions de Minuit, 1958. English translation © MacGibbon and Kee, 1960.

Feldheim Publishers Ltd., Jerusalem—New York: Excerpts from *Book of Knowledge* by Maimonides, translated by Moses Hyamson. Excerpts from *Duties of the Heart* by Bahya Ibn Paquda, translated by Moses Hyamson. By permission.

Hebrew Union College: Excerpts from "The Maimonidean Code of Benevolence" by Abraham Cronbach (translation of Maimonides's "Eight Degrees of Charity"), *Hebrew Union College Annual*, vol. 20. © 1947 by the Hebrew Union College.

Jewish Publication Society of America: Excerpts from *The Torah, A New Translation.* Copyright © 1962. Excerpts from *The Prophets, A New Translation.* Copyright © 1978. Excerpts from *The Five Megilloth, A New Translation.* Copyright © 1969. Excerpts from *The Book of Psalms, A New Translation.* Copyright © 1972. Excerpts from *The Holy Scriptures According to the Masoretic Text.* Copyright © 1917, 1955. Excerpts from *Mekilta de Rabbi Ishmael.* Copyright © 1933, 1961. Excerpts from *The Path of the Upright* by Moses Hayyim Luzzatto. Copyright © 1936. Excerpts from *Hebrew Ethical Wills* by Israel Abrahams. Copyright © 1926, 1954. Excerpts from *A Treasury of Responsa* by Solomon Freehof. Copyright © 1962. Excerpts from *Ma'aseh Book* vol. 2, by Moses Gaster. Copyright © 1934. Excerpts from Arthur E. Green, "A Contemporary Approach to Jewish Sexuality" and from David M. Feldman, "The Scope of Tradition and Its Application," in *The Second Jewish Catalog.* Copyright © 1976. All materials copyrighted by and used through the courtesy of the Jewish Publication Society of America.

Judaism: Excerpt from "Greater Love Hath No Man" by Louis Jacobs, vol. 6, no. 1 (Winter 1957). Copyright © 1957 The American Jewish Congress. Excerpts from "Sin, Crime, Sickness or Alternative Life Style?" by Hershel J. Matt, vol. 27, no. 1 (Winter 1978). Copyright © 1978 The American Jewish Congress.

Keter Publishing House: Excerpt from "Judaism and the Modern Attitude to Homosexuality" by Norman Lamm, in *Encyclopedia Judaica Yearbook* (1974). Copyright © 1974 by Keter Publishing House Jerusalem Ltd.

Ktav Publishing House, Inc.: Excerpts from *The Holy Letter of Nahmanides*, translated by Seymour J. Cohen. Copyright © 1976 Ktav Publishing House, Inc. Excerpt from *Faith After the Holocaust* by Eliezer Berkovits. Copyright © 1973 Ktav Publishing House, Inc. Excerpt from *Contemporary Halakhic Problems* by J. David Bleich. Copyright © 1977 Ktav Publishing House, Inc.

Lilith: The Independent Jewish Women's Magazine: Excerpts from "The Population Panic" by Shirley Frank. Copyright © 1978 by Lilith Publications, Inc. All rights reserved.

Macmillan Publishing Co., Inc.: Excerpts from Maimonides's "Letter on Astrology," translated by Ralph Lerner, in *Medieval Political Philosophy: A Sourcebook*, edited by Ralph Lerner and Muhsin Mahdi. Copyright © 1963 by The Free Press of Glencoe, a division of The Macmillan Company. Reprinted by permission of Macmillan Publishing Co., Inc.

New York University Press: Excerpt from *God's Presence in History: Jewish Affirmations and Philosophical Reflections* by Emile Fackenheim. © 1970 by New York University, published by New York University Press.

Philosophical Library, Inc.: Excerpts from *The Preservation of Youth* by Maimonides, translated by Hirsch L. Gordon. Copyright © 1958 by the Philosophical Library, Inc.

G. P. Putnam's Sons: Excerpt from "Boaz the Teacher," in *Some Laughter, Some Tears* by Sholom Aleichem. Copyright © 1968 by the Children of Sholom Aleichem. Reprinted by permission of G. P. Putnam's Sons.

Schocken Books, Inc.: Excerpts from *An Autobiography* by Solomon Maimon, edited and with an epilogue by Moses Hadas. Copyright 1947 by Schocken Books, Inc. Copyright renewed © 1975 by Schocken Books, Inc. Excerpts from *Tales of the Hasidim: Early Masters* by Martin Buber. Copyright 1947 by Schocken Books, Inc. Copyright renewed © 1975 by Schocken Books, Inc. Excerpts from *Tales of the Hasidim: Later Masters* by Martin Buber. Copyright © 1948 by Schocken Books, Inc. Copyright renewed © 1975 by Schocken Books, Inc. Excerpts from *Franz Rosenzweig: His Life and Thought* presented by Nahum N. Glatzer. Copyright © 1953, 1961 by Schocken Books, Inc. All reprinted by permission of Schocken Books, Inc.

Charles Scribner's Sons: Excerpts from *I and Thou* by Martin Buber, translated by Walter Kaufmann. Copyright © 1970 Charles Scribner's Sons. Courtesy of the publisher.

Sh'ma: A Journal of Jewish Responsibility: Excerpt from "When Justice Demands, Tradition Changes" by Sarah Roth Lieberman, vol. 9, no. 164 (December 22, 1978). Reprinted by permission of the publisher.

Seymour Siegel: Excerpt from "The Brown Baby and Jewish Tradition," in *United Synagogue Review* (Fall 1978). Excerpt from "The Ethical Dilemmas of Modern Medicine," in *United Synagogue Review* (Fall 1976).

Tradition: Excerpt from "The Jewish Attitude Toward Abortion" by Fred Rosner, vol. 10, no. 2 (Winter 1968). Copyright © 1968 by the Rabbinical Council of America.

University of Chicago Press: Excerpts from the translation of Job in *The Book of God and Man* by Robert Gordis. Copyright © 1965 by Robert Gordis. Reprinted by permission of the University of Chicago Press.

University of Wisconsin Press: Excerpt from *The Jews and the Crusaders* by Shlomo Eidelberg. Madison: The University of Wisconsin Press. Copyright © 1977 by the Regents of the University of Wisconsin.

Viking Penguin, Inc.: Henrietta Szold's Letter to Haym Peretz in *Henrietta Szold: Life and Letters* by Marvin Lowenthal. Copyright 1942 The Viking Press, Inc., © renewed 1970 by Herman C. Emer and Harry L. Shapiro, Executor for the Estate of Marvin Lowenthal. Reprinted by permission of Viking Penguin, Inc.

Rosamond Fischer Weiss: Excerpt from *Memoirs of Glueckel of Hameln,* translated by Marvin Lowenthal. Copyright © 1932, 1960 by Rosamond Fischer Weiss. Reprinted by permission.

Yale University Press: Excerpts from *The Fathers According to Rabbi Nathan,* translated by Judah Goldin. Copyright 1955 by Yale University Press. Excerpts from *Pesikta Rabbati*, translated by William G. Braude. Copyright © 1968 by Yale University. Excerpts from *The Tractate Mourning*, translated by Dov Zlotnick. Copyright © 1966 by Yale University. Excerpts from *The Code of Maimonides: Book IV—Women*, translated by Isaac Klein. Copyright © 1972 by Yale University Press; *Book V—Holiness*, translated by Louis I. Rabinowitz and Philip Grossman. Copyright © 1965 by Yale University; *Book XI—Torts*, translated by Hyman Klein. Copyright, 1954, by Yale University Press; *Book XII—Acquisitions*, translated by Isaac Klein. Copyright, 1951, by Yale University Press; *Book XIII—Civil Laws*, translated by Jacob J. Rabinowitz. Copyright, 1949, by Yale University; *Book XIV—Judges*, translated by Abraham M. Hershman. Copyright, 1949, by Yale University Press.

Contents

Surely, this instruction which I enjoin upon you this day is not too baffling for you, nor is it beyond reach. It is not in heaven, that you should say, "Who among us can go up to heaven and get it for us and impart it to us, that we may observe it?"

Neither is it beyond the sea, that you should say, "Who among us can cross to the other side of the sea and get it for us and impart it to us, that we may observe it?"

No, the thing is very close to you, in your mouth and in your heart, to observe it.

—Deuteronomy, chapter 30, verses 11–14

For my parents, my teachers,
Benjamin and Anna Lifton,
and for
Sarah
so you may "teach them to your children"

Acknowledgments

My debts to teachers, colleagues, friends, and family are enormous, and even printed acknowledgments cannot adequately thank them for the help and support that made this sometimes overwhelming project a reality.

Dr. Gerson D. Cohen set aside many hours, despite his grueling schedule at that time as Chancellor of the Jewish Theological Seminary, to review the entire book in manuscript form. His brilliant insights, his concrete criticisms, and his thoughtful reflections added immeasurably to the final work and to my own knowledge. Whatever errors may still have crept in are, of course, my own. I'm deeply grateful for all that he's done; he has always been and will always be my teacher as well as my friend.

Rabbi Seymour Siegel, Chairman of the Committee on Jewish Law and Standards of the Rabbinical Assembly, could not have been more generous in directing me to source materials, verifying legal matters, and sharing his own writings, course preparations, and thoughts with me. Rabbi Wolfe Kelman, Executive Vice-President of the Rabbinical Assembly, graciously allowed me to review all the files of Rabbinical Assembly responsa, including many unpublished questions and answers, and Rabbi Malcolm Stern, Director of Placements of the Central Conference of American Rabbis, kindly made that organization's responsa files available to me. Dr. Hayim Leaf, professor of Hebrew literature at Yeshiva University, translated some of the most difficult early responsa and commentaries in the book. Lawrence Kobrin gave me the benefit of his extensive knowledge of secular and Jewish law, and led me to many useful sources. David C. Whitney's ideas, comments, and editorial suggestions were invaluable, as were his patience and encouragement. And the staff of the Jewish Theological Seminary Library were consistently diligent and considerate in suggesting and locating books and articles.

At all stages in the preparation of this book, my Pantheon editor, Tom Engelhardt, was a delight to work with—wonderfully perceptive and exacting in his editing, cutting, and organizing. I thank him and his assistant, Nan Graham, for their commitment to the work; and Donna Bass, who copyedited the manuscript, for her care and dedication.

During the years I worked on this compilation, my husband and daughter must surely have felt displaced by my incessant involvement with sages and scholars of another age, and I'm so appreciative of their patient understanding and sustaining good humor throughout. And then, special gratitude goes to my father, who made countless suggestions, researched sources, checked citations, and—more than anything—inspired the love that led to this book.

—Francine Klagsbrun
New York City

On Jewish wisdom and ethics

For centuries, a child reared in a Jewish home grew up in a world defined by tradition. In that world, heroes and heroines of the Bible and Talmud were as much a part of the child's life as were the men and women who dwelled in the neighborhood. In that world, an ancient maxim came as easily to a parent's lips as did a lesson in cleanliness or good behavior. In that world, scholars and sages, confronted with issues for which they could find no legal precedent, would often advise one another to "go out and see how the people are accustomed to act." For in that world, the customs of the people and the teachings of the sages were linked one to the other.

The world in which I lived as a child was not very different from that world of tradition. In my home, the Bible, the Talmud, and books of Hebrew literature stood on bookshelves side by side with best-selling novels and contemporary biographies. In my school—a small Hebrew day school for girls—Judaic studies were not just part of the curriculum; they were a way of life. We learned the concept of loving one's neighbor, for example, from a biblical command, from a song we sang quoting the words of the famous scholar Rabbi Akiva, from a legend we read about the patient sage Hillel the Elder, and from the simple act of carrying coins to school on Fridays to place in the charity box that stood in every classroom as a reminder that giving charity is the finest expression of loving your neighbor.

We studied the Bible, struggling to understand its difficult Hebrew, to grasp the meaning behind its terse images. And when, as a class, we completed a book of the Bible, we celebrated the event with a party. We could barely contain our excitement as a student was called on to read and explain the final verse. Before she could even finish, we would rush to the open door of our classroom and shout at the top of our voices the traditional words of completion said in the synagogue: *hazak, hazak, v'nithazek* ("Be strong, be strong, and let us strengthen one another") for all the school to hear. Laughing, filled with pride, we then settled into our celebration. Young girls, at the brink of puberty, we looked forward to that moment at the classroom door no less than we did to a school dance or picnic. We had learned early not only the sheer joy of intellectual accomplishment but also the deep satisfaction of mastering the texts of our tradition.

I moved on from that world. We all did, on to college and graduate school; we learned about other people's religions, their myths and satisfactions. We married, had children, entered professions, and became involved in social movements. The exuberant young voices at the classroom door dimmed to a nostalgic memory.

Yet in my own life, the echo of those voices never completely faded. I continued my Hebrew studies at the Jewish Theological Seminary; and later, even while I became increasingly immersed in career and family, in friendships far removed from the homogeneous circle of childhood, I stayed close to the tradition. Apart from religious ceremonies and rituals, apart from holidays and festivals, what endured most meaningfully for me were the texts and teachings, and the power of their ethical principles and practical insights. That core of values that is the essence of Judaism was always there for me—balanced, within reach, yet motivated by inspired ideals; and I found that these values grew rather than diminished in meaning, even as I grew and changed, even as all of society was transformed.

It is with the values, the wisdom, and the moral teachings of Judaism that this book is concerned. Neither a compendium of Jewish law nor a guide to religious practices, it aims at presenting the Jewish ethic as a living, vital resource upon which we—perhaps the most determinedly secular of all generations—can continue to draw as did past generations, steeped as they were in religious belief.

The laws, legends, maxims, and anecdotes gathered here hold up to us a vision of how to live. On one level, it is a practical vision, emerging from knowledge and experience accumulated over thousands of years. We find among these writings and teachings ways of improving our relationships to others, of getting along better with our children, of protecting our bodies and preserving our health. But on another level, it is a vision of human possibilities, opening up perspectives that have become increasingly shut off from our lives. To our ever-deepening absorption in self, these teachings point to ways of reaching beyond ourselves and outside our own needs. To our unrelenting drive for power and success, they show us how to pull back, to take stock of the meaning and purpose of our existence. To our rootlessness, they offer a firm base built upon family, community, and shared responsibilities.

Because this book is intended as a guide to living, it is organized around such life themes as marriage, sex, health, education, and work. Like the Jewish ethic itself, it begins with the individual—with you and yourself—and moves outward to encompass broader issues and more universal themes. It focuses on life, but it ends with the inevitability of death.

The criteria for choosing the selections in the book were both intrinsic interest, and insights and applicability to life today. Within each section, the passages are presented the way people enveloped in the tradition have come to know them—the way I came to know them as a child—not in chronological order but as a totality, a broad tapestry whose parts are intricately interwoven. So, a talmudic parable, an old folktale, and a twelfth-century pietistic lesson might be juxtaposed in response to a problem, and arguments might rage across centuries and distant lands. Time becomes less important here than the ideas and attitudes that grew and became intertwined with one another.

But time is, of course, important in the sweep of Jewish life, and events do take place within a historical framework. It's useful to keep that framework in mind as you read this book, with its many passages that interpret and, sometimes, contradict one another. It's important, too, to be familiar with the great leaders of Judaism and to know something of the communities that created its classic texts. Jewish culture has shifted in time and space, taking on new forms from each civilization with which it has come into contact, yet it has remained true to itself and to the sources that nurtured it.

The Hebrew Bible has always been the lifeblood of the tradition. From it flowed the laws and moral precepts that defined Jewish attitudes, and to it were brought the loves and longings of a people who clung tenaciously to its teachings in spite of all obstacles. Jews generally do not refer to it as the Old Testament; for them, it is the only Testament. It consists of three major divisions, all represented in this anthology: The Five Books of Moses, or the Torah, revealed to Moses at Mount Sinai, according to tradition; The Prophets, including among its books the lofty moral teachings of Isaiah, Jeremiah, Ezekiel, and other prophets; and The Writings, or Hagiographa, consisting of the scrolls of Song of Songs, Ruth, Lamentations, Ecclesiastes, and Esther, and the books of Psalms, Proverbs, Job, Daniel, Ezra and Nehemiah, and Chronicles.

All together, these works make up the sacred texts of Judaism. But even in biblical days, a body of oral teachings began to grow up around the written codes, elaborating on their rulings, explaining difficult concepts, and adapting the law they laid down to changing social conditions. These interpretations and explanations are known as the oral law. They were not written down for generations to distinguish them from the holy Scriptures.

Of the sages who interpreted and expanded on the written law, Ezra is the first whose name we know. The book bearing his name describes the building of the Second Temple, about 2,500 years ago. The anonymous scribes and sages who continued his work were called *soferim* and were later referred to in the Talmud as "Men of the Great Assembly." The techniques they and scholars who followed them used to apply biblical principles to problems not explicitly covered by the Bible are known as *midrash*, meaning "inquiry" or "consultation." It is a term that has come to refer both to their method of ferreting out biblical meaning and to collections of such interpretive works. There are two kinds of *midrash: midrash halakha* are legal interpretations of scriptural texts, while *midrash aggadah* include homilies, anecdotes, parables, tales, and maxims aimed at making the Bible a living, meaningful part of each person's life. Such works as the *Mekhilta, Sifra*, and *Sifrei*, cited throughout the chapters that follow, are collections of *halakhic midrashim* (plural for *midrash*); the *Midrash Rabbah*, such as *Genesis Rabbah* and *Exodus Rabbah*, are made up of *aggadic midrashim*.

The oral law became a major force in Jewish life under the leadership of the Pharisees, a group of teachers and scholars who rose to prominence about 160 B.C.E. (The abbreviations B.C.E., meaning "Before the Common Era," and C.E., the "Common Era," are generally used in writings on Jewish topics instead of B.C. and A.D.) The teachings and interpretations of the Pharisees formed the main line of Jewish tradition as we know it today, and from the Pharisaic background came the great sages of the Mishnah and Talmud whose words appear again and again in the following pages. The Pharisees, many of whose members came from among the working classes and tradespeople, opposed the Sadducees, the aristocratic and priestly groups who ministered the Temple rituals. After the destruction of the Second Temple, in the year 70, the Sadducees lost their priestly functions and disappeared as a group, leaving the Pharisees as both the teachers of the Jewish community and the leaders of Jewish society.

The Pharisees regarded themselves and were regarded by the people as the spiritual heirs of the prophets. They believed that the oral law, along with the written law, had been revealed to Moses at Mount Sinai, and that the right to expound and interpret it had come down to them through Moses and Joshua, and from them through the judges, prophets, and scribes. In their lessons and in their lives, they emphasized purity of thought and conduct, care for the downtrodden and needy, and an egalitarianism that credited each person for his or her own deeds and knowledge rather than for inherited wealth or family position.

Although many of the beliefs of the Pharisees formed the basis for Christian doctrines, the view of them that has come to us through Christian writings is a negative one of haughty and self-righteous hypocrites, a view that may have been motivated by the desire of the young Christian church to break away and distinguish itself from its mother religion. In Jewish thought, the Pharisees are still revered as symbols of moral excellence and commitment to social justice.

The first great document that grew out of the oral tradition was the Mishnah. Tightly written, in crisp, clear Hebrew, the Mishnah is a compilation of legal decisions and rulings that, along with dissenting opinions, had accumulated over the centuries. The work is divided into six sections, called orders, and these, in turn, are subdivided into tractates—sixty-three in all. The most famous tractate of the Mishnah is the only one that includes no legalistic material:

Pirke Avot, the *Ethics of the Fathers*, a collection of maxims and statements that summarize what the rabbis consider to be the good life, a life governed by ethical values.

Many of the sages referred to in the Mishnah are known as *tannaim*, from the word *tanna*, meaning "a teacher of the law." Outstanding among them are the two sages you will meet many times in this book—Hillel and Shammai, who probably lived in the period just before and after the beginning of our era, and are usually considered the first of the *tannaim*. Their names appear without the titles "rabbi" or "rav," which came into use some years before the destruction of the Second Temple and were applied to *tannaim* of later generations such as Rabbi Akiva. Descendants of Hillel served as leaders of the Jewish people and heads of the Sanhedrin, the central legislative body in Palestine, for more than four hundred years. They were awarded the honorary title of "rabban," which means "our master."

Rabbi Judah the Prince (honored by being called simply Rabbi) compiled and edited the Mishnah at the beginning of the third century. Although from then on some written versions of it probably existed, it continued to be taught orally, recited in classrooms by students noted for their phenomenal memories—"baskets full of books" the sages loved to call them.

Even before the editing of the Mishnah ended, scholars were discussing, interpreting, and expanding on its teachings. These later scholars, known as *amoraim*, or expositors, analyzed the Mishnah the way the earlier *tannaim* had analyzed the Bible. Their discussions, laws, interpretations, and legends make up the Gemara; and together, the Mishnah and Gemara form the Talmud. (The name Talmud is also used, as it often is in this volume, for the Gemara alone; literally, Gemara is the Aramaic term for the Hebrew word Talmud.)

The story of the evolution of the Talmud is a tale of two countries, Palestine and Babylonia. After the death of Rabbi Judah the Prince, the power of Palestinian scholars began to wane as the country faced severe economic and political problems. At that time, many Jews emigrated to Babylonia, where a cohesive Jewish community had existed since the days of the Babylonian Exile. The influence of Babylonian scholarship became firmly established when, in the early 200s, Rabbi Abba ben Aivu, who was called Rav, opened an academy in Sura that attracted thousands of disciples from both Babylonia and Palestine. That academy and others at Nehardea and Pumbedita became major centers in the development of the Babylonian Talmud. Palestinian scholars also produced a Talmud, which was compiled a hundred years or so before the redaction of the Babylonian Talmud about the year 500. Generally called the Jerusalem Talmud, it does not bear the authority of the Babylonian one. When used alone, the name Talmud usually refers to the Babylonian Talmud.

The world of the Talmud is a world of disagreement and reconciliation, of beautiful legends and cut-and-dry legalisms, of precise logic and obscure arguments, of life in all its profundities and trivialities. Written in two languages—Aramaic, the popular language of the time, and Hebrew, to a lesser extent—the Talmud follows the organization of orders and tractates in the Mishnah but is much broader in scope. Ceremonial and ritual law, ethical principles, science, medicine, magic and folklore, sex, marriage, and child rearing, business and community matters—all are encompassed within this monumental work. In many ways, its discussions resemble the give and take of an academy of learning in which a lecture and ensuing debate, begun around a passage in the Mishnah, is carried from one subject to another by association and often ends up far afield from the original topic.

The Talmud has been compared to a sea, rich in the materials of life yet formless and unfathomable to those untrained in its ways. It is not true, as some people believe, that the talmudic masters were interested only in argument for the sake of argument. The Talmud has a logic of its own and a system of rules by which decisions and conclusions are arrived at. When the scholars Rav and Samuel disagree, for example, Rav's opinion is accepted on matters of ritual and Samuel's on matters of property. When Rabbi Meir and Rabbi Judah differ, Rabbi Judah's views are accepted; when Abbaye and Rava oppose one another, Rava's rulings are generally followed. In many cases, when the Talmud offers two possible solutions to a problem, the second is considered the decisive one. In other situations, the text simply states, "such and such is the law."

Still, the Talmud is not a law book. It presents a process of thinking, a dialectic that often does not have a resolution. "Every controversy that is for the sake of heaven will in the end endure," the sages said. Their debates and controversies are presented on these pages as they have endured, left for later ages to settle or to ponder.

The talmudic sages never envisaged themselves as innovators. They would have been horrified at the thought. All wisdom, they believed, had been revealed in the Torah, and the greatest accomplishment a scholar could perform was to uncover the truth embedded in the holy books. Always they cited "proof-texts" from the Bible, precedents to support their theories. And when a scholar could offer his master's or another sage's statements as a source of his information, he gladly did so. Time and again we find, "Rabbi Judah said in the name of Rav" or "Rabbi Assi said in Rabbi Johanan's name."

Yet, in spite of themselves, the rabbis of the Talmud changed the scope and impact of the Bible for all time. More than any other group of scholars, they revised, expanded on, and extrapolated from the Bible not only to meet new conditions in their society but to make it conform to their own ideals of justice and morality. In doing so, they established techniques for interpreting and reinterpreting Scripture that would keep it eternally meaningful.

In their responsiveness to the needs of their age, the sages were alert to the culture around them. They absorbed what was relevant and made it their own. Fables and folktales common to all ancient peoples became pathways for biblical and ethical lessons. Thousands of words of Greek and Latin origin were incorporated into their teachings and became part of talmudic literature. The rabbis used this vocabulary to communicate in terms Jews surrounded by Hellenism could understand. Greek and Roman academies became models for Jewish academies, and Greek and Roman table manners and customs became part of rabbinic lessons on politeness and proper conduct. But the talmudic sages never lost touch with the uniqueness of their own culture, with its emphasis on Scripture and scholarship. The Talmud and rabbinic values molded the thoughts, practices, hopes, attitudes, and ideals of generations of Jews scattered through many lands.

Babylonia dominated Jewish cultural life for almost seven hundred years. In time, the heads of the great academies at Sura and Pumbedita came to bear the title *gaon* (plural *geonim*) and to serve as leaders of the entire Jewish world. Students flocked to their schools, and the *geonim* themselves spread talmudic principles through the correspondence they maintained with many Jewish communities. Just as new issues had arisen in mishnaic and talmudic times that were not covered in the Bible, changing conditions once again raised problems not specifically dealt with in the Talmud. Troubled by an obscure passage or the application of a ruling to his own life, a rabbi or student would address his question to the *gaon*, whose answer then served as a precedent for the entire community. The letters of the *geonim*, with their decisions and explanations, were the beginnings of an important type of Hebrew literature known as responsa. Even in our own day, responsa from rabbis in all parts of the world have served as case studies and guidelines for Jewish law and practice. Several examples of such responsa literature appear in various chapters of this work.

As Jewish communities developed their own intellectual life and leaders, they became less dependent on the Babylonian academies. By the eleventh century, the influence of the *geonim* had waned, while two other centers of learning rose to leadership. One was in North Africa and Spain under Islamic rule, the other in Europe, in the Christian countries of Italy, France, and Germany. Now, too, in addition to informal responsa, scholars wrote more systematized commentaries to the Talmud, and codes of law that summarized and organized talmudic rules and regulations.

The greatest of the codifiers, as he was one of the greatest of all Jewish philosphers and scholars, was Rabbi Moses ben Maimon, known as Maimonides. Born in Spain in 1135, Maimonides spent much of his adult life in Egypt, where he, like other scholars of his time, was exposed to the powerful influence of Islamic culture. Maimonides wrote most of his works in Arabic, which had become the common language of Jews in Moslem lands. But he wrote his monumental *Code* in Hebrew because he regarded it as a basic supplement to Scripture, a work that would serve as the definitive compendium of Jewish law. In fact, he called it *Mishneh Torah*, a handbook to the Torah. In it, he presented talmudic decisions, omitting all discussions, legends, and other non-legal materials, and even the sources of his final rulings. This work, a model of logical thinking, is quoted often throughout *Voices of Wisdom*, both because of its clarity and because of the high position it holds in Jewish law. However, even Maimonides's *Code* could not become the final authority he intended it to be. In the tradition of the scribes and sages, other scholars over the years discussed, analyzed, and often disagreed with his work. Like the Talmud itself, Maimonides has become a classic source for study and comment.

Although the Talmud and legalistic studies remained at the heart of Jewish intellectual life until modern times, many other forms of expression grew up during the Middle Ages. Poetry flowered in Spain during a glorious golden age of Hebrew literature from the tenth to the twelfth centuries, and ethical and moralistic treatises became especially popular in Germany during the twelfth and thirteenth centuries. Legends and fables, always beloved, told and retold over generations, were added to and built upon by medieval fabulists, who borrowed freely from Greek, Arabic, and Indian sources.

And all along, sometimes lying dormant, sometimes bursting into wild and exotic fecundity, a mystical strain complemented and competed with all that was rational and logical in Jewish thought. Mystical tendencies characterize some of the most famous talmudic scholars, but it wasn't until the twelfth century that mysticism took shape as a body of literature, in the form of the Kabbalah. The teachings of the Kabbalah centered on esoteric interpretations of Scripture, investigation of the symbolic meaning of Hebrew letters, and speculation about the nature of God and the universe. Its major work was the *Zohar*, whose origins are as mysterious and romantic as some of its mystical symbols. The *Zohar* appeared in Spain at the end of the thirteenth century and was ascribed to Rabbi Simeon bar Yohai, a sage who had lived at the time of the *tannaim*. Many legends grew up about the authorship of the *Zohar*, but most scholars have come to attribute the work to the Spanish kabbalist Moses de Leon. The *Zohar* and the teachings it embodies have been condemned during some periods of Jewish history and glorified during others. In spite of its changing status, many of its most powerful and beautiful symbols and images have been incorporated—often unconsciously—into the mainstream of Jewish thought.

On the eve of modern times, mysticism became a backdrop for a movement whose major themes were religious spiritualism and emotionalism—the Hasidic movement. Hasidism emerged in Eastern Europe in the second half of the eighteenth century as a form of rebellion against the cold intellectualism and dry legalisms that had come to mark Jewish scholarship in that region. The Hasidim emphasized feelings and the joy and romance of religion. At their prayer services they sang and danced, and sometimes were moved to heights of mystical exaltation. In their teachings, they stressed love of God and the performance of good deeds above scholarship and rationalism. Israel Ba'al Shem Tov (the "Master of the Good Name") founded the movement. His descendants and those of other early Hasidic rabbis formed dynasties in which leadership was passed on from father to son or disciple. Followers of the Hasidic masters collected many of their sayings and many tales about them. These are noted for their gentle humor and accepting, homey approach to life.

The late-eighteenth and early-nineteenth centuries brought another form of intellectual rebellion, this one related to the emancipation of Jews, which was taking place in Europe. As Jews were given citizenship rights in many countries, they began to move freely into non-Jewish society and to assimilate into the general cultures in which they lived. Paralleling emancipation on an intellectual level, the enlightenment movement turned away from traditional religious and talmudic studies, and emphasized the importance of secular education and influences in Jewish life. In Eastern Europe, the enlightenment led to a flowering of Hebrew and Yiddish literature. From it later emerged the stories of Shalom Aleichem and other Yiddish writers whose humor, mixed with tender sympathy, have kept the world of the *shtetls* (small Jewish towns) alive for us today. In Germany, where the enlightenment began, the wish to modernize Judaism brought about the Reform movement. This broke with Orthodox devotion to the law and advocated, instead, the universal and social values of the prophets. Early Reform Judaism gave up many longstanding rituals of Judaism, but in recent years, it has become more accepting of tradition.

Reform Judaism was taken up in the United States toward the middle of the nineteenth century, while Conservative Judaism arose in Germany and the United States at the end of that century as a reaction against the extremes of Reform. Under the leadership of Solomon Schechter in the early 1900s, it developed its main ideology: dedication to traditional laws and practices but with a responsiveness to the changing needs of the Jewish community. In this respect it holds a middle ground between Reform Judaism and Orthodox Judaism, which adheres strictly to tradition.

Today, after the devastation of European Jewry by the Holocaust, Israel and the United States stand as the major centers of Jewish life. Hebrew literature flourishes in Israel; Jewish historical and talmudic studies continue in both countries. In many localities in which Jews live, rabbis still study the ancient texts to find precedents for coping with contemporary problems. Questions are asked, and responsa are written and published. The solutions offered today often reflect the differing philosophies of the three major branches of Judaism, and all three are represented throughout this book in discussions of such current issues as birth control, abortion, and euthanasia. But the process of ethical and legal interpretation remains what it has always been: a way of expanding and elaborating on a tradition that is open to new ideas even while its ideals continue, unchanged.

For me, the journey into tradition that was the making of this book was a voyage of discovery and rediscovery, of affirmation—and of questioning. Like many other Jewish women, I question the subordinate role women have held in this tradition, as they have in other religions and cultures. Although highly honored and respected by sages and scholars, for the most part women have been exempt from the most profound obligations and privileges of Jewish law and study, losing out, at the same time, on some of the deepest satisfactions of Jewish life. The great majority of passages in this book were written by men because it was always they who interpreted the texts, made the laws, and created the myths and legends.

The limitations on women's rights and roles do not negate the beauty and meaningfulness of the tradition as a whole, but they do pose a challenge that may not be ignored. All branches of Judaism have begun to grapple with this challenge within their own frameworks, just as rabbis and scholars of the past struggled with, and met, many other challenges to the validity and relevance of the Jewish tradition.

My daughter replaced me in the Hebrew school classroom, learning to master biblical texts, singing the melodies that span centuries. Her world is as different from mine as my world was from that of my parents. But that core of values that is the Jewish legacy—that solid mixture of ethics and wisdom, of what should be done and what can be done—will be there for her as it has been for me, to draw on, to learn from, to laugh with. It is timeless.

VOICES of WISDOM

1

YOU AND YOURSELF

"If I am not for myself, who is for me?"

On being yourself ✦ To gain perspective ✦ "This too is for the best" ✦ Defining the good life ✦ Controlling your temper ✦ Being flexible ✦ Guarding your tongue ✦ In search of wisdom ✦ Three wise rules for living ✦ Why it's futile to worry ✦ Where to turn for advice ✦ Striking a balance between humility and arrogance ✦ What is success?

If there is one quality more than any other that has been said to characterize our times, it is our involvement with ourselves. Accustomed through the techniques of psychoanalysis to examine every sensation we feel, to seek hidden meanings behind every mood, we've become experts at looking inward. Walk into any bookstore and you'll find shelves packed with the newest promises for self-improvement. Are you worried about being inefficient? You can learn techniques for increasing your productivity. Are you dissatisfied with your appearance? You can find dozens of guides to diet and exercise. Are you insecure about your decisions? You can discover methods of understanding your motives.

The implication behind our preoccupation with ourselves and the self-help literature that encourages it is that our problems are unique to us and our times. How is it possible, we wonder, for anyone else to have been tormented with our self-doubts, to have wrestled with our anxieties, or to have reached for self-fulfillment as we have?

Yet many of the issues we struggle with today are the same human issues that have occupied people of all times and places. Fears and worries, anger at ourselves and others, the search for wisdom, the meaning of happiness—these are subjects to which Jewish sages and teachers through the ages have devoted much attention. In fact, so important were these human problems considered in ancient times that special schools, known as wisdom schools, existed in Israel and other countries to teach ways of handling them. The young men who attended these schools came for practical as well as religious instruction that would help them lead full and successful lives. The authors of such "wisdom books" as Ecclesiastes and the Wisdom of Ben Sira, may have studied and later taught at these schools.

The writers of wisdom books, the talmudists, and the moralists who came after them offered commonsense, down-to-earth counsel as significant for us today as it was for people of their own times. "Trust your own judgment," advises Ben Sira. "A man's mind sometimes has a way of telling him more than seven watchmen posted high on a tower." "Do not worry about tomorrow's trouble," recommends a scholar, "for you do not know what the day may bring."

But beyond the hard-edged advice and quick insights into human nature lie deep and serious views of human goals that in many ways are far removed from the casual self-help guidance that abounds today. The sages stressed the importance of oneself because they considered every person's life precious: your life as valuable as your neighbor's, your needs as pressing as the next person's. But their focus did not remain fixed on the self. You become fulfilled, they maintained, only as you are able to expand your vision, giving of yourself to family, friends, and community; moving from understanding who you are to empathizing with a world outside your own ego.

In addition, the sages taught that to be a complete person you need to participate fully in life. When people are brought in for judgment in the world to come, one talmudic passage tells us, the first question they are asked is, "Were you honest in your business dealings?" Another is, "Did you engage in procreation?" Self-realization is not a matter of withdrawal from a corrupt world or narcissistic contemplation of oneself. An individual becomes a person by enjoying the world and contributing to it.

The individual who succeeds as a human being is also the one who keeps control over his or her emotions and actions. Respect yourself, we're told, but don't be arrogant; enjoy the good things life offers, but don't become a slave to your possessions; strive for success, but don't get puffed up with your own importance. Always there is a call for moderation, for a balance between cultivating your own abilities and overindulging yourself.

Finally, to be happy in this world, you need to be able to accept your life—not complacently but with the goal of making the most of it. The story is told of Rabbi Eleazar ben Pedat, who suffered great poverty. Once, when he had had nothing to eat, he became faint and fell into a deep sleep. He dreamed he saw God sitting at his side.

"How long will I suffer in this world?" he asked God.

"Eleazar, my son," the reply came, "would you like me to turn the whole world back to its very beginning? Perhaps then you will be born to a happier lot."

"All that trouble and then only 'perhaps' my life will be better," answered Eleazar. "I do not want it." And he chose to stay with the life he had.

There's no room in the sages' scheme of things for despair or self-pity. What you get out of life depends on what you bring to it.

On being yourself

Hillel the Elder, who lived about two thousand years ago, emphasized the importance of relying on yourself, both in his life and in his teachings. One of the great teachers in Israel, Hillel dedicated himself to his studies in spite of extreme poverty. Tradition has it that his brother Shebna, a merchant, offered to make Hillel his business partner and share his profits, but Hillel refused, determined to earn merit by devoting himself to the Torah without help from anyone.

Along with his belief in self-sufficiency, however, Hillel was often quoted for his saying, "Do not separate yourself from the community." His beautiful statement below encapsulates his ideals, and the selections that follow offer other insights into being your own person yet getting involved with life around you.

If I am not for myself, who is for me?
And if I am only for myself, what am I?
And if not now, when?

—Hillel, in *Ethics of the Fathers*,
chapter 1, paragraph 14

First a person should put his house together, then his town, then the world.

—Rabbi Israel Salanter (1810–1883), founder of the moralistic "musar movement" in Lithuania

---

Before he died, Rabbi Zusya said:

"In the world to come they will not ask me, 'Why were you not Moses?'

"They will ask me, 'Why were you not Zusya?' "

—Legend about Hasidic rabbi Zusya of Hanipoli (died in 1800)

When a person is brought in for judgment in the world to come he is asked:

Were you honest in your business dealings?
Did you set aside time for study?
Did you engage in procreation?
Did you look forward to salvation?
Did you engage in the dialectics of wisdom?
Did you look deeply into matters?

—Rava, in the Babylonian Talmud, tractate *Shabbat*, page 31a

To gain perspective

Part of keeping a balance in life, the following sayings and fables tell us, is accepting our own place in the larger scheme of things. The first selection gives a framework for this idea. Although not much is known about Akavyah ben Mahalalel, the Talmud portrays him as a man who lived firmly by his principles. When he was on his deathbed, his son asked him for a recommendation to the other sages. Akavyah refused, saying, "Your own deeds will bring you near to them, or your own deeds will push you away from them."

The talmudic fable of the fox in the vineyard and the much later fable by Berechiah ha-Nakdan are both based on Aesop and Oriental sources. Berechiah, the most famous Jewish fabulist of the Middle Ages, often put biblical verses into the mouths of the animals who inhabited his "fox fables." Translated from Hebrew into other languages, his fables circulated among Jews spread throughout Europe.

Mark well these three things, and you will not fall into the clutches of sin.

Know where you came from, where you are going, and to whom you are destined to give an account and reckoning.

"Where you came from?" A putrid drop.

"Where you are going?" To a place of dust, worms, and maggot.

"And before whom are you destined to give an account and reckoning?" Before the King of kings of kings, the Holy One, blessed be He.

—Akavyah ben Mahalalel,
in *Ethics of the Fathers*,
chapter 3, paragraph 1

The Bible says, "As he came out of his mother's womb, so must he depart at last, naked as he came" (Ecclesiastes 5:14).

This might be compared to a fox who found a vineyard that was closed on all sides, except for one small hole in it.

He tried to enter, but could not.

What did he do?

He fasted for three days until he became thin and scrawny. Then he entered through the hole. He ate from the vineyard and became sleek and fat.

When he wanted to leave, he could not get through

the hole. So he fasted another three days until he became thin and scrawny again.

Then he went out.

On leaving, he turned and looked at the place, saying, "O vineyard, vineyard, how beautiful you are, and how good is your fruit. All your produce is wonderful and worthy of praise. But what enjoyment have you given me? In the state in which one enters you, one must leave."

And so it is with the world at large.

—*Ecclesiastes Rabbah*,
chapter 5, section 14

A Hasidic rabbi gave this explanation to the talmudic saying "This world is like a wedding hall."

A man came to an inn in Warsaw. In the evening, he heard sounds of music and dancing coming from the next house.

"They must be celebrating a wedding," he thought to himself.

But the next evening he heard the same sounds, and again the evening after that.

"How can there be so many weddings in one family?" the man asked the innkeeper.

"That house is a wedding hall," answered the innkeeper. "Today one family holds a wedding there, tomorrow another."

"It's the same in the world," said the rabbi. "People are always enjoying themselves. But some days it's one person and other days it's another. No single person is happy all the time."

—Legend about Rabbi Hanokh
of Aleksandrow (1798–1870)

A season is set for everything, a time for every
 experience under heaven.
A time for being born, and a time for dying,
A time for planting and a time for uprooting the planted;
A time for slaying and a time for healing,
A time for tearing down and a time for building up;
A time for weeping and a time for laughing,
A time for wailing and a time for dancing;
A time for throwing stones and a time for gathering
 stones,
A time for embracing and a time for shunning embraces;
A time for seeking and a time for losing,
A time for keeping and a time for discarding;
A time for ripping and a time for sewing,
A time for silence and a time for speaking;
A time for loving and a time for hating;
A time for war and a time for peace.

—Ecclesiastes, chapter 3, verses 1–8

A small fish caught in a net said to the fisherman, "I am too little to be game. . . . Neither boiled nor roasted on the fire can I restore your soul. Let me go and refresh myself, and I will serve you two full years. Then will you find me in my river as before, large of stature and seven times as fat. If then I am boiled in water, it shall be as a festival in your house, and then can your heart be sustained with me."

Answered the fisherman, "Better is a little fish which is now within my grasp than a great leviathan which my neighbors will rule a year from now."

The parable is known in every city, and its interpretation is familiar upon the lips of every creature:

Better is a handful of satisfaction in your own palms than heaping handfuls of hope in the hands of another.

Better is a bird enclosed in a cage than two hopping on a hedge.

Take what is good, even if it is little; lay your hand upon it and grasp it and do not let it go.

Do not choose hope deferred for doubtful increase of advantage and blessing.

—Berechiah ben Natronai ha-Nakdan
(late 12th–early 13th century), French fabulist,
"Small Fish in a Net"

"This too is for the best"

A popular proverb in the *Ethics of the Fathers* says: "Who is rich? He who is content with his lot." Nahum of Gamzu, hero of many legends, became a symbol of this concept. His attitude of "all's for the best in this best of all possible worlds" was not meant to be taken literally but was the rabbis' way of emphasizing both faith and acceptance of what befalls you in life. The real Nahum was an early talmudic scholar who came from the town of Gimzo. As his piety and attitude toward life became known, legends grew up about him and his name was changed, as this tale relates.

There was a man nicknamed Nahum of Gamzu, because no matter what happened to him, he would always say, "This too is for the best," which in Hebrew is *Gam zu letovah*.

One time the Jews in the land of Israel wanted to send a gift to the emperor. After much discussion, they decided that Nahum should carry the gift because he had experienced many miracles. They sent him with a saddlebag filled with precious stones and pearls.

On the way he stopped at an inn overnight. While he slept, the people at the inn emptied his bag of its precious stones and filled it with earth. Next morning when Nahum discovered what had happened, he said, "This too is for the best!"

When Nahum arrived at his destination, and his gift was opened, it was found to be filled with earth.

"The Jews are mocking me," the emperor cried, and ordered Nahum put to death. Once again, Nahum exclaimed, "This too is for the best!"

At that moment Elijah the Prophet appeared disguised as one of the emperor's ministers and said, "Perhaps this is some of the earth of their patriarch Abraham. When he threw earth against his enemies it turned into swords, and when he threw stubble, it changed into arrows."

There was one province that the emperor had not been able to conquer. Now his men took some of the earth and threw it at the warriors in this province, and quickly defeated them.

The joyous emperor had Nahum taken to the royal treasury. There his bags were filled with precious stones and pearls, and he was sent home with great honor.

When he arrived at the inn where he had stayed before, the people asked him:

"What did you take to the emperor that you have been treated with such honor?"

"I brought only what I had taken from here," answered Nahum.

The innkeepers took some earth to the emperor and said to him, "The earth that was brought to you before belonged to us."

The emperor had the earth tested, but it had no power. And the innkeepers were put to death.

—Babylonian Talmud,
tractate *Ta'anit*, pages 21a–b

Defining the good life

Along with accepting the difficulties we suffer, we need to allow ourselves to enjoy the pleasures that come our way. The sages never hesitated to celebrate life and be grateful for the good it holds. The book of Ecclesiastes, in the second selection, encourages us to find happiness in what we have, though its praise of the good life is tinged with the skepticism that marks much of its teachings. The moralists, quoted next, sound a different note—a warning against excess and greediness. Finally, the Spanish philosopher and poet Judah Halevi suggests a middle path in which satisfaction in life is combined with self-discipline.

Beauty, strength, riches, honor, wisdom, old age, fullness of years, and children are becoming to the righteous and becoming to the world.

—*Ethics of the Fathers*, chapter 6, paragraph 8

Go, eat your bread in gladness, and drink your wine in joy; for your action was long ago approved by God.

Let your clothes be always freshly washed, and your head never lack ointment.

Enjoy happiness with a woman you love, all the fleeting days of life that have been granted to you under the sun—all your fleeting days.

For that alone is what you can get out of life and out of the means you acquire under the sun.

Whatever it is in your power to do, do with all your might. For there is no action, no reasoning, no learning, no wisdom in the netherworld where you are going. . . .

Even if a man lives many years, let him enjoy himself in all of them, remembering how many the days of darkness are going to be. The only future is nothingness!

—Ecclesiastes, chapter 9, verses 7–10; chapter 11, verse 8

There is no worldly pleasure but some sin follows upon its heels.

For instance . . . when a man gets into the habit of eating and drinking heartily, he is in distress if he happens to miss his regular meal. He will enter into the most arduous transactions and moneymaking schemes in order to maintain the kind of table to which he has become accustomed. Thus result dishonesty and greed, which are followed by false swearing and all the other sins that go with it. . . . Yet he would have been free from all these sins had he not allowed himself to be lured by the love of pleasures.

—Moses Hayyim Luzzatto (1707–1746),
Italian moralist, *The Path of the Upright*

The more flesh, the more worms.
The more possessions, the more worry.
The more wives, the more witchcraft.
The more maidservants, the more unchastity.
The more male servants, the more robbery. . . .

—Hillel, in *Ethics of the Fathers*,
chapter 2, paragraph 8

The pious man is nothing but a prince who is obeyed by his senses, and by his mental as well as his physical faculties, which he governs. . . .

He is fit to rule, because if he were the prince of a country, he would be as just as he is to his body and soul. He subdues his passions, keeping them in bonds, and at the same time giving them their share in order to satisfy them as regards food, drink, cleanliness and so on. . . .

If he, then, has satisfied each of them (giving to the vital organs the necessary amount of rest and sleep, and to the physical ones waking, movements, and world occupation), he calls upon his community as a respected prince calls his disciplined army, to assist him in reaching the divine degree.

—Judah Halevi (late eleventh century
to c. 1140), *Kuzari*, book 3, section 5

Controlling your temper

Jewish tradition has always accepted some kinds of anger as necessary and important—anger against social injustice, for example, or the anger of the prophets against the corruption of their times. But the uncontrolled anger of one person against another, the kind of anger in which people lose all sense of what they're saying or how they're affecting others, is condemned.

The *Book of the Pious*, a popular medieval collection of moral lessons, whose main author was Rabbi Judah the Pious of Regensburg, suggests two practical techniques for keeping your temper in check. An anecdote related in the *Fathers According to Rabbi Nathan* tells how Hillel kept control of himself in a situation that would have sent most people flying into a rage. Hillel is often contrasted with his quick-tempered colleague Shammai—"a person should always be gentle like Hillel and not passionate like Shammai."

A person's character can be judged by the way he handles three things: his drink, his money and his anger.

And some people say by the way he jokes also.

—Babylonian Talmud, tractate *Eruvin*, page 65b

There are four kinds of temperament:

Easily angered and easily appeased—his gain is canceled by his loss.

Hard to anger and hard to appease—his loss is canceled by his gain.

Hard to anger and easy to appease—the saint.

Easily angered and hard to appease—the wicked.

—*Ethics of the Fathers*, chapter 5, paragraph 14

He that in frenzy tears his clothes, or in frenzy smashes his furniture, will in the end worship idols.

For such is the art of the evil impulse: today it says to him, "Tear your clothes," and on the morrow it says to him, "Worship idols."

And he goes and worships idols.

—Rabbi Akiva, in *Fathers According to Rabbi Nathan*, chapter 3

There was a certain pious but hot-tempered man who, when people quarreled with him, would begin shouting and cursing instead of replying. After he calmed down, he would regret his actions.

The man went to a sage and asked, "What can I do to avoid cursing at people in my rage?"

The sage replied, "Take it upon yourself to say after cursing, 'May everything that I said about him come upon me.' Or, before cursing, say, 'May that which I am about to say to him come to me.' Then you will stop cursing."

But the man was unwilling to follow that advice. Instead, he took it upon himself that every time he yelled and cursed, he would give a certain amount to charity. The knowledge of how much it would cost him tended to keep him from cursing. In addition, giving charity was, for him, a way of atoning for his bad temper.

For charity, it was a source of profit.

—Judah the Pious (c. 1150–1217), *Book of the Pious*, section 127

The last in this series of irritating questions was especially designed to goad Hillel into anger because he was born in Babylonia, although he spent most of his adult life in Palestine.

Once two men decided to make a wager of four hundred *zuz* with each other. They said, "Whoever can put Hillel into a rage gets the four hundred *zuz*."

One of them went [to attempt it]. Now that day was a Sabbath eve, toward dusk, and Hillel was washing his head. The man came and knocked on his door.

"Where's Hillel? Where's Hillel?" he cried.

Hillel got into a cloak and came out to meet him. "My son," he said, "what is it?"

The man replied, "I need to ask about a certain matter."

"Ask," Hillel said.

The man asked, "Why are the eyes of the Tadmorites bleary?"

"Because," said Hillel, "they make their homes on the desert sands which the winds come and blow into their eyes. That is why their eyes are bleary."

The man went off, waited awhile, and returned and knocked on his door.

"Where's Hillel?" he cried. "Where's Hillel?"

Hillel got into a cloak and came out. "My son," he said, "what is it?"

The man replied, "I need to ask about a certain matter."

"Ask," Hillel said.

The man asked, "Why are the Africans' feet flat?"

"Because they dwell by watery marshes," said Hillel, "and all the time they walk in water. That is why their feet are flat."

The man went off, waited awhile, and returned and knocked on the door.

"Where's Hillel?" he cried. "Where's Hillel?"

Hillel got into a cloak and came out. "What is it you want to ask?" he inquired.

"I need to ask about some matter," the man said.

"Ask," Hillel said to him. In his cloak he sat down before him and said, "What is it?"

Said the man, "Is this how princes reply? May there be no more like you in Israel!"

"God forbid!" Hillel said. "Tame your spirit! What do you wish?"

The man asked, "Why are the heads of Babylonians long?"

"My son," Hillel answered, "you have raised an important question. Since there are no skillful midwives there, when the infant is born, slaves and maidservants tend it on their laps. That is why the heads of Babylonians are long. Here, however, there are skillful midwives, and when the infant is born, it is taken care of in a cradle and its head is rubbed. That is why the heads of Palestinians are round."

"You have put me out of four hundred *zuz*!" the man exclaimed.

Said Hillel to him, "Better that you have lost four hundred *zuz* because of Hillel than that Hillel lose his temper."

—*Fathers According to Rabbi Nathan*,
chapter 15

Being flexible

At all times let a man be supple as the reed and not rigid as the cedar:

A reed, when all the winds come and blow upon it, bends with them; when the winds are still, the reed is again upright in its place. And the end of this reed? Its good fortune is to be used as the pen that writes the Torah scroll.

The cedar, however, does not remain standing in its place; for as soon as the south wind blows, it uproots it and tears it down. And the end of the cedar? Loggers come upon it and chop it up and use it to cover the housetops—and what remains, they cast to the flames.

—Rabbi Simeon ben Eleazar, in
Fathers According to Rabbi Nathan,
chapter 41

Guarding your tongue

The rabbis emphasized self-control in speech as in other areas. A word once spoken, like an arrow shot, they said, can never be retracted.

Rabban Simeon ben Gamaliel said to his servant Tabbai, "Go to the market and buy me some good food."

The servant went and brought back a tongue.

He told him, "Go out and bring me some bad food from the market."

The servant went and brought back a tongue.

The rabbi said to him, "Why is it that when I said 'good food' you bought me a tongue, and when I said 'bad food' you also bought me a tongue?"

He replied, "It is the source of good and evil. When it is good, there is nothing better; when it is evil, there is nothing worse."

—*Leviticus Rabbah*,
chapter 33, section 1

A Persian king became deathly ill. His doctors told him that his only hope for survival was to drink the milk of a lioness. The king turned to his servants. "Who will bring me the milk of a lioness?" he asked.

"I will," answered one man, "if you will give me ten goats to take with me."

The man took the goats and found his way to a lion's den where a lioness was suckling her cubs. On the first day, the man stood at a distance and threw one of the goats to the lioness, who quickly devoured it. On the second day, he came a little closer and threw another goat. And so he continued. At the end of ten days, he made friends with the lioness, who allowed him to pet her, play with her cubs, and finally take some of her milk. And the man went on his way.

About halfway home, the man had a dream that all the parts of his body were fighting with one another. His legs said, "No part of the body is equal to us. Had we not walked to the lioness, this man would not have the milk to bring to the king."

The hands answered, "But had we not milked the lioness, he could not have had the milk for the king."

"But," said the eyes, "had we not shown the way, he couldn't have done anything."

"I'm better than all of you," cried the heart. "Had I not thought up the scheme, it wouldn't have mattered what you did."

"And I," answered the tongue, "am the best of all. For without speech, what can anyone do?"

"How dare you compare yourself to us," chimed in all the parts of the body. "You just spend your days in that dark, gloomy place, without even a bone in you, as the rest of us have."

"You'll see," said the tongue. "Today you'll say that I rule over all of you."

The man awoke and went on his way. When he entered the king's chambers he announced, "Here is the dog's milk I have brought for you."

"Dog's milk!" shouted the king. "I asked for lion's milk. Take this man away and have him hanged."

On the way to be hanged, all the parts of the man's body began to tremble. Then the tongue said to them, "I told you I'm superior to all of you. If I save you, will you admit that I rule over you?" They all quickly agreed.

"Return me to the king," shouted the tongue to the hangman. The man was brought back before the king.

"Why did you order me hanged?" demanded the man. "This milk will cure you. Don't you know that a lioness is sometimes referred to as a 'she-dog'?"

The king's physicians took the milk from the man, examined it, and found it to be, after all, the milk of a lioness. The king drank the milk and quickly recovered from his illness.

The man was handsomely rewarded for his efforts. Now all the parts of the body turned to the tongue.

"We bow down to you and you are our ruler," they said humbly.

And that is what is meant by the verse "Death and life are in the power of the tongue" (Proverbs 18:12).

—*Yalkut Shimoni*, on Psalms, section 721

In search of wisdom

Among the sages and scholars, wisdom traditionally meant common sense and good judgment in everyday matters—knowing, for example, when to speak and when not to, when to act and when not to. Always they emphasized that wisdom becomes meaningless when it is divorced from good deeds and day-to-day living.

Rabbi Eliezer ben Hyrcanus injects a note of caution into the general praise of wisdom. A brilliant scholar, Eliezer was also a rigid and stubborn man who refused to yield to even a majority of his colleagues on any matter of law. The other rabbis excommunicated him toward the end of his life, and his words may reflect the anger and hurt he felt.

Who is a wise man? He who learns from all men.

—Simeon ben Zoma, in
Ethics of the Fathers,
chapter 4, paragraph 1

The wise man does not speak before him that is greater than he in wisdom;

he does not break into his fellow's speech;
he is not in a rush to reply;
he asks what is relevant and replies to the point;
he speaks of first things first and of last things last;
of what he has not heard he says, "I have not heard,"

and he acknowledges what is true.
And the opposites apply to the clod.

—*Ethics of the Fathers*,
chapter 5, paragraph 9

He whose wisdom exceeds his works, to what may he be likened? To a tree whose branches are numerous but whose roots are few. The wind comes along and uproots it and sweeps it down. . . .

But he whose works exceed his wisdom, to what can he be likened? To a tree whose branches are few but whose roots are numerous. Then even if all the winds of the world come along and blow against it, they cannot stir it from its place.

As it is said: "He shall be like a tree planted by waters, sending forth its roots by a stream; it does not sense the coming of heat; its leaves are ever fresh; it has no care in a year of drought; it does not cease to yield fruit" (Jeremiah 17:8).

—Rabbi Eleazar ben Azariah, in
Ethics of the Fathers,
chapter 3, paragraph 22

Scripture says: "He who associates with the wise becomes wise, but the companion of fools shall be destroyed" (Proverbs 13:20).

To what may this be compared? To a person who goes into a spice shop. Although he buys nothing and takes nothing from the shop, the sweet odor clings to his clothes and does not leave him all day.

But if a man goes into a tannery, even though he buys nothing and takes nothing from the shop, his clothes become dirtied and the bad odor does not leave him all day.

—*Fathers According to Rabbi Nathan*,
version B, chapter 11

Keep warm, at the fire of the sages, but beware of their glowing coal, lest you be scorched:

For their bite is the bite of a jackal, and their sting the sting of a scorpion, and their hiss the hiss of a serpent.

And all their words are like coals of fire.

—Rabbi Eliezer ben Hyrcanus, in
Ethics of the Fathers,
chapter 2, paragraph 15

Three wise rules for living

A hunter once caught a bird that could speak seventy languages.

"Free me," said the bird, "and I'll teach you three wise sayings."

"First teach them to me," answered the man, "and I swear I will let you go."

"The first saying," said the bird, "is: After something is done, do not regret it.

"The second saying is: If a person tells you something you know cannot be true, do not believe it.

"And the third saying is: If you cannot climb up, do not waste your energy trying to climb up."

Then the bird said to the hunter, "Let me go." And the hunter set it free.

The bird flew off, perched on a high tree, and called out to the hunter:

"You silly man. You freed me and you didn't even know that in my caw I have a large, precious pearl worth thousands. That's what makes me so wise."

Distraught at having freed the bird, the hunter ran to the tree and started to climb it. But about halfway up, he fell and broke both his legs.

The bird laughed at him and cried:

"Fool! In just a few moments you forgot all the wise

sayings I taught you. I told you that once a thing was done you should not regret it. Yet you regretted freeing me. And I told you that if somebody tells you something you know cannot be true, don't believe it. Yet you believed that a little bird like me can have a huge and valuable pearl in its caw. And I told you that if you cannot climb something, you should not wear yourself out trying to climb. Yet you ran after me and tried to climb this tall tree, and fell and broke your legs.

"It is of you that the book of Proverbs says: 'A rebuke enters deeper into a man of understanding than a hundred stripes into a fool' " (Proverbs 17:10).

Then the bird flew away.

—From a medieval folktale
based on Oriental sources

Why it's futile to worry

One of the greatest Jewish scholars of all times, Rabbi Moses ben Maimon, known as Maimonides, or, in Hebrew, *Rambam*, was equally renowned as philosopher, talmudic expert, and physician. Always the rationalist, he wrote philosophic works with the same clarity and directness that he used in his medical treatises. Here he counsels the sultan of Egypt, whom he served as court physician, on the self-destructiveness of regrets and anxieties. Maimonides wrote from personal experience. When he was in his thirties, his brother David drowned with the family fortune while on a business trip, leaving Maimonides destitute. He then took up medicine to earn a livelihood and soon achieved fame for his work.

Do not worry about tomorrow's trouble, for you do not know what the day may bring.

Tomorrow may come and you will be no more, and so you will have worried about a world that is not yours.

—Babylonian Talmud,
tractate *Yevamot*, page 63b

Whatever a man thinks that hurts him while thinking it, and that brings him sadness, sighing and mourning, can only be one of two kinds: either he meditates upon what has been, as when he meditates upon money he had and lost, or upon the death of a person his heart grieves for; or he meditates upon what is going to happen in the future and dreams of what is going to happen, as when he imagines that he may suffer a loss.

And it is known through intellectual observation that reflection over what has happened and come to pass will be of no avail in any respect, and that mourning and sorrow over things that have passed are the activities of those who lack intellect. And there is no difference between a man who laments over the loss of money and the like, and he who laments the fact that he is a man and not an angel or a star or another of the things that are impossible.

. . . Whatever a man fears may happen to him is only a matter of probability—either it will happen or it will not happen. And just as it is possible that something painful, worrisome and fearful may happen, it is also possible that, because of his reliance on God, the reverse of what he feared may happen. Because, both what he feared and the reverse are possible.

—Maimonides (1135–1204), *The Preservation of Youth* (1198)

Where to turn for advice

The Wisdom of Ben Sira, never accepted as one of the sacred writings of the Hebrew Bible, is an important book of the Apocrypha. Talmudic scholars often quoted from its maxims and proverbs. The author, Simeon ben Jesus ben Sira, had a knack for using precise words and powerful images to strike at the heart of a matter.

Joseph ben Abba Mari Ibn Kaspi of Provençal was a prolific Hebrew writer during the fourteenth century. In his letter to his twelve-year-old son, Solomon, written before Kaspi left on a long trip, he gives typical parental advice about seeking advice: "Don't be afraid to ask if you don't know something."

Do not consult a man who is suspicious of you or reveal your intentions to those who envy you.

Never consult a woman about her rival or a coward about war,

a merchant about a bargain or a buyer about a sale,

a skinflint about gratitude or a hard-hearted man about a kind action,

an idler about work of any sort, a casual laborer about finishing a job, or a lazy servant about an exacting task—do not turn to them for any advice.

Rely rather on a god-fearing man whom you know to be a keeper of the commandments, whose interests are like your own, who will sympathize if you have a setback.

But also trust your own judgment, for it is your most reliable counselor.

A man's own mind sometimes has a way of telling him more than seven watchmen posted high on a tower.

But above all pray to the Most High to keep you on the straight road of truth.

—Wisdom of Ben Sira,
chapter 37, verses 10–15

I will confess . . . that though in my youth I learned a great portion of the Talmud I did not acquire a knowledge of the Posekim [experts on Jewish law].

Now that I am old and gray I often have to consult rabbis younger than myself. Why should I be ashamed of this? Can one man be skilled in every craft?

If, for instance, I want a golden cup, I go to the goldsmith, and I feel no shame; and so with other products,

I turn, in case of need, to those whom God has endowed with the requisite skill.

—Joseph ben Abba Mari Ibn Kaspi of Provençal, from "A Guide to Knowledge," dated Valencia, 1332

Striking a balance between humility and arrogance

Ben Sira states the need for self-confidence as well as anyone, but most of the sages were more concerned with overconfidence than with the lack of it. The rabbis considered arrogance one of the worst character traits a person could have, while humility, some said, "is the greatest virtue of all." Their enormous emphasis on humility may have been directed more at themselves and their disciples than at others. Treated with great honor and respect from the community, the rabbis did not always find it easy to resist getting carried away with their own importance.

The three anecdotes are, in a sense, stories the scholars told on themselves. The first deals with the historic rivalry between the followers of the sage Hillel and his contemporary Shammai. The School of Hillel usually took a liberal and lenient attitude toward interpreting the law, while the School of Shammai almost always held a strict, narrow line. Ultimately, the School of Hillel triumphed, and its interpretations became the accepted standards of law. The second story implies criticism of a saintly rabbi who used his name and influence for his own ends—although his only purpose was to save his life. And the last story has something to say about both self-respect and haughtiness in presenting an ordinary man who knows how to stand up to an arrogant scholar.

My son, in all modesty, keep your self-respect and value
yourself at your true worth.
Who will speak up for a man who is his own enemy?
Or respect one who disparages himself?

—Wisdom of Ben Sira, chapter 10, verses 28–29

An arrogant person is not accepted even in his own household....

At first members of his family jump to his every word; after awhile they find him repulsive.

—Babylonian Talmud,
tractate *Sotah*, page 47b

For three years the School of Shammai disputed with the School of Hillel.

The former said: "The law agrees with our views."

And the latter said: "The law agrees with our views."

Then a heavenly voice announced: "These and these are each the words of the living God, but the law agrees with the rulings of the School of Hillel."

Since both schools' rulings "are the words of the living God," why was the law fixed according to the rulings of the School of Hillel?

Because the followers of Hillel were kindly and modest. They not only studied the rulings of the School of Shammai, they even mentioned these rulings before their own....

This teaches you that whoever humbles himself, the Holy One, blessed be He, raises up, and whoever exalts himself, the Holy One, blessed be He, humbles.

From the person who seeks greatness, greatness flees. But the person who flees from greatness, greatness follows.

—Babylonian Talmud,
tractate *Eruvin*, page 13b

A certain man had a vineyard from which thieves stole constantly. The man was very distressed by the thefts and determined to stop the thieves. During the harvest season, Rabbi Tarfon came to the vineyard and ate some figs left behind on the vines by the vintner.

When the owner saw Rabbi Tarfon he believed he had found the thief who had been eating from his vineyard. He threw the rabbi in a sack and carried him off to fling into the river.

"Woe to Tarfon whom this man is about to murder," the rabbi cried when he realized what was happening to him.

Recognizing the name of the famous Rabbi Tarfon, the vintner quickly released him and fled.

All his life the pious rabbi regretted the incident because, he said, "I made profane use of my knowledge of the Torah." For the rabbis have said, "Whoever uses his knowledge of the Torah for his own ends is uprooted from the world."

What should he have done? Because he was wealthy himself, he should have paid the man for the losses he had suffered without ever revealing who he was. [In that way he would not have taken advantage of his position as a scholar.]

—Babylonian Talmud,
tractate *Nedarim*, page 62a

Once Rabbi Eleazar ben Simeon was coming from his teacher's house, riding leisurely on his ass and feeling happy and filled with great pride because he had studied much Torah. By chance he met an extremely ugly man who greeted him, "Peace be upon you, sir."

Instead of returning the greeting, he said to the man, "How ugly you are! Are all your fellow citizens as ugly as you?"

The man answered, "I don't know, but go tell the craftsman who made me, 'How ugly is the vessel you have made.' "

When Rabbi Eleazar realized what he had done, he bowed before the man and said, "I humble myself before you. Please forgive me."

But the angry man replied, "I will not forgive you until you go to the craftsman who made me and say to him, 'How ugly is the vessel you have made.' "

Rabbi Eleazar walked behind the man until he reached his own town. When the townspeople saw their rabbi, they greeted him with the words, "Peace be upon you O Teacher, O Master."

"Whom are you addressing that way?" the man asked.

"That man who is walking behind you," they answered.

"If that man is a teacher," the man cried out, "may there be no more like him in Israel!"

When the people asked why he spoke that way, he told them what had happened. "Nevertheless you should forgive him," they urged, "for he is a man greatly learned in the Torah."

"Because of you I'll forgive him," the man said finally. "But only on condition he never acts that way again."

—Babylonian Talmud,
tractate *Ta'anit*, pages 20a–20b

What is success?

The scholars have no quarrel with trying to succeed. Their observations are directed more at longings that become insatiable and ambitions that become all-encompassing. And, in the end, the last fable says, as outside trappings disappear, you have only yourself and the person you have become.

People never leave this world with even half their desires fulfilled.

Somebody who has a hundred wants to turn it into two hundred; and somebody who has two hundred wants to turn it into four hundred.

—*Ecclesiastes Rabbah*,
chapter 1, section 13

He who forces time is forced back by time, but he who yields to time finds time standing at his side.

—Babylonian Talmud,
tractate *Eruvin*, page 13b

The rabbi of Berdichev saw a man hurrying along the street, looking neither right nor left.

"Why are you rushing so much?" he asked the man.

"I'm rushing after my livelihood," the man answered.

"And how do you know," said the rabbi, "that your livelihood is running on before you so that you have to rush after it? Perhaps it's behind you, and all you need to do is stand still."

—Tale about Hasidic rabbi Levi Isaac
ben Meir of Berdichev (c. 1740–1810)

The more a man is disciplined, the less he is affected by both extremes, good times and bad, so that when he is favored by great fortune in this world, called by the philosophers "imaginary goodness," he does not get excited nor appear particularly great and good in his own eyes.

And when great misfortune and tribulation befall him, like the many tribulations that occur in the world and which the philosophers call "imaginary evils," he is neither startled nor terrified, but tolerates them well.

When one contemplates the true essence of things and the knowledge of the nature of reality, he attains a wisdom whereby he understands that the greatest good in this world does not stay with a man all his days because it is inferior in value, being perishable and destructible when a man reaches his end. For of what benefit is it to man, since he dies like other living creatures?

And so it is with the greatest of the evils in the world. When he considers death from which he cannot escape, every evil is less than the evil of death, undoubtedly. And therefore a change for the worse is less than a change for the worst, which one cannot escape.

—Maimonides, *The Preservation of Youth*

Once there was a lion, old and sick, whose loins were diseased, so that his spirit suffered; his fate was uncertain, whether he would live or die.

All the cattle and beasts, from the far ends of the earth, came to see this lion in his misery. Some came out of love for visiting the sick, some to gaze on his anguish, some to succeed to his rule, some to know who would reign after him.

He was so sick that none could tell whether he was still alive or already dead. The ox came and gored him, to try whether his strength was ended and empty; the heifer trampled him with her hoofs; the fox nipped at his ears with his teeth; the ewe brushed his mustaches with her tail, and said, "When will he die and his name perish?" And the cock pecked at his eyes and broke his teeth.

Then the lion's spirit returned, and he saw that his enemies were gloating over him, and he cried, "Alas for the day when my trusted counselors despise me, when my power and glory have turned against me, and my erstwhile slaves lord it over me. And they who loved me before have become my enemies."

The parable is of a man filled with riches and honor whose neighbors serve him. But when calamity comes upon him, when he is bowed down and humbled, they separate themselves from him whom they had once loved.

—Berechiah ha-Nakdan,
"Lion, Beasts, Cattle"

2

RELATING TO OTHERS

"Either companionship or death"

On loving your neighbor ✦ Accepting differences ✦ The value of friendship ✦ Choosing friends ✦ People to avoid ✦ When envy and hatred take over ✦ Making peace among friends ✦ Extending yourself for others ✦ Intervening to stop a wrong ✦ Ways of criticizing ✦ If you're asked for help ✦ How to be a good host/gracious guest ✦ Respecting others' privacy ✦ On being a good neighbor ✦ Returning lost property ✦ On shaming others ✦ When to bury the past ✦ Avoiding insults ✦ Gossip: "like the poison of a serpent" ✦ The dangers of overpraising ✦ If you know someone is a cheat ✦ Guarding a confidence ✦ Judging others ✦ Retaliating for an injury ✦ Bearing a grudge ✦ Forgiving your enemies

Shalom Aleichem once described his ability to get along well with people this way: "A man must always be considerate of the feelings of his neighbors. . . . So, for instance, if I went out to the fair . . . and did well, sold everything at a good profit, and returned with pocketsful of money, my heart bursting with joy, I never failed to tell my neighbors that I had lost every kopeck and was a ruined man. Thus I was happy, and my neighbors were happy. But if, on the contrary, I had really been cleaned out at the fair and brought home with me a bitter heart and a bellyful of green gall, I made sure to tell my neighbors that never since God made fairs had there been a better one. You get my point? For thus I was miserable and my neighbors were miserable with me."

It's not easy to be completely happy about another person's success or completely sympathetic with another's failure. Not that most of us wish one another harm; we simply prefer to have a little bit more and to do a little bit better than the next person.

Centuries before Shalom Aleichem, the medieval Spanish scholar Nahmanides expressed a similar thought in commenting on the commandment to "love your neighbor as yourself": "Sometimes a person will love his neighbor in certain matters, such as doing good to him in material wealth. . . . But if he loves him completely, he will want his beloved friend to gain riches, properties, honor, knowledge, and wisdom. However, he will still not want him to be his equal, for there will always be a desire in his heart that he should have more of these good things than his neighbor. Therefore, Scripture commanded that this degrading jealousy should not exist in his heart, but instead a person should love to do abundance of good for his fellow being as he does for himself."

Nahmanides's approach reflects that of many other Jewish sages and scholars. With down-to-earth realism they acknowledge human failings—the petty jealousies and large-scale envies, the veneration of power and disdain for weakness, that often determine the way we treat one another. Calling attention to these failings, the sages recognize that their advice might not always change our feelings, but it could, perhaps, influence our actions. The selections that follow urge that we show respect for all people, no matter how they differ from us. They examine the many aspects of friendship and wrestle with problems of helping and criticizing others. They lay out guidelines for good manners and hospitality, and focus in on the ways we hurt one another, sometimes through actions, more often with words. Throughout, these selections hone and polish our sensitivity to one another—even to the point of telling us: "If there has been a case of hanging in a person's family history, do not say to him, 'Hang up this fish for me.' "

Yet, for all their stress on caring for others, you will not find in them condemnation of any of us for caring about ourselves or, when necessary, for putting concern for ourselves ahead of concern for others. While the sages despised selfishness, they accepted self-interest as the starting point for every person, making it, in fact, the basis for some of their highest ethical teachings. As they saw it, you move from yourself outward. Because you know what it means to respect yourself, you become capable of respecting others. Because you understand how it feels to be hurt or humiliated yourself, you learn not to hurt or humiliate someone else. They rooted their teachings in the historical lessons of the Bible: "You shall not wrong a stranger, for you were strangers in the land of Egypt."

Even in the minute details of law, we are asked to use ourselves as a standard against which to gauge our behavior toward others. If, for example, you find something belonging to another person that you consider beneath your dignity to carry in public, you have no legal obligation to return it to its owner. But if you would have carried the lost object to your own home, had it belonged to you, then you are obliged to carry it to its owner.

Ultimately, the measure of how well we relate to others comes not when things go well but when there are difficulties, and the last several selections deal with matters of injury and retaliation. Here again, basic human feelings are used as a springboard for higher moral actions. Jewish tradition says, for example, that on the Day of Atonement, the holiest day of the year, people may expiate their sins by praying to God for forgiveness. However, God has no power to forgive wrongs committed by one person against another. The guilty party must personally ask the other's forgiveness. People who have been injured, either by words or actions, have a right to their anger and hurt, and a right to expect an apology. On the other hand, an injured person who refuses to forgive when asked to do so and who continues to bear a grudge is said to be cruel. When conflicts arise, both the wounder and the wounded must put themselves in the other's place and extend themselves to each other.

The English philosopher Thomas Hobbes described the human condition as one of "war, of everyone against everyone." While the Jewish sages would never accept such a negative view of humanity, they have no illusions about the selfishness and narrowness that sometimes motivate our behavior. But with unshakable optimism they insist that we can move far beyond these limitations. From getting along with our friends to dealing with our enemies, they teach us how to love and honor one another as we love and honor ourselves.

On loving your neighbor

"Love your neighbor as yourself," the book of Leviticus states, and this Golden Rule has been echoed by teachers and moralists through the ages. In the famous talmudic story below, Hillel presents the lesson in its negative form, telling a would-be convert how *not* to treat others. Some scholars have interpreted Hillel's statement as deliberately pragmatic. It's easier to learn to avoid hurting others than to learn to love them—or even treat them as though you love them—as yourself. Whether this was Hillel's intention, or whether he was simply restating the commandment in a different form, as many other scholars have suggested, he makes it clear that care for others forms the very heart of Jewish ethics.

The discussion that follows between Rabbi Akiva and his pupil Simeon ben Azzai bears out Hillel's position. To Akiva's emphasis on brotherly love, Ben Azzai adds the concept of the unity of all people: all, he reminds us, were created in the image of God.

A heathen once came before the sage Shammai. He said to him:

"I will convert to Judaism if you will teach me all the Torah while I stand on one foot."

Shammai pushed the man away with the builder's measure he held in his hand.

The man came before Hillel and repeated his request.

Hillel said to him:

"What is hateful to you do not do to your neighbor. That is the whole Torah. The rest is commentary—go and learn it."

—Babylonian Talmud,
tractate *Shabbat*, page 31a

"Love your neighbor as yourself" (Leviticus 19:18). Rabbi Akiva said: This is the greatest principle of the Torah.

Ben Azzai quoted the verse: "This is the book of the generations of Adam. In the day that God created man, in the likeness of God made He him" (Genesis 5:1). He said: This is a principle greater than that.

—*Sifra* on chapter 19, verse 18

Rabbi Eliezer said: Let the honor of your fellow be as dear to you as your own. . . .

How so? This teaches that even as one looks out for his own honor, so should he look out for his fellow's honor. And even as no man wishes that his own honor be held in ill repute, so should he wish that the honor of his fellow shall not be held in ill repute.

—Rabbi Eliezer ben Hyrcanus, in
Ethics of the Fathers, chapter 2,
paragraph 15; commentary from
Fathers According to Rabbi Nathan,
chapter 15

Accepting differences

The rabbis celebrated the differences among people as one of the miracles of creation. "A man strikes many coins from one die, and they are all alike," they explained. "But God strikes every person from the die of the first man, yet not one resembles the other." Respect and love for others, we learn, stem from recognizing and accepting the uniqueness of each individual.

A favorite saying of the rabbis of Jabneh was:

I am a creature of God and my neighbor is also a creature of God.

I work in the city and he works in the country.

I rise early for my work and he rises early for his work.

Just as he cannot excel in my work, I cannot excel in his work.

Will you say that I do great things and he does small things?

We have learned that it does not matter whether a person does much or little, as long as he directs his heart to heaven.

—Babylonian Talmud,
tractate *Berakhot*, page 17a

Despise no man and consider nothing impossible.

For there is no man who does not have his hour, and there is nothing that does not have its place.

—Simeon ben Azzai, in *Ethics of the Fathers*, chapter 4, paragraph 3

A person should not stay awake among people who are sleeping, or sleep among people who are awake;

not weep among people who are laughing, or laugh among people who are weeping;

not sit when others stand, or stand when others sit;

not read Torah when others are studying Mishnah, or Mishnah when others are reading Torah.

In short, a person should not depart from the customs of those around him.

—Minor tractate of the Talmud,
Derekh Erez Zuta,
chapter 5, paragraph 5

A person should always try to be on best terms with his friends and his relatives and with all people, even the heathen in the street, so that he may be beloved in heaven above and well-liked below, and accepted by his fellow creatures.

It has been said of Rabban Johanan ben Zakkai that no one ever greeted him first, before he greeted them, not even the heathen in the street.

—Abbaye, in the Babylonian Talmud,
tractate *Berakhot*, page 17a

The value of friendship

"Get yourself a companion," advised Joshua ben Perahyah. Later commentators explained that a person needs a companion "to eat with him, drink with him, study Scripture with him, study Mishnah with him . . . and reveal to him all his secrets, the secrets of the Torah and the secrets of worldly things."

The following legends illustrate the wisdom of the rabbis' advice. Honi the Circle-Drawer, hero of the first story, lived during the early days of the Roman Empire, in the first century B.C.E. An outstanding scholar, he was also regarded as a miracle worker, especially adept at calling forth rain. His nickname, the "Circle-Drawer," probably came from his most spectacular rain-making feat: he drew a circle on the ground, stood in it, and with his prayers, brought down just the right amount of rain needed for the crops. When sufficient rain had fallen, he prayed again, and it ceased.

According to the Roman Jewish historian Josephus, Honi died during a struggle among different factions of the Hasmonean dynasty, which ruled Judea at the time, but legend gives a different account of his death.

While traveling along a road, Honi the Circle-Drawer saw an old man planting a carob tree. He asked the man how long it would take for the tree to bear fruit, and the man told him seventy years.

Honi sat down to eat and felt himself overcome with drowsiness. He lay down and slept. And as his sleep deepened, rocks rose around him and enclosed him so that he was hidden from sight. He continued to sleep for seventy years.

When he awoke he saw a man gathering fruit from the carob tree.

"Are you the man who planted the tree?" asked Honi.

"No, I'm his grandson," the man answered.

"It's clear that I have slept for seventy years!" exclaimed Honi in amazement.

He then noticed that instead of his one mule, several generations of mules roamed the field.

Honi returned to where his home had been.

"Is the son of Honi the Circle-Drawer still alive?" he asked the people there.

"His son is no more," they said. "But his grandson is still living."

"I am Honi the Circle-Drawer," he said. But no one believed him.

Honi left his house and went to the house of study, where he could hear the scholars learning together.

"The law is as clear to us as in the days of Honi the Circle-Drawer," he heard them say. "For whenever Honi came to the house of study he would clarify for the scholars any difficulties they had with their texts."

"I am Honi," he called out to them excitedly.

But the scholars would not believe him, nor would they show him the honor he had received before.

Deeply hurt, Honi prayed for death. His prayers were answered, and he died.

Said the sage Rabbah: "From this tragedy comes the saying, 'Either companionship or death.' "

—Babylonian Talmud,
tractate *Ta'anit*, page 23a

A rich man had ten sons. He swore to them that when his time came to die he would leave each of them one hundred *dinars*.

As time went by, however, he lost part of his money, and all that remained was nine hundred and fifty *dinars*. So he gave a hundred *dinars* apiece to each of his nine elder sons. To his youngest son he said:

"I have only fifty *dinars* left, and I must put aside thirty of them for burial expenses. I can leave you only twenty. But I have ten companions, whom I will give to you, and they are better than a thousand *dinars*."

The man told his friends about his youngest son, and soon afterward he died and was buried.

The nine sons went their ways, and the youngest son gradually spent the few *dinars* that had been left to him. When he had only one left, he decided to spend it on a feast for his father's ten friends.

They ate and drank with him, and said to one another, "He is the only one of all the brothers who still cares for us. Let us show him kindness in return for his kindness."

So they each gave him a cow in calf and money. The cows gave birth and he sold them, and he used his money to start a business. The Lord blessed him and made him richer than his father.

Then he said, "Indeed, my father said truly that friends are better than all the money in the world."

—Legend in *An Elegant Composition Concerning Relief After Adversity*, compiled by Nissim ben Jacob ben Nissim Ibn Shahin (c. 990–1062)

There were two close friends who had been parted by war so that they lived in different kingdoms. Once one of them came to visit his friend, and because he came from the city of the king's enemy, he was imprisoned and sentenced to be executed as a spy.

No amount of pleas would save him, so he begged the king for one kindness.

"Your Majesty," he said, "let me have just one month to return to my land and put my affairs in order so my family will be cared for after my death. At the end of the month I will return to pay the penalty."

"How can I believe you will return?" answered the king. "What security can you offer?"

"My friend will be my security," said the man. "He will pay for my life with his if I do not return."

The king called in the man's friend, and to his amazement, the friend agreed to the conditions.

On the last day of the month, the sun was setting, and the man had not yet returned. The king ordered his friend killed in his stead. As the sword was about to descend, the man returned and quickly placed the sword on his own neck. But his friend stopped him.

"Let me die for you," he pleaded.

The king was deeply moved. He ordered the sword taken away and pardoned them both.

"Since there is such great love and friendship between the two of you," he said, "I entreat you to let me join you as a third." And from that day on they became the king's companions.

And it was in this spirit that our sages of blessed memory said, "Get yourself a companion."

—Legend in *Beit ha-Midrash*,
a collection by the Viennese scholar
Adolf Jellinek (1820–1893)

Choosing friends

The friendship of David and Jonathan, as described in the book of Samuel, is held up as the ideal—a friendship in which neither made demands on the other, yet each gave unstintingly of himself. But because such friendships are rare, we're urged to be cautious in choosing our friends.

Would you know who is your friend and who is your enemy?

Note what is in your own heart.

—Solomon Ibn Gabirol (c. 1020–c. 1057),
Spanish philosopher and poet,
Choice of Pearls

If love depends on some selfish end, when the end fails, love fails.

But if it does not depend on a selfish end, it will never fail.

. . . An example of love that did not depend on a selfish end? That was the love of David and Jonathan.

—*Ethics of the Fathers*,
chapter 5, paragraph 19

How have the mighty fallen
In the thick of battle—

Jonathan, slain on your heights!
I grieve for you,
My brother Jonathan.
You were most dear to me,
Your love was wonderful to me
More than the love of women.

—From David's lamentation over
Jonathan and Saul, in II Samuel,
chapter 1, verses 25–26

When you make a friend, begin by testing him, and be in no hurry to trust him.

Some friends are loyal when it suits them, but desert you in time of trouble.

Some friends turn into enemies and shame you by making the quarrel public.

Another sits at your table but is nowhere to be found in time of trouble; when you are prosperous, he will be your second self and make free with your servants, but if you come down in the world, he will turn against you and you will not see him again.

Hold your enemies at a distance, and keep a wary eye on your friends.

A faithful friend is a secure shelter; whoever finds one has found a treasure.

A faithful friend is beyond price; his worth is more than money can buy. . . .

Do not desert an old friend; a new one is not worth as much.

A new friend is like new wine; you do not enjoy drinking it until it has matured.

—Wisdom of Ben Sira,
chapter 6, verses 7–15;
chapter 9, verse 10

People to avoid

Our rabbis taught: There are four kinds of people who should not be tolerated: a poor man who is arrogant, a rich man who flatters, a lecherous old man, and a leader who lords it over his community without cause.

—Babylonian Talmud,
tractate *Pesahim*, page 113b

Make no friendship with a man who is given to anger.

—Proverbs, chapter 22, verse 24

There is the vain man who, because he regards himself as deserving of praise and considers himself unique and distinguished, deems it proper to assume a dignified bearing when he walks, when he sits, when he stands up, and whenever he says or does anything. . . . He speaks only with those of foremost rank, and even among them he utters only short sentences in oracular fashion. In all his behavior, in his gestures, in his eating, in his drinking, and in his dressing, he carries himself with great pompousness, as though his flesh were made of lead, and his bones of stone.

There is the proud man who thinks that because he possesses some superiority which entitles him to respect, he ought to inspire universal awe, and everyone ought to tremble before him. How dare an ordinary man speak to him or ask anything of him! He overawes with his voice those who dare approach him. He overwhelms people with his arrogant replies, and he scowls all the time. . . .

Another is the man who wants to be noted for his superior qualities and to be singled out for his behavior. He is not satisfied with having everyone praise him for the superior traits which he thinks he possesses, but he wants them also to include in their praises that he is the most humble of men. He thus takes pride in his humility and wishes to be honored because he pretends to flee from honor. . . . He refuses all titles of greatness and declines promotion in rank, but in his heart he thinks, "There is no one in all the world as wise and as humble as I." Conceited people of this type, though they pretend mightily to be humble, cannot escape some mishap which causes their pride to burst forth, like a flame out of a heap of litter. Such a man has been compared to a house filled with straw. The house being full of holes, the straw keeps on creeping through them, so that after a while, everyone knows what is within the house. The humility of his behavior is soon known to be insincere, and his meekness nothing but pretense.

—Moses Hayyim Luzzatto,
The Path of the Upright

When envy and hatred take over

"On the day of your friend's success, participate in his joy," the sages taught, with full awareness that envy is a more typical reaction than joy to a friend's success. Again and again they warned against envy, not only because it destroys any relationship, but because of its self-destructiveness, as Berechiah ha-Nakdan's disturbing fable shows.

A man is envious of everyone except his son and his disciple.

—Rabbi Yose ben Honi, in the
Babylonian Talmud, tractate
Sanhedrin, page 105b

There are some people so foolish that when they see a friend in luck they begin to brood and are so upset and distressed that even the good things they themselves possess no longer afford them pleasure, such is the effect that their friend's good fortune has on them.

Of them the wise Solomon said: "Envy is the rottenness of the bones" (Proverbs 14:30).

—Moses Hayyim Luzzatto,
The Path of the Upright

When God told Moses he was nearing the end of his life, he asked God why he must die.

"Because I have assigned Joshua to lead the Israelites into Canaan," God answered.

"Let him lead," said Moses. "I shall be his servant."

God agreed, but Joshua was not happy about the arrangement. "Do you not wish me to live?" Moses asked him. And Joshua consented to become the master of Moses.

When they were about to enter the Holy Tent, a cloud appeared. Joshua was allowed within the sacred spot, but Moses had to remain outside.

Said Moses, "A hundred deaths are preferable to one pang of jealousy." And he asked to die.

—*Chronicles of Moses*

There were two men, one covetous and the other envious.

Each hated his brother, and they uttered many recriminations against their Creator. . . .

The covetous man would speak as follows: "See how evil and bitter are all the works of God! He has brought the lofty low; why am I poor, whereas that man, my enemy and neighbor who dwells at my right hand, is rich? . . ."

Said the envious man with his wonted hatred, "God will not turn toward you nor listen to your voice to make you a prince over people. Let me die if you grow rich. . . ."

An angel of God found them in the wilderness of Leshem, and when the angel saw them he called to them and said:

"... Lo, I am sent before you to give each of you this day his request and fulfill his petitions. ... This is what I grant you: One of you shall have whatever his mouth utters; it shall come upon him in an instant. And a double portion of what he asks shall accrue to his fellow, who is last in order. This shall be the covenant which you must not violate." ...

And it came to pass ... that the angel departed from them, for the spirit bore him off; no eye saw him, nor were his footsteps perceived. Then did they understand that he was an angel of the Lord and that the law of truth was upon his lips.

The covetous one, who lusted for a double portion, said, "You ask first."

And the envious one answered him, "How shall I ask for a thing when you will emerge stronger than I? ..."

The covetous man grew angry ... and turned upon the envious man in fury and smote him with a high hand. ...

[*The two men continued to fight until finally the envious man spoke up.*]

Then spoke the envious man, saying:

"Please, Lord, do unto your servant the reverse of your kindness. ... Blind me of one of my two eyes, but my enemy of both. Make one of my hands to fail, and double the measure of my enemy."

And it came to pass, as he was speaking, that an awful darkness fell upon them and smote both with blindness.

The second man had double his fellow's measure. ... He turned his face to his fellow, and lo, both his eyes were darkened and his two hands hung from his sleeves so that his strength departed from him. ...

And so the two remained there, for shame and disgrace. Their lust was removed from them and also their hatred, for the covetous man ... did not any more covet the possessions of a lordly house, but only the grave. Nor did the envious man who hated his brother any longer begrudge others. His envy had departed at the ends of the members he had lost. . . . He was smitten to destruction.

—Berechiah ha-Nakdan,
"The Envious Man and the Covetous"

Making peace among friends

Conciliating friends who have quarreled is considered one of the finest deeds a person can perform. The rabbis regarded Aaron, brother of Moses, as a peacemaker to be emulated—even though his technique involved stretching the truth a bit.

Rabbi Beroka of Khuzistan often visited the market at Be Lapat. There he would meet Elijah the prophet [who, according to tradition, sometimes descended from heaven to appear to the pious on earth].

"Does anybody in this market have a share in the world to come?" Rabbi Beroka asked one day. . . .

While they were talking, two men came by.

Elijah said, "Those two have a share in the world to come."

Rabbi Beroka went to them and said, "What do you do?"

They said, "We are jesters. When we see a person depressed, we try to cheer him up. And when we see two people quarreling, we work hard to make peace between them."

—Babylonian Talmud,
tractate *Ta'anit*, page 22a

When two men had quarreled with each other, Aaron would go and sit down with one of them and say to him:

"My son, mark what your fellow is saying! He beats

his breast and tears his clothing, saying, 'Woe unto me! How shall I lift my eyes and look upon my fellow! I am ashamed before him, for I it is who treated him foully.' "

He would sit with him until he had removed all rancor from his heart, and then Aaron would go and sit with the other one and say to him:

"My son, mark what your fellow is saying! He beats his breast and tears his clothing, saying, 'Woe unto me! How shall I lift my eyes and look upon my fellow! I am ashamed before him, for I it is who treated him foully.' "

He would sit with him until he removed all rancor from his heart. And when the two men met each other, they would embrace and kiss each other.

—*Fathers According to Rabbi Nathan*, chapter 12

Extending yourself for others

How much should you inconvenience yourself for a friend? A neighbor? A person you barely know? Should you speak up for someone even if doing so might hurt you? The ideal as the sages saw it was always to reach as far beyond yourself as you could to help others. The patriarch Abraham set the example when he came before God to plead for the lives of the people of Sodom and Gomorrah, cities marked for destruction because of their sinfulness. In one of the most powerful scenes of the Bible, Abraham argues for justice and bargains for each life that might be saved.

Jewish scholars had countless ways of illustrating the evils of Sodom and Gomorrah. One legend states that the people of Sodom were so cruel that when they offered a stranger lodging, they gave him a standard-sized bed. If the visitor was too short for the bed, they stretched his legs to fit it; if he was too tall, they lopped off the part of his legs that hung over.

But many talmudic passages explain the real treachery of these people, not by their grossly wicked acts but by the subtleties of their relationships with others. For example, the rabbis said, the Sodomites would continually cheat a merchant of a shade less than a legally prosecutable amount of money so that they could not be brought to court; as a consequence, the merchant would eventually lose all he had. In the *Ethics of the Fathers* and commentaries on it, the "Sodom type" was seen as a person who insulated himself or herself from any of the cares and concerns of other people.

> Then the Lord said, "The outrage of Sodom and Gomorrah is so great, and their sin so grave! I will go down to see whether they have acted altogether according to the outcry that has come to Me! if not, I will know."
>
> . . . Abraham came forward and said: "Will You sweep away the innocent along with the guilty? What if there should be fifty innocent within the city; will You then wipe out the place and not forgive it for the sake of the innocent fifty who are living in it?
>
> "Far be it from You to do such a thing, to bring death upon the innocent as well as the guilty, so that innocent and guilty fare alike. Far be it from You! Shall not the judge of all the earth deal justly?"
>
> And the Lord answered, "If I find within the city of Sodom fifty innocent ones, I will forgive the whole place for their sake."
>
> Abraham spoke up, saying, "Here I venture to speak to the Lord, I who am but dust and ashes: What if the fifty innocent should lack five? Will you destroy the whole city for want of five?"
>
> And He answered, "I will not destroy if I find forty-five there."
>
> But he spoke to Him again, and said, "What if forty should be found there?" And He answered, "I will not do it, for the sake of the forty."
>
> And he said, "Let not the Lord be angry if I go on: What if thirty should be found there?" And He answered, "I will not do it, if I find thirty there."
>
> And he said, "I venture again to speak to the Lord: What if twenty should be found there?" And He answered, "I will not destroy, for the sake of the twenty."

And he said, "Let not the Lord be angry if I speak but this last time: What if ten should be found there?" And He answered, "I will not destroy, for the sake of the ten."

When the Lord had finished speaking to Abraham, He departed; and Abraham returned to his place.

—Genesis, chapter 18, verses 20–33

There are four types of men:

One who says, "Mine is mine, and yours is yours"—this is the commonplace type. But some say this is the Sodom type.

"Mine is yours and yours is mine"—the ignorant person.

"Mine is yours and yours is yours"—the saint.

"Mine is mine and yours is mine"—the wicked.

—*Ethics of the Fathers,*
chapter 5, paragraph 13

"The Sodom type": A person who lets no one enjoy what he has; once he gets into such a habit, he will eventually refuse to let people enjoy even what costs him nothing.

—Simeon ben Zemah Duran (1361–1444),
Magen Avot

Intervening to stop a wrong

Stepping in when you believe people are acting dishonestly or immorally is one form of extending yourself for them. "You shall surely rebuke your neighbor and not bear sin because of him," the book of Leviticus commands, emphasizing that once you're aware of a wrongdoing, you have some responsibility to try to stop it. The most powerful statement along these lines is Ezekiel's description of his prophetic mission from God; that mission was later translated into a course of action for all people.

Suppose, however, you're convinced that nothing you can do

will stop someone from cheating or lying or stealing. Should you still speak up? Here the Talmud moderates its position, and an eminent thirteenth-century scholar explains why. But the final legend still leaves us pondering the issue.

O mortal, I appoint you watchman for the House of Israel; and when you hear a word from My mouth, you must warn them for Me.

If I say to a wicked man, 'You shall die,' and you do not warn him . . . he, the wicked man, shall die for his iniquity, but I will require a reckoning for his blood from you. . . .

Again, if a righteous man abandons his righteousness and does wrong, when I put a stumbling block before him, he shall die . . . but because you did not warn him, I will require a reckoning for his blood from you. If, however, you warn the righteous man not to sin, and he, the righteous, does not sin, he shall live because he took warning, and you will have saved your own life."

—Ezekiel, chapter 3, verses 17–21

Whoever can prevent members of his household from committing a sin, but does not, is punished for the sins of his household.

If he can prevent his fellow citizens from committing sins, but does not, he is punished for the sins of his fellow citizens.

If he can prevent the whole world from committing sins, but does not, he is punished for the sins of the whole world.

—Babylonian Talmud,
tractate *Shabbat*, page 54b

Just as a person is commanded to speak up if he will be obeyed, so a person is commanded not to speak up if he will not be obeyed.

—Babylonian Talmud,
tractate *Yevamot*, page 65b

It is better for people to sin out of ignorance than to sin purposefully, after being warned that what they are doing is wrong. Therefore, if a person knows definitely that his warnings will not be accepted, he should not give them. But if he has some doubt about whether they will or will not be accepted, he should give them, in order to save his soul.

—Asher ben Jehiel (1250–1327),
Responsa, section 6, number 3

This legend relates to a vision of the destruction of the city of Jerusalem in the book of Ezekiel (chapter 9). According to tradition, because the righteous didn't protest, God changed His mind about separating them from the wicked.

The Holy One, blessed be He, said to His messenger Gabriel: "Go and mark a *taw* [the last letter of the Hebrew alphabet] in ink on the foreheads of the righteous people, so the angel of destruction may have no power over them; and mark a *taw* in blood on the foreheads of the wicked people, so the angel of destruction may have power over them."

The Attribute of Justice then stood before God and said:

"King of the Universe, how does the first group differ from the second?"

"The first are completely good," God replied, "and the second are completely evil."

"King of the Universe," argued Justice, "the righteous

had the power to protest the actions of the others, but they did not."

"It was known," God answered, "that had they protested, the wicked would not have listened to them."

"King of the Universe," replied Justice, "*You* knew they would not have changed. But did the righteous know that?"

—Babylonian Talmud,
tractate *Shabbat*, page 55a

Ways of criticizing

A person who rebukes another, whether for offenses against the rebuker himself or for sins against God, should administer the rebuke in private, speak to the offender gently and tenderly, and point out that he is speaking only for the wrongdoer's own good. . . .

If the wrongdoer accepts the rebuke, well and good. If not, he should be rebuked a second and a third time. And so one is bound to continue the admonition till the sinner assaults the admonisher and says to him, "I refuse to listen."

—Maimonides, *Code*, "Laws Concerning
Moral Dispositions and Ethical
Conduct," chapter 6, section 7

If you're asked for help

A biblical injunction against putting "a stumbling block before the blind" served the rabbis as a springboard for a variety of admonitions and regulations against deceiving people, offering misleading advice, or leading others into error, either intentionally or through lack of concern. For the rabbis, the blind and the deaf served as symbols of weakness, and they took special pains to protect anyone, who, like the disabled, was in a vulnerable position. In the ethical will he left his family, the eighteenth-century scholar Elijah de Veali emphasized discretion and modesty when helping those in need. His admonition stems from the talmudic view that reminding people of the good you've done for them is another form of holding a grudge against them.

Scripture says:

"You shall not insult the deaf or put a stumbling block before the blind. You shall fear your God: I am the Lord" (Leviticus 19:14).

"The blind" means somebody who is blind to a certain matter.

If, for example, someone asks you whether so-and-so's daughter may marry a priest, do not say that she may when really she may not. [Priests were forbidden to marry certain categories of women, such as divorcées.]

If a person asks for your advice, don't give advice that may cause harm. Don't tell him to get up early in the morning when you know he might be captured by bandits, or to go out at noontime when he might suffer sunstroke.

Don't advise someone to sell his field and buy a donkey with the money so that you can get the field for yourself.

You might argue: I'm giving good advice. But the thing is known in your heart. And therefore it is said: "But you shall fear your God; I am the Lord."

—*Sifra* on chapter 19, verse 14

If ye render a kindness to any man, do not recurrently remind him of it. This is a despicable habit.

So was Nehemiah punished—his book not being named after him because of his boast, "Remember unto me O God, for good, all that I have done for this people." [The biblical book of Nehemiah is considered part of the book of Ezra.]

But fix this maxim in your heart: "Do what you say, but say not what you do!"

—Elijah ben Raphael Solomon ha-Levi de Veali, rabbi of Alessandria in Northern Italy from 1738–1792, from his Testament

How to be a good host/gracious guest

In the Bible, Abraham became the model for welcoming and entertaining guests when—with help from his wife, Sarah—he quickly prepared an elaborate dinner for three messengers of God who appeared to him dressed as simple nomads. His graciousness was especially notable because he was still recuperating from the circumcision, which symbolized his covenant with God, at the age of ninety-nine. With him as their example, the rabbis praised the virtues of hospitality, especially hospitality to strangers. While they derived many of their rules from the Greeks and Romans among whom they lived, they stressed sincerity far more than mere formalities, and they concerned themselves with the behavior of guests as well as hosts—extending the obligations of a guest even to travelers in a foreign country.

There are many kinds of thieves.

First there are those who steal the hearts of people.

He who urges his neighbor to be his guest when in his heart he does not mean to invite him;

he who frequently offers gifts to his neighbor knowing well that they will not be accepted;

and he who makes his guest believe that he is opening a barrel of wine especially for him when in reality it has been sold to a shopkeeper. [Because wine spoiled quickly, people often arranged to have shopkeepers buy their wine once a barrel had been opened.]

—*Mekhilta of Rabbi Ishmael*, tractate "Nezikin," chapter 13

One Bar Yohania decided to give a banquet for the notables of Rome. He consulted with Rabbi Eliezer ben Yose ha-Gelili.

Said Rabbi Eliezer, "If you intend to invite twenty, prepare enough for twenty-five, and if you intend to invite twenty-five, prepare enough for thirty."

He, however, prepared only enough for twenty-four and then invited twenty-five.

The result was he was one dish short—some say it was artichokes.

He brought a gold dish and set it before the guest who was short. The guest threw it in his face, saying, "Do I eat gold?"

Bar Yohania went to Rabbi Eliezer ben Yose and said to him, "Indeed, I ought not to tell you this, for you told me what to do and I did not do it. But I want to know: Has God revealed to you scholars the secrets of the Torah and the secrets of entertaining as well?"

Rabbi Eliezer answered, "He has revealed to us the secrets of entertaining as well."

"How did you know what to do?" he asked.

Rabbi Eliezer answered, "From David, because it is written, 'When Abner came to David in Hebron, accompanied by twelve men, David made a feast for Abner and the men with him' (II Samuel 3:20). It doesn't simply say, 'He made a feast,' but it also says 'for the men with him.' "

—*Esther Rabbah*,
chapter 2, section 4

What does a good guest say?

"How much trouble my host has gone to for me. How much meat he has set before me. How much wine he has given me. How many cakes he has served me! And all this trouble he has gone to has been only for my sake!"

But what does a bad guest say?

"What kind of effort did this host make for me? I have eaten only one slice of bread. I have eaten only one piece of meat, and I have drunk only one cup of wine! Whatever trouble this host went to was done only for the sake of his wife and his children."

—Simeon ben Zoma, in the Babylonian Talmud, tractate *Berakhot*, page 58a

---

A guest eating in a house in which he has been offered hospitality should leave something on his plate to show that he was given more than enough. If he eats everything, people might say it is because he was not given enough.

If, however, the host said to him: "Please do not leave anything. Why throw the food to the dogs?" he should follow the wishes of his host and leave nothing on his plate. Furthermore, if they have to throw away the food he leaves, he will be guilty of wasting food.

—Judah the Pious, *Book of the Pious*, section 872

When the Israelites came to Edom they said to the king, "Allow us through your land . . . we will not drink the waters of a well" (Numbers 20:17). From this we learn good manners.

Even if a person traveling in a strange country has all his own supplies with him, he should not eat and drink what he brought with him.

Instead, he should buy what he needs from the local shopkeepers in order to improve trade.

What Moses meant when he spoke to the King of Edom was, "We will not drink from the well that we have with us [a legendary well that supposedly accompanied the Israelites on their journeys], and we will not eat the manna that has been given us. You won't be able to complain that we were nothing but trouble to you, because we will bring you business."

—*Tanhuma* (edited by Solomon Buber),
on Numbers, portion "Hukkat,"
page 61b

Respecting others' privacy

A biblical story tells how the soothsayer Balaam went out to curse the Israelites, but when he saw their encampment he blessed them instead. The scholars' interpretation of this was that when Balaam looked up he saw that the doors of the Israelites' tents were not directly opposite one another, and he blessed them for respecting one another's privacy. Jewish law legislates this high regard for privacy into prohibitions against even the most subtle forms of prying.

Do not appease your fellow in his hour of anger;
do not comfort him while the dead is still laid out before him;
do not question him in the hour of his vow;
and do not strive to see him in his hour of misfortune.

—Rabbi Simeon ben Eleazar, in
Ethics of the Fathers,
chapter 4, paragraph 23

A person should never enter another person's home without warning.

In this regard we can learn good manners from God, who remained outside the Garden of Eden and called to Adam before entering, as it is written: "The Lord God called out to man and said to him, 'Where are you?'" (Genesis 3:9).

—Minor tractate of the Talmud,
Derekh Erez Rabbah, chapter 5

When you make a loan of any sort to your neighbor, you must not enter his house to seize his pledge. You must remain outside, while the man to whom you made the loan brings the pledge out to you.

—Deuteronomy, chapter 24, verse 10

Come and hear: If a man's roof overlooks his neighbor's courtyard, he must build a railing round his roof that is four cubits high.

There is a special reason for this rule. The owner of the courtyard can say to the owner of the roof, "I use my courtyard only at fixed times, but you have no fixed times for using your roof. I have no way of knowing when you might go up on your roof so I can keep out of your sight and maintain my privacy."

—Babylonian Talmud,
tractate *Bava Batra*, page 2b

On being a good neighbor

In the Jewish legal system, many of the laws governing relations among neighbors stem directly from moral principles. For instance, if one neighbor can benefit from something and the other loses nothing, the second is obliged to go along with the wishes of the first. Typical of such moralistic laws is the "law of pre-emption," developed by the Babylonian sages. It states that a person selling his property must give first option on the sale to the owner of the property that lies immediately adjacent to his. The rationale for this law is the biblical command to "do what is right and good in the eyes of the Lord." In the eyes of the rabbis, it was "right and good" to give one's neighbor a first chance to acquire the land abutting his own.

But what happens when what seems "right" to one neighbor appears as an imposition to another? In the case history below, one homeowner would be inconvenienced if he acceded to his neighbor's request. While it might be generous of him to do so, the authorities say that legally he does not have to put his neighbor's comfort before his own.

Even if a man sells his land to another, the neighbor whose land is contiguous to the purchased land may repay the money to the purchaser and evict him thence. . . .

This law of pre-emption applies . . . even if the purchaser is a scholar, a neighbor, or a relation to the seller, and the owner of the adjacent field is an ignorant person and not related; the latter nevertheless has priority and can evict the purchaser. . . .

If one sells to orphans, the law of pre-emption does not apply because the "good and right" which results from kindness to them is greater than that which would redound to the owner of the adjacent land.

Thus, also, if one sells to a woman the law of pre-emption does not apply because it is not customary for a woman constantly to exert herself to buy; but now that she has bought, it is a kindness to her to let the land remain with her.

—Maimonides, *Code*, "Laws
Concerning Neighbors,"
chapter 12, sections 5, 13, and 14

A man once began to build a wall that faced his neighbor's window.

The neighbor said to him, "You are blocking off my light."

He answered, "I will close off the windows you have

and make new windows for you above the level of my wall."

"No," said the neighbor, "you will damage my wall if you do that."

"In that case," said the man, "I will tear down the wall in your house as far as the windows, and rebuild it with windows in it higher than my wall."

"A wall that is new on top and old on the bottom will not stand firmly," said the neighbor.

"If you wish," said the man, "I will tear down the entire wall and rebuild it with new windows in it."

"No," said the neighbor," a single new wall in an old house will not stand firmly."

"If so," he said, "let me tear down the whole house and build you a new one with windows in it."

"I have no place to live in the meantime," said the neighbor.

"I'll rent a house for you," said the man.

"I don't want to bother," said the neighbor.

Rabbi Hama said: The neighbor has every legal right to prevent the building of the wall.

—Babylonian Talmud,
tractate *Bava Batra*, page 7a

Returning lost property

Over the centuries, using a few brief, biblical verses, the sages extrapolated dozens of laws about things lost and found, always with the objective of encouraging people to go out of their way for one another. Returning lost property to non-Jews, whose laws did not make the same demands on them, was considered an act of special merit that sanctified God's name.

If you see your fellow's ox or sheep gone astray, do not ignore it; you must take it back to your fellow.

If your fellow does not live near you or you do not

know who he is, you shall bring it home and it shall remain with you until your fellow claims it; then you shall give it back to him.

You shall do the same with his ass; you shall do the same with his garment; and so too shall you do with anything that your fellow loses and you find: you must not remain indifferent.

—Deuteronomy, chapter 22, verses 1–3

Some found articles become the property of the finder immediately, and others have to be advertised.

The following become the property of the finder:

scattered fruits, scattered coins, small sheaves of corn lying in a public road, cakes of pressed figs, baker's loaves, strings of fish, pieces of meat, fleeces of wool in their natural state....

The following found articles must be advertised:

fruit in a vessel or an empty vessel, money in a purse or an empty purse, heaps of fruit, heaps of coins, three coins one on top of the other, small sheaves lying on private property, homemade loaves of bread, fleeces of wool that had been removed from a workshop. . . .

If someone finds something in a store it belongs to him; but if he finds it between the counter and the storekeeper's seat, it belongs to the storekeeper. . . .

—Mishnah, tractate *Bava Mezia*,
chapter 2, paragraphs 1, 2, and 4

Our rabbis taught: In former days whoever found a lost article would advertise it during the three festivals, and an additional seven days after the last festival. . . .

After the destruction of the Temple—may it be speedily rebuilt in our own day—the announcement was made in synagogues and schoolhouses.

But when men of violence increased, it was decreed

that the finder should inform his friends and neighbors, and that would suffice.

—Babylonian Talmud, tractate *Bava Mezia*, page 28b

If one finds a sack or a basket, the rule is as follows:

If he is a scholar or a respected elder who is not accustomed to taking such things in his hand, he need not concern himself with them. He must, however, examine his own conscience.

If he would have taken these things back for himself had they belonged to him, he must also return them when they belong to someone else. But if he would not have overlooked his dignity even had they belonged to him, he need not return them when they belong to another. . . .

If one follows the good and upright path and does more than the strict letter of the law requires, he will return lost property in all cases, even if it is not in keeping with his dignity.

—Maimonides, *Code*, "Laws Concerning Robbery and Lost Property," chapter 11, sections 13 and 17

On shaming others

"Wronging people with words," the masters said, is far worse than cheating them in financial matters, for while the one affects only their money, the other affects their entire being. Hurting another person, we're told, is a crime comparable to murder. Although in most cases of verbal assault, unlike physical assault, no legal penalties can be brought against the guilty person, God Himself hears and avenges the cries of the victim.

An tanna [a person who memorized oral teachings] recited before Rabbi Nahman ben Isaac:

"A person who publicly shames his neighbor is like someone who has shed blood."

To which Rabbi Nahman answered, "You have spoken well. I have seen that when someone is shamed, the color leaves his face and he becomes pale."

Abbaye asked Rabbi Dimi, "What do people in Palestine most carefully try to avoid?"

He answered, "Putting others to shame."

Three categories of people are condemned to eternal hell: he who commits adultery with a married woman; he who publicly shames his neighbor; and he who calls his neighbor by a degrading nickname, even if the other is accustomed to that name.

. . . It would be better for a man to throw himself into a fiery furnace than publicly put his neighbor to shame.

—Babylonian Talmud, tractate
Bava Mezia, pages 58b–59a

Rabbi Eleazar said: Since the destruction of the Temple, the gates of prayers are locked [making it harder for prayers to reach heaven].

But even though the gates of prayers are locked, the gates of tears are not.

Rabbi Hisda said: All gates are locked except the gates through which pass the cries of people who have been wronged.

—Babylonian Talmud, tractate
Bava Mezia, page 59a

In the years after the destruction of the Second Temple, a court of scholars was convened at various times to fix the months of the year and the festivals. This was known as intercalation of the year.

Once Rabban Gamaliel II said: "Send seven scholars to the upper chamber early in the morning" [to intercalate the year].

When he came in the morning he found eight.

"Whoever came without permission must leave," he announced.

Samuel the Little arose and said, "I am the one who came without permission. But I didn't come to take part in the intercalation; I came because I wanted to learn the law."

"Sit down, my son, sit down," said Rabban Gamaliel. "You are certainly worthy of intercalating the year, but the rabbis decreed that only those specifically appointed for that purpose may do so."

In reality, it was not Samuel the Little who had not been invited but another scholar. Samuel had taken the blame upon himself to save the other from embarrassment.

—Babylonian Talmud, tractate *Sanhedrin,* page 11a

It once happened, that while Rabbi [Judah the Prince] was giving a lecture, he smelled garlic in the room.

"The person who has eaten garlic must leave," he announced.

Rabbi Hiyya stood up and left, and then all the other scholars followed him out.

In the morning, Rabbi Simeon, the son of Rabbi, met Rabbi Hiyya and said, "Was it you who caused that annoying odor?"

"Heaven forbid!" said Rabbi Hiyya [but he and the other scholars wanted to keep the culprit from humiliation].

—Babylonian Talmud, tractate *Sanhedrin,* page 11a

If a man pulls another man's ears, plucks his hair, spits in his face, or removes his garments, or if he uncovers the head of a woman in the marketplace [married women always kept their heads covered as a sign of modesty], he must pay the other person four hundred *zuz*. . . .

It once happened that a man uncovered the head of a woman in the marketplace and when the case came before Rabbi Akiva, he ruled that the offender must pay the woman four hundred *zuz*.

The man said, "Rabbi, give me some time to pay." Rabbi Akiva agreed.

The man watched for the woman, and one day when he saw her standing outside the door of her courtyard, he broke a jug of oil in front of her.

The woman uncovered her head, collected the oil in her palms, and rubbed it on her head. The man had set up witnesses to the event and then appeared before Rabbi Akiva.

"Must I pay four hundred *zuz* to such a woman?" he asked [indicating that she showed no modesty herself by uncovering her head].

Said Rabbi Akiva, "Your argument carries no legal weight. Although it is forbidden for a person to injure himself, someone who does so need not pay a fine. But if others were to injure that person they would be liable.

"In the same way, a person who cuts down his own plants, although this is unlawful, does not pay a fine. But if others cut down his plants, they are liable."

—Mishnah, tractate *Bava Kamma*,
chapter 8, paragraph 6

When to bury the past

A truly thoughtful person, we are advised, does not even allude to subjects that might cause another's discomfort, does not even tolerate reminders of another's sin. The legendary account of the deaths of Resh Lakish and Rabbi Johanan ben Nappaha was used by the rabbis as a lesson in sensitivity to a person's past. An outstanding Palestinian scholar of the third century and a massive, powerful man, Resh Lakish (whose full name was Simeon ben

Lakish) had fought wild animals as a gladiator during his youth. Rabbi Johanan convinced him to give up that life and turn to study. He became a disciple and later an equal of Rabbi Johanan's.

If a man is a penitent, one must not say to him, "Remember your former deeds."

If he is the son of proselytes, he should not be taunted, "Remember the deeds of your ancestors."

If he is a proselyte and comes to study the Torah, one must not say to him, "Shall the mouth that ate unclean and forbidden foods . . . come to study the Torah that was spoken by the mouth of the All Powerful?"

—Babylonian Talmud, tractate *Bava Mezia*, page 58b

The book of Leviticus commands that if a man or woman commits bestiality, both the human and the animal must be killed. The talmudic sages were distressed at what seemed unfair treatment of the animal, who could not be held responsible, but gave this as an explanation:

If the man has sinned, in what way has the animal offended? . . .

[One] reason is that the animal should not walk through the streets, leading people to say, "This is the animal on whose account so-and-so was stoned."

—Mishnah, tractate *Sanhedrin*, chapter 7, paragraph 4

One day Rabbi Johanan was bathing in the Jordan River, when Resh Lakish saw him and leapt in after him. . . .

"Your strength should be devoted to the study of Torah," said Rabbi Johanan.

"And your beauty," said Resh Lakish, "should be for women."

"If you will repent," said Rabbi Johanan, "I will let you marry my sister, who is even more beautiful than I."

Resh Lakish repented, married Rabbi Johanan's sister, and studied with Rabbi Johanan, who taught him Bible and Mishnah and turned him into a great scholar.

One day there was a dispute in the house of study about when certain utensils—the sword, knife, dagger, spear, handsaw, and scythe—may become ritually unclean.

Rabbi Johanan ruled: when they are tempered in a furnace.

Resh Lakish insisted: when they have been scoured in water.

Rabbi Johanan, piqued, said, "A robber understands his trade" [referring to Resh Lakish's use of these weapons in his work as a gladiator].

To which Resh Lakish replied in anger, "And how have you helped me? There [at the Roman circus] I was called Master and here I am called Master."

Rabbi Johanan felt deeply hurt [by the implication that he had not helped Resh Lakish] and he refused to forgive him. As a result of this event Resh Lakish fell ill . . . and then died.

Rabbi Johanan sank into a profound depression . . . tearing his clothes and weeping, "Where are you O son of Lakisha? Where are you O son of Lakisha?" until he lost his mind.

Then the rabbis prayed for him to be freed of his misery, and he died.

—Babylonian Talmud, tractate
Bava Mezia, page 84a

Avoiding insults

Although the Talmud awards damages to a person who has been insulted only in specific cases where the insult can be proved false, rabbis in many communities meted out stiff punishment for insults and ridicule. In his responsum, Rabbi Solomon ben Jehiel Luria, a Lithuanian scholar, threatens excommunication for a man who had insulted a woman, even though he had whispered the insult to her privately. Rabbi Moses ben Isaac Alashkar, a Spanish talmudist, doesn't specify punishment in his responsum, but he makes it clear that he considers the implied insult discussed as serious an offense as an outright one.

I have seen the evidence against one Master Yakar bar Simeon, who whispered insults and obscenities in the ear of Mistress Rahana, wife of Rav Eleazar.

Here's what the man said: "You won't dance with me because I won't pay you three *gulden*, just the way you take money from a man in order to sleep with him."

. . . The woman is to be praised because she responded by crying out loud from embarrassment and modesty. Although he's the one who should have cried because of his great sin.

The man reduced this woman to the status of a prostitute with his words. And even though he insisted that the man he referred to from whom she extracted money is her husband, what kind of a person would make a statement like that—that a woman won't sleep with her own husband unless he pays her!

. . . And now I decree that Master Yakar should . . . ask forgiveness with these words: "I Yakar have sinned, and now I ask the Lord first and then Mistress Rahana and her husband, Eleazar, to forgive my obscenities. . . ."

. . . After asking forgiveness Yakar should spend four weeks in mourning. If he refuses to follow this ruling, he should be excommunicated.

—Solomon ben Jehiel Luria (1510?–1576),
Responsa, number 59

Rabbi Alashkar was asked the following question:

A man was quarreling with his friend, and in the midst of their words he cried out, "*I'm* not a bastard! *I'm* not an apostate! *I'm* not a sinner!" Isn't he implying by those words that his friend is a bastard, or apostate, or sinner—the hidden meaning being, "I'm not a bastard or sinner like *you*?"

The rabbi answered:

"It seems to me that the man's words carry the unspoken implication of I'm not a so-and-so like *you*. After all, his companion did not accuse him of being a bastard or sinner. There was no need for him to deny those appellations, except that he meant to imply, 'I'm not one but you are.' "

We can relate this to the tractate *Bava Mezia* in the Babylonian Talmud, page 33a. The discussion there concerns rulings about showing greater respect for one's teacher than for one's father. The Talmud records that Rabbi Hisda asked of his own teacher, Rabbi Huna, "What kind of respect should be shown by a disciple whose teacher needs him as much as he needs the teacher?"

Rabbi Huna took this question as a personal attack and cried out, "Hisda, Hisda, I don't need you, but you'll need me until you're forty years old." After that they remained angry and did not visit one another for many years.

Now, although Rabbi Hisda may have meant no insult at all by his words, they were interpreted as maligning by Rabbi Huna, and from his point of view they were as destructive as though Rabbi Hisda had openly insulted him.

The situation is similar in our case. It was as though the man had openly said, "I'm not a so-and-so, like *you*." He has insulted his friend without uttering an outright insult.

—Moses ben Isaac Alashkar,
(1466–1542), *Responsa*, number 81

Gossip: "like the poison of a serpent"

The sages said: "A large number of people commit robbery, either directly or indirectly, a small number commit incest, but just about everyone is guilty of slander." Because they recognized the universal appeal it has, they condemned gossip in the strongest terms, sometimes comparing it to idolatry or even murder. Maimonides summarizes their attitudes, and the moralist Jonah ben Abraham Gerondi adds that just listening to gossip is as bad as spreading it yourself. Ironically, Rabbi Gerondi spent a good part of his early life viciously criticizing Maimonides, who lived shortly before him and whose philosophy he violently opposed. He later regretted his attacks, publicly apologized, and supposedly wrote his best-known moralistic works as a form of repentance and a lesson to others.

Why is gossip like a three-pronged tongue? Because it kills three people: the person who says it, the person who listens to it, and the person about whom it is said.

—Babylonian Talmud, tractate *Arakhin*, page 15b

Whoever tells tales about another person violates a prohibition, as it is said: "Do not go about as a talebearer among your fellows" (Leviticus 19:16). . . .

Who is a talebearer? One who carries reports and goes about from one person to another and says, "So-and-so said this"; "I have heard such-and-such about so-and-so." Even if what he says or repeats may be true, the talebearer ruins the world.

There is a still graver offense that comes within this prohibition, namely, the evil tongue. This means talking disparagingly of anyone, even though what one says is true; but he who utters a falsehood is called a slanderer.

A person with an evil tongue is one who, sitting in company, says, "That person did such a thing"; "So-and-so's ancestors were so-and-so"; "I have heard this about him"; and then proceeds to talk scandal. . . .

There are modes of speech that may be styled "dust of the evil tongue": such remarks as "Who would have thought that so-and-so would be as he is now"; or, "Be silent about so-and-so. I don't want to tell what happened"; and so on. . . .

Equally reprehensible is the person who indulges in evil speech deceitfully, that is, speaks as though innocently, as if unaware that what he says is an evil utterance. . . .

—Maimonides, *Code*, "Laws Concerning Moral Dispositions and Ethical Conduct," chapter 7, sections 1–4

Take heed and know that a person who agrees with a slanderous statement when he hears it is as bad as the one who says it, for everyone will say: "That person who listened to what has been said agreed with it, and that shows it must be true."

Even if the hearer only turns to listen to the gossip and gives the impression of believing it to be true, he helps spread the evil, brings disgrace on his neighbor, and encourages slanderers to carry their evil reports to all people.

—Jonah ben Abraham Gerondi (c. 1200–1263), *Sha'arei Teshuvah*, section 3

The dangers of overpraising

So concerned were the sages about gossip of any kind that one scholar, Rabbi Dimi, even taught that no person should praise another, "for through too much praise he will bring about abuse."

Rabbi Gerondi questioned that teaching in light of the fact that Jewish tradition had always encouraged people to speak well of one another. He resolved the contradiction this way:

> The answer is this: A person should only praise another person in private, that is, when one person speaks to another, and not in public or at a large gathering, unless it is known to him that none of the people present hates or envies the man being praised.
>
> If, however, you want to praise someone who has an outstanding reputation and is known as a person who has no faults, it is proper to praise him even in the presence of his enemies or of people who are jealous of him, because they will not be able to speak evil of him. For everybody will know that the person who speaks evil lies and his words are hurting only himself.
>
> —Jonah ben Abraham Gerondi,
> *Sha'arei Teshuvah*, section 3

If you know someone is a cheat

No matter how scrupulously you might want to avoid gossiping, there are times when it becomes necessary to speak against somebody. Rabbi Israel Meir ha-Kohen, a Lithuanian scholar who devoted his life to investigating every possible aspect of gossip and slander, discusses such situations.

During the early 1870s, Rabbi Israel Meir published a definitive code of law on the subject called *Hafez Hayyim*, which won so much popularity that the author himself became known as the Hafez Hayyim. The name, which in English means "eager for life," comes from a verse in the book of Psalms: "Who is the man who is eager for life . . . Guard your tongue from evil."

> If a person knows that someone has committed an injustice to his friend—perhaps cheated him or stolen from

him or verbally fooled him—and he knows that the guilty person did not repay the theft or ask for forgiveness for his dishonesty, then the person who knows of these actions is permitted to tell others in order to help the injured party and protect others. But seven conditions must be present:

(1) The person needs to have evidence of the dishonesty himself and not merely to have heard rumors about it.

(2) The person must be very cautious and weigh the matter thoroughly to see whether it actually was a case of wrongdoing. And then he needs to think about it carefully before acting on his knowledge.

(3) He must admonish the dishonest person privately in a quiet, reassuring manner to see whether he will change his ways. If not, he may speak out publicly.

(4) He must not make the offense seem greater than it is.

(5) He needs to examine his own motives and make sure he's not slandering the person because of a private grudge, but is doing so in good faith and for constructive reasons.

(6) If there are any ways through which he can get around the situation without slandering the person, he should pursue those methods first.

(7) As a result of his action, he must not bring greater punishment on the guilty person than a court might order if the person were to be tried in court.

In addition, the person who publicly maligns someone else must himself be honest and not guilty of the same crimes for which he is criticizing another. . . . And he must be sure the people to whom he is speaking about the dishonesty are not evil people who indulge in the same practices themselves.

—Israel Meir ha-Kohen (1838–1933),
Hafez Hayyim, "M'kor Hayyim,"
rule 10

Guarding a confidence

Though Ben Sira recognized how hard it is to keep a secret, he and the later masters were unequivocal about respecting a confidence—personal or professional—perhaps indefinitely. Even mentioning a secret in private among people who know it is in poor taste, as the Hasidic Rabbi of Apta discovered.

Tell no tales about friend or foe; unless silence makes you an accomplice, never betray a man's secret.

Suppose he has heard you and learned to distrust you, he will seize the first chance to show his hatred.

Have you heard a rumor? Let it die with you. Never fear, it will not make you burst.

A fool with a secret goes through agony like a woman in childbirth.

—Wisdom of Ben Sira,
chapter 19, verses 8–11

Rumor had it that a certain disciple of Rabbi Ammi revealed a secret report he had been given in the house of learning twenty-two years earlier.

So Rabbi Ammi expelled him with the accusation: "This man reveals secrets!"

—Babylonian Talmud, tractate
Sanhedrin, page 31a

And how do we know that when leaving a trial, a judge must not say, "I was for acquittal, but my colleagues were for conviction, and what could I do since they were in the majority?"

Because of such a person, Scripture says, "Do not go

about as a talebearer among your fellows" (Leviticus 19:16).

—Mishnah, tractate *Sanhedrin*, chapter 3, paragraph 6

A respected and important woman once came to seek the advice of the Rabbi of Apta. The moment he looked at her the rabbi, who knew many things intuitively, cried out, "Adulteress! Just a short time ago you sinned, and now you dare enter my home!"

With great emotion the woman quickly answered:

"God has patience with the wicked. He does not punish them quickly and does not reveal their secret to anyone, lest they be ashamed to turn to Him. And He does not hide His face from them.

"Yet this rabbi sits in his office and cannot hold himself back for even a moment but must reveal what the Creator has kept hidden."

As a result of this incident, the rabbi used to say, "Nobody ever got the better of me, except one woman."

—Tale about the Hasidic rabbi Abraham Joshua Heschel of Apta (died in 1825)

Judging others

A certain amount of caution in dealing with people is suggested so that you don't unwittingly find yourself associated with someone with whom you would not want to be connected. But for the most part, Hillel's saying in the *Ethics of the Fathers* is considered to be a good rule of thumb to follow in forming an opinion about others: "Do not judge your fellow man until you have stood in his place." Or, going a step further, Joshua ben Perahyah urged: "Judge everyone with the scale weighted in his favor."

The cautious people of Jerusalem had these rules:

They would not sign a document unless they knew who was signing with them;

they would not sit on a court without knowing who would be sitting with them;

and they would not eat at a table unless they knew who their fellow diners would be.

—Babylonian Talmud, tractate *Sanhedrin*, page 23a

There was once a young girl who had been taken captive, and two saintly folk went after her to ransom her.

One of the men entered a harlot's house [where the girl was being held]. When he came out, he asked his companion:

"What did you suspect me of?"

The other replied, "Of finding out perhaps for how much money she is being held."

Said the first, "By the Temple service, so it was!" And he added, "Even as you did judge me with the scale weighted in my favor, so may the Holy One, blessed be He, judge you with the scale weighted in your favor."

—*Fathers According to Rabbi Nathan*, chapter 8

Retaliating for an injury

The biblical law of extracting "eye for eye," so harsh on its surface, had its counterpart in many ancient legal codes, including the Babylonian Code of Hammurabi. There was one crucial difference, however: in the other legal systems, a man may substitute a slave, or servant, or child to be punished in his stead. In the Bible, the guilty person—and that person alone—is punished for a crime, no matter how rich he is, how many slaves he may offer to replace him, or how much money he is willing to pay to buy his way out. Rich and poor are treated alike, and in that sense, the biblical law was meant to be universal and democratic. Later rabbis, repelled by the concept of physical retaliation for anyone, rich or poor, interpreted what they considered to be the spirit and intent of the law. Damages for a physical injury of any sort, they insisted, were meant to be compensated with a fixed amount of money, and the law was stated so severely only to teach a lesson: that a person who willfully injures another deserves to be injured in kind. They proved their point by using other biblical verses and their own logical arguments.

> If anyone maims his fellow, as he has done so shall it be done to him: fracture for fracture, eye for eye, tooth for tooth. The injury he inflicted on another shall be inflicted on him.
>
> —Leviticus, chapter 24, verses 19–20

> A person who injures another becomes liable to him for five items: for damages, for pain, for healing, for loss of time and for humiliation.
>
> How are damages estimated? If he poked out his eye, cut off his arm, or broke his leg, the injured person is considered as if he were a slave being sold in the market, and an appraisal is made as to how much he was worth before and how much he is worth now.
>
> Pain—If he burned him . . . we find out how much money a man of equal standing would accept to undergo so much pain.
>
> Healing—If he struck him, he is obligated to pay medical expenses. . . .
>
> Loss of time—To estimate the loss, the injured person is considered as though he were a watchman in a cucumber field. . . .
>
> Humiliation—To be estimated according to the status of the offended and of the offender.
>
> —Mishnah, tractate *Bava Kamma*, chapter 8, paragraph 1

You might think that where one person put out the other's eye, the offender's eye should be put out, or where he cut off his arm, the offender's arm should be cut off, or where he broke his leg, the offender's leg should be broken. But this is not so....

Note that Scripture says "You may not accept a ransom for the life of a murderer who is guilty of a capital crime; he must be put to death" [Numbers 35:31]. This implies that you may not accept compensation only when a murder has been committed, but you may take compensation for the destruction of parts of the body, even though these cannot be restored....

Rabbi Dostai ben Judah said: "Eye for eye" means monetary compensation. But perhaps this is not so and actual retaliation is meant? In that case, suppose the eye of one person was big and the eye of the other person was small. How, then, could you apply the principle of "eye for eye"? If you say, however, that monetary compensation was meant, you follow the Torah's teaching that "You shall have one standard of law" (Leviticus 24:22), implying that the standard of law is the same in all cases....

Rabbi Simeon bar Yohai said: "Eye for eye" means monetary compensation. But perhaps this is not so and actual retaliation is meant? In that case, how would you handle a situation in which a blind man put out someone's eye, or a cripple cut off someone's hand, or a lame person broke someone's leg? You cannot carry out the principle of retaliation in these cases, since the Torah says: "You shall have one standard of law," implying that the standard of law should be the same in all cases....

Abbaye said: The principle of compensation can be derived from the teaching of the school of Hezekiah. In that school it was taught, "eye for eye, life for life," but not "life and eye for eye." Now if you assume that the Bible meant actual retaliation, you might accidentally take an eye and a life as retribution for an eye because the shock of being blinded might cause a person to die. . . .

—Babylonian Talmud, tractate *Bava Kamma*, pages 83b–84a

Bearing a grudge

The Bible forbids us to "take vengeance or bear a grudge," and the sages, considering both terms, elaborated on the different ways people have of getting even with one another.

What is revenge and what is bearing a grudge?

If one person asks another to lend him his sickle and he refuses, and the next day the second person asks the first to lend him his axe and the first man answers, "I will not lend it to you just as you would not lend me your sickle"—that is revenge.

But if one person asks another to lend him his axe and that person refuses, and the next day the second person asks the first to lend him his jacket, and the first answers, "Here it is. I'm not like you who would not lend me what I asked for"—that is bearing a grudge.

—Babylonian Talmud, tractate *Yoma*, page 23a

The human heart in its perversity finds it hard to escape hatred and revenge.

A man is very sensitive to disgrace and suffers keenly when subjected to it. Revenge is sweeter to him than honey; he cannot rest until he has taken his revenge. . . .

The evil inclination always wants to excite us to anger and continually attempts to have us retain at least some remembrance of the evil our neighbor has done to us. . . .

He argues this way: "If you want to grant that man the favor which he refused you when you were in need, you do not have to grant it to him cheerfully. You may refuse to retaliate, but you do not have to be his benefactor or offer him help. . . ."

With these and similar sophistries the evil inclination endeavors to seduce our hearts. The Torah therefore lays down a general rule which takes all these possibilities into account:

"Love your neighbor as yourself"—as yourself without difference or distinction, without subterfuge and mental reservation, literally as yourself.

—Moses Hayyim Luzzatto,
The Path of the Upright

Forgiving your enemies

The ultimate expression of treating others as you would want to be treated is forgiving and accepting people who have hurt you. The sages had high praise for "those who are insulted but do not insult, hear their shame but do not reply." The story of Joseph receiving his brothers is an eloquent example of forgiveness and love. According to the Bible, Joseph's brothers had sold him into slavery in Egypt as a youth. There he rose to become one of the most powerful ministers of the land. When his brothers came to Egypt during a year of famine to request food, Joseph revealed himself to them.

If you have done your fellow a slight wrong, let it be a serious matter in your eyes; but if you have done your fellow much good, let it be a trifle in your eyes.

And if your fellow has done you a slight favor, let it be a great thing in your eyes; if your fellow has done you a great evil, let it be a little thing in your eyes.

—*Fathers According to*
Rabbi Nathan, chapter 41

Rejoice not when your enemy falls,
  And let not your heart be glad when he stumbles....
If your enemy is hungry, give him bread to eat,
  And if he is thirsty, give him water to drink.

—Proverbs, chapter 24, verse 17; chapter 25, verse 21

In that hour when the Israelites crossed the Red Sea, the ministering angels wanted to sing a song of praise before God.

But He said to them: "My handiwork [the Egyptians] is drowning in the sea, yet you want to sing a song before me!"

—Babylonian Talmud, tractate *Sanhedrin*, page 39b

Who is mighty? He who makes of his enemy a friend.

—*Fathers According to Rabbi Nathan*, chapter 23

Joseph could no longer control himself before all his attendants, and he cried out, "Have everyone withdraw from me!"

So there was no one else about when Joseph made himself known to his brothers. His sobs were so loud that the Egyptians could hear, and so the news reached Pharaoh's palace.

Joseph said to his brothers, "I am Joseph. Is my father still well?" But his brothers could not answer him, so dumbfounded were they on account of him.

Then Joseph said to his brothers, "Come forward to me." And when they came forward, he said, "I am your brother Joseph, he whom you sold into Egypt.

"Now, do not be distressed or reproach yourselves because you sold me hither; it was to save life that God sent me ahead of you. It is now two years that there has been famine in the land, and there are still five years to come in which there shall be no yield from tilling.

"God has sent me ahead of you to insure your survival on earth and to save your lives in an extraordinary deliverance. So it was not you who sent me here, but God; and He has made me a father to Pharaoh, lord of all his household, and ruler over the whole land of Egypt."

—Genesis, chapter 45, verses 1–8

3

LOVE, SEX, AND MARRIAGE

"When love is strong, a man and woman can make their bed on a sword's blade"

On the joys of love ✦ In praise of marriage ✦ Sex and the Evil Impulse ✦ "A woman's voice is a sexual incitement" ✦ On rape ✦ Attitudes toward homosexuality ✦ The question of sex without marriage ✦ The time to marry ✦ Choosing a mate ✦ Accepting fate ✦ Matchmaker, matchmaker ✦ Wooing a woman ✦ Honoring the bride and groom ✦ Making marriage work ✦ A husband's obligations to his wife ✦ If a husband beats his wife ✦ A wife's traditional role ✦ The ideal wife ✦ Challenging the traditions ✦ Enjoying the "marital duty" ✦ On adultery ✦ Getting along with in-laws ✦ Grounds for divorce ✦ Saving a marriage ✦ Keeping peace between husband and wife

One of the most romantic stories in literature, told in the book of Genesis, is the story of the patriarch Jacob and his beautiful cousin Rachel.

It opens with Jacob resting near a well during his flight to Mesopotamia to escape the wrath of his brother, Esau. As he chats with some shepherds, he sees a lovely young woman leading her flock to the well and is told that she is Rachel, the daughter of his mother's brother.

It's love at first sight. When Jacob is introduced to Rachel, he is so overcome by emotion that he impulsively kisses her and then breaks into tears. (Later biblical interpreters explained that at that moment he saw in a vision that Rachel, who would die before him, would not be buried near him, and he cried with sorrow.) Jacob accompanies Rachel home and agrees to earn her hand by working without pay for her father, Laban, over a period of seven years. "Jacob served seven years for Rachel, and they seemed to him but a few days because of his love for her," the Bible relates. But the sly Laban tricks Jacob into marrying his elder daughter, Leah, first. Then Jacob must work yet another seven years for the privilege of wedding his beloved.

With its emphasis on love and devotion, tenderness and honesty of feelings, this ancient love story still has much to say to us today. But it also has another side that seems far removed from our own lives. Although the narrative revolves around Rachel, we neither hear her speak nor learn anything about her as a person before her marriage. Does she love Jacob as he loves her? We don't know and will never find out. How does she feel when her elder sister is substituted for her in the bridal chamber? We're not told and, by implication, should not be asking. Rachel exists as her father's daughter, totally dependent, according to ancient law, on his wishes for her. He has the right to marry her to whomever he pleases, although he may ask for her consent before doing so. He also has the right to sell her, if he needs to, in order to pay off a debt.

This contrast between the loftiness of Jacob's love and the lowly status of Rachel, the object of his love, is a contrast that characterizes relationships between men and women throughout centuries of Hebrew literature, as it does world literature in general. Within the framework of Jewish law, women were and, in many respects, continue to be second-class citizens. As daughters, like Rachel, they were subject to the will and whim of their fathers. As wives, they were expected to serve and obey their husbands. They could not inherit property directly from their husbands or initiate divorce proceedings, and they had only limited rights to give legal testimony. They were not formally educated, nor were they required to take part in many of the most important rituals and religious practices incumbent upon men.

Yet, within their accepted roles, and in everyday life, women received great respect and honor, and often much power. "If your wife is short, bend down to hear her whisper," was the way one sage encouraged men to seek their wives' counsel. Marriage itself was seen as one of the highest attainments in life, so much so that the love relationship between God and Israel—the holiest of relationships in Jewish tradition—was equated in several passages of the Talmud with the love of a husband and wife, and marital sex was regarded as a joyous and beautiful experience. Long before modern psychiatry, the sages recognized the importance of female sexuality, and many details of domestic law revolve around satisfying women's sexual needs.

In reading the selections here, these contrasting attitudes toward women need to be taken into consideration. The voices we hear are almost exclusively male voices: men talking about their own feelings, men discussing women, men setting standards for their wives' behavior. Not until contemporary times do women begin to make themselves heard, and then they raise their voices to protest their status and call for change.

Still, at a time when almost one out of every two marriages ends in divorce, there's special meaning in a passage telling us that when a man divorces his wife, the very altar in the sanctuary weeps in sorrow—and this within a tradition that does not condemn divorce as a sin. At a time when sexual problems are among the chief complaints therapists hear from married couples, there's something to be learned from the medieval Jewish scholar who wrote that "a man should never force himself upon his wife and never overpower her, for the Divine Spirit never rests upon one whose conjugal relations occur in the absence of desire, love, and free will."

Other contrasts characterize these selections. As in so many areas, the talmudic scholars strove to expand and liberalize biblical rulings concerning women. In matters of adultery and divorce, marriage arrangements and inheritance laws, they used compassion and creativity to ease some of the legal restrictions on women. However, from the Middle Ages on, many of these liberalizing talmudic tendencies ossified as Jewish scholars came ever more strongly under the influence of cultures around them and tended toward stricter interpretations and less sweeping changes. Today, controversies of interpretation have arisen on many matters relating to women, sex, and marriage, with disputing groups finding precedents for their viewpoints within the various lenient or strict traditions that have accumulated through the ages.

Though you will find many biases and contradictions in the passages that follow, you will also find an unwavering commitment to marriage and family living, and a firm conviction that they can succeed only when based on deep mutual love and respect.

On the joys of love

A celebration of love between man and woman, the Song of Songs exudes passion and sensuality as does no other biblical book. It was accepted into the sacred canon because the talmudic authorities considered it an allegory of God's love for Israel written by the wise King Solomon. Interpreting even the most erotic verses symbolically, they could view the work, in the words of Rabbi Akiva, as the "holiest of the holy."

There is little doubt, however, that along with their spiritual interpretation, the sages did recognize the more literal meanings of these love poems. According to an old tradition, a husband reads the Song of Songs to his wife on the Sabbath eve, a time set aside, explained the great commentator Rashi, for "pleasure, rest, and physical enjoyment."

Many scholars today regard the Song of Songs as a collection of lyric love poems, possibly written over a long period of time, in the style of other ancient Near Eastern poetry glorifying love, courtship, and marriage.

I am a rose of Sharon,
A lily of the valleys.
Like a lily among thorns,
So is my darling among the maidens.
Like an apple tree among trees of the forest,
So is my beloved among the youths.
I delight to sit in his shade,
And his fruit is sweet to my mouth. . . .

My beloved spoke thus to me:
"Arise, my darling;
My fair one, come away!
For now the winter is past,
The rains are over and gone,
The blossoms have appeared in the land,
The time of pruning has come;
The song of the turtledove
Is heard in our land.
The green figs form on the figtree,
The vines in blossom give off fragrance,
Arise, my darling;
My fair one, come away!" . . .

How sweet is your love,
My own, my bride!
How much more delightful your love than wine,
Your ointments more fragrant
Than any spice!
Sweetness drops
From your lips, O bride;
Honey and milk

Are under your tongue;
And the scent of your robes
Is like the scent of Lebanon....

Let me be a seal upon your heart,
Like the seal upon your hand.
For love is fierce as death,
Passion is mighty as Sheol;
Its darts are darts of fire,
A blazing flame.
Vast floods cannot quench love,
Nor rivers drown it.
If a man offered all his wealth for love,
He would be laughed to scorn.

—Songs of Songs,
chapter 2, verses 1–3, 10–13;
chapter 4, verses 10–11;
chapter 8, verses 6–7

In praise of marriage

The sages believed marriage to be the ideal path to love and sexual fulfillment. Although procreation was considered one of the major functions of marriage, it was not seen as the sole purpose. "A religious deed that leaves the body pure is to marry a woman when one already has children," the talmudists said, extolling the many gratifications of marriage and decrying the emptiness that exists without it.

Hence a man leaves his father and mother and clings to his wife, so that they become one flesh.

—Genesis, chapter 2, verse 24

The Bible describes how Isaac married Rebekah and lived with her in the tent that had belonged to his mother: "Isaac loved her, and thus found comfort after his mother's death" (Genesis 24:67). To this, Rabbi Yose made the following comment:

Isaac mourned his mother Sarah for three years. At the end of those years he married Rebekah and stopped mourning his mother.

Thus we see that until a man takes a wife, he directs his love toward his parents. Once he marries, he directs his love toward his wife.

—*Pirkei de-Rabbi Eliezer*,
chapter 32, section 2

A man who does not have a wife lives without joy, without blessing, and without goodness.

In the West they said: "Without Torah and without moral protection."

Rabba ben Ulla said: "And without peace."

—Babylonian Talmud, tractate
Yevamot, page 62b

As soon as a man takes a wife his sins are buried, for it is said: "Who finds a wife finds a great good, and obtains favor from the Lord" (Proverbs 18:22).

—Babylonian Talmud, tractate
Yevamot, page 63b

Where there is no union of male and female, men are not worthy of beholding the *Shekhinah* [Divine Presence].

—*Zohar*, volume 3, portion
"Aharei Mot," page 59a

There are three sights which warm my heart and are beautiful in the eyes of the Lord and of men:

concord among brothers, friendship among neighbors, and a man and wife who are inseparable.

—Wisdom of Ben Sira,
chapter 25, verse 1

The world becomes darkened for a man whose wife dies. . . . His steps grow short. . . . His wits collapse.

—Babylonian Talmud, tractate
Sanhedrin, page 22a

Sex and the Evil Impulse

We get two views of sex in Jewish tradition. On the one hand it is presented as a good, even noble part of life, a gift given us by God. Even during periods when asceticism dominated Jewish philosophic thought, celibacy was frowned upon as unnatural, and mystics spoke of sexual relations between husband and wife as a holy union in which the Divine Spirit is present. On the other hand, sexuality is referred to time and again as the "Evil Impulse" or "Evil Inclination," with dangerous powers to corrupt a person. The scholars themselves saw little contradiction in these two views. As long as we master our sexual impulses and not they us, they advised, sex is positive and beautiful. It is when sexual drives become uncontrolled and immoderate that they can destroy individuals and even societies.

Though Isaac Bashevis Singer has his own perspective on sex, the importance he attributes to it in the final selection is not out of line with the mainstream of Jewish thought.

Know that the sexual intercourse of man with his wife is holy and pure. . . . No one should think that sexual intercourse is ugly and loathesome. . . .

We the possessors of the Holy Torah believe that God, may He be praised, created all, as His wisdom decreed, and did not create anything ugly or shameful. For if sexual intercourse were repulsive, then the reproductive organs are also repulsive. . . . If the reproductive organs are repulsive, how did the Creator fashion something blemished? If that were so, we should find that His deeds were not perfect. . . . But this matter is as has been expressed. God is omniscient. . . . Seeing in the end nothing which is faulty or loathesome, He created man and woman. He created and formed all their organs, placed them in their form. And He did not create anything repulsive. . . .

. . . The mystery of man includes in his being the mystery of wisdom, understanding and knowledge. Know that the male is the mystery of wisdom and the female is the mystery of understanding. And the pure sex act is the mystery of knowledge. . . . If so, it follows that proper sexual union can be a means of spiritual elevation when it is properly practiced, and the mystery greater than this is the secret of the heavenly bodies when they unite in the manner of man and woman.

—*The Holy Letter*, often attributed to Nahmanides (Rabbi Moses ben Nahman, 1194–1270)

There is a wee little organ in man.
Feed it, and you whet its appetite for more;
Starve it, and it will act sated.

—Babylonian Talmud, tractate *Sukkah*, page 52b

At first the Evil Impulse is as fragile as the thread of a spider, but eventually it becomes as tough as cart ropes.

—Rabbi Assi, in the Babylonian Talmud, tractate *Sukkah*, page 52a

Legend says that the people of Israel once prayed diligently to have the Evil Desire for Idolatry turned over to them and in that way rid themselves of any temptation to worship idols. After fasting for three days and three nights, they were rewarded and given the Evil Idolater. They quickly locked him in a lead pot, thus freeing Israel of idolatry from that day on. Flushed with victory, the people decided to go a step further.

They said, "Since this is a time of grace for us, let us pray that the Evil Impulse be handed over to us."

They prayed and he was given to them.

But the prophet Elijah warned them: "Understand, that if you kill the Evil Impulse, the whole world will collapse."

Nevertheless, they imprisoned the Evil Impulse for three days. But when they looked for a fresh egg, none could be found in all of the land of Israel.

"What shall we do?" the people asked one another. "Shall we kill him? But without the Evil Impulse, the world cannot survive. Shall we beg for a half-mercy [allowing the impulse to survive but preventing it from tempting people]? But they do not grant such half-mercies in heaven."

So they put out his eyes and let him go ["blinding" the sex impulse to keep it under control].

—Babylonian Talmud, tractate *Yoma*, page 69b

Were it not for the Evil Impulse, no man would build a house, marry a wife, or beget children.

—*Genesis Rabbah*, chapter 9, section 7

The sage Abbaye once heard a certain man saying to a certain woman, "Let us arise and travel together."

"I will follow them," thought Abbaye, "and keep them from sinning with one another."

He followed them across the meadows. When they were about to separate he heard one of them say, "Your company was pleasant, and now the way is long."

"If it had been I," Abbaye thought, "I could not have restrained myself."

In deep despair, he went and leaned against a doorpost. An old man came up to him and taught him: "The greater the man, the greater his Evil Impulse."

—Babylonian Talmud, tractate *Sukkah*, page 52a

. . . In sex and in love human character is revealed more than anywhere else.

Let's say a man tries to play a very strong man: a big man, a dictator. But in sex he may become reduced to a child or to an imp. The sexual organs are the most sensitive organs of the human being. The eye or the ear seldom sabotage you. An eye cannot stop seeing if it doesn't like what it sees, but the penis will stop functioning if he doesn't like what he sees. I would say that the sexual organs express the human soul more than any other part of the body. They are not diplomats. They tell the truth ruthlessly. . . They are even more *meshuga* than the brain.

—Isaac Bashevis Singer, from an interview with Richard Burgin in *The New York Times*, November 26, 1978

"A woman's voice is a sexual incitement"

Members of Israel's Cabinet once suggested to Golda Meir, then Minister of Labor, that a curfew be imposed on women because of a growing number of assaults taking place on the streets. Mrs. Meir objected: "Men are attacking women, not the other way around. If there is going to be a curfew, let the men be locked up, not the women."

Her response was a break from the traditional attitude of the sages, who placed restrictions on women in order to prevent men from being tempted into sin. During talmudic times and for hundreds of years afterwards, women were expected to keep their arms, legs, and heads covered, and to confine themselves to their homes as much as possible. To protect themselves from women's snares, men were advised to speak to them only when absolutely necessary, and if the Evil Impulse became especially strong, to sublimate it by immersing themselves in study. There was, however, special advice for men who absolutely could not resist temptation.

We have almost no record of women's reactions to this view of them as temptresses. But we do have one report of a woman's biting response to a man who engaged her in conversation. The woman, Beruryah, was the brilliant wife of the scholar Rabbi Meir, who probably lived in the second century. The fact that the Talmud records this incident attests to the high regard in which Beruryah was held; it also reminds us that for all their earnest concern about the seductiveness of women, the rabbis were able to laugh at themselves.

When the Evil Impulse sees a man who swaggers [so that women will notice him], shows off his clothes, and smooths his hair-locks, he says to himself, "This man belongs to me!"

—*Genesis Rabbah,*
chapter 22, section 6

Rabbi Hisda said: A woman's leg is a sexual incitement....

Samuel said: A woman's voice is a sexual incitement....

Rabbi Sheshet said: A woman's hair is a sexual incitement. . . .

—Babylonian Talmud, tractate *Berakhot*, page 24b

Turn your eyes away from your neighbor's charming wife, lest you be caught in her net. Do not visit with her husband and share wine and strong drink with him.

For through the form of a beautiful woman, many were destroyed.

—Babylonian Talmud, tractate *Yevamot*, page 63b

Beruryah is quoted several times in the Talmud, each showing her great learning and influence. That influence may have been too great for later, more conservative generations to accept. A legend that appeared almost a thousand years after her death states that because Beruryah scoffed at the rabbis for calling women light-headed, her husband tested her by sending one of his students to seduce her. She finally gave in and then committed suicide out of shame. There is no factual basis for this legend. It seems to have been created to counter the power this strong-minded woman exerted.

The following exchange was Beruryah's way of sarcastically teaching a lesson from the Ethics of the Fathers *to a young scholar. The lesson: "Talk not overmuch with women."*

Once Rabbi Yose the Galilean was on a journey and he met Beruryah.

"By what road do we go to Lydda?" he asked her.

"You foolish Galilean," she answered. "Didn't the sages say, 'Talk not overmuch with women'? You should have said, 'How to Lydda?'" [and thus avoid too many words with a woman].

—Babylonian Talmud, tractate *Eruvin*, page 53b

My son, if this repulsive creature, the Evil Impulse, attacks you, lead him to the house of study. If he is stone, he will dissolve; if he is iron, he will shiver into fragments.

—Babylonian Talmud, tractate *Kiddushin*, page 30b

If a man sees that his Evil Impulse is conquering him, he should go to a place where he is unknown, put on black clothes, wrap himself in a black cloak, and do what his heart desires, but let him not publicly profane the name of heaven.

—Rabbi Ilai the Elder, in the Babylonian Talmud, tractate *Kiddushin*, page 40a

On rape

In spite of their warnings about the seductiveness of women, the sages never fell into the trap—still common among law enforcers—of blaming women themselves for rapes or assaults committed on them. The penalties they assigned for rape, however, were in keeping with their own patriarchal society.

The book of Deuteronomy spells out the conditions under which a man may be charged with rape. Because a girl who was betrothed had almost the same status as a married woman, violating her was equivalent to adultery. And because a virgin "belonged" to her father, he had to be compensated for his dishonor. Forcing a rapist to marry his victim was a way of assuring marriage for a girl who, no longer a virgin, would probably have a difficult time finding a mate. The talmudic authorities later ruled that a girl did not have to marry her assailant if she didn't want to, but if she did want him he had to marry her "even if she is lame, even if she is blind, and even if she is afflicted with boils." Once married, he was not permitted to divorce her, but she could demand a divorce if she wanted it.

The Bible says little about the rape of a married woman. In Jewish law, a woman who commits adultery is considered a harlot, with whom her husband may no longer associate, and the talmudists wondered whether a woman who has been raped also becomes tainted and forbidden to her husband. They ruled that unless her husband is a priest, she does not. Then they extended that ruling even to a woman who, after an initial struggle, voluntarily succumbs to her attacker.

> In the case of a virgin who is pledged to a man—if a man comes upon her in town and lies with her, you shall take the two of them out to the gate of that town and stone them to death; the girl because she did not cry for help in the town, and the man because he violated his neighbor's wife. Thus you will sweep away evil from your midst.
>
> But if the man comes upon the engaged girl in the open country, and the man lies with her by force, only the man who lay with her shall die, but you shall do nothing to the girl. The girl is not guilty of a capital offense, for this case is like that of a man attacking another and murdering him. He came upon her in the open; though the engaged girl cried for help, there was no one to save her.
>
> If a man comes upon a virgin who is not engaged and he seizes her and lies with her, and they are discovered, the man who lay with her shall pay the girl's father fifty *shekels* of silver, and she shall be his wife. Because he has violated her, he can never have the right to divorce her.
>
> —Deuteronomy,
> chapter 22, verses 23–29

> The fine of fifty *shekels* of silver constitutes payment for the enjoyment of the intercourse alone. The seducer [who has the victim's consent] must also pay, in addition to this

fine prescribed by the Torah, compensation for the humiliation and the blemish. The violater [who forces his victim] must pay, in addition to all these, compensation for the pain, for a woman who submits to intercourse willingly suffers no pain, whereas if she is violated she does suffer pain.

—Maimonides, *Code*, "Laws Concerning a Virgin Maiden," chapter 2, section 1

Any woman whose rape began under duress though it ended with her consent—and even if she said, "Leave him alone!" and that if he had not made the attack on her she would have hired him to do it—is permitted to her husband.

What is the reason?

The rapist plunged her into an uncontrollable passion.

—Babylonian Talmud, tractate *Ketubbot*, page 51b

Attitudes toward homosexuality

The Mishnah records a dispute among the sages: Rabbi Judah said that two bachelors are not permitted to sleep together under the same blanket; the other sages, however, permitted it. Jews, they explained, are not suspected of homosexuality. Their reasoning was true of their own age and true for centuries afterward. Prohibited by biblical law, homosexuality was considered one of the most serious and perverse of crimes. So pervasive were feelings against it that when the sixteenth-century scholar Joseph Caro ruled that men should avoid being alone together because "in these days, so many loose people abound," he was severely criticized by his contemporaries who argued, as had earlier talmudic sages, that such acts were unheard of in the Jewish community.

The Bible presents a graphic picture of homosexuality among the people of Sodom, who were destroyed for their sinful ways. In one narrative in the book of Genesis, all the Sodomites gather outside the home of Abraham's nephew Lot and demand that his two male guests be given to them for sexual abuse. The term "sodomy" comes from this incident, and Judaism's strong aversion to homosexuality is related to it. The fact that male prostitution was an integral part of many pagan religious cults added to the intense negative attitude of Jewish authorities.

Lesbianism received less attention than homosexuality in Jewish codes and moral writings. The Talmud refers to it as a transgression only once, and Maimonides is one of the few later authorities to take up the issue. As he outlines the laws, lesbianism is forbidden but is considered a lesser crime than male homosexuality, perhaps because there is no specific biblical injunction against it.

The traditional attitudes toward homosexuality and lesbianism are being reexamined today as the views of society as a whole are changing. Rabbis and scholars have had to confront such issues as whether homosexuality should be considered an alternative lifestyle, whether homosexual marriages should be performed, and whether separate homosexual religious congregations should be recognized. Hershel J. Matt, a Conservative rabbi, raises some of these questions and proposes his own solutions to them. Rabbi Norman Lamm, president of Yeshiva University, takes a stricter position, treating homosexuality as an aberration that calls for sympathy but not acceptance. His point of view is shared by most leaders in all branches of Judaism. The Reform movement has, however, accepted affiliations with gay synagogues, but neither the Orthodox nor Conservative has done so.

> Do not lie with a male as one lies with a woman; it is an abhorrence. . . . If a man lies with a male as one lies with a woman, the two of them have done an abhorrent thing; they shall be put to death—their bloodguilt is upon them.
>
> —Leviticus, chapter 18, verse 22; chapter 20, verse 13

A woman must not put on a man's apparel, nor shall a man wear woman's clothing, for whoever does these things is abhorrent to the Lord your God.

—Deuteronomy, chapter 22, verse 5

Women are forbidden to engage in lesbian practices with one another, these being "the doings of the land of Egypt" against which we have been warned. . . .

Our sages have said: "What did they do? A man would marry a man or a woman a woman or a woman would marry two men." Although such an act is forbidden, the perpetrators are not liable to a flogging, since there is no specific negative commandment prohibiting it, nor is actual intercourse of any kind involved here. Consequently, such women are not forbidden to the priesthood on account of harlotry [priests may marry them], nor is a woman prohibited to her husband because of it, since this does not constitute harlotry.

It behooves the court, however, to administer the flogging prescribed for disobedience, since they have performed a forbidden act. A man should be particularly strict with his wife in this matter, and should prevent women known to indulge in such practices from visiting her, and her from going to visit them.

—Maimonides, *Code*, "Laws Concerning Forbidden Intercourse," chapter 21, section 8

. . . A truly Torah approach . . . would acknowledge that . . . God alone . . . has the ability and right to judge a person's culpability; and that none of us humans, therefore, ought to presume to judge a homosexual or automatically regard a homosexual as a sinner. . . .

Furthermore, a Torah approach would look with deep compassion upon the plight of many homosexuals in our society....

... A genuinely Jewish approach to homosexuality would require us to *demonstrate* such feelings of compassion by willingly associating with homosexuals and engaging in acts of kindness and friendship....

But even more is required.... We should work for the immediate repeal of laws, rules and practices that exclude or discriminate against homosexuals....

For the organized Jewish community a further problem arises in connection with a request ... that national synagogue organizations accept congregations of homosexuals as local affiliates.... Our responses to this dilemma would be threefold: a) it would be far preferable for homosexuals to be welcome and feel welcome in existing congregations ... b) since the present reality, however, is that such a welcome is not assured and is perhaps even unlikely, the formation of gay congregations is legitimate; and c) a gay congregation, to be eligible for affiliation with a union of congregations, however, must not—by rule, name, practice, or implication—restrict its own membership or leadership to homosexuals.

—Hershel J. Matt, from "Sin, Crime, Sickness or Alternative Life Style? A Jewish Approach to Homosexuality," in *Judaism* (Winter 1978)

First, society and government must recognize the distinctions between the various categories [of homosexuality]. It must offer its medical and psychological assistance to those whose homosexuality is an expression of pathology, who recognize it as such, and are willing to seek help. We must be no less generous to the homosexual than to the drug addict, to whom the government extends various forms of therapy....

Second, jail sentences must be abolished for all homosexuals, save those who are guilty of violence, seduction of the young, or public solicitation.

Third, the laws must remain on the books, but by mutual consent of judiciary and police, be unenforced. This . . . is the nearest one can come to the category so well known in the *halakhah* [Jewish law] whereby strong disapproval is expressed by affirming a *halakhic* prohibition, yet no punishment is mandated. It is a category that bridges the gap between morality and law. . . .

For the Jewish community as such, the same principles, derived from the tradition, may serve as guidelines. . . . Certainly, there must be no acceptance of . . . synagogues set aside as homosexual congregations. . . .

. . . Regular congregations and other Jewish groups should not hesitate to accord hospitality and membership, on an individual basis, to those "visible" homosexuals who qualify for the category of the ill. . . . But to assent to the organization of separate "gay" groups under Jewish auspices makes no more sense, Jewishly, than to suffer the formation of synagogues that cater exclusively to idol worshippers, adulterers, gossipers, tax evaders, or Sabbath violators.

—Norman Lamm, from "Judaism and the Modern Attitude to Homosexuality" in *Encyclopedia Judaica Yearbook* (1974)

The question of sex without marriage

"No prohibition in all the Torah is as difficult to keep as that of forbidden unions and illicit sexual relations," wrote Maimonides—words that are probably far more applicable today than in his own time. While the sages lauded and encouraged sex within marriage, they strongly prohibited sex outside of marriage. Surprisingly, the prohibitions cannot be traced directly to biblical law. Although the Bible condemns an adulterous woman to death, it says little about premarital sex. Even in post-biblical times, in ancient Judea, families took a relaxed attitude toward premarital sex among betrothed couples, allowing the young people to spend as much time as they wished alone, with few questions asked. But in the Galilee, in northern Palestine, standards were much stricter, with young men and women carefully separated until marriage, and it was the Galilean practices and outlooks that eventually became accepted throughout Jewish society.

The talmudic masters and, to an even greater extent, the rabbis who came after them were unbending in their emphasis on sexual chastity for both men and women before marriage and strict fidelity in marriage. That the sages were aware of the "sweetness" of "stolen waters" is clear from the first selection, but that anecdote also illustrates the lengths to which they were prepared to go to preserve a woman's chastity. Maimonides codified the dominant point of view, portraying a sexual relationship without marriage as one that degrades the woman and is sinful for the man. A contemporary authority on sexuality in Jewish law, Rabbi David M. Feldman, explains and reaffirms Maimonides's position, while another contemporary scholar, Dr. Arthur E. Green, challenges the traditional Jewish approach to sex in light of the sweeping changes in sexual mores that have taken place in recent decades. His solution, however, would still be considered unacceptable to most rabbinic authorities.

> A man once developed an overwhelming longing for a certain woman, and he became sick with desire for her.
>
> The doctors consulted declared, "He will be cured only if she submits."
>
> But the sages said, "Let him die rather than have her submit."
>
> The doctors then said, "Let her stand nude before him."
>
> To which the sages answered, "Sooner let him die."
>
> "Then," said the doctors, "let her speak with him from behind a fence."
>
> "Let him die," the sages maintained, "rather than even have her speak with him from behind a fence."
>
> Why not have the man marry her?
>
> Marriage would not satisfy his passion, even as Rabbi Isaac said: Since the destruction of the Temple, sexual

pleasure has been taken away from those who practice it lawfully and given to sinners, as it is written: "Stolen waters are sweet, and bread eaten in secret is pleasant" (Proverbs 9:17).

—Babylonian Talmud, tractate *Sanhedrin*, page 75a

Before the revelation of the Torah, when a man would encounter a woman in the street, if both consented to marriage, he would bring her into his house and would have intercourse with her in privacy, and thereby she would become his wife.

Upon the revelation of the Torah, the people of Israel were commanded that if a man wishes to marry a woman, he must first acquire her in the presence of witnesses, and only thereafter does she become his wife, as it is said: "A man marries a woman and cohabits with her. . . ." (Deuteronomy 22:13).

—Maimonides, *Code,* "Laws Concerning Marriage," chapter 1, section 1

Maimonides . . . sees the marriage bond as the Torah's advance over laws of primitive society. . . . The Torah, Maimonides means to say, has institutionalized the relationship—not to shackle it, but to raise it from what it was in prebiblical and precivilization days. Marriage is an institution to protect the partners from the uncertainties of changing moods and the lure of competing claims on their affections. Marriage thus prevents the ultimate human relationship from being trivialized; it does the same for sex itself. . . .

—David M. Feldman, from "The Scope of Tradition and Its Application," in *The Second Jewish Catalog* (1976)

> Living in a world where we cannot advocate either ideal sex or no sex as the alternatives, what we must begin to evolve is a *sliding scale* of sexual values. . . . At the top of the scale would stand the fully knowing and loving relationship . . . while rape—fully unconsenting and anonymous sexuality—would stand at the bottom. Somewhere near the middle of the scale, neither glorified nor condemned, would be the relationship of two consenting persons, treating one another with decency, fulfilling the biological aspects of one another's love-needs, while making no pretense at deeper intimacy. Given such a scale, a Jew might begin to judge his/her own sexual behavior in terms of a series of challenges which he/she might want to address. . . .
>
> —Arthur E. Green, assistant professor of religious studies, The University of Pennsylvania, from "A Contemporary Approach to Jewish Sexuality," in *The Second Jewish Catalog* (1976)

The time to marry

With the great importance they attached to premarital chastity, Jewish leaders constantly urged men to marry young. "The reason I am superior to my colleagues," said the third-century Babylonian scholar Rabbi Hisda, "is that I married at sixteen. And had I married at fourteen, I would have said to Satan: Fie on you!"

The attitude toward young women was somewhat different. Most fathers were only too anxious to betroth their daughters at an early age to ensure a good marriage. The rabbis frowned upon such child marriages and ruled that a minor girl (under the age of twelve) may have her marriage annulled merely by announcing that she refuses to live with her husband. After she reaches maturity, however, she must receive a divorce in order to end her marriage. How seriously the rabbis' advice and rulings were actually taken depended greatly on circumstances in individual families and communities. In times of persecution, for example, parents tried to marry off their daughters as quickly as possible, while they still had dowry money to give them.

Until a young man reaches the age of twenty, God sits and waits.

When will he take a wife?

As soon as he turns twenty and has not married, God exclaims, "May his bones be blasted!" . . .

While you still have influence over your son—between the ages of sixteen and twenty-two—marry him off.

—Babylonian Talmud, tractate
Kiddushin, pages 29b and 30a

A man who passes the age of twenty and is not yet married spends his days in sin.

In sin! Is that really so?

Rather say, he spends all his days in sinful thoughts.

—Babylonian Talmud, tractate
Kiddushin, page 29b

The difference of opinion, in the following selection, reflects the different economic conditions of Jews in Babylonia and Palestine. Beset by economic problems, Palestinians like Rabbi Johanan found it extremely difficult to devote time to study while supporting a wife and family.

If a person wants to study Torah and to get married, he should first study and then marry.

But if he cannot live without a wife, he should marry first and then study.

Rabbi Judah said in the name of Samuel: The rule is: a man marries first and then studies.

Said Rabbi Johanan: With a millstone round his neck, should a man study Torah!

—Babylonian Talmud, tractate *Kiddushin*, page 29b

A father may not betroth his daughter while she is a minor.

He must wait until she is grown up and says, "I want so-and-so."

—Rabbi Judah, in Rav's name, in the Babylonian Talmud tractate *Kiddushin*, page 41a

Choosing a mate

"Let not a quite young man take to wife one who has reached forty years," the German moralist Judah the Prince advised, and generally, we're told, happy marriages are more likely to result when people come from similar backgrounds. The sages unequivocably opposed marrying for money, but they did value family affiliation. And because they regarded scholarship and all that it implied—love of learning, an emphasis on ethics and right living—as one of the highest callings in life, they considered scholarly families the very best ones to marry into, if you could arrange it.

During the period of the Second Temple, about two thousand years ago, Jews celebrated the fifteenth day of the Hebrew month of Av—which falls about mid-August—as a festival for young people. Unmarried girls, ordinarily confined to their homes or closely chaperoned outside, dressed in white and danced in the vineyards with young, eligible bachelors, calling on them to choose a wife. The holiday was celebrated because, among other reasons, it marked the date on which an old law forbidding members of various tribes from intermarrying was abrogated. A similar dance for young men and women also took place on the Day of Atonement.

If he was young and she old or if he was old and she young, he is told, "What would you with a young woman?" or "What would you with an old woman? Go to one who is of the same age as yourself and create no strife in your home!"

—Babylonian Talmud, tractate *Yevamot*, page 44a

An abnormally tall man should not marry an abnormally tall woman, lest their offspring look like a mast [tall and skinny].

A male dwarf should not marry a female dwarf, lest their offspring be an even smaller dwarf.

An abnormally pale man should not marry an abnormally pale woman, lest their offspring be extremely pale.

A very dark complexioned man should not marry an equally dark complexioned woman, lest their offspring be jet black.

—Resh Lakish, in the Babylonian Talmud, tractate *Beḳhorot*, page 45b

---

When a divorced man marries a divorced woman, there are four minds in bed.

—Babylonian Talmud, tractate *Pesahim*, page 112a

A man who takes a wife for the sake of money will have unworthy children.

—Babylonian Talmud, tractate *Kiddushin*, page 70a

A man who wants to take a wife should inquire about her brothers. . . .

It was taught: Most children resemble their mother's brother.

—Babylonian Talmud, tractate
Bava Batra, page 110a

A man should sell all his possessions in order to marry the daughter of a scholar.

If he cannot marry the daughter of a scholar, let him marry the daughter of one of the great men of the generation.

If he cannot marry the daughter of one of the great men of the generation, let him marry the daughter of the head of synagogues in his town.

If he cannot marry the daughter of the head of synagogues, let him marry the daughter of the town's charity treasurer.

If he cannot marry the daughter of the charity treasurer, let him marry the daughter of a schoolteacher.

But let him not marry the daughter of an ignoramus. . . .

—Babylonian Talmud, tractate
Pesaham, page 49b

There were no greater days of joy in Israel than the fifteenth of Av and the Day of Atonement. On these days the daughters of Jerusalem used to go out in white dresses they had borrowed so as not to shame those who had none. . . .

They danced in the vineyards calling out, "Young man, lift up your eyes and see which maiden you want to choose for yourself. Do not look for beauty, but look for family background, for 'Grace is deceitful and beauty is vain, but a woman who fears the Lord shall be praised' " (Proverbs 31:30).

—Mishnah, tractate *Ta'anit,*
chapter 4, paragraph 8

Accepting fate

For all the care necessary in choosing a suitable marriage partner, we can't always control our own destiny—and certainly not that of our children.

It is told that King Solomon had a beautiful daughter. In all the earth there was no one as beautiful as she.

The king studied the stars to find out what young man would be worthy to marry his daughter. And he discovered that a poor and simple youth, from the poorest of his people, was destined to wed his beautiful daughter.

To foil fate, Solomon built a huge tower in the middle of the sea, and surrounded it with strong walls on every side. Then he placed his daughter in the tower and left seventy eunuchs from among the elders of Israel to guard her and care for her. He stocked the tower with every kind of food and drink imaginable so that nothing would be lacking. He bolted all the doors and gates with locks of iron, allowing no one to come in or go out.

"Now," said the king, "I shall see God's acts and deeds, and whether the prediction of the stars will come true."

In the city of Acre there lived a poor boy. One night, he left his native town and set out on a journey to explore the world beyond. He was starving and barefoot as he traveled, his clothes in rags, only the earth and the stones serving as his bed and pillow.

One cold, rainy night, he saw the carcass of an ox lying on the ground, and crept in to protect himself. While he slept, a great eagle swooped down, and carried the carcass with the boy inside to the roof of the tower in which the maiden lived. The bird began to pick off scraps of meat from the carcass, but the boy awoke and shooed it off.

In the morning the princess came out to the roof and discovered the youth. "Who are you?" she asked. "And who brought you here?"

The boy told her his story, and the kind-hearted princess took him to her room, where she washed, clothed and fed him. And when she looked at him, she saw that he was more handsome than anyone she had ever seen. Soon she discovered that he was witty and wise too, and pure in heart. The princess kept the boy hidden in her room, so that the elders knew nothing about him.

Now, the maiden and the youth fell deeply in love. One day they agreed to marry. The boy let out blood from his arm, and with the blood he wrote her a marriage contract, and he said, "The Lord is witness and His angels Michael and Gabriel are our witnesses this day."

They lived together as man and wife, and the girl became pregnant. When the elders noticed that she was with child, they became terrified of the king's anger. But as much as they questioned her, she would tell them nothing. The elders sent for the king, pleading for mercy and swearing their innocence.

The angry king summoned his daughter to him, and asked what had happened. "God sent me a good and handsome man, a scholar and scribe," she told him, "and he has taken me for his wife." The king had the boy brought to him, and the young man showed him the marriage contract that he had sealed in blood as proof of his love. The king asked him details about his parents and family and the city in which he had lived. And from the youth's answers, Solomon knew that this was the young man whom he had learned about from the stars.

Then the king's anger subsided, and he rejoiced. "Blessed be God," he said, "who gives a man his wife!"

—Based on a legend in the
Midrash Tanhuma

Matchmaker, matchmaker

Marriages may be made in heaven, but, even for God, it seems pairing the right man with the right woman is no easy task. The profession of matchmaker (*shadkhan*) came into existence during the twelfth century, when Jews, persecuted and scattered in small communities throughout Europe, turned to intermediaries to seek mates for themselves or their children. Early matchmakers, usually scholars or respected members of the community, worked hard for modest fees. In later years, matchmaking often deteriorated into a pastime for people out to make quick money. The satirical writer Mendele Mocher Seforim describes one such venture in the last selection.

A Roman matron asked Rabbi Yose ben Halafta, "How many days did it take God to create the world?"

"It took Him six days," was the answer.

"And from then until now, how does He spend His time?" she asked.

"The Holy One, blessed be He," answered Rabbi Yose, "sits and pairs off couples—this one's daughter with this one's son."

"That's His work?" she asked incredulously. "I can easily do the same thing. I have a number of male and female slaves, and in a single hour I can pair them all off."

"It may appear easy to you," said the rabbi, "yet every marriage is as difficult for God as was the parting of the Red Sea."

Rabbi Yose went his way. And what did the matron do?

She gathered a thousand slaves, male and female, arranged them in rows, and said, "This one will marry this one, and this one will marry this one," until she had paired them all off in a single night.

The next morning they came to her—this one's arm was cut, this one's eye blackened, this one's leg broken.

"What happened?" she asked.

One said, "I don't want her." And the other cried, "I don't want him."

The matron immediately sent for Rabbi Yose and said

to him, "Rabbi, your Torah is true and exalted, and everything you spoke you spoke well."

—*Genesis Rabbah,*
chapter 68, section 4

The narrator in this story has come to a fair to sell old prayer books but quickly realizes that there's little profit in his merchandise. With a daughter to marry off and a dowry to be paid, he decides to try his hand at the more profitable business of matchmaking.

I had made up my mind to turn matchmaker and to bring about a marriage between two well-to-do merchants, one of them being Reb Eliakim Sharogroder, and the other Reb Getzel Greidinger. . . .

. . . There is hope and there are prospects. I am running from Reb Getzel to Reb Eliakim and from Reb Eliakim to Reb Getzel. I am running hither and thither, thank God, like other businessmen, very busy, no worse than other Jews; I am working hard, for the business *must* succeed, and at once, that is to say, here at the fair. There is no better opportunity for a marriage than a fair. Well then, quickly, in a hurry, the business is arranged. The fathers of the young people have seen each other and both are very willing; well, what more do you want, since both parties are ready and willing? I am swelling with pride and joy, counting my profits which I look upon as if I had them already in my pocket. I am already calculating how much dowry I would be able to give my girl.

On the strength of my profits I buy drilling for bedding and am on the point of bargaining for a velvet overcoat with a secondhand clothes dealer. . . . Well, never mind; but listen what happened. I tell you, if you have no luck it is better you had never been born. I had no luck, for when we were already on the point of settling the business and breaking plates, and were incidentally thinking of bride and bridegroom—well, guess what happened! It is a shame and a heartache to relate, but it turned out nothing; no, worse than nothing; it turned out topsy-turvy. Listen to my misfortune, to God's punishment; it turned out that both fathers had—what do you think they had?—both had boys!

—Mendele Mocher Seforim (pseudonym for Shalom Jacob Abramowitsch, 1835–1917), from "Matchmaking at a Fair," in *Fishke the Lame*

Wooing a woman

One day King Solomon the wise overheard a male bird talking to a female.

"If you want me to," said the little bird, "I will destroy the throne upon which the mighty King Solomon sits."

Infuriated by the arrogance of the bird, Solomon had him brought before him. "How dare you boast about destroying my throne," the king scolded.

"Oh Solomon," answered the bird, "where is your famous wisdom? Don't you know that to win a woman's admiration men always exaggerate their powers and boast of wonderful abilities?"

—Legend

The interpretation of the rooster's words in the following passage comes from his gesture of spreading his wings toward the ground before mating, as if describing a long cloak, and shaking his head after mating.

If the Torah had not been given, we could have learned modesty from the cat, honesty from the ant, chastity from the dove, and good manners from the rooster, who first coaxes, then mates.

How does the rooster coax his mate?

. . . He tells her, "Come to me and I will buy you a gown of many colors that will reach your feet."

After they mate he says, "May I lose my crest if when I get some money I don't buy you such a thing."

—Babylonian Talmud, tractate *Eruvin*, page 100b

Honoring the bride and groom

The tradition of wholehearted rejoicing at a wedding goes back to earliest times, even to the marriage of Adam and Eve. When the prophet Jeremiah wanted to portray the redemption of Israel, the symbol of happiness he used was of the voices of bridegroom and bride. And the talmudic masters considered cheering the bridal party as it passed through the streets so important that they could interrupt their study of Torah to do so.

The dispute between the conservative School of Shammai and the more flexible School of Hillel about how to describe an unattractive bride has been the basis for many scholarly treatises on the subject of telling white lies. Since the law almost always follows the School of Hillel, the lesson that grows from this controversy is that there are times when it is morally more important to avoid hurting someone than to be relentlessly truthful.

Thus said the Lord: Again there shall be heard in this place, which you say is ruined, without man or beast—in the towns of Judah and the streets of Jerusalem that are desolate, without man, without inhabitants, without beasts—

The voice of mirth and the voice of gladness,

The voice of the bridegroom and the voice of the bride.

The voice of those who cry, "Give thanks to the Lord of Hosts, for the Lord is good, for His kindness is everlasting!" . . .

—Jeremiah, chapter 33, verses 10–11

The book of Genesis uses the phrase "And He brought her to the man" after describing God's creation of Eve. The rabbis gave this interpretation:

This teaches that God served as Adam's best man. Here the Torah teaches a lesson in behavior. That is, that an important man can act as best man to a less important man without seeing his role as belittling him.

—Babylonian Talmud, tractate *Berakhot*, page 61a

It was the custom in ancient Judea that a cedar tree was planted when a boy was born and an acacia tree when a girl was born. When they grew up and married, their wedding canopy was made of branches woven from both trees.

—Babylonian Talmud, tractate *Gittin*, page 57a

If two scholars sit and study Torah and before them passes a bridal procession . . . if there are enough in the procession they ought not to neglect their study, but if not let them get up and cheer and hail the bride. . . .

Once as Rabbi Judah bar Ilai sat teaching his disciples, a bride passed by. So he took myrtle twigs in his hand and cheered her until the bride passed out of his sight.

Another time as Rabbi Judah bar Ilai sat teaching his disciples, a bride passed by. "What was that?" he asked them.

"A bride passing by," they replied.

"My sons," he said to them, "get up and attend upon the bride. For thus we find concerning the Holy One, blessed be He, that He attended upon a bride, as it is said: 'And the Lord God built the rib' (Genesis 2:22). If He attended upon a bride, how much more so we!" [*The text goes on to explain that in some regions, the Hebrew word for build is similar to the word for braiding. Thus, God "fixed Eve's hair and outfitted her as a bride and brought her to Adam."*]

—*Fathers According to Rabbi Nathan*, chapter 4

In kabbalistic philosophy, the Shekhinah *is the feminine principle in the divine world. Here it is equated with a bride:*

Therefore must the bride below have a canopy, all beautiful with decorations prepared for her, in order to honor the Bride above, who comes to be present and participate in the joy of the bride below. For this reason it is necessary that the canopy be as beautiful as possible, and that the Supernal Bride be invited to come and share in the joy.

—*Zohar*, volume 2, portion "Terumah," page 169a

Everyone knows why a bride enters the bridal chamber.

But if someone makes obscene comments about it, even if that person was destined for seventy years of happiness, the decree is changed to one of unhappiness.

—Babylonian Talmud, tractate *Shabbat*, page 33a

This discussion grew out of the practice at traditional Jewish weddings of dancing and singing before the seated bride and groom.

Our rabbis taught: How does one dance before the bride?

The School of Shammai say: You describe the bride as she is.

The School of Hillel say: You praise her as a beautiful and graceful bride.

The School of Shammai said to the School of Hillel: If she were lame or blind would you still say of her, "Beautiful and graceful bride," since it is written in the Torah, "Keep far from a false matter"? (Exodus 23:7).

Said the School of Hillel to the School of Shammai: According to your view, if a person made a bad purchase in the market, should you praise it in front of him or should you deprecate it? Surely you should praise it!

Therefore the sages said: A person should always have a pleasant disposition with others.

—Babylonian Talmud, tractate
Ketubbot, pages 16b–17a

This is how they sing before the bride in Palestine: "No powder and no paint, and no waving of the hair, and still a graceful gazelle."

—Rabbi Dimi, in the
Babylonian Talmud, tractate
Ketubbot, page 17a

Making marriage work

Because Jewish law gives the husband most of the legal and financial power within a family, the sages make a point of reminding men that love and kindness, not authority, are the stuff of which happy marriages are made. At the same time, recognizing that in spite of their legal disabilities, women have a major influence on marriage and family life, the scholars describe the traits which, to their minds, make for a good or bad wife.

When love is strong, a man and woman can make their bed on a sword's blade. When love grows weak, a bed of sixty cubits is not large enough.

—Babylonian Talmud, tractate
Sanhedrin, page 7a

If your wife is short, bend down to hear her whisper.

—Babylonian Talmud, tractate *Bava Mezia*, page 59a

Of a man who loves his wife as himself, honors her more than himself, guides his sons and daughters in the right path, and arranges for them to be married after they reach puberty, Scripture says: "And you shall know that your tent is in peace" (Job 5:24).

—Babylonian Talmud, tractate *Yevamot*, page 62b

A man should always be careful not to wrong his wife, for since she cries easily, she is quickly hurt. . . .

A man must be careful about the respect with which he treats his wife, because blessings rest on his home only on account of her.

And this is what Rava said to the townspeople of Mahoza: Honor your wives so that you may be enriched.

—Babylonian Talmud, tractate *Bava Mezia*, page 59a

There was once a man who married a woman who had a stump for one hand, but the man never noticed the deformity until the day she died.

Rabbi said: "How modest this woman must have been that her husband never saw her deformity."

Rabbi Hiyya said to him: "It was natural for her to hide her hand, but how modest this man must have been, for he never examined his wife's body."

—Babylonian Talmud, tractate *Shabbat*, page 53b

There was once a pious man who was married to a pious woman, and they did not have any children.

They said, "We are of no use to God," and they divorced one another.

The man went and married a wicked woman, and she made him wicked.

The woman went and married a wicked man, and she made him good.

This proves that all depends on the woman.

—*Genesis Rabbah*,
chapter 17, section 7

How can you define the term a "bad wife"?

Abbaye said: A woman who prepares a tray for her husband, and has her tongue also ready.

Rava said: A woman who prepares a tray for her husband and turns her back on him. . . .

Rava further stated: A bad wife is as troublesome as a very rainy day, for it is said: "A continual dropping in a very rainy day and a contentious woman are alike" (Proverbs 27:15).

—Babylonian Talmud, tractate
Yevamot, page 63b

There is nothing so bad as a bad wife; may the fate of the wicked overtake her!

It is as easy for an old man to climb a sand-dune as for a quiet husband to live with a nagging wife. . . .

A good wife makes a happy husband; she doubles the length of his life.

A staunch wife is her husband's joy; he will live out his days in peace.

A good wife means a good life; she is one of the Lord's gifts to those who fear Him. . . .

A wife's charm is the delight of her husband, and her womanly skill puts flesh on his bones. . . .

As bright as the light on the sacred lamp-stand is a beautiful face in the settled prime of life.

Like a golden pillar on a silver base is a shapely leg with a firm foot.

—Wisdom of Ben Sira,
chapter 25, verses 19–20;
chapter 26, verses 1–3, 13,
and 17–18

A husband's obligations to his wife

As much as they could, the talmudic sages worked to expand the rights of women within the legal framework of the Bible as they saw it. For example, they made husbands responsible for supporting their wives, allowing a husband, in exchange, the right to his wife's earnings. As Maimonides explained, however, a woman may waive her rights to maintenance and keep her own earnings. On the other hand, a man is not permitted to waive his rights to a woman's earnings and in that way free himself of the obligation to support her.

To further protect women, in about the year 75, the sages instituted the *ketubbah*, a marriage contract that spells out the payment a woman receives in case of divorce or the death of her husband. Similar documents existed since earliest ancient times, but now the marriage contract was established as a written, formal guarantee for women. The *ketubbah* is still used in traditional marriages, but it is usually ceremonial and standardized according to an old rabbinic formula. In Israel, however, it does carry some legal weight.

During the Middle Ages, a major legal and psychological step toward advancing the rights of women was an ordinance by the German scholar Rabbenu Gershom ben Judah (960–1028) prohibiting polygamy. Although, after biblical times, it had become rare for Jewish men to take more than one wife, the practice had never been officially outlawed until Rabbenu Gershom's time. His prohibition was binding on Jews in Germanic countries but not in Oriental ones.

When a man marries a woman . . . he obligates himself to her for ten things. . . .

Of the ten, three are found in the Torah: her food, her clothes and her conjugal rights. Her *food* signifies her maintenance; her *clothes*, what the term implies; her *conjugal rights*, sexual intercourse with her, according to the ways of the world.

The other seven are of scribal origin. . . . The first is the statutory *ketubbah*: the rest are called "conditions contained in the *ketubbah*." They are the following: to treat her if she falls ill; to ransom her if she is captured; to bury her if she dies; to provide for her maintenance out of his estate; to let her dwell in his house after his death . . . ; to let her daughters sired by him receive their maintenance out of his estate after his death, until they become espoused; to let her male children sired by him inherit her *ketubbah*. . . .

The Sages have further enacted that a wife's earnings are chargeable against her maintenance. . . .

Therefore, if the wife says, "I want neither maintenance nor work," her wish must be respected and she may not be coerced. On the other hand, if the husband says, "I will neither support you nor take any of your earnings," no attention need be paid to him, perchance her earnings will not suffice for her support. It is because of this enactment that the obligation of maintenance is regarded as one of the conditions contained in the *ketubbah*.

—Maimonides, *Code*, "Laws Concerning Marriage," chapter 12, sections 1, 2, and 4

If a man's position rises, a woman may enjoy all the benefits of the rise; but if he suffers setbacks, she is not legally required to lower her standard of living from what she enjoyed before her marriage, although she may certainly do so if she wishes.

A woman rises with her husband but does not go down with him. . . .

Rabbi Eleazar said the proof is from the verse, "She was the mother of all the living" [about Eve, in Genesis 3:20]. She was given to her husband to live, but not to suffer pain.

—Babylonian Talmud, tractate *Ketubbot*, page 61a

A man may not force his wife to move from a town or city in one country to a town or city in another country. He may force his wife to move from one town to another in the same country or one city to another in the same country, however.

But he may not force her to move from a town to a city or from a city to a town.

A man may take his wife from an inferior dwelling to a superior one, but not from a superior one to an inferior one. Rabban Simeon ben Gamaliel ruled: He may not even force her to move from an inferior dwelling to a superior one because the change to a superior dwelling is disruptive.

—Mishnah, tractate *Ketubbot*, chapter 13, paragraph 10

If a husband beats his wife

One of the most shocking pieces of advice in all of Maimonides's writings is his reference to "scourging" one's wife if she refuses to do her work. It may have reflected common practice in the twelfth-century Islamic world, of which Maimonides was a part, or his own stern outlook. But it fell far out of line with Jewish tradition, and both contemporary and later commentators were quick to point that out. The thirteenth-century scholar Rabbi Meir ben Baruch of Rothenburg represents the accepted attitude, not only among authorities but within Jewish family life over the centuries.

A wife who refuses to perform any kind of work she is obligated to do may be compelled to perform it, even by scourging her with a rod.

—Maimonides, *Code*, "Laws Concerning Marriage," chapter 21, section 10

I have never heard of women being scourged with a rod!

—Abraham ben David Posquières (c. 1125–1198), commentary on Maimonides

Wife beating is unheard of among the children of Israel!

—Rabbenu Tam (Jacob ben Meir Tam, c. 1100–1171), French talmudist

The rabbi was questioned about a man who habitually struck his wife.

A Jew must honor his wife more than he honors himself. If one strikes his wife, he should be punished more severely than he would be for striking another person. For a man is enjoined to honor his wife, but is not enjoined to honor the other person. . . .

If this man persists in striking his wife, he should be excommunicated, lashed, and suffer the severest punishment, even to the extent of amputating his arm. If his wife is willing to accept a divorce, he must divorce her and pay the *ketubbah*.

—Meir ben Baruch of Rothenburg, *Responsa*, "Even ha-Ezer," number 297

A wife's traditional role

Legally, a husband gets four financial benefits from his wife in return for the ten duties he has toward her. He may demand a certain amount of housework, and if she earns money from her work, he keeps those earnings. He owns anything she gains or finds by chance, he gets the income from her property, and he is the only heir to her estate when she dies. Any of these rights may be changed, however, by mutual agreement.

Outside the legal sphere, a Jewish woman's role has been similar in many respects to the traditional role of women in society as a whole. She helps her husband, cares for her children, cleans, and cooks. But there's another dimension: she also performs the rituals and preserves the religious ideals that make her home a place of peace and contentment for her family.

The best catalog of a woman's work and family responsibilities comes from the book of Proverbs. The talmudic view of the work required of a woman in return for her husband's support, though geared to its own time, has a contemporary ring in its insistence that a woman find some work to occupy her even if her husband would rather she does not. Rabbi Jonah Gerondi spells out a woman's responsibilities as seen through the eyes of a medieval male moralist.

A woman of valor who can find?
For her price is far above rubies.
The heart of her husband does safely trust in her,
And he has no lack of gain.
She does him good and not evil
All the days of her life.
She seeks wool and flax,
And works willingly with her hands.
She is like the merchant-ships;
She brings her food from afar.
She rises also while it is still night,
And gives food to her household,
And a portion to her maidens.

She considers a field and buys it;
With the fruit of her hands she plants a vineyard.
She girds her loins with strength,
And makes strong her arms.
She perceives that her merchandise is good;
Her lamp goes not out by night.
She lays her hand to the distaff,
And her hands hold the spindle.
She stretches out her hand to the poor;
Yea, she reaches forth her hand to the needy.
She is not afraid of the snow for her household;
For all her household are clothed in scarlet.
She makes for herself coverlets;
Her clothing is fine linen and purple.
Her husband is known in the gates,
When he sits among the elders of the land.
She makes linen garments and sells them;
And delivers girdles unto the merchant.
Strength and dignity are her clothing;
And she laughs at the time to come.
She opens her mouth with wisdom;
And the law of kindness is on her tongue.
She looks well to the ways of her household,
And eats not the bread of idleness.
Her children rise up and call her blessed;
Her husband also, and he praises her:
Many daughters have done valiantly,
But you exceed them all.
Grace is deceitful, and beauty is vain;
But a woman that fears the Lord, she shall be praised.
Give her of the fruit of her hands;
And let her works praise her in the gates.

—Proverbs, chapter 31,
verses 10–31

These are the kinds of work that a woman must perform for her husband: grind corn, bake bread, wash clothes, cook, nurse her child, make her husband's bed and work in wool.

If she brought one servant [with her when she married—or money to pay one], she need not grind or bake or wash.

If she brought two servants, she need not cook or nurse her child.

If she brought three servants, she need not make the bed or work in wool.

If four, she may sit in an easy chair [and do nothing].

Rabbi Eliezer said: Even if she brought a hundred servants, her husband should insist that she do woolwork, for idleness leads to unchastity.

Rabban Simeon ben Gamaliel said: If a man forbade his wife to do any work at all, he must divorce her and pay her ketubbah, for idleness leads to madness.

—Mishnah, tractate *Ketubbot*,
chapter 5, paragraph 5

A woman must see to it that there is peace between herself and her husband, and that she is loving and kind to her husband.

A woman must see to it that she prays morning, afternoon, and evening for her sons and her daughters that they learn to fear heaven, and that her sons succeed in the study of the Torah and in doing the commandments.

For the essence of woman's merit for attaining the world to come is that her children fear God's name, and do the will of God. And when she is in her eternal home, and her children have the fear of heaven in their hearts, this is accredited to her as though she were alive and carrying out all the commandments herself, and she is on the highest steps leading to the world to come.

—Jonah ben Abraham Gerondi,
Iggeret Teshuvah

The ideal wife

Rachel, Rabbi Akiva's wife, served as an inspiration for Jewish women in ghettos and small towns throughout Europe down to the days of the Holocaust. Like her, many of them took on the dual burdens of caring for their families and providing financial support for their husbands, who devoted much of their time to the study of Torah.

Although the legend is exaggerated, it has some basis in fact. Rabbi Akiva did begin his career as a poor shepherd who later turned to scholarship. For several years he studied away from home at the rabbinical academy at Lydda, and he rose to become one of the great scholars and patriots in Israel. Rachel is given credit for contributing to his many achievements through her patience and loyal encouragement.

In his youth, Rabbi Akiva was a shepherd for the rich Kalba Savu'a of Jerusalem. This man had a beautiful and modest daughter, and seeing how noble the shepherd was, she said to him:

"If I betroth myself to you, will you go out and study Torah?" He replied: "Yes, with all my heart."

They married secretly, and he went off to study Torah. But when her father heard what she had done, he drove her from his house, vowing that she should not benefit from his property as long as he lived.

Akiva stayed away for twelve years. When he returned, he brought with him twelve thousand disciples. As he reached home he heard an old man say to his wife:

"How long will you go on living the life of a living widow?" His wife answered: "If he would listen to me, my husband would go away and continue his studies for another twelve years."

Hearing this, Akiva went away to study at the academy

for another twelve years. When he returned this time, he brought with him twenty-four thousand disciples.

Told of his return, his wife went out to greet him. Her neighbors said, "Borrow some clothes from us so that you will not look so shabby." But she refused. When she reached him, she fell on her face and kissed his feet. His pupils were about to push her away, but Rabbi Akiva cried, "Leave her alone. All that is mine and yours is hers," meaning that it was because of her that they had achieved what they had.

When her father Kalba Savu'a learned that a great scholar had come to town, he said to himself, "I will go to him, and perhaps he will free me of my vow," which he had come to regret.

"Would you have made your vow if you knew that your son-in-law was a great scholar?" Rabbi Akiva asked him.

"If he had known even one chapter or one law," said the other, "I would not have made that vow."

Then Rabbi Akiva said, "I am the shepherd who tended your flock, and it was because of your daughter that I went out to study."

When Kalba Savu'a heard this, he fell at Akiva's feet, and gave him half his wealth.

—Babylonian Talmud, tractate *Ketubbot*, pages 62b–63a

Challenging the traditions

To people who question the traditional attitudes toward women, the learned and outspoken Beruryah, and not the self-sacrificing Rachel, has become the ideal. Jewish feminists, even within Orthodoxy, argue that women should be included in all aspects of legal, ritual, and religious life on an equal basis with men. Here, historian Paula E. Hyman outlines many of the restrictions Judaism has placed on women as she sees them. Novelist Cynthia Ozick decries the exclusion of women from serious Jewish study, for centuries the most important and most prestigious occupation of men. Judith Hauptman, the first woman to teach Talmud at the Jewish Theological Seminary, argues that Jewish law and legend are broad enough to allow women full rights. And educator Sarah Roth Lieberman presents the case for admitting women to the rabbinate. The Reform movement has ordained women as rabbis since 1972, and the Reconstructionist since 1974. In the Conservative movement, with the largest membership among American Jews, the issue was debated from 1977 to 1983, when the first women were admitted to the rabbinical school of the Jewish Theological Seminary. The first woman was ordained as a Conservative rabbi in 1985. The issue has not been taken up among the Orthodox, who generally hold that it would not be permissible to ordain women.

> Within the framework of traditional Judaism, women are not independent legal entities. Like the minor, the deaf-mute, and the idiot, they cannot serve as witnesses in Jewish court. . . . They do not inherit equally with male heirs; they play only a passive role in the Jewish marriage ceremony; and they cannot initiate divorce proceedings. . . .
>
> Within the family the woman may have had a necessary and noble task to fulfill. But the heart and soul of traditional Judaism remained communal prayer and study. And prayer and study were the pursuits almost exclusively of men. No wonder, then, that Jewish sages from Rabbi Eliezer to Maimonides considered women as frivolous, ignorant beings, wasting their husbands' time, for they were not engaged in that most worthy and significant of Jewish endeavors, sacred study. . . . No wonder, then, that the birth of a male child was cause for celebration, the birth of a female, for stoic acceptance. . . .
>
> What Jewish feminists are seeking . . . is not more apologetics but change, based on acknowledgment of the ways in which the Jewish tradition has excluded women

from entire spheres of Jewish experience and has considered them intellectually and spiritually inferior to men.

—Paula E. Hyman, assistant professor of modern Jewish history, Columbia University, from "The Other Half: Women in the Jewish Tradition," in *Conservative Judaism* (Summer 1972)

If *halakhah* aids in suppressing the scholars who can grow to create it, that is a kind of self-decimation. If the Jewish communal conscience continues to amputate half its potential scholarship, that is akin to cultural self-destruction. When half the brain is idling, the other half is lame.

Until Jewish women are in the same relation to history and Torah as Jewish men are and have been, we should not allow ourselves ever again to indulge in the phrase "the Jewish genius." There is no collective Jewish genius.

Since Deborah the Prophet we have not had a collective Jewish genius. What we have had is a Jewish half-genius. That is not enough for the people who choose to hear the Voice of the Lord of History.

We have been listening with only half an ear, speaking with only half a tongue, and never understanding that we have made ourselves partly deaf and partly dumb.

—Cynthia Ozick, from "The Jewish Half-Genius," in the *Jerusalem Post*, July 7, 1978

. . . We renounce the view held by many, both men and women, that the Jewish tradition, having been shaped by men, is totally biased in their favor. It was the rabbis, members of the very class of people who were more equal than others, who voluntarily extended some of their privileges to those who were not so fortunate. . . .

What troubles Jewish women today is that the movement for equalization ended before real equalization was reached. . . . These problems would have been solved centuries ago had not a new trend of status quo conquered the progressive trend, perhaps under the influence of other cultures. Status quo in a society that is moving forward turns into retrogression. . . .

Jewish women lament the fact that the igenious techniques worked out by the rabbis for continual ethical refinement of legal institutions have fallen into disuse, that women today are suffering from legal and social injustices, and that the Jewish tradition is very frequently the target of criticism. We hope that we will soon see a reinstitution of the process so admirably evolved and applied by the earlier rabbis, an improvement in the lot of women, and a vindication of the essential Jewish tradition.

—Judith Hauptman, professor of Talmud, Jewish Theological Seminary of America, from "Women's Liberation in the Talmudic Period," in *Conservative Judaism* (Summer 1972)

In biblical times, Jewish leaders were not rabbis, nor cantors, nor sextons, nor directors of education. Each role evolved as the need arose. In biblical times leaders were priests, prophets, and wise persons. In addition, there were female judges, prophets, rulers, and teachers. Women were even, like the rabbi of modern times, professional mourners—skilled in dirges, delivering eulogies in poetic metre. . . . The rabbis of today have taken away from women what was theirs by tradition.

. . . The full-time professional rabbi as we know him appeared only recently in Jewish life at the end of the eighteenth-century in Germany when demands of secular education, preaching in the vernacular, and theological inquiry beyond the *halakhah* became the norm. In perspective, the modern rabbi is a relatively recent institution in Jewish life, the result of development and response to the needs of the Jewish community. And now the Jewish community, in continuing responsiveness to its needs, is considering the woman to serve as rabbi. . . .

The Jewish community needs that vast and rich reservoir of Jewish knowledge, expertise, and commitment found in its Jewish women. . . . What does the contemporary rabbi do which a woman is not capable of doing? A woman can engage in scholarly pursuits, counsel couples and families, lead in study and prayer. . . . But above all—she can be a role model, exemplary in moral and religious conduct, which together with learning is the basic requirement of clergy.

—Sarah Roth Lieberman, in
Sh'ma (December 22, 1978)

Enjoying the "marital duty"

Rabbi Simeon ben Halafta, an early sage, once described the male sex organ as the "peacemaker of the home," lamenting the fact that with old age it had ceased functioning. The sages regarded it as a husband's duty to give his wife sexual pleasure, even going so far as to construct a schedule of minimal sexual activity for men of different occupations! That is not to say that they reduced sex to a rigid formula. On the contrary, they discussed ways of making it more enjoyable, encouraging both men and women to be good lovers. The most poetic view of marital sex comes from the *Zohar*, the major work of the mystical Kabbalah movement, which portrays a male as incomplete without a female. Mystical approaches to marital sex also inform *The Holy Letter*, attributed to Nahmanides, except that its instructions are quite down-to-earth.

In the final selection, Maimonides states early mishnaic rules about a "rebellious" husband or wife who refuses to have sex. Not all scholars have taken such a hard line on the penalties due a rebellious wife. Some have suggested that while she forfeits her *ketubbah*, she does keep her dowry money and the property she owns.

The marital duty as set forth in the Torah is:

for men who have no occupation, every day;

for laborers, twice a week;

for donkey-drivers [who travel about during the week], once a week;

for camel-drivers [who travel for long periods], once every thirty days;

for sailors [who may travel for months], once in six months.

—Mishnah, tractate *Ketubbot*, chapter 5, paragraph 5

Friday night, the Sabbath eve, is regarded as a time of intense spirituality, and with it, physical—and especially sexual—enjoyment.

Suppose a man wants to change occupations from a donkey-driver to camel-driver [which keeps him away from home longer, although it pays more]?

The answer: A woman prefers less money with enjoyment to more money with abstinence.

. . . How often should scholars perform their marital duty? Rabbi Judah said in the name of Samuel: Every Friday night.

—Babylonian Talmud, tractate *Ketubbot*, page 62b

. . . A man may not treat his wife the way the Persians do, who perform their marital duties with their clothes on.

Rabbi Huna ruled: A husband who says, "I will not perform my marital duty unless she wears her clothes and

I wear mine," must give his wife a divorce [if she wants it] and pay her ketubbah money.

—Babylonian Talmud, tractate *Ketubbot*, page 48a

A person may not drink out of one goblet and think of another [sleep with one woman and fantasize about another].

—Babylonian Talmud, tractate *Nedarim*, page 20b

A man is forbidden to force his wife to the marital obligation. . . .

Whoever forces his wife to the marital obligation will have unworthy children.

—Babylonian Talmud, tractate *Eruvin*, page 100b

A woman who solicits her husband to the marital obligation will have children the like of whom did not exist even in the generation of Moses. . . .

Rabbi Isaac ben Avdimi stated: While a husband solicits with his speech, a wife solicits with her heart, this being a fine trait among women. In other words, she entices him [without speaking openly of her desire].

—Babylonian Talmud, tractate *Eruvin*, page 100b

In the following passage, Maimonides is not implying that a husband is permitted to force his wife into any form of sex he wishes but that both are free to enjoy one another physically.

Since a man's wife is permitted to him, he may act with her in any manner whatsoever. He may have intercourse with her whenever he so desires, and kiss any organ of her body he wishes, and he may have intercourse with her naturally or unnaturally, provided that he does not expend semen to no purpose. Nevertheless, it is an attribute of piety that a man should not act in this matter with levity, and that he should sanctify himself at the time of intercourse....

—Maimonides, *Code*, "Laws Concerning Forbidden Intercourse," chapter 21, section 9

All the time that a man is on his travels, he should be very careful of his actions, in order that the celestial partner may not desert him and leave him defective, through lacking the union with a female. If this was necessary when his wife was with him, how much more so is it necessary when a heavenly partner guides him on the way all the time until he returns home. When he does reach home again it is his duty to give his wife some pleasure, because it is she who acquired for him this heavenly partner.

It is his duty to do this for two reasons. One is that his pleasure is a religious pleasure and one which gives joy to the *Shekhinah* also, and what is more, by its means he spreads peace in the world. . . . The other is, that if his wife becomes pregnant, the celestial partner imparts to the child a holy soul....

—*Zohar*, volume 1, portion "Bereshit," pages 49b–50a

. . . A husband should speak with his wife with the appropriate words, some of erotic passion, some words of fear of the Lord....

A man should never force himself upon his wife and never overpower her, for the Divine Spirit never rests upon one whose conjugal relations occur in the absence of desire, love, and free will. . . .

One should never argue with his wife, and certainly never strike her on account of sexual matters. The Talmud . . . tells us that just as a lion tears at his prey and eats it shamelessly, so does an ignorant man shamelessly strike and sleep with his wife. . . .

A man should not have intercourse with his wife while she is asleep, for then they cannot both agree to the act. It is far better to arouse her with words that will placate her and inspire desire in her.

To conclude, when you are ready for sexual union, see that your wife's intentions combine with yours. Do not hurry to arouse her until she is receptive. Be calm . . . as you enter the path of love and will.

—*The Holy Letter*,
attributed to Nahmanides

A man may not withhold from his wife her conjugal rights. If he transgresses and does so withhold in order to torment her, he has violated a negative commandment of the Torah. . . .

If he has become ill or enfeebled so that he is unable to have sexual intercourse, he may wait six months . . . perchance he will recover. After that, he must either obtain her consent or divorce her and pay her her ketubbah.

The wife who prevents her husband from having intercourse with her is called a "rebellious wife," and should be questioned as to the reason for her rebelliousness. If she says, "I have come to loathe him, and I cannot willingly submit to his intercourse," he must be compelled to divorce her immediately, for she is not like a captive woman who must submit to a man that is hateful to her.

She must, however, leave with forfeiture of her ketubbah, but may take her worn-out clothes that are still on hand....

If she rebels against her husband merely in order to torment him, and says, "I am going to make him suffer in this way because he has done thus and thus to me," ... the court should send her a message stating as follows: "Be it known to you that if you persist in your rebellion, your *ketubbah* . . . will stand forfeited."

—Maimonides, *Code*, "Laws Concerning Marriage," chapter 14, sections 7–9

On adultery

The Seventh Commandment—"You shall not commit adultery"—is directed at both men and women, but with inequalities. In Jewish law, a married woman is considered an adulteress any time she has sexual relations outside her marriage; a married man is branded an adulterer only if his relations are with a married woman. This emphasis on the unfaithfulness of the woman stems both from her early legal status as a possession of her husband and from the fact that for centuries men were free to marry more than one wife.

The Bible imposes a humiliating ordeal on a woman accused of adultery—the only instance of trial by ordeal in Jewish law. Although in practice this ordeal and, certainly, the death penalty for a guilty woman were discontinued long before Rabban Johanan ben Zakkai officially abolished them after the destruction of the Second Temple in the year 70, later talmudic authorities continued to analyze the ceremony and build legends around it. Distressed by its one-sidedness, they found ways to prove that the woman's lover and her husband—if he himself had been unfaithful—were punished along with her. Maimonides explains their reasoning.

As the law was finally fixed, a woman could be convicted of adultery only if she had been warned against it by two witnesses who then saw her in the act—not a likely circumstance. But to underline the severity of the crime, the law considers a woman convicted of adultery unfit for her husband and forbidden to her lover. And while a child born out of wedlock is considered legitimate in Jewish law, an infant born of an adulterous relationship is regarded as a bastard, who may never marry within the Jewish community.

> If a man is found lying with another man's wife, both of them—the man and the woman with whom he lay—shall die. Thus you will sweep away evil from Israel.
>
> —Deuteronomy, chapter 22, verse 22

The primitive ordeal to which a woman suspected of adultery was subjected had magical implications along with elaborate ritual. A priest gave the woman a potion to drink and warned her of the curses that would come upon her if she were guilty.

> The priest shall put these curses down in writing and rub it off into the water of bitterness. He is to make the woman drink the water of bitterness that induces the spell, so that the spell-inducing water may enter into her to bring on bitterness....
>
> Once he has made her drink the water—if she has defiled herself by breaking faith with her husband, the spell-inducing water shall enter into her to bring on bitterness, so that her belly shall distend and her thigh shall sag; and the woman shall become a curse among her people. But if the woman has not defiled herself and is pure, she shall be unharmed and able to retain seed.
>
> —Numbers, chapter 5, verses 23–28

There were two sisters who looked very much alike. Each married and moved to different cities. The husband of one sister accused his wife of adultery, and sought to have her drink of the bitter waters in Jerusalem. The woman fled to her sister's city.

"What has happened?" her sister asked. "Why are you here?"

"My husband wants me to drink of the bitter waters," she replied, "and I am guilty."

Her sister answered, "Don't be afraid. I will take your place and drink the waters. And since I'm innocent, you will never be found out."

The innocent woman dressed in her sister's clothes and took her place at the ordeal. She drank the bitter waters and was found pure.

She returned to her sister's house. Her sister ran forward to greet her, and the two women embraced.

As they kissed, the guilty sister inhaled the odor of the bitter waters—and died immediately.

—*Numbers Rabbah*, chapter 9, section 9

At the very hour that an adulterous woman died, her paramour, on whose account she was made to drink of the water, likewise died, wherever he happened to be, and whatever befell her—the swelling of the belly and the falling away of the thigh—befell him also.

All this applied only if her husband had never indulged in illicit intercourse. If he had, the water could not test his wife....

If the husband who had thus transgressed caused his wife to drink of the water, he thereby added another sin to his iniquity in that he . . . discredited the efficacy of the water. For his wife was bound to tell other women that she had played the harlot, and yet the water had no effect upon her, seeing that she was unaware that her husband's own doings were responsible for the water's failure to test her.

—Maimonides, *Code*, "Laws Concerning the Wayward Woman," chapter 4, sections 17–18

When adulterers increased in number, the ritual of the bitter waters ceased.

It was Rabban Johanan ben Zakkai who brought it to an end, citing this verse:

"I will not punish their daughters for fornicating, nor their daughters-in-law for committing adultery; for they themselves turn aside with whores, and sacrifice with prostitutes. . . ." (Hosea 4:14).

—Mishnah, tractate *Sotah*,
chapter 9, paragraph 9

Getting along with in-laws

The extended families of earlier days are no longer common, but friction between young married couples and their parents still stirs up conflicts. The rabbis affirm that loyalty to your spouse comes before loyalty to your parents, even if that means angering or hurting your parents. Solomon Maimon, who describes his personal solution to in-law problems, was a brilliant, outspoken, and rebellious scholar. He was married at the age of twelve, and with his wife he went to live in the home of his widowed mother-in-law, Rissia. The two fought constantly, often spending mealtimes flinging bowls and plates at one another. Finally, as described in the last selection, he devised a way of bringing peace to his household.

If one's parents constantly argue with one's wife and if the person were to tell his wife to be silent she would become quarrelsome with him and refuse intercourse with him, then he should keep silent himself. . . . Don't place yourself between two hot tempers. . . .

And if his father and his mother are quarrelsome people who pick on his wife, and he knows that his wife is in the right, he should not rebuke his wife so as to please his parents.

—Judah the Pious,
Book of the Pious,
section 952

If a man says to his wife, "I do not wish to have your father, your mother, your brothers or your sisters come to my house," his wish is to be honored, and she should visit them instead. . . . They, however, should not visit her, unless something has happened to her, such as illness or a delivery, for no man may be compelled to let others enter his premises.

Thus, also, if she says, "I do not wish to have your mother or your sisters visit me, nor do I wish to reside in the same courtyard with them, because they cause me harm and annoyance," her wish is to be honored, for no person may be compelled to let other people reside with him on his premises.

—Maimonides, *Code*, "Laws Concerning Marriage," chapter 13, section 14

I rose about midnight, took a large earthenware vessel, crept with it under my mother-in-law's bed, and began to speak aloud into the vessel in the following fashion:

"O Rissia, Rissia, you ungodly woman, why do you treat my beloved son so ill? If you do not mend your ways, your end is near, and you will be damned to all eternity."

Then I crept out again, and began to pinch her cruelly; and after a while I slipped silently back to bed.

The following morning she got up in consternation and told my wife that my mother had appeared to her in a dream, and had threatened and pinched her on my account. In confirmation she showed the blue marks on her arm.

When I came from the synagogue I did not find my mother-in-law at home, but found my wife in tears. I asked her the reason, but she would tell me nothing.

My mother-in-law returned, with a dejected look and eyes red with weeping. She had gone, as I afterwards learned, to the Jewish place of burial, thrown herself on my mother's grave, and begged for forgiveness of her fault. . . . She also fasted the whole day, and towards me showed herself extremely amiable.

—Solomon Maimon (c. 1753–1800), *Autobiography*

Grounds for divorce

The great emphasis on the importance of marriage and family life made divorce a rare occurrence among Jewish couples until contemporary times. Yet divorce is easier to obtain under Jewish law than under almost any other legal system. Neither party has to prove the other guilty; both need only agree to end their marriage. The law seems to recognize that if family ties and social pressures are not strong enough to hold a marriage together, legal barriers can only make matters worse.

The Bible gives a man the power to divorce his wife at will. The talmudic sages, following the School of Hillel rather than the School of Shammai, perpetuated the ease of divorce for men; but to protect women, they instituted the *ketubbah* contract, obligating a husband to pay his wife a specified amount of money if they divorced. For the first time, they also established broad grounds upon which a woman could seek a divorce. The difference was, however, that she could not divorce her husband directly. The "bill of divorcement," called a *get*, had to come from him. If he didn't agree to the divorce, she had to apply to a rabbinic court, which would then try to convince the man to accept her wishes. Members of the rabbinic courts often were not above using physical force to "persuade" a recalcitrant husband; and with little compunction, Maimonides gives the rationale for their actions.

A significant advance for women came during the eleventh century, when an ordinance by the great German leader Rabbenu Gershom established that a woman may not be divorced against her will. In a situation in which a woman is incapable of consenting to a divorce because of mental illness or other disability, the husband must obtain a release signed by a hundred rabbis before he may take another wife.

The fact that a bill of divorcement must come from the man still causes problems in Israel, where Jewish family law is the law of the land. Some men have extorted large sums from wives before agreeing to a divorce; and in some cases, men have abandoned their wives, who may not remarry without a religious divorce. If they do, they have the status of an adulteress, and their children are considered illegitimate. In the United States, both the Orthodox and Conservative movements require a religious divorce along with a civil one. Both have sought ways to ease the disadvantages of women in matters of divorce.

> A man takes a wife and possesses her. She fails to please him because he finds something obnoxious about her, and he writes her a bill of divorcement, hands it to her, and sends her away from his house.
>
> —Deuteronomy, chapter 24, verse 1

> The School of Shammai said: A man may not divorce his wife unless he found something unchaste about her. . . .
>
> The School of Hillel said: He may divorce her even if she spoiled a dish for him. . . .
>
> Rabbi Akiva said: Even if he found another woman more beautiful than she. . . .
>
> —Mishnah, tractate *Gittin*, chapter 9, paragraph 10

The "serpent" in Rav's epigram refers to the husband.

> Rav stated: If a husband says, "I will neither maintain nor support my wife," he must divorce her and pay her ketubbah money.
>
> Rabbi Eleazar reported this statement to Samuel, who said, ". . . Rather than forcing him to divorce her, let him be forced to support her."
>
> What was Rav's reason for ordering divorce?
>
> "No one can live with a serpent in the same box."
>
> —Babylonian Talmud, tractate *Ketubbot*, page 77a

The following may be compelled to divorce their wives: A man who is afflicted with boils, or has a goiter, or gathers dog excrements [for use in tanning], or is a coppersmith or a tanner [whose work makes him smell bad], whether these conditions existed before they married or arose after marriage.

About all these Rabbi Meir said: Although the husband may have made an agreement with her that she marry him in spite of these defects, she may plead, "I thought I could endure him, but I cannot." . . .

—Mishnah, tractate *Ketubbot*, chapter 7, paragraph 10

If a woman says, "He is repulsive to me," she should not be pressured to remain married to the man.

Mar Zutra ruled: She should be pressured. Such a case once occurred, and Mar Zutra convinced the woman to remain married. As a result of the reconciliation, Rabbi Hanina of Sura [an outstanding scholar] was born.

Still, this was not the right thing to do. The happy results came about only with the help of heaven.

—Babylonian Talmud, tractate *Ketubbot*, page 63b

If a man refuses to give a woman a divorce, he is forced until he declares, "I am willing."

—Babylonian Talmud, tractate *Kiddushin*, page 50a

Why is a divorce given under duress not considered null and void?

Because . . . he whose evil inclination induces him to

. . . commit a transgression, and who is lashed until he does what he is obligated to do, or refrains from what he is forbidden to do, cannot be regarded as a victim of duress; rather he has brought duress upon himself by submitting to his evil inclination. Therefore, this man who refuses to divorce his wife . . . has only been overwhelmed by his evil inclination—once he is lashed until his inclination is weakened and he says, "I consent," it is the same as if he had given the *get* voluntarily.

—Maimonides, *Code*, "Laws Concerning Divorce," chapter 2, section 20

Saving a marriage

Although the decision to divorce is accepted as a personal one, the aim is to keep marriage intact, using all possible resources; a Hasidic rabbi calls on tradition to help him plead his cause with his wife, and a clever woman finds her own way to win back her husband.

All things can be replaced except the wife of one's youth.

—Babylonian Talmud, tractate *Sanhedrin*, page 22a

If a man divorces his first wife even the altar sheds tears, as it is written:

"And this you do as well: You cover the altar of the Lord with tears, weeping and moaning. . . . Because of what? Because the Lord is a witness between you and the wife of your youth with whom you have broken faith, though she is your partner and covenanted spouse" (Malachi 2:13–14).

—Babylonian Talmud, tractate *Gittin*, page 90b

Rabbi Zusya's wife was unhappy in their marriage, and persistently asked for a divorce. One night the rabbi called to her, "Hendel, look here." He showed her that his pillow was wet.

"The Talmud tells us that if a man divorces his first wife, the altar itself sheds tears for him. My pillow is wet with those tears. Now, do you still insist that we divorce?"

From then on, Rabbi Zusya's wife became happy and contented.

—Tale about Rabbi
Zusya of Hanipoli

Legally, a man may divorce a woman if she doesn't bear children after ten years of marriage, and both are free to remarry, for, says the Talmud, "it is possible that it was he who was unworthy to have children from her."

A couple who lived in Sidon had been married for ten years without having children. The husband demanded a divorce, and the couple went to see Rabbi Simeon bar Yohai. The rabbi, who strongly opposed divorces, tried to convince them to stay together. But the husband was adamant.

"Since you are resolved to divorce," the rabbi told them, "you should give a party to celebrate your separation just as you gave one to celebrate your wedding."

The couple agreed. During the course of the party, the husband, who had drunk much wine, said to his wife, "My dear, before we separate, choose whatever you consider most precious in this house, and take it with you when you return to your father's house to live."

After her husband had fallen into a drunken sleep, the woman ordered her servants to carry him to her father's house and put him to bed there. In the middle of the night, the husband awoke.

"Where am I?" he called out.

"At my father's house," his wife replied. "You told me to take with me whatever I considered most precious to me. There is nothing in the world more precious to me than you."

Moved by his wife's love, the husband decided to remain married, and they lived together happily after that.

—*Song of Songs Rabbah*, chapter 1, section 4

Keeping peace between husband and wife

Once again, as in the case of the unattractive bride, absolute truth takes second place to a higher value: *shalom bayit*, maintaining peace in the home.

In the book of Genesis, when God tells Sarah she is to have a son, she laughs and says, "Now that I am withered, am I to have enjoyment—with my husband so old?"

When God relates the incident to Abraham, He is recorded as saying, "Why did Sarah laugh, saying, 'Shall I in truth bear a child, old as I am?' "

According to the rabbis, God deliberately changed Sarah's words in telling them to Abraham so as not to reveal that his wife had complained of his old age.

At the school of Rabbi Ishmael it was taught:

Great is the cause of peace, seeing that for the sake of peace even the Holy One, blessed be He, deviated from the truth and modified a statement.

For at first it is written: "with my husband so old."

And then it is written: "old as I am."

—Babylonian Talmud, tractate *Yevamot*, page 65b

Rabbi Meir used to give public sermons every Friday evening. A certain woman, who enjoyed his lectures greatly, attended regularly. One evening, his sermon was especially long, and when the woman returned home, she found her house darkened and her husband angrily standing at the door.

"Where have you been?" he shouted at her.

"To hear the rabbi preach," the woman replied.

"Since the rabbi's preaching has pleased you so much," the husband said, "I vow that you will not enter this house until you have spat in his eyes. That's his reward for the entertainment he has given you," he added sarcastically.

The husband barred the doorway, and refused to allow his wife to enter. The astonished woman went to live with a neighbor.

When word of the incident reached Rabbi Meir, he sent for the woman. Pretending to have pain in both his eyes, the rabbi asked her if she knew of a cure for his illness.

The simple woman nervously said, "No."

"Spit seven times in my eyes," said the rabbi, "perhaps that will heal them."

The woman hesitated, but then did as Rabbi Meir requested.

"Now go home," he told her, "and say to your husband: 'You told me to spit once, but I have spat seven times.' "

When the rabbi's disciples complained of the indignity he had allowed himself to suffer, he chided them, "No act is disgraceful if it promotes the peace and happiness of husband and wife."

—Based on a legend in
Deuteronomy Rabbah,
chapter 5, section 15

4

FAMILY RELATIONSHIPS

"As my father worked for me, I work for my children"

For the sake of the children ✦ The importance of having children ✦ A parent's love ✦ On losing a child ✦ What parents owe children ✦ On having daughters ✦ Sibling love and rivalry ✦ Adopted children and orphans ✦ "I'm lucky—I'm an orphan" ✦ A father's advice ✦ How parents influence children ✦ Stern vs. permissive discipline ✦ Striking a child ✦ Reaching out to a child ✦ When a child is defiant ✦ Punishing a "stubborn and rebellious" son ✦ What children owe parents ✦ Ways of showing respect ✦ About model children ✦ Should children support parents? ✦ On growing old ✦ Caring for elderly parents ✦ If parents are senile ✦ Limits of parental authority ✦ Parents and children: choosing priorities

The relationships within a family are probably the most complex of all relationships. In spite of the myriad of learned books and popular manuals on the subject, parents and children in every generation find themselves wrestling with many of the same problems: how to communicate with one another; how to show love and respect for one another; how to let go of one another when the time comes. And in every generation, the child-rearing pendulum swings. We shift from insisting that children should be "seen and not heard" to maintaining that children must be free to express themselves at all times. And then we shift back again.

The changing attitudes about parent-child relationships appear as well in the teachings of the Jewish sages. Parents themselves, they were influenced, as parents always are, by their own experiences and by the environment in which they lived. "Break in your son while he is young, beat him soundly while he is still a child" was Ben Sira's advice, reflecting the harsh discipline that was the norm in ancient times. About a thousand years later, the Spanish talmudist Judah ben Asher wrote: "My father and mother left me to do what was right in my own eyes . . . wherefore I have never been wont to chide others . . . even my own sons."

Many of the selections that follow have meaning today not because they offer new insights into child development but because their insights mirror the struggles of parents everywhere. We read them with a nod of recognition. More important, however, the passages have meaning for us because of the ideals they convey.

First, children are deeply wanted and loved. "Be fruitful and multiply," the book of Genesis commands, and that command was treated with great seriousness and great joy in every generation.

Second, children are accepted and valued in and of themselves. They remain our children even when they disappoint or defy us.

In this the rabbis used God as an example, pointing out that although the Israelites sinned, the Bible still refers to them as God's children.

Finally, the responsibility for children's actions and attitudes is placed squarely on the shoulders of their parents. One Hasidic rabbi compares a parent to a passenger on a ship that is constantly tossed at sea. Just as the passenger cannot get away from the turmoil of the sea, parents can never entirely cut themselves off from the care of their children.

Responsibilities of parents and children flow in two directions, and in the second part of this chapter we look at the obligations of children to their parents. Basing their teachings on the Fifth Commandment to "Honor your father and your mother," Jewish scholars through the ages insisted on strict obedience to and respect for parents. At times their viewpoint seems extreme and, in today's terms, almost certain to provoke guilt. How many of us can be like Rabbi Tarfon, who used his hands as shoes for his mother to walk on? How many like Dama ben Netina, who risked losing a hundred gold pieces because he refused to disturb his parents' sleep in order to make a sale?

Yet, even if we cannot—or may not want to—fulfill all the sages' requirements for honoring our parents, the intensity of their demands does not detract from the essence of their teachings. They stress a sense of connection with the elderly that has been almost forgotten today. Old people count in this tradition, and they may not be ignored or shunted aside for the convenience of the young. Parents count, and they are not derided for having expectations of their children.

Then, too, limits are set, even in this area of debts and duties. Nowhere are we asked to disregard our own needs in order to accommodate the needs of our parents. If parents make demands that are unreasonable, if they behave immorally, if they interfere with what we know is best for ourselves, we're advised by most authorities to go our own way. We do so gently, trying to cause as little hurt as possible. But in any event, we do so.

Ultimately, both parents and children are seen as individuals. For all their claims on one another, each is entitled to a life separate and distinct from the other.

For the sake of the children

Children are singled out in this legend because only through them can our beliefs and traditions be preserved.

When the people of Israel stood at Mount Sinai ready to receive the Torah, God said to them, "Bring Me good securities to guarantee that you will keep it, and then I will give the Torah to you."

They said, "Our ancestors will be our securities."

Said God to them, "I have faults to find with your ancestors. . . . But bring Me good securities and I will give it to you."

They said, "King of the Universe, our prophets will be our securities."

He replied, "I have faults to find with your prophets. . . . Still, bring Me good securities and I will give the Torah to you."

They said to Him, "Our children will be our securities."

And God replied, "Indeed, these are good securities. For their sake I will give you the Torah."

Hence it is written: "Out of the mouth of babes and sucklings You have founded strength" (Psalms 8:3).

—*Song of Songs Rabbah,*
chapter 1, section 4

The importance of having children

When the Roman historian Tacitus wanted to describe the "strange" customs of the Jews in the Roman Empire, he pointed to their strong desire to have children, which made it "a crime among them to kill any child." His astonishment at the Jewish ways was shared by many Greeks and Romans, among whom the exposure of unwanted infants to the elements to die of hunger and cold was common practice. Jews regarded the pagan ways as unconscionable and considered the life of every child, like that of every adult, sacred.

Children were seen both as a blessing and as a means of ensuring the survival of the people. Although the authorities legislated a minimum number of children they considered necessary for a couple to have in order to fulfill the commandment to "Be fruitful and multiply," they encouraged larger families, even urging older couples to have children if possible.

> A person who does not engage in the propagation of the race is like someone who has shed blood.
>
> —Rabbi Eliezer, in the Babylonian Talmud, tractate *Yevamot*, page 63b

---

The bachelor scholar Simeon ben Azzai elaborated on Rabbi Eliezer's words, adding that a person who does not have children diminishes the image of God. His colleagues called him to account for his own failure to have children.

> They said to Ben Azzai, "Some people preach well and act well; others act well but do not preach well. You, however, preach well but do not act well."
>
> Replied Ben Azzai, "But what can I do if my soul is in love with the Torah? The world can be carried on by others."
>
> —Babylonian Talmud, tractate *Yevamot*, page 63b

Hezekiah is considered one of the great rulers of the ancient kingdom of Judah, His son Manasseh, who reigned after him, was one of the worst, and Manasseh's son Amon, the Bible says, surpassed even his father in evil. Still, the talmudic rabbis would not accept the idea that Hezekiah should have refrained from having children in order to prevent future calamities. (The king's reasoning in this legend has parallels in today's argument that it is a crime to bring children into our terrible world.) The sages' lesson is built around the words of the prophet Isaiah to King Hezekiah, who had become ill: "Set your affairs in order, for you are going to die; you will not live" (Isaiah 38:1). The Bible says Hezekiah was granted another fifteen years of life after pleading for mercy, and legend holds that he married Isaiah's daughter and that Manasseh was the offspring of that marriage.

What is the meaning of "You are going to die, you will not live"? It means "you will die in this world and not live in the world to come."

When Hezekiah heard Isaiah's words he asked, "Why such a severe punishment?"

Isaiah replied, "Because you did not try to have children."

Said Hezekiah, "The reason was that I saw with the help of the Divine Spirit that the children issuing from me would not be virtuous."

Isaiah answered, "What have you to do with the secrets of the All Merciful? You have your duty and let the Holy One, Blessed be He, do what pleases Him." . . .

—Babylonian Talmud, tractate *Berakhot*, page 10a

Tradition in this dispute follows the School of Hillel.

A man may not refrain from fulfilling the commandment "Be fruitful and multiply" unless he already has children.

The School of Shammai ruled that he must have two sons.

The School of Hillel ruled: a son and a daughter, for it is written: "Male and female He created them" (Genesis 5:2).

—Mishnah, tractate *Yevamot*, chapter 6, paragraph 6

If a man married in his youth he should marry again in his old age; if he had children in his youth, he should also have children in his old age.

For it is said: "Sow of your seed in the morning, and don't hold back your hand in the evening, since you don't know which is going to succeed, the one or the other, or if both are equally good" (Ecclesiastes 11:6).

—Babylonian Talmud, tractate *Yevamot*, page 62b

A parent's love

In its own way, each of these selections presents a classic picture of parental love. David pitiably mourns his son Absalom, who has been killed leading a rebellion against his father. The matriarch Rachel is symbolically portrayed weeping for the Children of Israel as they are exiled from their homeland to Babylonia. God's love for Israel is compared to a father's love. And a scholar stops short of placing a ban on the miracle worker Honi the Circle-Drawer for his cavalier demands for rain from on high because Honi is like a favorite son, pampered and loved even when he is demanding. Finally, a Hasidic rabbi reminds us that the other side of parental love is anxiety, and it remains with us even after our children are grown.

On some levels, passages such as these have provided the psychological roots for the "Jewish mother" we hear so much about. In spite of the excesses and overprotectiveness ascribed to her, the "Jewish mother" does stem from a tradition of truly caring about one's children.

David has been told that Absalom is dead.

The king was shaken. He went up to the upper chamber of the gateway and wept, moaning these words as he went: "My son Absalom! O my son Absalom! If only I had died instead of you. O Absalom, my son, my son!"

... And the victory that day was turned into mourning for all the troops, for that day the troops heard that the king was grieving over his son. The troops stole into town that day like troops ashamed after running away in battle.

The king covered his face, and the king kept crying aloud, "O my son Absalom! O Absalom, my son, my son!"

—II Samuel, chapter 19, verses 1–5

The prophet Jeremiah pictures Rachel crying from her grave as the Babylonian exiles pass her. The talmudic sages amplify the image.

A cry is heard in Ramah—
Wailing, bitter weeping—
Rachel weeping for her children.
She refuses to be comforted
For her children who are gone.

—Jeremiah, chapter 31, verse 15

What was Jacob's reason for burying Rachel on the road to Ephrath? Jacob foresaw that the exiles would pass there. He buried her in that spot so that she might pray for mercy for them.

Thus it is written: "A cry is heard in Ramah. . . . Rachel weeping for her children. . . . Thus said the Lord: Restrain your voice from weeping. . . . And there is hope for your future" (Jeremiah 31:15–17).

—*Genesis Rabbah*,
chapter 82, section 10

The book of Exodus describes how God protected Israel from Egypt and uses the phrase "how I bore you on eagles' wings." This is a rabbinic commentary:

How is the eagle distinguished from other birds? All the other birds carry their young between their feet, because they're afraid of the birds flying above them. But the eagle is afraid only of men who might shoot at him. Therefore he prefers to have the arrows lodge in him rather than in his children.

To give a parable: A man was going on the road with his son walking in front of him. If robbers, who might seek to capture the son, come from in front, he takes the boy from before himself and puts him behind himself. If a wolf comes from behind, he takes his son from behind and puts him in front. If robbers come from in front and wolves from behind, he takes the son and puts him on his shoulders.

—*Mekhilta of Rabbi Ishmael*,
tractate "Bahodesh," chapter 2

Were you not Honi, I would order you excommunicated....

But what shall I do with you who acts petulantly before God and He grants your wishes, as a son who acts petulantly before his father and he grants his wishes; so that if the son says to him, "Bathe me in warm water," the father bathes him in warm water; "Wash me in cold water," he washes him in cold water; "Give me nuts, peaches, almonds and pomegranates," he gives him nuts, peaches, almonds and pomegranates.

—Babylonian Talmud, tractate
Ta'anit, page 23a

The Hasidic rabbi of Radamsko gave this parable:

A passenger on a ship impatiently awaited the day when it would reach port. When the ship neared the harbor, a storm drove it back to sea, much to the dismay of the traveler.

In the same way, a man is filled with anxiety for his

sons and daughters until he succeeds in rearing them to maturity. Then he hopes to be freed from worry about them. But his oldest son comes with his troubles, seeking paternal advice, and the father's retirement is delayed. The daughter also comes with her problems, and once more his hope for a quiet life is postponed.

Few of us are ever entirely freed from worry and the necessity of continuous labor in this world.

—Solomon ha-Kohen Rabinowich
of Radamsko (1803–1866)

On losing a child

This famous talmudic legend reminds us that no matter how much our children mean to us, ultimately they don't belong to us.

Rabbi Meir was delivering a sermon in the house of study on a Sabbath afternoon. While he was away, his two sons died. Their mother, Beruryah, placed them on a bed and spread a linen cloth over them. At the close of the Sabbath, Rabbi Meir returned.

"Where are the boys?" he asked.

"They went to the house of study," she answered.

"I didn't see them there."

She gave him a cup of wine and he made the *Havdalah* blessing that ends the Sabbath. Then he asked again.

"Where are the boys?"

"They must have gone some place else. They'll be back soon," she said.

She brought him his food, and he ate and said the blessing. Then she said, "I have a question to ask you."

"Ask it," he said.

"Some time ago, a man came and gave me something to keep for him," she said, "and now he wants it back. Should we return it?"

"Wife," he said, "anybody who has received something on trust must surely return it to its owner when asked."

"If you had not stated your opinion, I would not have returned it," she told him.

Then she took him by the hand and led him to the room and to the bed where their sons lay. When she removed the cloth he saw both his sons lying dead upon the bed. He began to weep and cry, "Oh my sons, my sons, my teachers, my teachers. My sons after the fashion of the world, and my teachers because they brightened their father's face with their knowledge of Torah."

Then his wife said to him, "Rabbi, did you not say that I had to return our pledge to its owner? And does it not say: 'The Lord gave, and the Lord has taken away; Blessed be the name of the Lord'?" (Job 1:21).

—*Yalkut Shimoni*, on
Proverbs, section 964

What parents owe children

Jewish tradition assumes that having children imposes such binding moral obligations on parents that their actions should not be governed strictly by legal requirements. Legally, the obligation to maintain a child falls primarily on the father; he must support his children until the age of six, and great pressure was brought on him to continue his support long after that, even if he were poor. Traditionally, it is also a father's duty to teach his son a trade so that the young man can support a family of his own, whereas a father's duties to his daughter include clothing her so she can attract a man who will marry and support her.

A man should always eat and drink less than his means allow, dress according to his means, and honor his wife and children beyond his means, because they are dependent on him, and he is dependent on the One who spoke and the world came into being.

—Babylonian Talmud, tractate
Hullin, page 84b

Once the emperor Hadrian was walking along the road near Tiberias in Galilee, and he saw an old man working the soil to plant some fig trees.

"If you had worked in your early years, old man," he said, "you would not have to work now so late in your life."

"I have worked both early and late," the man answered, "and what pleased the Lord He has done with me."

"How old are you?" asked Hadrian.

"A hundred years old," the man answered.

"A hundred years old, and you still stand there breaking up the soil to plant trees!" said Hadrian. "Do you expect to eat the fruit of those trees?"

"If I am worthy, I will eat," said the old man. "But if not, as my father worked for me, I work for my children."

—*Leviticus Rabbah*,
chapter 25, section 5

A father is obligated to circumcise his son, redeem him, teach him Torah, take a wife for him, and teach him a trade.

Some authorities say to teach him to swim, also. . . . What is the reason? His life may depend on it. . . .

He who does not teach his son a craft teaches him to be a thief.

—Babylonian Talmud, tractate
Kiddushin, pages 29a and 30b

A father must provide for his daughter clothing and covering and must also give her a dowry so that people may be anxious to woo her and so proceed to marry her. And to what extent? . . . Up to a tenth of his wealth.

—Babylonian Talmud, tractate
Ketubbot, page 52b

When a father who refused to support his child was brought before Rabbi Hisda, he would say:

"Make a public announcement and proclaim: 'The raven cares for its young, but this man does not care for his young.' "

—Babylonian Talmud, tractate *Ketubbot*, page 49b

On having daughters

Probably the first feminist protest in history occurs in the book of Numbers when the daughters of a man named Zelophehad argue that the biblical law allowing sons but not daughters to inherit from their fathers needs to be modified when there are no sons. They win their case. Probably the first complaint of reverse discrimination appears in the Talmud when a scholar named Admon protests a ruling that sons must support their sisters from their inherited estates, even to their own disadvantage. He loses his case despite the prestigious support of Rabban Gamaliel.

There's no question that sons were considered preferable to daughters, and the sages were as ambivalent about having girls as they were about women in general. But they did treat daughters with affection and made every effort to expand their rights within the structure of biblical law.

The daughters of Zelophehad, of Manassite family . . . came forward. The names of the daughters were Mahlah, Noah, Hoglah, Micah, and Tirzah. They stood before Moses, Eleazar the priest, the chieftains, and the whole assembly, at the entrance of the Tent of Meeting, and they said, "Our father died in the wilderness . . . and he has left no sons. Let not our father's name be lost to his clan just because he had no son! Give us a holding among our father's kinsmen!"

Moses brought their case before the Lord.

And the Lord said to Moses, "The plea of Zelophehad's daughters is just: you should give them a hereditary holding among their father's kinsmen; transfer their father's share to them.

"Further, speak to the Israelite people as follows: 'If a man dies without leaving a son, you shall transfer his property to his daughter.' "

—Numbers, chapter 27, verses 1–8

If a man dies and leaves sons and daughters, and his estate is large, the sons inherit and the daughters receive maintenance from it. But if the estate is small, the daughters receive maintenance, and the sons go a-begging.

Admon said, "Am I to be the loser because I am a male?" Rabban Gamaliel said, "I agree with Admon!"

—Mishnah, tractate *Ketubbot*,
chapter 13, paragraph 3

Ewe follows ewe: a daughter's acts are like those of her mother.

—Babylonian Talmud, tractate
Ketubbot, page 63a

A daughter is a vain treasure to her father.

Through anxiety on her account, he can't sleep at night.

When she's a child, he worries that she'll be seduced; as an adolescent, that she'll be promiscuous; as an adult, that she won't get married; as a married woman, that she won't have children; if she grows old, that she'll engage in witchcraft.

—Babylonian Talmud, tractate
Sanhedrin, page 100b

Sibling love and rivalry

The ideal of loving your friend or neighbor stems from the ideal of brotherly—or sisterly—love within a family. The book of Psalms expresses the ideal, but real-life difficulties in sibling relationships are graphically illustrated by three biblical narratives: the stories of Cain and Abel, Jacob and Esau, and Joseph and his brothers. In each, the conflict grows from jealousy and the wish to be the parents'—or God's—favorite child. The relationship between Moses and Aaron offers a happy contrast. Separated for years, they greeted each other warmly when they met and together undertook their mission to lead the Israelites out of Egypt. Biblical commentators love to explain that Aaron felt no jealousy on hearing that his younger brother would lead the people of Israel, and Moses was delighted when he learned that his elder brother would be appointed high priest. The last selection, a simple, popular legend, is another reminder of the positive side of having a sibling.

How good and how pleasant it is that brothers sit together.

—Psalms, psalm 133, verse 1

In the course of time, Cain brought an offering to the Lord from the fruit of the soil; and Abel, for his part, brought the choicest of the firstlings of his flock. The Lord paid heed to Abel and his offering, but to Cain and his offering He paid no heed. Cain was much distressed and his face fell....

... And when they were in the field, Cain set upon his brother Abel and killed him. The Lord said to Cain, "Where is your brother Abel?" And he said, "I do not know. Am I my brother's keeper?"

Then He said, "What have you done? Hark, your brother's blood cries out to Me from the ground!"

—Genesis, chapter 4,
verses 3–4, and 8–10

Jacob tricks his father, Isaac, into thinking that he is the first-born son, Esau, and in that way gets the blessing intended for Esau. When Isaac discovers the mistake, he tells Esau, who is shocked.

When Esau heard his father's words, he burst into wild and bitter sobbing, and said to his father, "Bless me, too, Father!" But he answered, "Your brother came with guile and took away your blessing."

Esau said ". . . First he took away my birthright and now he has taken away my blessing!" And he added, "Have you not reserved a blessing for me?"

Isaac answered, saying to Esau, "But I have made him master over you: I have given him all his brothers for servants, and sustained him with grain and wine. What, then, can I still do for you, my son?"

And Esau said to his father, "Have you but one blessing, Father? Bless me, too, Father!" And Esau wept aloud.

—Genesis, chapter 27,
verses 34–38

Joseph's brothers, jealous of his favored position and the coat of many colors their father gave him, planned a way to get rid of him.

When Joseph came up to his brothers, they stripped Joseph of his tunic, the ornamental tunic that he was wearing, and took him and cast him into the pit. The pit was empty; there was no water in it.

Then they sat down to a meal. Looking up, they saw a caravan of Ishmaelites coming from Gilead, their camels bearing gum, balm, and ladanum to be taken to Egypt. Then Judah said to his brothers, "What do we gain by killing our brother . . . ? Come, let us sell him to the Ishmaelites, but let us not do away with him ourselves. After all, he is our brother, our own flesh."

His brothers agreed. . . . They sold Joseph for twenty

pieces of silver to the Ishmaelites, who brought Joseph to Egypt.

—Genesis, chapter 37,
verses 23–28

The Lord said to Aaron, "Go to meet Moses in the wilderness." He went and met him at the mountain of God, and he kissed him. Moses told Aaron about all the things that the Lord had committed to him and all the signs about which He had instructed him.

Then Moses and Aaron went and assembled all the elders of the Israelites. Aaron repeated all the words that the Lord had spoken to Moses, and he performed the signs in the sight of the people, and the people were convinced. When they heard that the Lord had taken note of the Israelites and that He had seen their plight, they bowed low in homage.

—Exodus, chapter 4,
verses 27–31

There were two brothers who were farmers. One lived with his wife and children on one side of a hill, and the other, unmarried, lived in a small hut on the other side of the hill.

One year the brothers had an especially good harvest. The married brother looked over his fields and thought to himself:

"God has been so good to me. I have a wife and children, and more crops than I need. I am so much better off than my brother, who lives all alone. Tonight, while my brother sleeps, I will carry some of my sheaves to his field. When he finds them tomorrow he'll never suspect that they came from me."

On the other side of the hill, the unmarried brother looked at his harvest and thought to himself:

"God has been kind to me. But I wish He had been as

> good to my brother. His needs are so much greater than mine. He must feed his wife and children, yet I have as much fruit and grain as he does. Tonight, while my brother and his family sleep, I will place some of my sheaves in his field. Tomorrow, when he finds them, he will never know that I have less and he has more."
>
> So both brothers waited patiently until midnight. Then each loaded his grain on his shoulders and walked toward the top of the hill. Exactly at midnight, they met one another at the hilltop. Realizing that each had thought only of helping the other, they embraced and cried with joy.
>
> —Legend

Adopted children and orphans

Jewish law has no mechanism for the adoption of children, but to all intents and purposes, it recognizes the status of an adopted child as the son or daughter of the adoptive parents.

The sages looked with favor on the adoption of children, especially orphaned children. Their guiding principle in determining custody of abandoned children, orphans, or children of divorced parents was simply to do what was in the best interest of the child. In case of divorce, for example, they considered it best for children under six to remain with their mothers; above that age, boys went to their fathers and girls stayed with their mothers. But if an arrangement proved harmful to a child, it could be changed, no matter what a parent wanted. This emphasis on the child's welfare is reflected in the responsa of Rabbi David ben Solomon Ibn Abi Zimra, who was a major force in Jewish life under Ottoman rule.

> Whoever brings up an orphan in his home is regarded, according to Scripture, as though the child had been born to him.
>
> —Babylonian Talmud, tractate *Sanhedrin*, page 19b

He who brings up a child is to be called its father, not he who gave birth.

—*Exodus Rabbah*,
chapter 46, section 5

If a man opens his door to another, that person is obligated to honor him more than his father and mother.

—*Exodus Rabbah*,
chapter 4, section 2

Question: Reuben's wife died and left him with a small, sickly son. The child is being cared for by his mother's mother. Reuben wants to have the child live with him, although he is not married and is poor. When he is out of the house, he would leave the child with neighbors. Is it more advisable to have the child stay with his grandmother or with his father?

Answer: In ordinary circumstances it is clear that a child should be with his mother and not with his grandmother. But if the court sees that it is in the child's best interest to be with his grandmother, because she will have more compassion than anyone else, he should be left with her. And even if Reuben says, "Give me my son, and I will do with him whatever I wish, and if he dies, so be it," we do not listen to him. It makes no difference whether he wants to leave the boy with his neighbor or with anyone else when he goes out to work. There is no doubt in our mind that his grandmother is preferable to others. . . .

In general, it is up to the court to decide what is best for the child's welfare.

—David ben Solomon Ibn Abi Zimra
("Radbaz"; 1479–1573), *Responsa*,
volume 1, number 123

"I'm lucky—I'm an orphan"

Aside from issues of adoption or custody, orphans are singled out, along with widows, for extra care and solicitude because of their helplessness and dependency, Maimonides's beautiful statement derives from biblical teachings. Shalom Aleichem, however, can't resist telling of some of the "benefits" of being an orphan.

> You shall not mistreat any widow or orphan. If you do mistreat them, I will heed their outcry as soon as they cry out to Me, and My anger shall blaze forth and I will put you to the sword, and your own wives shall become widows and your children orphans.
>
> —Exodus, chapter 22, verses 21–23

> A man ought to be especially heedful of his behavior toward widows and orphans, for their souls are exceedingly depressed and their spirits low. Even if they are wealthy, even if they are the widow and orphans of a king, we are specifically enjoined concerning them. . . .
>
> How are we to conduct ourselves toward them? One must not speak to them otherwise than tenderly. One must show them unvarying courtesy, not hurt them physically with hard toil, or wound their feelings with harsh speech. . . .
>
> This applies only where a person afflicts them for his own ends. But if a teacher punishes orphan children in order to teach them Torah or a trade or lead them in the right way—that is permissible. And yet, he should not treat them like others but make a distinction in their favor. He should guide them gently, with the utmost tenderness and courtesy, whether they are bereft of a father or mother. . . .

To what age are they to be regarded in these respects as orphans? Till they reach the age when they no longer need an adult on whom they depend to train them and care for them, and when each of them can provide for all his wants, like other grown-up persons.

—Maimonides, *Code*, "Laws Concerning Moral Dispositions and Ethical Conduct," chapter 6, section 10

Never before in my life have I been the privileged character I am now. What is the reason for this?

As you know, my father, Peisi the cantor, died the first day of Shevuos and I was left an orphan. . . .

I sleep with my mother now in the bed my father had slept in—the only piece of furniture left in the house. She lets me have most of the blanket.

"Cover yourself," she says to me, "and go to sleep, my poor little child. You might as well try to sleep; I have no food to give you."

I cover myself with the blanket, but I can't fall asleep. I keep repeating the words of *Kaddish* [the mourner's prayer] to myself.

I don't go to *heder* [Hebrew school] these days. I am not learning anything these days. I don't even pray, I don't sing in the choir.

I'm lucky. I'm an orphan. . . .

How my brother Elihu found out that I have been going fishing I don't know. When he did find out he almost pulled my ear off. It was lucky that Fat Pessie, our neighbor, saw him do it. One's own mother couldn't take up for her child any better.

"Is that the way to treat an orphan?" she cried.

My brother Elihu is ashamed and lets go of my ear. Everybody takes up for me these days.

I'm lucky. I'm an orphan. . . .

It is agreed that I should live at Pessie's for the time being. . . . Everyone in this house has a nickname. . . .

I have a nickname too. . . . And just because I can't stand it they keep on teasing me and calling me by it all the time. Nothing can make them stop. First I was "Motel with the Lips," then "The Lips," and finally just "Lippy."

"Lippy, where have you been?"

"Lippy, wipe your nose."

It annoys me and then it hurts me so that I start to cry. Seeing me, their father, Pessie's husband, Moishe the bookbinder, asks, "Why are you crying?"

I answer, "Why shouldn't I cry? My name is Motel and they call me Lippy." . . .

. . . He laid them down one by one and gave each one a good whipping with the cover of a prayer book.

"You rascals!" he cried. "I'll show you how to make fun of an orphan! The devil take every one of you!"

And so it goes. Everybody comes to my defense. Everybody takes up for me.

I'm lucky. I'm an orphan.

—Shalom Aleichem, from
"I'm Lucky—I'm an Orphan"

A father's advice

The Talmud records the last, brief words of advice of some of the sages to their children. These sayings were forerunners of the medieval ethical wills in which fathers left moral advice and admonitions to their children.

My son, do not sit and study at the busiest point of a town [where you won't be able to concentrate];

do not live in a town whose leaders are scholars [too preoccupied with their studies];

do not enter your own house suddenly, and especially not your neighbor's house;

and do not go without shoes.

Rise up early and eat, in summer because of the heat and in winter because of the cold;

treat your Sabbath like a weekday rather than be dependent on any man [don't borrow money in order to buy special foods and make the Sabbath festive];

and strive to be on good terms with someone upon whom the fortune of the hour smiles.

—Rabbi Akiva's testament to his son, Rabbi Joshua, in the Babylonian Talmud, tractate *Pesahim*, page 112a

---

Do not take drugs; do not leap over ditches; do not have a tooth extracted; and do not anger either a snake or a Syrian.

—Rav to his son, Rabbi Hiyya, in the Babylonian Talmud, tractate *Pesahim*, page 113a

---

Rise up early and stay up late, and go to the synagogue, so that you may prolong your life.

—Rabbi Joshua ben Levi to his children, in the Babylonian Talmud, tractate *Berakhot*, page 8a

How parents influence children

An example may be learned from a man who opened a perfumery for his son in a marketplace frequented by prostitutes. The businesses in the area went their own way; the prostitutes went their way; and the young man went his way—to a bad end.

His father came, and catching him with the prostitutes began to shout, "I'll kill you! I'll kill you!"

A friend who was present said to the father, "You caused your son to go astray and now you're shouting at him. You ignored all other trades and taught him the perfume business, and you ignored all other business streets, and opened a shop for him in the middle of the red light district. What can you expect?"

—*Exodus Rabbah*,
chapter 43, section 7

The Zhitomer rabbi was once walking along with his son when they saw a drunken man and his drunken son both stumbling into the gutter.

"I envy that father," said the rabbi to his son. "He has accomplished his goal of having a son like himself. I don't know yet whether you will be like me. I can only hope that the drunkard is not more successful in training his son than I am with you."

—Tale about the Hasidic rabbi Ze'ev
Wolf of Zhitomer (died in 1800)

Rabbi Nahman once asked Rabbi Isaac to bless him as they were saying goodbye. Rabbi Isaac replied:

"Let me give you a parable. A man traveled a long way in the desert. He felt hungry, weary and thirsty, when suddenly he came upon a tree filled with sweet fruits, covered with branches that provided delightful shade, and watered by a brook that flowed nearby.

"The man rested in the tree's shade, ate of its fruits, and drank its water. When he was about to leave, he turned to the tree and said:

" 'O tree, beautiful tree, with what shall I bless you? Shall I wish that your shade be pleasant? It is already pleasant. Shall I say that your fruits should be sweet? They are sweet. Shall I ask that a brook flow by you? A brook does flow by you. Therefore I will bless you this way: May it be God's will that all the shoots taken from you be just like you.'

"So it is with you," Rabbi Isaac said to Rabbi Nahman. "What can I wish you? Shall I wish you learning? You have learning. Wealth? You have wealth. Children? You have children.

"Therefore I say: May it be God's will that all your offspring be like you."

—Babylonian Talmud, tractate *Ta'anit*, pages 5b–6a

Stern vs. permissive discipline

Train up a child in the way he should go, and even when he is old, he will not depart from it.

—Proverbs, chapter 22, verse 6

Discipline your family to the simple needs of life. Hence the Torah teaches a rule of conduct—that a person should not accustom his son to meat and wine.

—Babylonian Talmud, tractate *Hullin*, page 84a

A child . . . should be pushed aside with the left hand and drawn closer with the right hand.

—Babylonian Talmud, tractate *Sotah*, page 47a

A person should not promise to give a child something and then not give it, because in that way the child learns to lie.

—Babylonian Talmud, tractate *Sukkah*, page 46b

A man should never single out one son among his others, for on account of the sela weight of silk [the coat of many colors] that Jacob gave Joseph in excess of his other sons, his brothers became jealous of him, and the matter resulted in our forefathers' exile in Egypt.

—Babylonian Talmud, tractate *Shabbat*, page 10b

A child from Bene-Berak broke a flask. His father threatened to box his ears. In terror of his father, the child went off and threw himself into a well. The matter was brought before Rabbi Akiva, who ruled: "No burial rites whatever are to be denied to him" [as they ordinarily would be in the case of suicide].

As a result of this, the sages said: "A man should never threaten his child. He should punish the child at once, or else hold his peace and say nothing."

—Minor tractate of the Talmud, *Mourning*, chapter 2, paragraph 5

A man who spoils his son will bandage every wound and will be on tenterhooks at every cry.

An unbroken horse turns out stubborn, and an unchecked son turns out headstrong.

Pamper a boy and he will shock you; play with him and he will grieve you.

Do not share his laughter, for fear of sharing his pain, you will only end by grinding your teeth.

Do not give him freedom while he is young or overlook his errors....

Discipline your son and take pains with him, or he may offend you by some disgraceful act.

—Wisdom of Ben Sira, chapter 30, verses 7–11 and 13

Now because of the weakness of my eyesight, my father and mother left me to do whatever was right in my own eyes; they never punished or rebuked me. Wherefore I have never been wont to chide others; for they taught me not how; even my own sons I knew not how to reprove.

If they reprove not themselves, they will receive no reproofs from me. Nor have I the face to admonish them by words of mouth, lest I put them to blush, even though evil unto me was the evil of their ways. No joy of mine on earth equals my happiness at their well-doing, no pain or distress can compare with my grief at their misconduct.

—Judah ben Asher (1270–1349),
rabbi of Toledo, from his
Testament

Striking a child

The sages generally shared the view expressed in the book of Proverbs that "He who spares the rod hates his son." However, they recognized that sometimes, instead of remedying a situation, a spanking becomes a "stumbling block" to good behavior, inciting the child—especially an older one—to more rebellious action. They even legislated that if a man were caught beating a grown child, he was to be placed under a ban—ostracized by the community for at least a month.

A man who loves his son will whip him often so that when he grows up he may be a joy to him. . . .

Break him in while he is young, beat him soundly while he is still a child, or he may grow stubborn and disobey you and cause you vexation.

—Wisdom of Ben Sira,
chapter 30, verses 1 and 12

If you strike a child, strike him only with a shoelace.

—Babylonian Talmud, tractate *Bava Batra*, page 21a

When you lead your sons and daughters in the good way, let your words be tender and caressing, in terms of discipline that wins the heart's assent. . . .

. . . Sometimes one sows on stone, the stony heart into which no seed enters at all, and it is necessary to strike the stone until it is split. Therefore, I have bidden you to strike your children if they refuse to obey you.

—Elijah ben Solomon Zalman, the Gaon of Vilna (1720–1797), from a letter to his family

---

One of the maidservants in the house of Rabbi noticed a man beating his grown-up son and said, "Let that fellow be placed under a ban because he has violated the word of Scripture—'You shall not place a stumbling block before the blind' " (Leviticus 19:14).

For it has been taught that that verse applies to a man who beats his grown-up son [and in that way incites him to worse behavior].

—Babylonian Talmud, tractate *Mo'ed Katan*, page 17a

It would seem that "grown-up son" is not meant to be taken literally, but according to the temperament of the child, if it is believed that he will react violently. Even if the child is not yet Bar Mitzvah [thirteen years old], it is not right that he be incited to strike or curse his father. Rather, he ought to be spoken to and won over. The

Talmud speaks of a "grown-up son" only because it is more natural for a mature son [to rebel at being hit].

—Yom Tov ben Abraham Ishbili
("Ritba"; c. 1250–1330),
commentary on *Mo'ed Katan*,
page 17a

Reaching out to a child

This story can be interpreted in many ways. On its most immediate level, it offers insight into communicating with a child who seems to live in a dream world.

There was once a king whose son imagined he was a turkey. He believed he had to sit under the dining room table nude and scratch around for leftover crumbs and old food.

The worried king tried all the doctors in his kingdom, but none could help his son. One day, a wise man came to the king and volunteered to help the boy.

The man undressed and sat beneath the table with the king's son. When the boy asked him what he was doing under the table, the wise man answered, "I am a turkey."

"I, too, am a turkey," said the king's son. So the two of them sat naked beneath the table for a few days, getting acquainted with one another.

One day, the wise man had some shirts thrown down to them.

"Do you think a turkey cannot wear a shirt?" he asked the boy. "Of course a turkey can wear a shirt and still remain a turkey."

A few days later the wise man had some pants thrown down to them.

"Do you think that just because someone wears pants he can't be a turkey?" he asked the boy.

And they both put on the pants.

The wise man continued in this way until both were fully clothed.

Then he had some human food thrown down from the table.

"Do you think," he asked the boy, "that if you eat good food you cannot be a turkey? Of course you can be a turkey and eat good food."

So they ate together.

Finally, the wise man said, "Do you think a turkey has to sit under the table all the time? You know, it's possible to be a turkey and still sit at the table."

And that is how the wise man went along, step by step, until he brought the boy back to the real world.

—Tale told by one of the great Hasidic leaders, Rabbi Nahman of Bratslav (1772–1810)

When a child is defiant

First, two rabbis give their impressions of the hurt that comes when children turn against their parents. Then, using God's relationship to Israel as a metaphor, the second selection emphasizes that our children remain our children even when they are "foolish."

Rabbi Judah ben Nahmani said: "It is like a man who bought a knife to cut meat. The knife fell on his finger and cut it. He said, 'I bought this knife to cut with—did I buy it to cut my finger?' So, too, a man produces offspring to honor him, and they curse him."

Rabbi Levi said: "It is like a man who lights a candle in order to use its light, and it falls down and burns his coat. He said, 'I lit this candle to enjoy its light, not to be burned by it.' So, too, a man produces offspring to honor him, and they curse him."

—Midrash Samuel, chapter 7, section 1

How do we interpret the verse, "You are children of the Lord your God"? (Deuteronomy 14:1).

In Rabbi Judah's view, if you behave the way children ought to behave, you are called "children." If you do not behave the way children ought to, you are not called "children."

But Rabbi Meir said: In either case you are called children. For it is written, "they are foolish children" (Jeremiah 4:22). And it is also written: "They are children with no loyalty in them" (Deuteronomy 32:20).

—Babylonian Talmud, tractate *Kiddushin*, page 36a

A man once complained to the Ba'al Shem Tov about his son. The youth had turned completely away from religion, a great blow to his father.

"What shall I do, Rebbe?" asked the distraught man.

"Do you love your son?"

"Of course I do."

"Then love him even more."

—Tale about Rabbi Israel ben Eliezer Ba'al Shem Tov (c. 1700–1760), founder of Hasidism

Punishing a "stubborn and rebellious" son

The Bible orders death by stoning for a son who so defies his parents that no form of discipline can control him. But, unlike Roman law, which gave fathers power of life and death over their children, biblical law orders parents to bring their child to the elders of the city for judgment. Later scholars went much further in limiting parental power. They built in so many conditions for identifying a rebellious son and isolating his crime that they had to conclude that capital punishment for such a child "never happened and never will happen."

If a man has a stubborn and rebellious son who does not heed his father or mother and does not obey them even after they discipline him, his father and mother shall take hold of him and bring him out to the elders of his town at the public place of his community.

They shall say to the elders of the town, "This son of ours is stubborn and rebellious; he does not heed our voice. He is a glutton and a drunkard."

Thereupon the men of his town shall stone him to death....

—Deuteronomy, chapter 21,
verses 18–21

When does someone become liable for the penalty of being a "stubborn and rebellious" son?

From the time he produces two hairs until he grows a beard right round, by which is meant the hair of the genitals, not of the face. . . . For Scripture speaks of a "stubborn and rebellious son." This refers to a son . . . but not a full-grown man. Yet a minor [under the age of thirteen] is exempt from the penalty, since he is not responsible for upholding the commandments.

When does he become liable? When he eats a tartemar [a specific measure] of meat and drinks half a log of Italian wine. . . . For Scripture says: "This son of ours . . . is a glutton and a drunkard."

If his father wants him punished, but not his mother, or the reverse, he is not treated as a "stubborn and rebellious" son. . . . Rabbi Judah said: If his mother is not fit for his father, he does not become a "stubborn and rebellious" son.

—Mishnah, tractate *Sanhedrin*,
chapter 8, paragraphs 1–5

What is meant by "if his mother is not fit"? . . . After all, his father is his father and his mother is his mother.

It means that she is physically not like his father. . . . Rabbi Judah said: If his mother is not like his father in voice, appearance and stature, he does not become a "stubborn and rebellious" son.

Why is this so? Because Scripture says: "He does not heed our *voice*" [using the singular], and since they must be alike in voice, they must also be alike in appearance and structure. . . .

Rabbi Simeon said: Because a person eats a tartemar of meat and drinks half a log of Italian wine, shall his father and his mother have him stoned? But it never happened and never will happen. Why then was this law written? That you may study it and receive reward.

—Babylonian Talmud, tractate *Sanhedrin*, page 71a

What children owe parents

The first duty children have to parents derives from the Fifth Commandment to "Honor your father and your mother." On its most fundamental level, Berechiah's fable teaches that honoring our parents means accepting them as they are, in spite of their shortcomings.

There are three partners in man: the Holy One, blessed be He, the father and the mother.

When a person honors his father and his mother, God says, "It is as though I had dwelt among them and they had honored Me."

—Babylonian Talmud, tractate *Kiddushin*, page 30b

"Honor your father and your mother." I might understand that because the father precedes in the text, he should actually take precedence over the mother. But in another passage, "You shall each revere his mother and his father" (Leviticus 19:3), the mother precedes. Scripture thus declares that both are equal.

—*Mekhilta of Rabbi Ishmael*,
tractate "Pisha," chapter 1

A man should honor his father and mother more for the moral instruction they gave him than for their having brought him into the world. For in bringing him into the world, their own pleasure was their motive.

—Israel ben Joseph Al-Nakawa
(died in 1391), Spanish
moralist, *Menorat ha-Ma'or*,
chapter 4, page 18

A mule walking by the way was met by a fox who had never before seen him. The fox observed the majesty of his face and that his eyes were bright and his ears long, and said in his heart: "Who is this I now behold? What is the nature of this creature? I have never seen a picture like him, nor himself, until this moment. . . ."

The fox . . . asked the mule who had given him birth, and the mule answered: "My uncle walked in pride; he was the horse upon whom the king rode. On the day of battle and destruction he leapt and pranced, and he pawed the earth with stormy passion. His neck was clothed with a mane, and his lordly neighing was terrible. His hoofs were like flint; they thirsted for hot battle and hungered for destruction. . . . His eyes were like flame, like flashing lightning. He was a tower of strength for his rider and strode with neck outstretched. . . . Such is the genealogy of the mule."

The parable is for a man magnificently attired from head to foot . . . and he preens himself on his grandeur. But when they ask him his name and birth, because it suits not his splendor to tell of his father and mother, he mentions his relative who ennobles him, and makes no mention of him who begot him. . . .

I have searched but never found a true man among those who say of father and mother, "I have never seen them."

—Berechiah ha-Nakdan,
"Mule and Fox"

Ways of showing respect

It's not just what you do for your parents but how you go about doing it that is important in honoring them.

A man may feed his father fattened chickens and inherit Gehenna [Hell], and another may put his father to work treading a mill and inherit the Garden of Eden.

How is it possible for a man to feed his father fattened chickens and still inherit Gehenna?

There was a man who used to feed his father fattened chickens. Once his father said to him, "My son, where did you get these?" He answered, "Old man, old man, shut up and eat, just as dogs shut up when they eat." Such a man feeds his father on fattened chickens but inherits Gehenna.

How is it possible for a man to put his father to work in a mill and still inherit the Garden of Eden?

There was a man who worked in a mill. The king ordered that millers be brought to work for him. Said the man to his father, "Father, you stay here and work in the mill in my place, and I will go to work for the king. For if insults come to the workers, I prefer that they fall on me and not on you. Should blows come, let them beat me and not you." Such a man puts his father to work in a mill yet inherits the Garden of Eden.

—Jerusalem Talmud, tractate
Kiddushin, chapter 1, paragraph 7

A man must not dishonor his father in his speech. How so? For example, if the father is old and wants to eat early in the morning, as old men do, and he asks his son for food, and the son says, "The sun has not yet risen, and you're already up and eating!" . . .

Or when the father says, "My son, how much did you pay for this coat or for this food you bought for me?" And the son says, ". . . I bought it and have paid for it; it is no business of yours to ask about it!"

Or when he thinks to himself, saying, "When will this old man die and I shall be free of what he costs me?"

—Israel ben Joseph Al-Nakawa, *Menorat ha-Ma'or*, chapter 4, page 16

If a parent unwittingly transgresses a law of the Torah, his child should not reprimand him, "Father, you have transgressed a law." He should say, "Father, is that what it says in the Torah?"

But in the end, aren't both expressions equally insulting?

Yes. What he should really say is, "Father, the Torah says such-and-such" [stating the verse and allowing his father to draw his own conclusions].

—Babylonian Talmud, tractate *Sanhedrin*, page 81a

About model children

The talmudic sages loved to tell anecdotes about the extremes to which some people went in order to honor their parents. Impressed by the emphasis on filial piety in the Hellenistic world around them, they did not hesitate to use the pagan Dama ben Netina as their prime example of a devoted son. Their expectation was not that everybody can do the same, but that heroes like Dama would serve as models for the young.

Rabbi Eliezer was asked: "How far is one to go in honoring one's father and mother?" He replied: "Let you and me ask Dama ben Netina." . . .

One time the jasper stone representing the Tribe of Benjamin [in the breastplate of the High Priest] was lost. The sages asked, "Who has a precious stone like it?" and were told, "Dama ben Netina has."

They went to him and agreed on a purchase price of one hundred *dinars*. He went upstairs because he wanted to fetch it for them, and found his father and mother asleep. Some say his father's feet were upon the box in which the jasper lay. Some say the key to the box was in his father's fingers.

He went to the sages and said, "I cannot give it to you." They said to one another, "Maybe he wants more money," and decided among themselves to raise the price to a thousand *dinars*. When his father and mother awoke, he went up and brought the jasper down to the sages.

They were about to give him the larger sum they had decided on, but he said, "What, shall I sell you the honor due to one's father and mother for money? I will not take any kind of profit as a reward for honoring my parents."

—*Pesikta Rabbati,*
Piska 23/24

Rabbi Tarfon's mother once walked in the courtyard on the Sabbath and her sandal split and fell off. Rabbi Tarfon placed his two hands under her feet so that she walked on them until she reached her bed.

One time he became ill, and the sages came to visit him. His mother said to them, "Pray for Rabbi Tarfon, my son, for he honors me more than he should." They asked her what he did for her and she told them what had happened.

They said to her, "Even if he were to do that a thousand times, he would not have given you even half the honor demanded by the Torah."

—Jerusalem Talmud, tractate
Kiddushin, chapter 1, paragraph 7

When Rabbi Joseph heard his mother's footsteps he would say, "I will rise before the approaching *Shekhinah*" [Divine Presence].

—Babylonian Talmud, tractate
Kiddushin, page 31b

Should children support parents?

Ben Sira offers practical advice to parents on how to avoid becoming dependent on their children, but the talmudic authorities rule that children have an obligation to see that their parents are fed and cared for. The Palestinian and Babylonian talmudists disagree among themselves, however. The Palestinians hold that children must actually support their parents even if they themselves are poverty-stricken. The Babylonians maintain that money for caring for parents may come from the father's estate, if he has one. If the father is poor, however, his children may be forced to support him, at the very least, from the money they are obliged by law to give to charity. The medieval scholar Rabbi Meir of Rothenburg upholds the Babylonian position but points out that treating parents as if they were another form of charity is far from ideal. The "greenhorn" writing to the "Bintel Brief" gives us a glimpse into the conflicts of young immigrants on New York City's Lower East Side, who were torn between wanting a new life for themselves and feeling responsible for the folks back home. The "Bintel Brief" advice column appeared in the Yiddish newspaper, the *Jewish Daily Forward*, from 1906 on.

As long as you live, give no one power over yourself—son or wife, brother or friend.

Do not give your property to another, in case you change your mind and want it back. . . .

It is better for your children to ask from you than for you to be dependent on them.

—Wisdom of Ben Sira,
chapter 33, verses 19 and 21

Great is the honor one owes one's parents—for God raises it even above the honor one owes Him.

In one place it says: "Honor your father and your mother" (Exodus 20:12). In another it says: "Honor the Lord with your substance and with the first fruits of your increase" (Proverbs 3:9).

How do you honor God? With the wealth in your possession—you give the gleanings to the poor . . . you feed the hungry, and give drink to the thirsty. If you do not have the means you are not obliged.

But with "Honor your father and your mother," it is not so: whether you have the means or you do not, honor your father and your mother; even if you must become a beggar at the door.

—Jerusalem Talmud, tractate
Kiddushin, chapter 1, paragraph 7

What is respect and what is honor?

Respect means that a son must neither stand nor sit in his father's place, nor contradict his words, nor side with his opponent in an argument.

Honor means that a son must give his father food and drink, clothe and cover him.

The scholars asked: At whose expense?

Rabbi Judah said: At the son's expense.

Rabbi Nahman ben Oshia said: At the father's expense.

The rabbis ruled that it must be at the father's expense.

—Babylonian Talmud, tractate
Kiddushin, page 32a

Rabbi Meir was asked whether a widow could demand support from her three sons. He answered:

It is the accepted law that children are obligated to support their widowed mother only out of the possessions they inherited from their father. . . . Therefore, any son who would himself be thrown upon charity were he forced to support his mother cannot be forced to do so. But those sons who have means should support their mother in proportion to their wealth. These . . . can be forced to do so out of the money they are usually obliged to give to charity, although they would thus incur the curse of the rabbis, who say, "Cursed be he who feeds his father out of the poor man's tithe."

—Meir ben Baruch of Rothenburg,
Responsa, "Yoreh De'ah,"
number 197

Esteemed Editor: I am a "greenhorn," only five weeks in the country and a jeweler by trade. I come from Russia, where I left a blind father and a stepmother. Before I left, my father asked me not to forget him. I promised that I would send him the first money I earned in America.

When I arrived in New York, I walked around for two weeks looking for a job. . . . In the third week I was lucky, and found a job at which I earn eight dollars a week. I worked, I paid my landlady board, I bought a few things to wear, and I have a few dollars in my pocket.

Now I want you to advise me. . . . Shall I send my father a few dollars for Passover, or should I keep the little money for myself? In this place the work will end soon and I may be left without a job. . . .

—Your thankful reader,
I.M.

Answer: The answer to this young man is that he should send his father the few dollars for Passover because, since he is young, he will find it easier to earn a living than would his blind father in Russia.

—From the "Bintel Brief,"
Jewish Daily Forward, 1906

On growing old

Abraham might have considered old age a mark of distinction, as this legend says, but later teachers recognized the physical deterioration and emotional depression that often accompanies it. One of the most powerful descriptions of aging ever written appears in the book of Ecclesiastes. The author uses metaphors to describe the various parts of the body: the "guards of the house" are the arms; "men of valor," the legs; "maids that grind," the teeth; "ladies that peer through the windows," the eyes; and the "doors to the street," the ears. The book of Psalms has a softer, pleading tone, and some of these verses have been included in the Yom Kippur prayer service.

Until Abraham's time, the young and the old were not distinguished from one another. A man could live a hundred or two hundred years and not look old. Abraham said, "My son and I enter a town, and nobody knows who is the father and who the son."

So Abraham said to God, "King of the Universe, there must be some outward sign of distinction between a father and a son, between an old man and a youth." And God said, "I will begin with you."

Abraham went to sleep and when he awoke in the morning, he saw that his hair and beard were white. He said, "King of the Universe, You have made me an example."

—*Tanhuma*, on Genesis, portion
"Hayye Sarah," paragraph 1

Rabbi Yose ben Kisma said: Woe for the one thing that goes and does not return.

What is that?

One's youth.

Rabbi Dimi said: Youth is a crown of roses, old age a crown of heavy willow rods.

—Babylonian Talmud, tractate
Shabbat, page 152a

So appreciate your vigor in the days of your youth, before
those days of sorrow come and those years arrive of
which you will say, "I have no pleasure in them";
before sun and light and moon and stars grow dark,
and the clouds come back again after the rain:
When the guards of the house become shaky,
And the men of valor are bent,
And the maids that grind, grown few, are idle,
And the ladies that peer through the windows grow dim,
And the doors to the street are shut—
With the noise of the hand mill growing fainter,
And the song of the bird growing feebler,
And all the strains of music dying down;
When one is afraid of heights
And there is terror on the road. . . .
Before the silver cord snaps
And the golden bowl crashes,
The jar is shattered at the spring,
And the jug is smashed at the cistern.
And the dust returns to the ground
As it was,
And the lifebreath returns to God
Who bestowed it.

—Ecclesiastes, chapter 12,
verses 1–7

Do not cast me off in old age;
 when my strength fails, do not forsake me! . . .
I come with praise of Your mighty acts, O Lord God;
I celebrate Your beneficence, Yours alone.
You have let me experience it, God, from my youth;
 until now I have proclaimed Your wondrous deeds,
And even in hoary old age do not forsake me, God,
 until I proclaim Your Strength to the next generation.

—Psalms, psalm 71,
verses 9 and 16–18

Caring for elderly parents

You shall rise before the aged, and show deference to the old; you shall fear your God; I am the Lord.

—Leviticus, chapter 19, verse 32

It is natural for old people to be despised by the general population when they can no longer function as they once did, but sit idle, and have no purpose. The commandment "Honor your father and your mother" was given specifically for this situation.

—Gur Aryeh ha-Levi (seventeenth century), commentary on the Fifth Commandment, in *Melekhet Mahshevet*

Among the storks, the old birds stay in the nests when they are unable to fly while the children fly . . . over sea and land, gathering from every quarter provisions for the needs of their parents. . . .

With this example before them, may not human beings, who take no thought for their parents, deservedly hide their faces for shame?

—Philo Judaeus (c. 20 B.C.E.–50 C.E.), recognized as the father of Jewish philosophy, *On the Decalogue*, sections 115–118

According to all the standards we employ . . . the aged person is condemned as inferior. . . . Conditioned to operating as a machine for making and spending money, with all other relationships dependent upon its efficiency, the moment the machine is out of order and beyond repair, one begins to feel like a ghost without a sense of reality. . . . Regarding himself as a person who has outlived his usefulness, he feels as if he has to apologize for being alive.

May I suggest that man's potential for change and growth is much greater than we are willing to admit, and that old age be regarded not as the age of stagnation but as *the age of opportunities for inner growth.*

The years of old age . . . are indeed formative years, rich in possibilities to unlearn the follies of a lifetime, to see through inbred self-deceptions, to deepen understanding and compassion, to widen the horizon of honesty, to refine the sense of fairness.

—Abraham Joshua Heschel (1907–1972), American rabbi, teacher, and philosopher, from "To Grow in Wisdom," in *Judaism* (Spring 1977)

If parents are senile

The Talmud tells of Rabbi Assi, who had a demanding, senile mother. He gave in to all her demands until she said, "I want a husband as handsome as you." Then he left her and his home in

Babylonia and fled to Palestine, where he settled. With this story as his guide, Maimonides lays down his rule about caring for a senile or mentally ill parent. By no means does he free children of the responsibility for such a parent, but he eases the personal burden —and the guilt.

> If the mind of his father or his mother is affected, the son should make every effort to indulge the vagaries of the stricken parent until God will have mercy on the afflicted.
>
> But if the condition of the parent has grown worse, and the son is no longer able to endure the strain, he may leave his father or mother, go elsewhere, and delegate others to give the parent proper care.
>
> —Maimonides, *Code*, "Laws Concerning Rebels," chapter 6, section 10

Limits of parental authority

Even if parents are bad—so bad that they "have been condemned to death and are on their way to execution," Joseph Caro's *Shulhan Arukh*, or *Code of Jewish Law*, tells us, we are not permitted to hit or curse them. That much we owe them. But we do not owe a bad parent respect in the way we otherwise would. More, we do not owe any parent blind obedience to the point where we violate our own conscience. These selections list some of the circumstances under which we must break with our parents.

> The Torah says, "You shall each revere his mother and his father, and keep My Sabbaths. . . ."
>
> "You shall each revere"—I might think that a person must obey his parents even if they told him to violate a commandment.
>
> Therefore the Torah says, "and keep My Sabbaths."

You are all [parents and children] required to honor Me above everything.

—*Sifra* on chapter 19, verse 3

Parents may not hinder a son's marriage so that he may continue to work for them; let him take a wife and remain with them still....

If he can pay for the support and care of his parents, then he has a right to seek a wife and settle elsewhere, only let him see to it that she is not such as is repugnant to the parents' feelings.

If his choice falls on a worthy girl of honorable parentage, but his father and his mother wish to force him to take one not worthy, because her relatives offer money, he need by no means yield to his parents' wishes, for their methods are blameworthy.

—Judah the Pious,
from his Testament

If Rabbi Eliezer's story, which follows, had not ended well, he still would have been considered within his rights to have left home in order to pursue his studies.

What were the beginnings of Rabbi Eliezer ben Hyrcanus?

He was twenty-two years old and had not yet studied Torah. One time he resolved, "I will go and study Torah with Rabban Johanan ben Zakkai." Said his father Hyrcanus to him, "Not a taste of food shall you get before you have plowed the entire furrow."

He rose early in the morning and plowed the entire furrow [and then departed for Jerusalem]. . . .

When Hyrcanus his father heard of him, that he was studying Torah with Rabban Johanan ben Zakkai, he declared, "I shall go and ban my son Eliezer from my possessions."

It is told: That day Rabban Johanan ben Zakkai sat expounding in Jerusalem and all the great ones of Israel sat before him. When he heard that Hyrcanus was coming, he appointed guards and said to them, "If Hyrcanus comes do not let him sit down." Hyrcanus arrived and they would not let him sit down. But he pushed on ahead . . . [and sat among the wealthy and elite city leaders].

It is told: On that day Rabban Johanan ben Zakkai fixed his gaze upon Rabbi Eliezer and said to him: "Deliver the exposition."

"I am unable to speak," Rabbi Eliezer pleaded.

Rabban Johanan pressed him to do it and the disciples pressed him to do it. So he arose and delivered a discourse upon things which no ear had ever before heard. As the words came from his mouth Rabban Johanan ben Zakkai rose to his feet and kissed him upon his head and exclaimed, "Rabbi Eliezer, master, you have taught me the truth!"

Before the time came to recess, Hyrcanus his father rose to his feet and declared, "My masters, I came here only in order to ban my son Eliezer from my possessions. Now, all my possessions shall be given to Eliezer my son. . . ."

—*Fathers According to Rabbi Nathan*, chapter 6

Parents and children: choosing priorities

The remarkable woman Glueckel of Hameln began her memoirs to relieve her depression after the death of her first husband. She put them aside for years while carrying on various successful business ventures and rearing her twelve children, then returned to them in old age at the urging of her children. She wrote in Yiddish and laced her account with parables and folktales, which both offer moral insights and paint a colorful picture of German-Jewish life and thought during the seventeenth century.

A father's love is for his children; the children's love is for their own children.

—Babylonian Talmud, tractate *Sotah*, page 49a

A bird once set out to cross a windy sea with his three fledglings. The sea was so wide and the wind so strong that the father bird was forced to carry his young, one by one, in his claws. When he was halfway across with his first fledgling, the wind turned to a gale, and he said, "My child, look how I am struggling and risking my life in your behalf. When you are grown up, will you do as much for me and provide for my old age?"

The fledgling replied, "Only bring me to safety, and when you are old I shall do everything you ask of me."

Whereat the father bird dropped his child into the sea, and it drowned, and he said, "So shall it be done for such a liar as you."

Then the father bird returned to the shore, set forth with the second fledgling, asked the same question, and receiving the same answer, drowned the second child with the cry, "You, too, are a liar!"

Finally, he set out with the third fledgling, and when he asked the same question, the third and last fledgling replied:

"My dear father, it is true you are struggling mightily and risking your life in my behalf, and I shall be wrong not to repay you when you are old, but I cannot bind myself. This, though, I can promise: when I am grown up and have children of my own, I shall do as much for them as you have done for me."

Whereupon the father bird said, "Well spoken, my child, and wisely; your life I will spare and I will carry you to safety."

—Glueckel of Hameln (1645–1724), *Memoirs*

5

HEALTH AND MEDICINE

"The body is the soul's house"

The body as a reflection of the universe ✦ Caring for your body ✦ Developing good eating habits ✦ The dangers of overeating ✦ On eating meat ✦ Drinking and drugs ✦ The importance of cleanliness ✦ Keeping fit ✦ Emotions and health ✦ On visiting the sick ✦ If you're in pain ✦ About miracle doctors ✦ A physician's responsibilities ✦ The work and ideals of a physician ✦ The fees doctors charge ✦ The patient as a person ✦ When a patient is dying ✦ Taking medical risks ✦ Autopsies and medical research ✦ About test-tube babies

Many outstanding rabbis and Jewish scholars also achieved fame as prominent physicians. The Talmud records the medical teachings of a number of sages. Best-known among them was Mar Samuel, a judge, expert in civil law, and head of a prestigious academy of learning, who is credited with discovering an ointment for curing certain eye diseases. At a later date, the brilliant Hebrew poet-philosopher Judah Halevi became a highly influential and sought-after doctor in his native Spain; and, of course, Maimonides, probably the greatest of all Jewish scholars, wrote numerous medical works and served as personal physician to the family of Sultan Saladin of Egypt.

It is not by chance that men immersed in Jewish law and learning chose to take up medicine as a profession. The sages saw a close connection between medicine and religion—between the body and the soul. Our bodies, they taught, belong to God and have been given to us on loan, as it were, during our stay on earth. Caring for your body by keeping it clean and healthy is a religious duty that honors God; neglecting your body or intentionally abusing it is a sin that profanes Him.

This view of the body as holy and precious made medicine a high calling; and scholars, who refused to be paid for their rabbinic duties, were proud to take it up as a vocation. Emphasis on the importance of the body also led the sages, both those who were physicians and those who were not, to detailed investigations into matters of health and medicine. They approached questions of nutrition or body care as earnestly as they did complex laws of religious ritual; and though sometimes naïve and unscientific, their conclusions as often were concrete and remarkably contemporary.

In matters of health, as in so many areas of life, the sages call for moderation. The scholar Nahmanides put it plainly. It's easy, he said, to become a "sordid person" without violating a single precept of the law. All it takes is doing everything permitted—eating, drinking, enjoying sex—to excess, to the point at which you lose control over your appetites.

Moderation is the guide word for the behavior of physicians as well. Charged with the sacred trust of our bodies, physicians receive much power and praise. But physicians who take themselves too seriously, whose fees are too high and manners too arrogant, come in for their share of ridicule and angry criticism. The example to follow was set by Amatus Lusitanus, a sixteenth-century practitioner, who wrote: "I have regard for this one thing, namely, that I might in some measure provide for the health of mankind."

The great respect given our bodies and the important role of the physician take on special significance today when major scientific breakthroughs raise issues of medical ethics undreamed of by earlier generations. Surely the old traditions cannot give definitive solutions to such new areas of concern as experimental drugs or test-tube babies. But the process of Jewish legal decision is still very much alive, and the perspectives that formed earlier traditions continue to shape the responses of rabbis, physicians, and patients to each development that arises.

A talmudic anecdote relates that Rabbi Huna once urged his son Rabbah to study with the scholar Rabbi Hisda.

"Why should I study with him?" answered Rabbah. "He lectures only on secular matters."

Questioned further, Rabbah explained that the teacher devoted his entire lecture to a discussion of bodily functions.

"He treats of health matters and you call that secular!" exclaimed his father. "All the more reason to study with him."

The body as a reflection of the universe

"The human figure," says the *Zohar*, the principle work of Jewish mysticism, "unites all that is above and all that is below; therefore, the Ancient of Ancients has chosen it for His form."

The Holy One, blessed be He . . . created the heavens and the earth, the beings on high and those down below, and formed in man whatever He created in His world:

He created forests in the world and He created forests in man: to wit, man's hair. . . .

He created channels in the world and He created channels in man: to wit, man's ears;

He created a wind in the world and He created a wind in man: to wit, man's breath. . . .

A sun in the world and a sun in man: to wit, man's forehead;

Salt water in the world and salt water in man: to wit, man's tears;

Streams in the world and streams in man: to wit, man's urine;

Walls in the world and walls in man: to wit, man's lips; . . .

Towers in the world and towers in man: to wit, man's neck;

Masts in the world and masts in man: to wit, man's arms;

Pegs in the world and pegs in man: to wit: man's fingers; . . .

Pits in the world and a pit in man: to wit, man's navel;

Flowing waters in the world and flowing waters in man: to wit, man's blood;

Trees in the world and trees in man: to wit, man's bones;

Hills in the world and hills in man: to wit, man's buttocks;

Pestle and mortar in the world and pestle and mortar in man: to wit, man's joints;

Horses in the world and horses in man: to wit, man's legs. . . .

Mountains and valleys in the world and mountains and valleys in man: erect, he is like a mountain; recumbent, he is like a valley.

Thus you learn that whatever the Holy One, blessed be He, created in His world, He created in man.

—*Fathers According to Rabbi Nathan*, chapter 31

Caring for your body

Each selection strikes the same theme: the sanctity of the human body.

The body is the soul's house. Shouldn't we therefore take care of our house so that it doesn't fall into ruin?

—Philo Judaeus, *The Worse Attacks the Better*, section 10

Once when the sage Hillel had finished a lesson with his pupils, he accompanied them partway home.

"Master," they asked, "where are you going?"

"To perform a religious duty," he answered.

"What duty is that?"

"To bathe in the bathhouse."

"Is that a religious duty?" they asked.

"If somebody is appointed to scrape and clean the statues of the king that stand in the theaters and circuses, is paid for the work, and even associates with the nobility," he answered, "how much more should I, who am created in the image and likeness of God, take care of my body!"

—*Leviticus Rabbah*, chapter 34, section 3

Since by keeping the body in health and vigor one walks in the ways of God—it being impossible during sickness to have any understanding or knowledge of the Creator —it is a man's duty to avoid whatever is injurious to the body and cultivate habits conducive to health and vigor.

—Maimonides, *Code*, "Laws Concerning Moral Dispositions and Ethical Conduct," chapter 4, section 1

Developing good eating habits

Superstition and folk remedies are mixed with practical advice to teach a simple lesson: eat wisely.

Thirteen things were said concerning eating bread in the morning:

It protects against heat and cold, winds and demons.

It makes the simple wise, causes a person to win lawsuits, and helps a person to study and teach Torah, to have his words heeded, and to retain scholarship.

A person who eats in the morning doesn't exhale a bad odor and lives with his wife without lusting after other women.

Morning bread also kills the worms in a person's intestines.

And some people say it gets rid of jealousy and encourages love. . . .

A proverb says: "Sixty runners speed along but cannot overtake the person who breaks bread in the morning."

—Babylonian Talmud, tractate *Bava Mezia*, page 107b

Have you found honey? Eat so much as is sufficient for you, lest you be filled with it, and vomit it.

—Proverbs, chapter 25, verse 16

Rav said: A meal without salt is no meal.

Rabbi Hiyya bar Abba said: A meal without soup is no meal.

—Babylonian Talmud, tractate *Berakhot*, page 44a

Five things were said of garlic:

It satisfies your hunger.

It keeps the body warm.

It makes your face bright.

It increases a man's potency.

And it kills parasites in the bowels.

Some people say that it also encourages love and removes jealousy.

—Babylonian Talmud, tractate *Bava Kamma*, page 82a

A person should not speak at meals lest his windpipe act before his gullet and his life become endangered because of it.

—Babylonian Talmud, tractate *Ta'anit*, page 5b

He who eats foods that do not agree with him transgresses three commandments, in that he has despised himself, despised the foods, and recited a blessing improperly.

—Rabbi Akiva, in *Fathers According to Rabbi Nathan*, chapter 26

The dangers of overeating

The sages joked that two of their colleagues, Rabbi Ishmael and Rabbi Eleazar, were so fat that when they stood together, waist to waist, a yoke of oxen could pass beneath them and not touch them at all. Such obesity was far from approved of, however. Ben Sira gives specific advice on how to control oneself at a large dinner party overflowing with tempting food. And in a treatise on health written especially for the Sultan of Egypt, Maimonides speaks of the need to regulate one's diet.

If you are sitting at a grand table, do not lick your lips and exclaim, "What a spread!" . . .

Do not reach for everything you see or jostle your fellow-guest at the dish; judge his feelings by your own and always behave considerately. . . .

If you are dining in a large company, do not reach out your hand before others.

A man of good upbringing is content with little, and he is not short of breath when he goes to bed.

The moderate eater enjoys healthy sleep; he rises early, feeling refreshed.

But sleeplessness, indigestion, and colic are the lot of the glutton.

—Wisdom of Ben Sira,
chapter 31, verses 12–15 and 18–20

If a man would take care of his body as he takes care of the animal he rides on, he would be spared many serious ailments. For you will not find a man who would give too much hay to his animal, but he measures it according to its capacity. However, he himself will eat too much without measure and consideration. Man is very attentive to his animal's movement and fatigue in order that it should continue in a state of health and not get sick, but he is not attentive to his own body. . . .

One should eat only when justified by a feeling of hunger, when the stomach is clear and the mouth possesses sufficient saliva. Then one is really hungry. A man must not drink water unless he is truly justified by thirst.

This means that if one feels hungry or thirsty he should wait a little, as occasionally one is led to feel so by a deceptive hunger and deceptive thirst.

—Maimonides,
The Preservation of Youth

On eating meat

Most contemporary Bible critics are convinced that vegetarianism was the biblical ideal, and that people were permitted to slaughter animals for food only as a concession to human weakness and desires. Isaiah's vision for the end of days when the "lion, like the ox, shall eat straw" seems to corroborate this theory, and the talmudic interpretation of biblical events further bears it out. Over the centuries, meat has been accepted and has become a symbol of festivity for the Sabbath and holidays. Still, Nahmanides cautions against excessiveness.

A person should not eat meat unless he has a special appetite for it.

—Babylonian Talmud, tractate
Hullin, page 84a

Adam was not permitted to eat meat, for it is written: "See, I give you every seed-bearing plant that is upon all the earth. . . . And to all the animals on land, to all the birds in the sky, and to everything that creeps on earth . . . I give all the green plants for food" (Genesis 1:29, 30). The implication is that the beasts of the earth shall not be for man to eat.

But at the time of the sons of Noah meat was permitted, for it is said: "Every creature that lives shall be yours to eat. . . ." (Genesis 9:3).

—Babylonian Talmud, tractate
Sanhedrin, page 59b

> The Torah has admonished us against immorality and forbidden foods, but permitted sexual intercourse between man and his wife, and the eating of meat and wine.
>
> If so, a man of desire could consider this to be permission to be passionately addicted to sexual intercourse . . . and to be among winebibbers, and among gluttonous eaters of flesh . . . and thus he will become a sordid person within the permissible realm of the Torah!
>
> Therefore, after having listed the matters which He prohibited altogether, Scripture followed them up by a general command that we practice moderation even in matters that are permitted.
>
> —Nahmanides, commentary on Leviticus, chapter 19, "Ye Shall Be Holy"

Drinking and drugs

"Wine cheers the hearts of men," said the biblical psalmist, but the sage Rabbi Meir taught that "the forbidden tree from which Adam ate was a grapevine, for nothing brings as much woe to man as wine." Both views have their place in Jewish thought. While wine and liquor have always been used to make holidays and special occasions festive, overindulgence is regarded as vulgar and debilitating. The remarkably low rate of alcoholism among Jews until our own day, with its widespread assimilation, is connected to this insistence on balance and moderation.

The case against drugs is stated in the last selection by a twelfth-century rabbi, one of the few references to drugs in the traditional literature.

> There are eight things that taken in large quantities are bad but in small quantities are helpful:
>
> Travel, sex, wealth, work, wine, sleep, hot baths and bloodletting.
>
> —Babylonian Talmud, tractate *Gittin*, page 70a

The benefits of wine are many if it is taken in the proper amount, as it keeps the body in a healthy condition and cures many illnesses.

But the knowledge of its consumption is hidden from the masses. What they want is to get drunk, and inebriety causes harm. . . .

The small amount that is useful must be taken after the food leaves the stomach. Young children should not come close to it because it hurts them and causes harm to their body and soul. . . .

The older a man is, the more beneficial the wine is for him. Old people need it most.

—Maimonides,
The Preservation of Youth

When Noah went to plant a vineyard Satan appeared before him.

"What are you planting?" asked Satan.

"A vineyard," answered Noah.

"What is it like?" asked Satan.

"Its fruits are always sweet, whether fresh or dry, and wine is made of them to gladden the heart," Noah replied.

"Let us form a partnership in this vineyard," Satan proposed.

"Very well," said Noah.

What did Satan do?

He brought a sheep and a lamb, and slew them under the vine.

Then he brought in turn a lion, a pig, and a monkey and slew each so that their blood dripped into the vineyard and drenched the soil.

In that way Satan hinted that before a person drinks wine he is simple like a sheep and quiet like a lamb.

When he has drunk in moderation, he is strong as a lion and thinks that nobody in the world is as strong as he.

When he has drunk more than enough, he becomes like a pig, wallowing in filth.

And when he is completely drunk, he makes a monkey of himself, dancing about, spewing out obscenities, and unaware of anything he's doing.

—*Tanhuma*, on Genesis,
portion "Noah," paragraph 13

Do not take drugs because they demand periodic doses and your heart will crave them. You will also lose money. Even for medicinal purposes do not take drugs if you can find a different medicine that will help.

—Samuel ben Meir (1085–1158),
commentary on the Talmud,
tractate *Pesahim*, page 113a

The importance of cleanliness

Keeping your body clean is considered so important that a variety of religious rituals have been attached even to the simple act of washing hands before and after meals. Nahmanides explains, interpreting a biblical verse in terms of the cleanliness of body and spirit.

Uncleanliness of the head causes blindness.
Uncleanliness of clothes causes madness.
Uncleanliness of the body causes boils and ulcers.
So beware of uncleanliness.

—Babylonian Talmud, tractate
Nedarim, page 81a

Washing your hands and feet in warm water every evening is better than all the medicines in the world.

—Babylonian Talmud, tractate
Shabbat, page 108b

The words "you shall sanctify yourselves and be holy, for I am holy" are from Leviticus, chapter 11, verse 44.

"And you shall sanctify yourselves." This refers to the washing of hands before meals.

"And be you holy." This refers to the washing of hands after meals.

"For I am holy." This alludes to the spiced oil [which was rubbed into the hands after a meal].

. . . Scripture's main intention is to warn us . . . that we should be clean and pure, and separated from the common people who soil themselves with luxuries and unseemly things.

—Nahmanides, commentary on
Leviticus, chapter 19,
"Ye Shall Be Holy"

Keeping fit

Amusing but very questionable medical advice from the Talmud is followed here by sound counsel from Maimonides.

Do not sit too much, for sitting aggravates hemorrhoids;
Do not stand too much, for standing hurts the heart;
Do not walk too much, for walking hurts the eyes.
So, spend one third of your time sitting, one third standing, and one third walking.

—Babylonian Talmud, tractate
Ketubbot, page 111a

One does not consider exercise, though it is the main principle in keeping one's health and in the repulsion of most illnesses. . . .

And there is no such thing as excessive body movements and exercise. Because body movements and exercise will ignite natural heat and superfluities will be formed in the body, but they will be expelled. However, when the body is at rest, the natural heat is suppressed and the superfluities remain....

Exercise removes the harm caused by most bad habits, which most people have. And no movement is as beneficial, according to the physicians, as body movements and exercise.

Exercise refers both to strong and weak movements, provided it is a movement that is vigorous and affects breathing, increasing it. Violent exercise causes fatigue, and not everyone can stand fatigue nor needs it. It is good for the preservation of health to shorten the exercises.

—Maimonides,
The Preservation of Youth

Emotions and health

Do not give yourself over to sorrow or distress yourself deliberately.

A merry heart keeps a man alive, and joy lengthens his span of days....

Envy and anger shorten a man's life, and anxiety brings premature old age.

A man with a gay heart has a good appetite and relishes the food he eats.

—Wisdom of Ben Sira, chapter 30,
verses 21–22 and 24–25

Eat a third and drink a third and leave the remaining third of your stomach empty.

Then, when you get angry, there will be sufficient room for your rage.

—Babylonian Talmud, tractate
Gittin, page 70a

Three things drain a person's health: worry, travel, and sin.

—Babylonian Talmud, tractate *Gittin*, page 70a

Three things restore a person's good spirits: beautiful sounds, sights, and smells.

—Babylonian Talmud, tractate *Berakhot*, page 57b

Emotional experiences cause marked changes in the body which are clear and visible to all and bear witness in clear testimony.

You see a man strongly built whose voice is powerful and pleasant and whose countenance is splendid. When he is affected all of a sudden by a feeling of great disgust, his facial expression falls and loses its luster. The light of his countenance changes, his posture becomes low and his voice hoarse and weak. . . . His strength weakens, occasionally he trembles from great debility, his pulsating blood vessels become thin and powerless. . . .

You see quite the reverse in a man whose body is weak, whose appearance is strange and whose voice is low. When something happens to him which causes him to rejoice greatly, you will see how his body becomes strong, his voice rises, his face brightens, his movements become rapid, his pulsating vessels become strong and wide, his body surface becomes warm, and joy and gladness become manifest in his face and eyelids. . . .

. . . When one is overpowered by imagination, prolonged meditation and avoidance of social contact, which he never exhibited before, or when one avoids pleasant experiences which were in him before, the physician should do nothing before he improves the soul by removing the extreme emotions.

—Maimonides,
The Preservation of Youth

On visiting the sick

The model for visiting sick people is God, whom the book of Genesis tells us visited Abraham when the patriarch was recuperating from his circumcision. To visit a person who is ill became a religious obligation, and in every Jewish community, down to our own day, special societies have been formed to visit poor or lonely patients who may not have others to depend on.

It was taught: There is no measure for visiting the sick.

What does "no measure" mean?

Rabbi Joseph explained: [This means] the rewards for doing so are unlimited.

But Abbaye said: Is there a definitive measure of reward for carrying out any commandment? . . . Rather, "no measure" means that even a great person must visit a lowly one who is sick.

Rava said: A person must visit the sick even a hundred times a day.

—Babylonian Talmud, tractate
Nedarim, page 39b

It once happened that one of Rabbi Akiva's disciples became ill, and none of the sages visited him.

Then Rabbi Akiva himself went to the disciple's house, and because he saw to it that the floor was swept and sprinkled with water, the man recovered.

"My master, you have restored me to life," the disciple said.

Akiva went out and taught: He who does not visit the sick is like someone who sheds blood.

Rabbi Dimi said: He who visits the sick causes him to recover, and he who does not visit the sick causes him to die.

—Babylonian Talmud, tractate *Nedarim*, page 40a

An enemy should not visit his enemy during his sickness, and should not comfort him in mourning, for the sick man may think that his enemy rejoices in his misfortunes.

The enemy may, however, attend the funeral of a dead enemy, and should not worry that people think he came to rejoice, since this is the end of every mortal.

—Solomon Ganzfried, *Condensed Code of Jewish Law,* chapter 193, section 1

A visitor came to see a sick man and asked him what ailed him. After the sick man told him, the visitor said:

"Oh, my father died of the same disease."

The sick man became extremely distressed, but the visitor said, "Don't worry, I'll pray to God to heal you."

To which the sick man answered:

"And when you pray, add that I may be spared visits from any more stupid people."

—From *Path of Good Men,* ethical stories and sayings, edited by Zevi Hirsch Edelmann (1805–1858)

If you're in pain

Not only does no conflict exist between religion and medicine, but the sages expect physicians to help nature along, and even improve on it when possible. About the physicians themselves, however, we find more ambivalent attitudes.

If you're in pain, go to a physician!

—Babylonian Talmud, tractate
Bava Kamma, page 46b

Once Rabbi Ishmael and Rabbi Akiva were strolling in the streets of Jerusalem along with another man. They met a sick person who said to them, "Masters, tell me how I can be healed." They quickly advised him to take a certain medicine until he felt better.

The man with them turned to them and said, "Who made this man sick?"

"The Holy One, blessed be He," they replied.

"And do you presume to interfere in an area that is not yours?" the man exclaimed. "He is afflicted and you heal?"

"What is your occupation?" they asked the man.

"I'm a tiller of the soil," he answered, "as you can see from the sickle I carry."

"Who created the field and the vineyard?"

"The Holy One, blessed be He."

"And you dare to move into an area that is not yours? He created these and you eat their fruit!"

"Don't you see the sickle in my hand?" the man said. "If I did not go out and plow the field, cover it, fertilize it, weed it, nothing would grow!"

"Fool," the rabbis said. ". . . Just as a tree does not grow if it is not fertilized, plowed and weeded—and even if it already grew but then is not watered it dies—so the body is like a tree, the medicine is the fertilizer and the doctor is the farmer."

—*Midrash Samuel*,
chapter 4, section 1

Honor the doctor for his services, for the Lord created him.

His skill comes from the Most High, and he is rewarded by kings.

The doctor's knowledge gives him high standing and wins him the admiration of the great.

The Lord has created medicines from the earth, and a sensible man will not disparage them. . . .

The Lord has imparted knowledge to men, that by their use of His marvels He may win praise; by using them the doctor relieves pain and from them the pharmacist makes up his mixture.

There is no end to the works of the Lord, who spreads health over the whole world.

—Wisdom of Ben Sira,
chapter 38, verses 1–8

It is forbidden to live in a town that does not have a physician.

—Jerusalem Talmud, tractate
Kiddushin, chapter 4, paragraph 12

The knavish doctor is the colleague of the angel of death.

—Isaac Abrabanel (1437–1508),
commentary on Genesis,
chapter 41

The best of physicians belongs in hell!

—Mishnah, tractate *Kiddushin*,
chapter 4, paragraph 14

Many rationalizations have been given for the harsh condemnation, above, and Rashi, one of the greatest of all commentators, offers one. The criticism may simply have been written into the Mishnah in exasperation with some doctors, or it may reflect feelings that were common among philosophers in the ancient world.

> This applies only to a physician who does not humble himself to trust in heaven, who sometimes causes the death of his patients, and who can afford to treat the poor without charging a fee but doesn't do so.
>
> —Rashi (Rabbi Solomon ben Isaac; 1040–1105), commentary on Mishnah, tractate *Kiddushin*, chapter 4, paragraph 14

> When you need a physician, you esteem him a god;
> When he has brought you out of danger, you consider him a king.
> When you have been cured, he becomes human like yourself;
> When he sends you the bill, you think him a devil.
>
> —Jedadiah ben Abraham Bedersi (c. 1270–1340), French poet and philosopher

About miracle doctors

Lack of scientific knowledge may have led scholars of different periods to accept medical remedies that we would consider quackery today. But within the realm of their knowledge, Jewish leaders have always insisted on the use of recognized medical and scientific practices in treating illnesses. The Talmud branded reliance on faith healing or magical incantations, such as the one included in the first selection, as forms of idolatry. The medieval folk story reflects that tradition.

The following do not have a share in the world to come. . . . Anyone who whispers a mystical charm over a wound and says, "I will not bring upon you any of the diseases that I brought upon the Egyptians, for I the Lord am your healer" (Exodus 15:26).

—Mishnah, tractate *Sanhedrin*, chapter 10, paragraph 1

There once lived a Jew who was led astray by a wizard. The Jew was lame and could not walk. One day he was told that there lived in a certain town a man who by means of an ointment enabled the lame to walk, the blind to see, and all the sick to be healed. So he said he would also like to go to that town so that he might be cured.

Now the man who healed the people was a demon, may God protect us from them! The Jew went to that city, and when he arrived there, he saw a man walking about in the night and healing the sick.

The man said to the demon, "I am a Jew and have heard that you heal all the sick and make all the lame walk. Therefore, I have come to you that you may cure my lameness also."

The man replied, "Do you know who I am? I am a demon and have assumed the form of a physician to lead all the people astray who follow sorcery, in order to destroy them. Now, your time had come to be cured of your lameness, but because you allowed yourself to be led astray by sorcerers, the Lord has decreed that you should remain lame all your life."

—Medieval legend, included in the *Ma'aseh Book*, edited by Moses Gaster (1856–1939)

A physician's responsibilities

Joseph Caro's *Code of Jewish Law* explains the responsibilities and liabilities of a doctor. More lenient than common law, Jewish law does not hold the physician legally liable for injuring a patient, although he is considered morally accountable. He is responsible, however, for the death of a patient through negligence, though he is treated as an accidental rather than a willful murderer.

The Torah grants physicians permission to heal. Healing is, in fact, a religious duty that falls under the rules for saving a life.

If a physician withholds treatment when he is able to give it, he is regarded as a murderer, even if there is someone else who can heal a patient, because it may be that in this case it is the special merit of this physician to provide the healing for this patient.

However, a person should not practice medicine unless he is an expert, and there is no one immediately available who is more competent than he; otherwise, he is regarded as a murderer.

If a person gives medical treatment without the permission of a Jewish court [or today, a medical license], he is subject to payment of indemnities, even if he is an expert.

If he had the proper credentials but he erred in his judgment and negligently injured the patient, he is exempt from the laws of man but is held responsible by the laws of heaven. If the physician caused a death because of negligence, he is exiled according to the laws that deal with a person who killed another accidentally. [In early days such a person was banished to a city of exile, where the murdered person's family was not permitted to pursue him.]

—Joseph Caro, *Code of Jewish Law*, "Yoreh De'ah," chapter 336, section 1

Many physicians treat their patients with criminal neglect; nevertheless, the patients do not die but are saved. And

I have seen those who have prescribed asparagus, a strong purgative, for one who did not need even a mild one . . . yet the patient got well again.

But the physician should not take it for granted that a physician causes little injury and say: "As this error in great measure did not cause death, it will surely cause no harm if the physician errs a little in the amount of food and drink." But this is not so. . . .

And the error of the physicians is equal in both directions, for sometimes they commit a grave error and the patient is saved, and occasionally the error in treatment is very mild and the patient thinks that it is of little consequence, yet it will prove the cause of his death. Let every intelligent man keep his eye on this.

—Maimonides,
The Preservation of Youth

The work and ideals of a physician

Two physicians describe their work and the standards they set for themselves. Maimonides's portrayal of his busy day is from a letter he wrote to Samuel Ibn Tibbon, translator of many of Maimonides's works. The letter's purpose was to dissuade Samuel from visiting, because, as Maimonides explained, they would not have a minute alone, "either by day or night." Amatus Lusitanus wrote his piece as an oath appended to one of his medical treatises. Born in Portugal, Amatus held prominent medical positions in Belgium and later in Italy, where he treated Pope Julius III. His parents were Marranos who had been forced to convert to Christianity, but Amatus retained his Jewish ties and eventually openly returned to the practice of Judaism in the city of Salonika.

I dwell in Fustat, and the Sultan resides in Cairo [Maimonides served as physician to the Sultan of Egypt and his family]. . . . My duties to the ruler are very heavy. I am obliged to visit him every day, early in the morning; and when he or any of his children, or any of the inmates of his harem is indisposed, I dare not quit Cairo, but must stay during the greater part of the day in the palace.

It also frequently happens that one or two of the royal officers fall sick, and I must attend to their healing the entire day. Hence, as a rule, I repair to Cairo very early in the day, and even if nothing unusual happens, I do not return to Fustat until the afternoon. . . . Then I am almost dying with hunger. I find the antechambers filled with people, both Jews and Gentiles, important and unimportant people, theologians and bailiffs, friends and foes—a mixed multitude, who await the time of my return.

I dismount from my animal, wash my hands, go forth to my patients, and beg and entreat them to bear with me while I partake of some slight refreshment, the only meal I take in the twenty-four hours. Then I go forth to attend my patients, write prescriptions and directions for their several ailments. Patients go in and out until nightfall, and sometimes even, I solemnly assure you, until two hours in the night or even later. I converse with, and prescribe for them while lying down on my back from sheer fatigue; and when night falls, I am so exhausted, I can scarcely speak.

—Maimonides, from a letter to
Samuel Ibn Tibbon, 1199

I swear that I have always striven after one thing, namely, that benefit might spread forth to mankind. . . .

Concerning the remuneration, furthermore, which is commonly given to physicians, I have not been anxious for this, but I have treated many, not only zealously, but even without pay; and have unselfishly and unswervingly refused several rewards offered by many people; and have rather sought that the sick might, by my care and diligence, recover their lost health than that I might become richer by their liberality. All men have been considered equals by me of whatever religion they were, whether Hebrews, Christians, or followers of the Moslem faith.

> . . . I have never brought about sickness; in diagnosis I have always said what I thought to be true. I have unduly favored no vendors of drugs, except perhaps those whom I knew to surpass the others by reason of their skill in their art or because of their natural qualities of mind. In prescribing drugs I have exercised moderation in proportion as the powers of the sick man allowed. I have revealed to no one a secret entrusted to me. . . .
>
> . . . I have published my books on medical matters with no desire for profit, but I have had regard for this one thing, namely, that I might in some measure provide for the health of mankind. . . .
>
> —Amatus Lusitanus (1511–1568),
> from his "Oath," written in 1559

The fees doctors charge

Theoretically, doctors, like rabbis and religious teachers, were not permitted to receive fees for their actual services but only for the interruption of their time, as Joseph Caro's *Code of Jewish Law* explains. In practice, however, doctors did receive fees from the earliest times, whatever the rationale. The Talmud records a popular proverb of the period, warning that you better not depend on the service you get from a physician who doesn't charge. The physician Isaac Israeli takes the idea a step further in the advice he gives his colleagues—in-group advice that sounds all too contemporary. Treatment of the poor, however, was another matter. Physicians are urged again and again not to demand payment from patients who cannot afford it nor to avoid treating poor patients. The very same Isaac Israeli conveys that message to fellow physicians, and the Talmud presents Abba the Bloodletter as a model for all medical people.

> A physician may not accept a fee for giving advice to a patient, because in sharing learning and wisdom with his patient, he performs the religious duty of restoring health to a person who has lost it. And just as God performs his services gratuitously, so should a physician. However, a

physician may accept payment for the time he spends in visiting a patient, and the trouble he takes to write prescriptions.

—Joseph Caro, *Code of Jewish Law*, "Yoreh De'ah," chapter 336, section 2

A doctor who charges nothing is worth nothing!

—Babylonian Talmud, tractate *Bava Kamma*, page 85a

The more you demand for your service, the greater will it appear in the eyes of the people. Your art will be looked down upon by people you treat for nothing.

—Isaac Israeli (c. 855–c. 955), Egyptian physician and philosopher, *Doctor's Guide*, number 40

Make it your special concern to visit and treat poor and needy patients, for in no way can you find more meritorious service.

—Isaac Israeli, *Doctor's Guide*, number 30

Abba the Bloodletter [he bled people for medicinal purposes] placed a box in his office out of public view in which patients could put their fees. People who could afford to pay placed their fees in the box; those who could not afford to pay didn't have to, and were not ashamed.

Whenever a poor young scholar came to him for medical advice, Abba would not only treat him without charging, he would also give the young man some money and say, "Here, use this to regain your strength."

—Babylonian Talmud, tractate
Ta'anit, page 21b

The patient as a person

Maimonides knew that not just science and medicine but the intangibles—music, a pleasant atmosphere—could make all the difference in regaining health. Eight hundred years later, Professor Abraham Heschel, in a speech before the American Medical Association, again spoke of intangibles in an illness—this time the unique relationship between doctor and patient.

In order to strengthen the vital powers, one should employ musical instruments and tell patients gay stories which will make the heart swell and narratives that will distract the mind and cause them and their friends to laugh.

One should select as attendants and caretakers those who can cheer up the patient. This is a must in every illness....

—Maimonides,
The Preservation of Youth

While medical science is advancing, the doctor-patient relationship seems to be deteriorating. In fairness to physicians, the relationship has changed because medicine has changed. The doctor of old may have had little more to offer the patient than understanding, sympathy, personal affection.

The great advances in medicine have made it necessary for men to specialize if they wish to remain abreast of any particular field of medicine, and this specialization has forced a change in the image of the practitioner. Yet there is no necessary clash between specialization and compassion, between the use of instruments and personal sensitivity....

The doctor is not simply a dispenser of drugs, a computer that speaks. In treating a patient he is morally involved. What transpires between doctor and patient is more than a commercial transaction, more than a professional relationship between a specimen of the human species and a member of the A.M.A.: it is a profoundly human association, involving concern, trust, responsibility....

The doctor enters a covenant with the patient, he penetrates his life, affecting his mode of living, often deciding his fate. The doctor's role is one of royal authority, while the patient's mood is one of anxiety and helplessness. The patient is literally a sufferer, while the doctor is the incarnation of his hope.

—Abraham Joshua Heschel, from
"The Patient as a Person,"
Conservative Judaism (Fall 1974)

When a patient is dying

A beautiful legend says that when Moses had to inform his brother Aaron of Aaron's impending death, he sat down with him and read the narrative of the creation of the world in the book of Genesis. As they read of the creation of each day, Moses exclaimed, "How beautiful and good was the creation of this day!" But when they reached the description of the creation of Adam, Moses said, "I don't know what to say about the creation of man. How can I call it beautiful and good when the end of man is death?" Aaron quickly replied, "We must resign ourselves to the will of God," and that answer gave Moses an opening in which to tell Aaron about his own approaching death.

In the series below, the prophet Isaiah is criticized for his abrupt way of announcing the death of King Hezekiah of Judah. The rebuke comes in the form of fictionalized conversations between Isaiah and Hezekiah indicating how a terminally ill patient should be addressed. The approach of the early sages was later formalized in the *Code of Jewish Law*. The issue here is not hiding the truth but presenting it in a way that can be absorbed and eventually accepted by the patient.

> In those days, Hezekiah fell dangerously ill. The prophet Isaiah, son of Amoz, came and said to him, "Thus said the Lord. Set your affairs in order, for you are going to die; you will not live."
>
> Thereupon Hezekiah turned his face to the wall and prayed to the Lord. "Please O Lord," he said, "remember how I have walked before You sincerely and wholeheartedly, and have done what is pleasing to You." And Hezekiah wept profusely.
>
> Then the word of the Lord came to Isaiah: "Go and tell Hezekiah: Thus said the Lord, the God of your father David: I have heard your prayer, I have seen your tears. I hereby add fifteen years to your life. . . ."
>
> —Isaiah, chapter 38, verses 1–5

The rabbis reconstructed this rebuke:

> Hezekiah said to Isaiah, "Son of Amoz, finish your prophecy and go! This tradition I have learned from my ancestor, King David: Even if a sharp sword is placed at a person's neck, he should not stop praying."
>
> Rabbi Hanan said: Even if a person dreams that the next day he will die, he should not stop praying.
>
> —Babylonian Talmud, tractate *Berakhot*, pages 10a–b

An additional rabbinic elaboration on the biblical text:

> When Hezekiah became ill, the Holy One, blessed be He, told the prophet Isaiah, "Go and tell him: Set your affairs in order, for you are going to die; you will not live."

Said Hezekiah to the prophet, "Isaiah, the customary way of the world is for a person who is visiting another who is sick to say, 'May heaven have mercy upon you.' And the physician continues to tell him to eat this, to drink this and not drink that.

"Even when the physician realizes that his patient approaches death, he does not say to him, 'Arrange your affairs,' lest the person's mind faint. But you, Isaiah, say to me, 'Set your affairs in order, for you are going to die; you will not live.' "

—*Ecclesiastes Rabbah*,
chapter 5, section 6

It is permitted to tell a person who is seriously ill that he should turn his attention to his affairs. If he has lent money or deposited it with someone, or if others have lent him money or deposited their money with him, he should see that everything is in order. But he should be told that he need not fear that death is imminent because of these questions. . . .

When death draws near he is advised to confess. And we reassure him, "Many have confessed and then not died, just as many have not confessed and died. In the merit of your confessing you might be granted life."

—Joseph Caro, *Code of Jewish Law*, "Yoreh De'ah," chapter 335, section 7; chapter 338, section 1

Taking medical risks

Should an experimental drug be given to a terminally ill patient to prolong life, with the knowledge that the drug itself may cut that life short? Should a surgeon risk an operation in which a patient might die because the operation is necessary to save the patient's life?

Such questions have grown pressing with the rapid advances in medical experimentation. A precedent for coping with them in Jewish tradition stems from a strange talmudic discussion about whether a heathen physician may be permitted to treat a Jew. Because they were convinced that the pagan physicians of their time employed idolatrous forms of magic, the talmudic authorities generally forbade treatment by non-Jewish physicians. But they did make an exception for a situation in which a patient most probably would die without such treatment. Their ruling became the basis for a responsum on the subject by the eighteenth-century scholar Rabbi Jacob Reischer. His decision—that a certain amount of risk could be incurred to save a person's life—has become the major source for most contemporary discussions of this subject by Jewish scholars. Rabbi Reischer spoke of the use of a new drug, but his ruling has been extended to include many kinds of medical procedures if the risk involved holds out real hope for improving the patient's condition.

> When we are in doubt about whether a patient will live or die, we must not allow idolators to heal. But if the patient certainly will die, we may allow them to heal.
>
> But shouldn't we consider momentary life [the few hours left to the patient] and not jeopardize that?
>
> In a situation like this, momentary life is not to be considered.
>
> —Babylonian Talmud, tractate *Avodah Zarah*, page 27b

Rabbi Reischer received an inquiry from a doctor concerning a patient who was close to death. All the physicians agreed that there was one medication that might cure him, but if it failed, he would probably die immediately. Question: Were they permitted to administer the drug or should they do nothing? Reischer responded:

> Since this is in reality a capital case, one is required to be very cautious. . . .

Upon first consideration, it would seem that it is preferable to refrain from taking any action, for we are concerned with momentary life, even when a person is actually moribund. . . . Maimonides wrote, for example, that if one even closes the eyes of a dying person (and hastens his death), it is as though he were spilling blood. And such is the consensus of all rabbinic authorities. . . .

However, if it is possible that by administering the medicine to this patient, he might be completely cured of his illness, we certainly cannot be concerned with momentary life. Clear support for this distinction is found in the Talmud, tractate *Avodah Zarah* [cited above]. . . .

In this case, too, since the patient would surely die, we set aside the certainty of death and grasp the doubtful possibility of curing him.

Nevertheless, we enjoin the physicians from acting in the usual manner but urge extreme caution in this situation. That is, they should consult with expert physicians in town and follow the majority opinion—which means a substantial two-to-one majority—because one has to be wary of casual opinions. And . . . they must also have the consent of the local rabbinic authority.

—Jacob ben Joseph Reischer, (1670–1733), *Responsa, Shevut Yaakov*, volume 3, number 75

Autopsies and medical research

There has been a longstanding aversion to autopsies among Jewish authorities, which stems from the biblical verse, below, ordering the body of a criminal who has been executed to be removed and buried the same day. The sages interpreted that passage as a directive to treat all corpses with honor; and on this basis, they forbade disfiguring a corpse in any way, and most especially with an autopsy. The question of permitting autopsies for medical research was raised at many times, but the prohibition remained fixed. Rabbi Ezekiel Landau's response of two hundred years ago became the most authoritative on the subject, permitting an autopsy only if it could be shown that there is a person "at hand" who might benefit directly from it.

In recent years, when all branches of Judaism have generally permitted transplanting organs from a deceased to a living person, and when increasing numbers of people have begun to will parts of their bodies for medical research after their death, the question of autopsies has been discussed and debated again and again. Rabbi Immanuel Jakobovits, chief rabbi of Great Britain and a well-known Orthodox scholar of medical issues, shows how a more lenient interpretation of Rabbi Landau and earlier scholars might lead to saving many lives. Although not all authorities agree with him, many Orthodox and most Conservative and Reform rabbis have taken more permissive positions than in the past. Reform leaders usually leave the decision about whether an autopsy is to be performed to the family. A responsum of the Conservative Rabbinical Assembly, prepared in 1958 by Rabbi Isaac Klein, states that where medical science claims that an autopsy or the use of part of a dead body may save lives, "it is not only permitted, but is actually a *mitzvah* [duty]. There should always, however, be a respectful attitude to the human body, and burial should be piously performed wherever possible."

> If a man is guilty of a capital offense and is put to death, and you impale him on a stake, you must not let his corpse remain on the stake overnight but must bury him the same day. For an impaled body is an affront to God.
>
> —Deuteronomy, chapter 21,
> verses 22–23

Rabbi Landau was asked whether an autopsy might be performed on a man who had died during a gallstone operation in order to improve the technique for future operations. The rabbi questions whether this autopsy will help save other lives.

The principle that even a possibility of saving a life waives all biblical commandments except in three cases applies only when there is before us concretely such a possibility, as for instance a person sick with that same ailment. In our case, however, there is no patient at hand whose treatment calls for this knowledge. It is only that people want to learn this skill for the future possibility that a patient who will need this treatment might come before us. For such a slight apprehension we do not nullify a biblical commandment or even a rabbinic prohibition. . . .

—Ezekiel ben Judah Landau of Prague (1713–1793), *Responsa, Noda bi-Yehudah, Tinyana*, "Yoreh De'ah," number 210

In applying the basic principles laid down by Rabbi Ezekial Landau . . . one has to take into account the following new circumstances:

In these days of speedy communications, patients are "at hand" everywhere awaiting the findings of anatomical research, and what is discovered in one place today may save a life in another tomorrow.

The need for autopsies to conquer some of the worst scourges, such as cancer and heart disease, is, according to medical opinion, incontestable. Indeed, any autopsy nowadays . . . is more likely to help in the saving of life than in any "at-hand" case permitted two hundred years ago, when medical science was primitive by comparison. . . .

The anticipated benefits from autopsies now include not only the hope of finding cures for obscure diseases but . . . testing the safety of the constant output of new drugs, whose effects cannot otherwise be ascertained, and discovering errors of diagnosis and treatment. . . .

While no blanket sanction can be given for the indiscriminate surrender of all bodies to post-mortem examination, it is equally unrealistic to limit the sanction

> to obscure causes of death only. It should be broadened to include controlled tests of new medications and cases of reasonable suspicion that a diagnosis was mistaken. . . .
>
> Just as it is the duty of rabbis to urge relatives not to consent to autopsies where life-saving considerations do not apply . . . they are religiously bound to advocate and encourage autopsies in cases where human lives may thereby be saved, in the same way that the suspension of the Sabbath laws in the face of danger to life is not merely optional but mandatory.
>
> —Immanuel Jakobovits,
> *Jewish Medical Ethics*
> (1975)

About test-tube babies

The concept of human life being created outside a mother's womb was beyond even the realm of speculation for early sages, so that the guidance Jewish tradition can offer on a subject such as test-tube babies must stem from attitudes toward other issues that can be related to it. One such issue is artificial insemination. The Talmud records an unusual question asked of the sage Ben Zoma: May a high priest, permitted to marry only a virgin, wed a virgin who is pregnant? The answer is yes. But how, it is asked, can a virgin be pregnant? And the answer to that is: by conceiving in a public bath into which a man has discharged semen.

Medically unsound as this brief reference may be, it is often cited in discussing the permissibility of artificial insemination. Rabbi Seymour Siegal, a Conservative authority on Jewish law, refers to it in his essay written immediately after the birth of the first known test-tube baby to a British couple named Brown in July 1978. In this case, the mother's egg was fertilized in a test tube by the father's sperm, and the fertilized egg was then implanted in the mother's uterus, where it grew to a full-term normal baby. Rabbi Siegal extends his discussion beyond legal matters to take up the social and moral implications of the birth.

The birth of the Brown baby has raised many important questions in the minds of thinking men and women. . . . The ethical question is whether it is right to conceive a child in a test tube outside the mother's body. The theological question is whether human beings have the right to radically tamper with nature. The public policy question is whether the Brown baby event opens the door to the use of more radical procedures, such as creating artificial wombs to gestate children, the use of host wombs . . . and the ordering of children according to specifications of sex, intelligence and so on.

From the standpoint of Jewish tradition:

The ethical question . . . is a variation on the question of artificial insemination. . . . The Brown case resembles the situation known as AIH [artificial insemination husband], since there is no third party involved. The Talmud discusses this problem in rather peculiar circumstances . . . but it does reflect the opinion of the rabbis that artificial impregnation is not prohibited. Though not all rabbinic authorities sanction AIH, the majority do not object to impregnating the wife with the seed of her husband if conception is impossible otherwise. This attitude is related to the Jewish view that to have children is a great *mitzvah.* If conception cannot be accomplished in the usual way, then let it be done artificially. . . . Therefore, there would be no *halakhic* [legal] objection to joining sperm and ovum of a married couple in a test tube. . . .

The theological question involves our relationship to nature. In the biblical viewpoint, nature, like man, is a creature of God. Nature is not divine as the pagans believed. . . . We are called upon to accept and care for nature. We are also called upon to use our ingenuity, our imagination, and intelligence to improve nature when human happiness is being thwarted. . . . This is, of course, the basis of the whole medical enterprise. . . . When we can use our knowledge to help us overcome the obstacles nature has put in our way, we are bidden to do so. If some anatomical quirk has made it impossible for Mrs.

Brown to conceive a child, then let us try to "outwit" nature. To do otherwise is to resign ourselves to sickness, deformity, and abnormalities. . . .

More difficult is the public policy issue. The Brown baby deserves our congratulations. But does her birth open the door to other procedures which would be morally objectionable? This . . . dilemma is the basis of the "slippery slope" argument, which says that it is not good policy to start something which might be perfectly acceptable if it can lead to outcomes that would be objectionable. . . . There is persuasive force in this argument. However, it can also be used to thwart all progress. . . . As in other areas of biomedical experimentation, the good sense and the ethical sensitivity of scientists operating under the regulatory powers of government acting in the interests of the public can establish the ground rules that will encourage research and avoid the dehumanization we all fear.

—Seymour Siegel, professor of theology and ethics, Jewish Theological Seminary, from "The Brown Baby and Jewish Tradition," in *United Synagogue Review* (Fall 1978)

6

STUDY, SCHOLARSHIP, AND SUPERSTITION

"A person who has knowledge has everything"

On the importance of knowledge ✦ "Ask your father" ✦ Scholars and ordinary folk ✦ The study of Torah ✦ Educating boys/educating girls ✦ Gaining wisdom from the elderly ✦ Student-teacher relationships ✦ Good and bad teaching ✦ Tips for teaching ✦ Developing study habits ✦ "At the tip of a pen" ✦ It's never too late to learn ✦ Delving into the unknown ✦ The dark side of knowledge ✦ Interpreting dreams ✦ Looking to the stars

A boy's first visit to a classroom and the first lessons he received were traditionally enveloped in emotion and ceremony. Dressed in new clothes, the child was carried to the schoolroom by a rabbi or learned man. There he received a clean slate on which letters of the Hebrew alphabet or a simple biblical verse had been written in honey. The child licked off the slate while reciting the name of each letter, and afterward he ate treats of honey cake, apples, and nuts—all aimed at making his introduction to his studies sweet and tempting.

Though this custom has long since fallen into disuse, the sentiment behind it still characterizes Jewish attitudes toward education. Knowledge is sweet; learning is to be approached with excitement and awe, lapped up eagerly, and savored long after the initial lesson is over.

Such emphasis on the importance of education goes back to the Bible, where the Israelites are commanded again and again to study all the laws and commandments they have been taught: "Gather the people—men, women, and children, and the strangers in your communities—that they may hear and so learn," Moses ordered the elders. And God's first charge to Joshua, Moses' successor as leader of the people, was "Let not this Book of Teaching cease from your lips, but recite it day and night, so that you may observe faithfully all that is written in it."

By talmudic times, learning and study had come to be regarded as so important that scholars stood out as the elite of Jewish society. Scholars, rather than princes or warriors, held authority over community organization and activities. Scholars, not businessmen or financiers, were sought after as the most desirable marriage partners for young women of upper-class families.

The scholarly world was tightly structured. Rabbinic schools—the highest educational institutions—had many similarities to the philosophic academies of the Hellenistic world in which the rabbis lived. Like the Hellenistic philosophers, Jewish teachers held absolute authority, while their disciples waited upon them, intent on learning everything, from how the master ate to what he thought about the most complicated subjects. So crucial was education that the relationship between teacher and pupil even took precedence over the relationship between father and son.

This high regard for knowledge sometimes led the Jewish scholars, as it did the Greek and Roman philosophers, to overbearing pride and to great intolerance of the uneducated. But for the rabbis, impatience with ignorance did not stem only from intellectual achievement and certainly not from deprecation of occupations other than scholarship. The sages received no fees for their teaching, earning their livings, instead, as tailors and cobblers, as blacksmiths and bakers. If they looked down on the uneducated, it was mostly because as teachers they worked hard to make learning widely available and had little sympathy for people who failed to take advantage of this.

Beginning in the last century before the destruction of the Second Temple (about a hundred years before the start of the Roman Empire), Jewish communities in Palestine and Babylonia had public schools for boys between the ages of seven and thirteen, and youths of scholarly bent could move on to academies of advanced studies. (Girls did not go to school. Their education, discussed later in this chapter, consisted mainly of learning domestic skills.) In the schools the boys attended, Bible and Talmud were the main subjects taught, though arithmetic, geometry, logic, astronomy, and, in some localities, philosophy and foreign languages were also offered. For adults, there were regular sermons on Sabbath and festivals; and in the summer and fall, special gatherings, called *ḳallahs*, presented lecture series by heads of academies of learning.

With their great interest in teaching and study, the sages had strong ideas about educational techniques that sound progressive even today. For example, a teacher was not permitted to teach more than twenty-five students; if a class was larger, an assistant teacher had to be hired. Teachers were advised to seat slow learners near quicker ones, who might help them in their studies. And stress was placed on rewarding students for their accomplishments rather than punishing them for their failures.

The educational plans laid down during the talmudic period continued to guide Jewish communities for hundreds of years. Many of their schools, however, fell far short of the goals outlined. In the *heders*—the one-room schools—of small East European ghettos, as both Solomon Maimon and Shalom Aleichem describe them, the system often deteriorated into one of classroom corruption and cruelty by teachers who had almost no pedagogic training and even less feeling for children. But at their best, the ideals of Jewish education centered around learning and diligent study, simply for the sake of knowing.

And yet . . . another tradition of knowledge existed. Magic, superstition, and folk beliefs found their place in Jewish life as they did in the cultures of most people. While the rabbis railed against these beliefs, they themselves were not immune from fear of the evil eye, from the lure of arcane dream interpretation, or from the intrigue of astrological fortune telling. A sampling of some of the most prevalent and perisistent of these superstitions, in the final sections of this chapter, offers a glimpse into a world of demons and spirits, of strange dreams and mysterious forebodings: a world that refused to be suppressed even in the midst of the most dedicated commitment to knowledge and wisdom and meticulous scholarship.

On the importance of knowledge

Hillel's statement about ignorance encapsulates the value of education in the Jewish tradition. His own commitment to learning served as a model for all future generations.

. . . God appeared to Solomon and said to him, "Ask what I shall give you."

And Solomon said to God, "You have shown great kindness to David, my father, and have made me king in his stead. . . . Give me now wisdom and knowledge, that I may go out and come in before this people; for who can judge these your people, that are so great?"

And God said to Solomon, "Because this was in your heart, and you have not asked for riches, wealth or honor, nor for the life of those who hate you, neither have you asked for long life, but for wisdom and knowledge for yourself . . . wisdom and knowledge is granted to you, and I will give you riches, and wealth, and honor, such as none of the kings have had before you, neither shall any after you have the like."

—II Chronicles,
chapter 1, verses 7–12

No one is poor except he who lacks knowledge. . . .

A person who has knowledge has everything. A person who lacks knowledge, what has he?

Once a person acquires knowledge, what does he lack? If a person does not acquire knowledge, what does he possess?

—Babylonian Talmud, tractate
Nedarim, page 41a

An ignorant person cannot be pious; the timid cannot learn; nor can the quick-tempered teach.

—Hillel, in *Ethics of the Fathers*,
chapter 2, paragraph 6

Study leads to precision, precision leads to zeal, zeal leads to cleanliness, cleanliness leads to restraint, restraint leads to purity, purity leads to holiness, holiness leads to humility, humility leads to fear of sin, fear of sin leads to saintliness, saintliness leads to possessing the holy spirit, the holy spirit leads to eternal life.

—Babylonian Talmud, tractate
Avodah Zarah, page 20b

Although sages like Shemaiah and Avtalyon were not paid for their teaching, the fee charged in this legend was to maintain the school building.

The rabbis taught: If a person comes before the heavenly court and says, "I was too poor and busy earning my livelihood to study," he is asked, "Were you poorer than Hillel?"

Hillel the Elder was a poor man. He worked every day and earned only half a *dinar*. He gave half of this to the guard at the house of study and used the other half to support himself and his family.

One day, on the Sabbath eve, he earned no money, and the guard at the house of study would not permit him to enter. He climbed up to the roof and put his head against the skylight, where he could hear the words spoken by the sages Shemaiah and Avtalyon. As he lay on the roof, heavy snow began to fall on him, but Hillel remained in his place all night.

Next morning, Shemaiah said to Avtalyon, "Brother, this house is light every day, but today it is dark. Is it perhaps cloudy outside?"

They looked up and saw the figure of a man in the skylight. They climbed to the roof and found Hillel, covered with snow and almost frozen to death. They carried him down, bathed and anointed him, and placed him near the fire.

And they said, "This man is worthy of having the Sabbath profaned because of him."

—Babylonian Talmud, tractate
Yoma, page 35b

"Ask your father"

Education begins with learning our own traditions and culture. The Bible stresses telling and retelling the story of the exodus from Egypt so that the young may learn and remember. From our own heritage we move outward, absorbing knowledge from people and events in our lives. Rabbi Meir continued to learn from his former teacher, the brilliant scholar Elisha ben Avuyah, even after Elisha broke with Judaism. The Talmud refers to Elisha as "Aher," meaning "deviant," because he completely removed himself from the fold, but it quotes many of his teachings, often transmitted by Rabbi Meir.

> Take to heart these words with which I charge you this day. Impress them upon your children. Recite them when you stay at home and when you are away, when you lie down and when you get up. Bind them as a sign on your hand and let them serve as a symbol on your forehead; inscribe them on the doorposts of your house and on your gates.
>
> —Deuteronomy, chapter 6, verses 6–9

> And when, in time to come, your son asks you, saying, "What does this mean?" you shall say to him, "It was with a mighty hand that the Lord brought us out of Egypt, the house of bondage...."
>
> —Exodus, chapter 13, verse 14

> Remember the days of old,
> Consider the years of ages past;
> Ask your father, he will inform you,
> Your elders, they will tell you.
>
> —Deuteronomy, chapter 32, verse 7

Rabbi Meir continued to learn traditions at the mouth of Aher.

But how could he do that?

Rabbi Meir found a pomegranate; he ate the fruit within it, and then threw away the seeds [he took the best, and rejected what was bad].

—Babylonian Talmud, tractate *Hagigah*, page 15b

The rabbi of Sadgora once said to his Hasidim, "We can learn something from everything, and not only everything God has created. What man has made also has something to teach us."

"What can we learn from a train?" one Hasid asked.

"That because of one second a person can miss everything."

"And from the telegraph?"

"That every word is counted and charged."

"And the telephone?"

"That what we say here is heard there."

—Saying of the Hasidic rabbi Abraham Jacob of Sadgora (1819–1883)

Scholars and ordinary folk

Some of the sages wondered why it was that scholars rarely raised sons who themselves became scholars. One authority ventured that this was their punishment for acting "highhandedly toward the community."

With the great value placed on scholarship, it was hard for scholars to avoid attitudes of superiority. But many were able to recognize their own failings in this regard and consequently made every effort to spread learning to the people. Hillel's democratic view of education rather than Shammai's elitist one became the norm.

A bastard who is learned takes precedence over an ignorant high priest.

—Mishnah, tractate *Horayot*,
chapter 3, paragraph 8

A scholar takes precedence over a king of Israel, for if a scholar dies no one can replace him, while if a king dies, all Israel is eligible for kingship.

—Babylonian Talmud, tractate
Horayot, page 13a

Emperor Hadrian's daughter said to Rabbi Joshua ben Hananiah, a learned but homely scholar, "Such great wisdom in such an ugly vessel!"

He answered, "Learn from your father's palace. In what kinds of vessels is wine stored?"

"In earthen jars," she said.

"Earthen jars! But that's what common people use," he answered. "You should store your wine in gold and silver vessels."

The girl went and had the wine transferred to gold and silver jars, and it all turned sour.

"You see," he said to her, "the Torah is the same way."

"But aren't there handsome people who are also learned?" she asked.

"Yes," he retorted. "But if they were ugly, they would be even more learned!"

—Babylonian Talmud, tractate
Nedarim, page 50b

The School of Shammai says: One ought to teach only a person who is talented and meek and of distinguished ancestry and rich.

But the School of Hillel says: One ought to teach every man, for there were many sinners in Israel who were drawn to the study of Torah and from them descended good, pious, and worthy folk.

—*Fathers According to Rabbi Nathan*, chapter 3

In a year of food shortages, Rabbi [Judah the Prince] opened his warehouse and announced that only men who had studied Scripture, or Mishnah, or Gemara, or Law, or Lore may enter and fill their needs. But the unlearned may not enter.

Rabbi Jonathan ben Amram, disguised so he could not be recognized, forced his way in and asked for food.

"My son," said Rabbi, "did you study Scripture? Did you study Mishnah?"

"No," answered the scholar.

"Then why should I feed you?"

"Feed me as one feeds a dog or a raven," came the reply.

And Rabbi fed him.

Later Rabbi regretted having shared his bread with an unlearned man.

"But perhaps," said one of his disciples, "this was really your pupil Jonathan ben Amram, who has made a principle of not allowing himself to gain material benefit from his knowledge of Torah."

The matter was investigated and found to be true.

After that, Rabbi opened his warehouse to everybody.

—Babylonian Talmud, tractate *Bava Batra*, page 8a

The study of Torah

The term "Torah" includes not just the Bible but the Talmud, the commentaries, and all of Jewish learning through the ages. It was this study of Jewish knowledge that the sages considered the essence of learning—all else is peripheral. The *Zohar* presents a mystical picture of the elusive yet deeply rewarding nature of the Torah for those who truly want to know it. Rabbi Hiyya, a second-century scholar, describes his personal efforts to keep Jewish learning alive in Palestine under Roman rule. The early-twentieth-century philosopher Franz Rosenzweig writes from the perspective of a Jew who had been on the verge of converting to Christianity before he decided to immerse himself in Jewish learning. Rosenzweig speaks of the Emancipation, which, beginning in the late eighteenth century, not only gave Jews political freedom in many of the European countries in which they lived but also exposed them to broad areas of Western culture from which they had previously been cut off. Many Jews reacted to emancipation by rejecting traditional Jewish values and teachings. Rosenzweig calls for a return to a serious study of the Torah, not in a parochial way but by bringing to it knowledge acquired from secular fields.

> These are the things whose fruits a person eats in this world while the capital remains for him in the world to come: honoring one's parents, the practice of loving-kindness, hospitality to strangers, and making peace between a person and his neighbor. And the study of Torah surpasses them all.
>
> —Babylonian Talmud, tractate *Kiddushin*, page 39b

> Like unto a beautiful woman hidden in the interior of a palace who, when her friend and beloved passes by, opens for a moment a secret window and is seen only by him, then again retires and disappears for a long time, so the doctrine shows herself only to the elect, but not even to these always in the same manner. In the beginning, deeply veiled, she only beckons to one passing. . . .
>
> Later, she approaches him somewhat nearer and whispers to him a few words, but her countenance is still hidden in the thicket of her veil, which his glances can

hardly penetrate. Still later, she converses with him, her countenance covered with a thinner veil.

After he has accustomed himself to her society, she finally shows herself to him, face to face, and entrusts him with the innermost secrets of her heart.

—*Zohar*, volume 2, portion
"Mishpatim," pages 99a–b

There was once a man in Israel who had a son who had no interest in learning. His teachers finally gave up and taught him no more than the book of Genesis. Eventually soldiers came to town, took the boy captive, and imprisoned him in a faraway city.

It so happened that Caesar came to the city where the boy was held and visited that very prison. He asked to see the books in the prison and among them saw one he did not know how to read.

"This can only be a book of the Jews," he said. "Is there someone here who knows how to read it?"

"Yes," answered the keeper. "I shall bring him to you."

The keeper called the boy. "If you do not know how to read this book," he said, "the king will have your head. It would be better for you to die here in prison than to have the king cut off your head."

"My father taught me how to read only one book," said the boy.

The keeper took him from prison, dressed him in beautiful clothes, and brought him to Caesar. The emperor set the book before the boy, and the young man read it from the word "In the beginning" until he reached "This is the history of the heavens" [the first chapter and part of the second chapter of Genesis].

When Caesar heard him he said, "Clearly the Holy One, blessed be He, stirred up His world only in order to return this child to his father." So he gave the boy silver and gold and appointed two guards to escort him back to his father.

When the sages heard this tale they said, "Even though this boy's father taught him only a single book, the Holy One, blessed be He, rewarded him. Think, then, what a reward will come to a person who goes to the trouble of teaching his children Scripture and Mishnah and Legend."

—Legend

Rabbi Hiyya said: To make sure the Torah would not be forgotten in Israel, what did I do?

I sowed flax, and from the flax cords I made nets. With the nets I trapped deer, gave their meat to orphans to eat, and from their skins prepared scrolls.

On the scrolls I wrote the five books of Moses. Then I went to a town that had no teachers and taught the five books to five children, and the six orders of the Mishnah to six children.

I instructed them, "Until I return, teach each other the Torah and the Mishnah." And that is how I kept the Torah from being forgotten in Israel.

—Babylonian Talmud, tractate
Bava Mezia, page 85b

It is to a book, the Book, that we owe our survival—the Book which we use, not by accident, in the very form in which it has existed for millenia: it is the only book of antiquity that is still in living use as a scroll. The learning of this book became an affair of the people, filling the bounds of Jewish life completely. Everything was really within this learning of the Book. . . .

Then came the Emancipation. At one blow it vastly enlarged the intellectual horizons of thought and soon, very soon afterwards, of actual living. Jewish "studying" or "learning" has not been able to keep pace with this rapid extension. . . .

. . . "Learning"—the old form of maintaining the relationship between life and the Book—has failed. . . .

A new "learning" is about to be born—rather it has been born.

It is a learning in reverse order. A learning that no longer starts from the Torah and leads into life, but the other way round: from life, from a world that knows nothing of the Law, or pretends to know nothing, back to the Torah. That is the sign of the time.

. . . There is no one today who is not alienated or who does not contain within himself some small fraction of alienation. All of us to whom Judaism, to whom being a Jew, has again become the pivot of our lives . . . we all know that in being Jews we must not give up anything, not renounce anything, but lead everything back to Judaism. From the periphery back to the center, from the outside in. . . .

. . . The oneness of the center is not something that we possess clearly and unambiguously, not something we can be articulate about. Our fathers were better off in that respect. We are not so well off today. We must search for this oneness and have faith that we shall find it. Seen from the periphery the center does not appear invariably the same. In fact, the center of the circle looks different from each point of the periphery. There are many ways that lead from the outside in. Nevertheless, the inside is oneness and harmony. Only the outset, only the point of departure, will be different for everyone. . . .

—Franz Rosenzweig (1886–1929), German philosopher and theologian, from the draft of a speech at the opening of the "Free Jewish House of Learning," which he founded in Frankfort on the Main, 1919

Educating boys/educating girls

"Above all, we pride ourselves on the education of our children," wrote the ancient historian Josephus. The talmudic teachers wrestled with many problems familiar to educators today: At what age should formal education begin? How many pupils can one teacher handle? How far should children be expected to travel for their lessons?

Attributed to the high priest Joshua ben Gamla, the educational system that became standardized sometime during the final years before the destruction of the Second Temple remained a model for Jewish educators for years afterward. However, it was by no means universal education, since it applied only to boys. From ancient times until modern, girls in most countries were excluded from formal Jewish education. There were a number of women through the ages who managed to become learned scholars by studying on their own or by being taught by fathers or brothers. But most women were given only a rudimentary Jewish education, focused on laws and customs relating to home life and to rules of purity for women. Few could read or write in Hebrew, or even understand the prayer book.

The education of women was not prohibited by law; the law simply did not obligate women to study or be taught, as it did men. To be sure, the dogmatic stand of Rabbi Eliezer ben Hyrcanus against teaching women Torah has been cited by later authorities as justification for denying women a Jewish education. But neither his position nor the opposite one advocated by Ben Azzai was a majority view among the talmudic sages or later rabbis. Maimonides, for example, opposed educating women, but he did acknowledge that some would study and be rewarded for their efforts. For the most part, scholars felt that there was no obligation to teach women the intricacies of the Bible or Talmud, since their lives centered around home and family, and their domestic duties took up almost all their time.

Over the years, girls—usually of well-to-do families—began to receive secular educations, in some countries achieving a far broader background than boys, whose studies were confined to Jewish subjects. As secular education for girls spread, Jewish leaders began to change their attitudes toward religious education. By the early twentieth century, separate religious schools for girls were established in some countries; there also arose a scattering of coeducational schools. Today, many Jewish day and afternoon schools in the United States and other parts of the world finally do provide equal coeducation in all aspects of Jewish studies.

He who studies as a child, to what may he be likened? To ink written on fresh paper.

But he who studies as an old man, to what may he be likened? To ink written on worn-out paper.

—Elisha ben Avuyah, in
Ethics of the Fathers,
chapter 4, paragraph 25

The world endures only for the sake of the breath of schoolchildren....

Schoolchildren must never be made to neglect their studies, not even for the building of the Temple. . . .

Every town that has no schoolchildren will be destroyed.

—Judah the Prince, in the
Babylonian Talmud, tractate
Shabbat, page 119b

Rav said to Rabbi Samuel ben Shilat: Do not accept pupils who are less than six years old, but from that age on you can accept them and stuff them with learning the way you would stuff an ox.

—Babylonian Talmud, tractate
Bava Batra, page 21a

At first if a child had a father, the father taught him, but if he had no father, he received no education.

Then it was decreed that teachers of children would be appointed in Jerusalem and fathers would take their sons to Jerusalem to be taught. But, again, fatherless children received no instruction.

Then it was resolved that teachers would be appointed in each district and that boys would receive formal education from the age of sixteen or seventeen. But as it happened, when a teacher punished a student, the student would often rebel and leave school.

Finally, Joshua ben Gamla organized an educational system in which teachers were appointed in every district and every town, and children entered school at the age of six or seven.

—Babylonian Talmud, tractate *Bava Batra*, page 21a

The Hebrew word tiflut *in this text has been variously defined as "obscenity," "frivolity," or "blasphemy." The implication is that women will corrupt the learning they receive. Interestingly, Rabbi Eliezer was married to a highly learned woman, Imma Shalom.*

Ben Azzai said: A man is obligated to teach his daughter Torah. . . .

Rabbi Eliezer said: Whoever teaches his daughter Torah teaches her obscenity [*tiflut*].

—Mishnah, tractate *Sotah*, chapter 3, paragraph 4

Let the words of the Torah be burned rather than entrusted to women!

—Rabbi Eliezer ben Hyrcanus, in the Jerusalem Talmud, tractate *Sotah*, chapter 3, section 4

How do we know that others are not commanded to teach women?

Because it is written: "And teach them to your sons" (Deuteronomy 11:19)—your sons, but not your daughters.

—Babylonian Talmud, tractate *Kiddushin*, page 29b

How do women earn merit?

By making their children go to the synagogue to learn Scripture, and their husbands to the house of study to learn Mishnah, and by waiting for their husbands until they return from the house of study.

—Babylonian Talmud, tractate *Berakhot*, page 17a

A woman who studies Torah will be rewarded but not in the same measure as a man, for study was not imposed on her as duty, and one who performs a meritorious act which is not obligatory will not receive the same reward as one upon whom it is incumbent and who fulfills it as a duty, but only a lesser reward.

—Maimonides, *Code*, "Laws Concerning the Study of the Torah," chapter 1, section 2

It seems that all this applied only in times gone by, where everyone lived near his father and our tradition was very strong for each and every one to conduct himself in the ways of our forefathers. As the sages say: "Ask your father and he will tell you." In this situation, we can say that a woman may not be taught Torah and she will learn how to conduct herself by watching her righteous father.

But today, when our father's tradition has become very weak and it is common practice not to live with our fathers, and women learn to read and write a secular language, it is certainly a great deed to teach them Bible and the moral traditions of our sages . . . so that the truth of our holy heritage and religion will become known to them, for if we do not do this they might completely leave the way of the Lord and transgress the tenets of our religion, Heaven forbid!

—Israel Meir ha-Kohen,
Likutei Halakhot,
"Sotah," page 21a

Gaining wisdom from the elderly

Legend says that Rabbi Eleazar ben Azariah was only eighteen years old when he was appointed head of the Sanhedrin, the highest legal body in Palestine. To ensure him the respect his position called for, a miracle occurred, and eighteen rows of white hair grew around his chin. As a result, he said, "Behold, I am like a man of seventy years old." (His words, in the Talmud, are repeated in the Passover *Haggadah*.) Age connotes wisdom, and studying with an elderly scholar, we're told, may benefit us more than studying with a young one.

He who learns from the young, to what may he be likened? To one who eats unripe grapes and drinks wine from the vat [new wine].

But he who learns from the old, to what may he be likened? To one who eats ripe grapes or drinks wine that's aged.

—*Ethics of the Fathers*,
chapter 4, paragraph 26

The older scholars grow, the more wisdom they acquire . . . but the ignorant, as they wax older grow more foolish.

—Babylonian Talmud, tractate
Shabbat, page 152a

If you have not gathered wisdom in your youth, how will you find it when you are old?

> Sound judgment sits well on gray hairs, and wise advice comes well from older men.
>
> Wisdom is fitting in the aged, and ripe counsel in men of eminence.
>
> Long experience is the old man's crown, and his pride is the fear of the Lord.
>
> —Wisdom of Ben Sira, chapter 25, verses 5–6

Student-teacher relationships

A student may bring out the best in a teacher just as a teacher may bring out the best in a student; each owes the other loyalty and respect. Like the Hellenistic philosophers, the rabbis considered a teacher the most exalted person in a student's life, worthy of even greater honor than that given a parent. But this relationship too has its limits: you stop short of doing anything for a teacher that might violate your own conscience.

> Disciples increase the teacher's wisdom and broaden his mind. The sages said, "Much wisdom I learned from my teachers, more from my colleagues, from my pupils most of all." Even as a small piece of wood kindles a large log, so a pupil of small attainment sharpens the mind of his teacher, so that by his questions, he elicits glorious wisdom.
>
> —Maimonides, *Code*, "Laws Concerning the Study of the Torah," chapter 5, section 13

When Rabbi Akiva was imprisoned for teaching Judaism against Roman orders, his pupil Simeon bar Yohai pleaded with him to continue his teaching from his prison cell. Akiva refused to endanger his student's life in that way but assured Simeon of his own powerful desire to teach, using the following imagery, which has come to symbolize a teacher's need for his pupil:

More than a calf wishes to suck does the cow desire to suckle.

—Babylonian Talmud, tractate *Pesahim*, page 112a

There are four types of students:

Quick to understand but quick to forget—his gain is canceled by his loss.

Understands with difficulty but forgets with difficulty—his loss is canceled by his gain.

Quick to understand and forgets with difficulty—the wise.

Understands with difficulty and quick to forget—this is an evil lot.

—*Ethics of the Fathers*, chapter 5, paragraph 15

There are four types among those who sit in the presence of sages: the sponge, the funnel, the strainer, and the sifter.

The sponge soaks up everything.

The funnel takes in at one ear and lets out at the other.

The strainer lets the wine pass and retains the dregs.

The sifter holds back the coarse and collects the fine flour.

—*Ethics of the Fathers*, chapter 5, paragraph 18

Let the honor of your student be as dear to you as your own, and the honor of your comrade as the fear of your teacher, and the fear of your teacher as the fear of God.

—*Ethics of the Fathers*, chapter 4, paragraph 15

A person who teaches Torah to his friend's child may be regarded, according to Scripture, as though the child had been born to him, as it says: "This is the line of Aaron and Moses" (Numbers 3:1), and then it goes on to say: "These were the names of Aaron's sons." This teaches us that Aaron bore children and Moses taught them, and therefore they were called by Moses' name also.

—Babylonian Talmud, tractate *Sanhedrin*, page 19b

If a person goes looking for property lost by his father and property lost by his teacher, his teacher's takes precedence over his father's because his father brought him into the world, but his teacher, who taught him wisdom, brings him into the world to come. . . .

If his father and his teacher each carries a heavy burden, he must help his teacher first and then his father.

If his father and his teacher were kidnapped, he must ransom his teacher first and then his father.

—Mishnah, tractate *Bava Mezia*, chapter 2, paragraph 11

The refrain, from the book of Exodus, "Keep far from a false matter," is brought in to reinforce the lesson that telling the truth takes precedence even over honoring teachers. A disciple may not shade the truth in the slightest, let alone openly lie, to help his teacher.

How do we know that a disciple who sits before his master and sees that a poor man is right and a wealthy man is wrong [although his master ruled the other way] should not remain silent? Because it is said: "Keep far from a false matter" (Exodus 23:7). . . .

And suppose a master says to a disciple: You know that if I were given a hundred *manehs* I would not tell a lie. Now, so and so owes me one *maneh* . . . I definitely have one witness against him. [At least two witnesses are required by Jewish law to force someone to repay a debt.] You stand in court and pretend to be a witness. You need not say anything so that you will not be telling a lie [but your presence may be enough to make him think you're a witness, and perhaps lead him to pay his debt]. Even so, it is prohibited, because it says: "Keep far from a false matter."

—Babylonian Talmud, tractate *Shevu'ot*, page 31a

Good and bad teaching

In spite of the high standards set, the model teacher has always been a rarity, to be cherished when found. At all times there have been too many teachers like those sketched by Solomon Maimon and Shalom Aleichem. Maimon tells about a ghetto school in Poland at the end of the eighteenth century. Shalom Aleichem describes a similar situation about a hundred years later in his *heder* in a small town in the Ukraine. He breaks off his story in the middle but leaves us with the clear impression that we needn't worry—cruel teachers *do* get their just desserts.

Rav once came to a certain town and ordered the people to fast and pray in order to bring down rain. But no rain fell.

The Reader of the congregation then went before the Ark and recited the words from the prayer book, "He causes the wind to blow," and immediately the wind began to blow. He then recited, "He causes the rain to fall," and rain began to fall.

Rav asked him, "What special deed have you done to merit such reward?"

The Reader answered, "I teach young children, those

of the poor as well as those of the rich. I take no fees from anyone who cannot afford to pay. Also, I have a fish pond, and if a child does not want to study, I give him some fishes to keep and win him over in that way so that soon he becomes eager to learn."

—Babylonian Talmud, tractate *Ta'anit*, page 24a

Rabbi Samuel ben Shilat was known as an outstanding and dedicated teacher.

Rav once found Samuel ben Shilat in a garden and said to him, "Have you deserted your teaching post?"

He replied, "I have not seen this garden for thirteen years, and even now my thoughts are with the children."

—Babylonian Talmud, tractate *Bava Batra*, page 8b

Rava said: If you have one teacher who is competent and another who is better, you do not replace the first teacher with the second, because under those circumstances the second might become lazy for lack of competition. But Rav Dimi of Nehardea said that the second would work even harder if appointed, in accordance with the saying, "Jealousy among scribes increases wisdom" [he would work hard to outshine the other].

Rava further said: If there are two teachers, and one goes through the lessons quickly but with mistakes and the other goes slowly but without mistakes, we appoint the one who goes quickly, because mistakes correct themselves in time. But Rav Dimi of Nehardea disagreed. He said we must appoint the one who goes slowly without mistakes, because once a mistake is fixed in a student's mind, it can never be eradicated.

—Babylonian Talmud, tractate *Bava Batra*, page 21a

A child may be transferred from one teacher to another who is more competent in reading or grammar, only, however, if both the teacher and the pupil live in the same town and are not separated by a river. But we must not send the child to school in another town nor even across a river in the same town unless it is spanned by a firm bridge, not likely to collapse soon.

—Maimonides, *Code*, "Laws Concerning the Study of the Torah," chapter 2, section 6

It is forbidden for a teacher to be up at night and attend school in the daytime, or to fast at the time of teaching, or to overeat, because these things impair his health and result in neglect in teaching children.

—Joseph Caro, *Code of Jewish Law*, "Yoreh De'ah," chapter 245, section 8

I must . . . say something of the condition of Jewish schools in general. The school is commonly a small, smoky hut, and the children are scattered, some on benches, some on the bare earth. The master, in a dirty blouse, sits on the table and holds between his knees a bowl in which he grinds tobacco into snuff with a huge pestle like the club of Hercules, while at the same time he wields his authority. The ushers give lessons, each in his own corner, and rule those under their charge quite as despotically as the master himself. Of the breakfast, lunch, and other food sent to the school for the children, these gentlemen keep the largest share for themselves. . . . Here the children are imprisoned from morning to night and have not an hour to themselves, except only an afternoon on Fridays and at the New Moon.

—Solomon Maimon,
Autobiography

———◆———

I was much too young to hate, but nevertheless I already hated my *rebbe*, Boaz.

How could I not hate him? How could one not hate a *rebbe* who did not let you raise your head? It was forbidden. Don't stand here! Don't go there! Don't talk to him! How could one not hate a man who didn't have a spark of compassion, who rejoiced at another's pain, bathed in his tears? . . .

One would think there was no greater humiliation than a whipping. But was there anything more embarrassing than being stripped stark naked and told to stand in the corner? No, even that wasn't enough for Boaz. Boaz demanded that you strip, remove your shirt and underwear, lay yourself face down without any help—and leave the rest to him.

Backside
whacks,
Backside
smacks . . .

. . . We sighed and groaned over our lot, which was as miserable and bitter as the Exile. We muttered and talked and sought means for ending this awful tyranny. . . .

[*The author describes a strike planned by the students in which every one of them would claim to be sick one day and not attend school. He refuses to tell us outright whether the plan came off, but we know that the students' lot must have improved because he concludes:*]

I just want to tell you briefly that Boaz is still alive. But, alas and alack, what a life it is. Years have passed since he taught a class. What does he do? How does he make a living? Ah me, he has to go begging from door to door. If you meet him some day . . . give him a donation, won't you? It's a pity. The poor man is down at the heels—a has-been!

—Shalom Aleichem, from
"Boaz the Teacher"

Tips for teaching

A variety of pedagogic suggestions are presented. Jesus' name, which appears in the last legend, was censored from most editions of the Talmud but is referred to in some early ones. The legend itself does not shy away from self-criticism by the rabbis. It has no historical basis, but it is meant to make a point: Teachers should think carefully about how they rebuke their students so that they don't alienate them as Joshua ben Perahyah did Jesus. Joshua probably lived a hundred years before Jesus; the author of the legend might have mistakenly telescoped the two periods because of the similarities in Hebrew of the names of Joshua ben Perahyah and Jesus, whom the rabbis sometimes called Jesus ben Pantira. (Pantira may have been another name for Jacob, father of Joseph, Mary's husband.)

"Train up a child in the way he should go," the book of Proverbs teaches. This means, if you see a child making progress in Bible studies, but not in Talmud, do not try to push him by teaching him Talmud, and if he understands Talmud, do not push him to learn Bible. Train him in the things that he knows.

—Judah the Pious,
Book of the Pious,
section 824

If the teacher taught and his pupils did not understand, he should not be angry with them or fall into a rage, but should repeat the lesson again and again until they have grasped its full meaning. . . .

A disciple should not feel ashamed before his fellow students who grasp the lesson after hearing it once or twice, while he needs to hear it several times before he knows it. . . . These observations apply only, however, when the students' lack of understanding is due to the difficulty of the subject or to their mental deficiency. But if the teacher clearly sees that they are negligent and indolent in their study of Torah and that this is the cause of their failure to understand, it is his duty to scold them and shame them with words of reproach, and so stimulate them. . . .

A teacher should set "pitfalls" before his pupils, both in his questions and in what he does in their presence, in order to sharpen their wits and ascertain whether they remember what he has taught them or do not remember it. Needless to add that he has a right to question them on a subject other than that on which they are at the moment engaged, in order to stimulate them to be diligent in study.

—Maimonides, *Code*, "Laws Concerning the Study of the Torah," chapter 4, sections 4, 5, and 6

Let not the teacher impose his yoke heavily on them [children], for instruction is only efficient when it is conveyed easily and agreeably. Give the children small presents of money and the like, to please them—this helps their studies.

—Elijah ben Solomon Zalman, the Gaon of Vilna, from a letter to his family, mid-eighteenth century

---

An attentive pupil will read on his own, and if one student is inattentive, put him next to a studious one.

—Babylonian Talmud, tractate *Bava Batra*, page 21a

When a person teaches children—some of whom are more brilliant than others—and sees that it is disadvantageous for all of them to study together inasmuch as the brilliant children need a teacher for themselves alone, he should not keep quiet. He ought to say to the parents, "These children need a separate teacher," even if he loses by making the division.

—Judah the Pious,
Book of the Pious,
section 823

One way of keeping students alert is by rousing them with startling statements as Judah the Prince did.

Rabbi was once lecturing when he noticed that his audience was falling asleep. Searching for ways to rouse them, he suddenly called out, "A woman in Egypt gave birth to six thousand children all at once."

One student, Rabbi Ishmael ben Yose, stirred out of his boredom, asked, "Who could that be?"

Said Rabbi loudly, "It was Jochebed, when she gave birth to Moses, because he is equal to six thousand people."

—*Song of Songs Rabbah*,
chapter 1, section 15

The dispute in this legend arose because of the double meaning of the word aksania, *which denotes either an inn or a female innkeeper.*

Our rabbis taught: Always let the left hand push away and the right hand draw closer. Not like . . . Joshua ben Perahyah, who thrust his disciple Jesus the Nazarene away with both his hands. . . .

What was the incident with Joshua ben Perahyah?

He once found himself in a certain inn, on the way from Alexandria to Jerusalem, and the owners paid him great respect.

"How beautiful is this *aksania*," he said, referring to the inn.

"My master, her eyes are too narrow," said his disciple Jesus, referring to the innkeeper.

"Wicked person," cried Joshua, "is that all you think about?"

Joshua sent forth four hundred horns and excommunicated Jesus [horns were blown at excommunication ceremonies].

The disciple came to him many times, pleading, "Receive me!" But Joshua refused to notice him.

One day while Joshua was praying, Jesus came to him again. The rabbi intended to receive him this time, motioning with his hand to wait until he had finished his prayers.

But his disciple thought he was being rejected once again. So he went and worshipped the moon. . . .

—Babylonian Talmud, tractate
Sanhedrin, page 107b

Developing study habits

Hillel's famous words "If not now, when?" are restated more specifically here. The legend about Rabbi Rehumei cautions that even studying, this most important of all activities, needs to be tempered by consideration for others.

Say not, "When I have leisure I will study." Perhaps you will have no leisure.

—Hillel, in *Ethics of the Fathers*,
chapter 2, paragraph 5

The advantages of reviewing are unlimited.

The person who has reviewed his chapter a hundred times is not to be compared with the person who has reviewed it a hundred and one times.

—Babylonian Talmud, tractate *Hagigah*, page 9b

Rabbi Rehumei, who studied at an academy away from home, used to return home on the eve of every Day of Atonement.

One year, he forgot to return home. His wife was waiting impatiently for him. Every moment she kept saying, "Now he's coming! Now he's coming!" When he didn't arrive, she became so depressed that tears flowed from her eyes.

At that moment, the rabbi was sitting on a roof. The roof collapsed under him and he was killed.

—Babylonian Talmud, tractate *Ketubbot*, page 62b

"At the tip of a pen"

Man's wisdom is at the tip of his pen
His intelligence is in his writing.
His pen can raise a man to the rank
That the scepter accords to a king.

—Samuel ha-Nagid (993–1055), Spanish poet and statesman

He who is able to write a book and does not write it is as one who has lost a child.

—Rabbi Nahman of Bratslav

Not everything that is thought should be expressed, not everything that is expressed verbally should be written, and not everything that is written should be published.

—Rabbi Israel Salanter

If you write anything, read it through a second time, for no man can avoid slips. Let not any consideration of hurry prevent you from revising a short epistle.

Be punctilious as to grammatical accuracy in conjunctions and genders. A man's mistakes in writing bring him into disrepute; they are remembered against him all his days. . . .

Be careful in the use of conjunctions and adverbs and how you apply them and how they harmonize with the verbs. . . . Endeavor to cultivate conciseness and elegance; do not attempt to write verse unless you can do it perfectly. Avoid heaviness, which spoils a composition, making it disagreeable alike to reader or audience.

—Judah Ibn Tibbon
(c. 1120–c. 1190),
author and translator,
from his Testament

It's never too late to learn

Legend tells us that Rabbi Akiva was a poor shepherd who didn't begin his studies until the age of forty, but then rose to become one of the greatest of all Jewish scholars. Anecdotes about his education appear in many sources.

It has been said that Rabbi Akiva learned nothing until he was forty years old. After he married the daughter of the wealthy Kalba Savu'a, she urged him to go to Jerusalem to study Torah.

"I'm forty years old," he said to her. "What can I accomplish? They'll laugh at me because I know nothing."

"Let me show you something," his wife said. "Bring me an ass whose back is injured."

When Akiva brought the ass, she covered its sore back with dust and earth and herbs so that it looked ridiculous.

The first day they took the ass to market, people laughed at it. They laughed the second day too. But on the third day nobody laughed any more.

"Go and study Torah," said Akiva's wife. "Today people will laugh, tomorrow they will not laugh, and the day after they'll say, 'That's his way.' "

—Legend

Delving into the unknown

An abiding mystical strain runs through all of Jewish literature, a powerful undercurrent beneath the surface of rational, legalistic discussions. By the twelfth century, this mystical leaning flowered into the Kabbalah, whose rich symbols and esoteric teachings have had a profound influence on the development of Jewish thought.

The poetic selection from the book of Job argues that while the human mind can, and should, try to understand the world around us, ultimate mysteries will always remain out of our reach. The talmudic sages endorsed that position and strongly opposed mystic delvings, but the very number of admonitions in the Talmud against searching out the secrets of the universe only proves how strong the pull of such studies was among the sages. The last passage hints that there are some chosen few, like Rabbi Akiva, who can penetrate the unknown yet escape unharmed.

Man puts his hand to the flinty rock
  and overturns mountains by the roots.
He hews out channels in the rocks,
  and his eye sees every precious thing.
He binds up the flow of rivers,
  and what is hidden he brings to light.
But Wisdom, where may she be found,
  and where is the place of Understanding?

Man does not know her place,
  nor is she found in the land of the living.
The Deep says, "Not in me,"
  the Sea says, "Nor with me."
She cannot be acquired for gold,
  and silver cannot be weighed as her price....
For she is hidden from the eyes of all living things,
  concealed even from the birds of the air.
Abaddon and Death say,
  "We have heard only her echo."
But God understands her way
  and He knows her place,
For He looks to the ends of the earth
  and sees everything under the heaven.
When He gave the wind its weight
  and meted out the waters by measure,
when He made a law for the rain
  and a way for the thunderbolt,
then He saw Wisdom, and described her;
  He established her and searched her out.
But to man He said,
  "To be in awe of the Lord—that is wisdom,
  and to avoid evil—that is understanding."

—Job, chapter 28,
verses 9–15 and 21–28

Whoever ponders on four things, it were better for him if he had not come into the world: what is above, what is below, what was before time, and what will be hereafter.

—Mishnah, tractate *Hagigah*,
chapter 2, paragraph 1

Each of the scholars in this passage was famous and highly regarded but none was as knowledgeable or as equipped to deal with the mysteries of the "Garden" they visited as Rabbi Akiva. The Garden is usually interpreted as the Garden of Eden; the visit, a metaphor for the attempts of these and other sages to reach mystical heights through contemplation and even ecstasy.

> Four men entered the Garden: Simeon ben Azzai, Simeon ben Zoma, "Aher" [Elisha ben Avuyah], and Rabbi Akiva.
>
> Ben Azzai looked and died; Ben Zoma looked and became demented; "Aher" cut off the shoots [a reference to his conversion]; Rabbi Akiva entered in peace and left in peace.
>
> —Babylonian Talmud, tractate *Hagigah*, page 14b

The dark side of knowledge

Superstition, rather than mysticism, is the subject of these passages, although some of the demons and spirits of folklore have their origins in mystical imaginings. Folk belief and superstition have always created their own reasons for happenings that seem to have no rational explanations. Even scholars sometimes became caught up in helping people protect themselves against unknown forces: the evil eye cast by a jealous person or a frightening demon lurking in the shadows.

> Blessings can come only to those things hidden from the Eye.
>
> —Babylonian Talmud, tractate *Ta'anit*, page 8b

> Just as the fishes in the sea are covered with water and the Evil Eye has no power over them, so the Evil Eye has no power over anyone descended from the seed of Joseph [anyone who can trace ancestry back to Joseph of Egypt].
>
> —Babylonian Talmud, tractate *Berakhot*, page 20a

If a person is afraid of the Evil Eye, let him take the thumb of his right hand in his left hand, and the thumb of his left hand in his right hand, and say, "I so-and-so am of the seed of Joseph, over which the Evil Eye has no power."

—Babylonian Talmud, tractate *Berakhot*, page 55b

Six things are said concerning demons: In regard to three they are like the ministering angels, and in regard to three they are like human beings.

In regard to three they are like the ministering angels: they have wings like the ministering angels, they fly from one end of the world to the other like the ministering angels, and they know what will happen like the ministering angels.

In regard to three they are like human beings: they eat and drink like human beings, they propagate like human beings, and they die like human beings.

—Babylonian Talmud, tractate *Hagigah*, page 16a

When a person takes extra care about demons they go out of the way to vex him. When a person is not very concerned about them, they do not bother him.

Nevertheless, people should be cautious.

—Babylonian Talmud, tractate *Pesahim*, page 110b

It is forbidden for one man to greet another at night for fear he may be a demon.

—Babylonian Talmud, tractate *Megillah*, page 3a

It once happened in our town that Abba Yose of Zaythor was sitting and studying near a fountain. A certain spirit that lived there appeared to him and said:

"You know, I have lived here for many years, and although you and your family came here morning and evening I never harmed you. Now a certain evil spirit wants to live here, and he will hurt people."

"What shall we do?" asked Abba Yose.

"Go and warn the townspeople," said the spirit. "Tell them that they should come here tomorrow with their hoes and shovels and watch the surface of the water. When they notice the water moving, all together they should strike their irons and cry, 'Ours wins!' And they must not leave until they see a clot of blood appearing on the surface of the water."

Abba Yose went and did what the spirit told him, and all the townspeople appeared with their hoes and shovels at the fountain. When they noticed a movement in the water, they struck at once, crying, "Ours wins! Ours wins!" And they remained there until they saw a clot of blood on the water's surface.

We learn from this that if spirits that were not created to receive help still need it, how much more do we who were created to receive help need it. And that is the meaning of the verse, "The Lord . . . send forth your help from the sanctuary" (Psalms 20:2–3).

—*Leviticus Rabbah*,
chapter 24, section 3

Interpreting dreams

In the Bible, Joseph rose to fame and an exalted position in the Egyptian government by interpreting Pharaoh's dreams. Some of the later sages took a more skeptical attitude toward dream interpretation. Rabbi Meir declared simply, "Dreams are of no consequence." And Rabbi Bana'ah described taking the same dream to twenty-four interpreters in Jerusalem and receiving twenty-four different interpretations. Still, many of the scholars put great stock in dreams, as did most ordinary people. Some of their interpretations sound uncannily Freudian; others seem like sheer fantasy. The story of Rava and the dream interpreter Bar Hedya shows the rabbis laughing at the "profession" of dream interpretation, yet being sufficiently drawn to it to want their own dreams interpreted.

A dream that is not interpreted is like a letter that is not read....

Neither a good dream nor a bad dream is ever entirely fulfilled....

Just as there can be no wheat without some straw, there can be no dream without some nonsense.

While a part of a dream may be fulfilled, the entire dream never is....

A person should wait for a good dream to be fulfilled for as long as twenty-two years....

Three kinds of dreams come true: a dream you have in the early morning, a dream a friend has about you, and a dream that is interpreted in the middle of another dream. Some add a dream that is repeated. . . .

A person sees in his dreams only what is suggested by his own thoughts.

—Babylonian Talmud, tractate *Berakhot*, pages 55a–b

Our rabbis taught: If a person sees a reed in a dream, he may hope for wisdom; if he sees several reeds, he may hope for understanding....

Pumpkins appear in dreams only to people who fear heaven with all their might.

If a person sees a donkey in a dream, he may hope for salvation....

If someone sees a white horse in a dream, whether

walking slowly or galloping, it is a good sign; if someone sees a red horse and it is walking slowly, it is a good sign; if galloping, it is a bad sign....

If a person sees a camel in a dream, death had been decreed for that person, but he has been delivered from it....

If a man dreams of having sex with his mother, he can expect to get understanding, for it is written, "Yea, you will call understanding 'mother'" (Proverbs 2:3)....

If a man dreams of having sex with his sister, he may expect to get wisdom, for it is written, "Say to wisdom, 'You are my sister'" (Proverbs 7:4)....

If a man sees a rooster in a dream, he may expect a son; if several roosters, several sons....

If a man dreams he is shaving his head, it is a good sign for him; his head and his beard, it is a good sign for him and his family....

If a person dreams he climbs up to a roof, he will gain a high position. If he dreams that he goes down, he will be degraded....

All kinds of drinks are a good sign in a dream except wine, because sometimes you can drink it and it turns out good, and sometimes you can drink it and it turns out bad....

All kinds of beasts are a good sign in a dream except the elephant, the monkey, and the long-tailed ape....

All kinds of fruits are a good sign in a dream except unripe dates. All kinds of vegetables are a good sign except turnip tops....

All kinds of colors are a good sign in a dream except blue.

—Babylonian Talmud, tractate
Berakhot, pages 56b–57b

Bar Hedya was an interpreter of dreams. He gave a favorable interpretation to people who paid him and an unfavorable one to people who didn't. Abbaye and Rava each had a dream. Abbaye gave him a *zuz*, and Rava gave him nothing.

They said to him, "In our dream we each had to read the verse, 'Your ox shall be slaughtered before your eyes' " (Deuteronomy 28:31). To Rava he said, "Your business will be a failure, and you'll be so unhappy, you won't be able to eat." To Abbaye he said, "Your business will prosper and you won't be able to eat from sheer joy."

Then they said to him, "We had to read in our dream the verse, 'Though you beget sons and daughters, they shall not remain with you' " (Deuteronomy 28:41). To Rava he interpreted the words literally, in their unfavorable meaning. To Abbaye he said, "You have many sons and daughters, and your daughters will be married and go away, so that you will feel as though they have gone into captivity."

[*They gave him a series of other verses, to which he gave opposing interpretations.*]

Later Rava went to him alone and said, "I dreamed that the outside door fell off." Bar Hedya answered, "Your wife will die."

Rava said, "I dreamed that my front and back teeth fell out." Bar Hedya said, "Your sons and daughters will die."

Rava said, "I saw two pigeons flying." He answered, "You will divorce two wives." . . .

Finally Rava went to Bar Hedya and paid him a fee. He said to the interpreter, "I saw a well fall down." Bar Hedya answered, "You will accumulate wealth without end." Rava said, "I dreamed that Abbaye's house fell down and the dust covered me." Bar Hedya answered, "Abbaye will die and you will be asked to become head of his academy." Rava said, "I saw my own house fall, and everyone came and took a brick." Bar Hedya replied, "Your teachings will spread throughout the world." . . .

Once Bar Hedya and Rava were traveling in a boat. As

they were disembarking, Bar Hedya dropped a book. Rava picked it up and found written in it: "All dreams follow the mouth" [their meaning comes from the mouth of the interpreter].

"You wretch!" cried Rava. "It all depended on you, and you gave me so much pain!"

—Babylonian Talmud, tractate *Berakhot*, page 56a

Looking to the stars

Many of the sages, like people in all generations, believed in the power of the stars to influence individual lives. Yet they managed to incorporate popular beliefs about astrology into their overall view of the world, maintaining that the stars and constellations, like everything else in the universe, are subject to the will of God. Even the most dire predictions of the astrologers, the story of Rabbi Akiva's daughter assures us, can be overcome with charity and good deeds.

Long after the days of the talmudic sages, the belief in the stars continued—and continues. The Hebrew word for star or planet, *mazal*, is still used to mean luck, as in *mazaltov*, or "good luck." Over the years, several Jewish thinkers became caught up in astrological speculation. One twelfth-century Spanish philosopher, Abraham bar Hiyya, devoted an entire book, *Megillat ha-Magalleh*, to interpreting history through astrology. He also became involved in a bitter dispute with a contemporary, Judah ben Barzillai, by insisting on postponing a wedding because the stars were not right. Maimonides was one of the few Jewish scholars who, in his time or for years afterward, spoke out against astrology, contrasting it with the "true science" of astronomy. He even made the somewhat startling statement that Jerusalem and the Second Temple had been destroyed because the people had become involved in astrological predictions. The letter he wrote to a group of French rabbis who questioned him about the validity of astrology stands out as a staunch defense of reason by an unequivocating man of science.

There is not a single blade of grass that has not its own star in heaven that strikes it and says, "Grow."

—*Genesis Rabbah*,
chapter 10, section 6

Not the constellation of the day but that of the hour is the determining influence.

A person born under the influence of the Sun will be distinguished. He will not depend on others, and he will be open. If he tries to steal, he will not succeed.

A person born under the influence of Venus will be rich and adulterous, because fire was created through that constellation.

A person born under the influence of Mercury will be wise, with a retentive memory, because Mercury is the Sun's scribe.

A person born under the influence of the Moon will suffer evil, will build and destroy, and again destroy and build, eating and drinking that which is not his own. His secrets will remain hidden, and if he tries to steal he will be successful. [This person is compared to the moon itself, which waxes and wanes and is generally secretive and dark because it has no light of its own.]

A person born under the influence of Saturn will be frustrated in his plans. Others say, all schemes against him will be frustrated.

A person born under the influence of Jupiter will be a righteous person.

A person born under the influence of Mars will be a shedder of blood. Rabbi Ashi remarked: either a surgeon, a thief, a butcher, or a circumciser.

—Babylonian Talmud, tractate
Shabbat, page 156a

Rava's statement falls out of line with the traditional view that the blessings of life come as a reward for good deeds. It reflects Rava's own mystical leanings and the folk belief that no matter who you are, you've got to have a little luck in life.

The length of a person's life, his children, and his wealth do not depend on merit but on the stars.

Compare the cases of Rabbah and Rabbi Hisda. Both were saintly rabbis; when either prayed for rain, it came. But Rabbi Hisda lived to the age of ninety-two, and Rabbah only to the age of forty.

In Rabbi Hisda's house there were sixty weddings; in Rabbah's house, there were sixty deaths.

In Rabbi Hisda's house even the dogs ate bread made of fine flour, and there was plenty to spare. In Rabbah's house, the people had only barley bread to eat, and not even enough of that.

—Rava, in the Babylonian Talmud,
tractate *Mo'ed Katan*, page 28a

Astrologers told Rabbi Akiva that on the day of his daughter's marriage, as she entered the bridal chamber, a snake would bite her and she would die. The rabbi worried a great deal about this.

On her wedding day, as she entered the bridal chamber, the girl removed a brooch she was wearing and pinned it to the wall. Unknowingly she pressed the pin of the brooch through the eye of a poisonous snake hidden in the wall. Next morning, as she removed the pin from the wall, she found the snake, dead.

"What good deed did you do?" asked her father, when told of the incident.

"A poor man came to the door on my wedding night," the girl answered, "and everybody was so busy at the wedding feast that no one paid attention to him. So I took my portion and gave it to him."

"You have done a very good deed," said Rabbi Akiva.

And from then on he taught that "righteousness delivers from death" (Proverbs 10:2). And not only from unnatural death, but from death itself.

—Babylonian Talmud, tractate *Shabbat*, page 156b

Know, my masters, that it is not proper for a man to accept as trustworthy anything other than one of these three things:

The first is a thing for which there is a clear proof deriving from man's reasoning—such as arithmetic, geometry, and astronomy.

The second is a thing that a man perceives through one of the five senses—such as when he knows with certainty that this is red and this is black. . . .

The third is a thing which a man receives from the prophets or from the righteous.

Every reasonable man ought to distinguish in his mind and thought all the things that he accepts as trustworthy and say: "This I accept as trustworthy because of tradition, and this because of sense perception, and this on grounds of reason." . . .

Thus you ought to know that fools have composed thousands of books of emptiness and nothingness. Any number of men, great in years but not in wisdom, wasted all their days in studying these books and imagined that these follies are science. . . .

This is why our kingdom was lost and our Temple was destroyed and why we were brought to this; for our fathers sinned and are no more because they found many books dealing with these themes of the stargazers, these things being the root of idolatry. . . .

Know, my masters, that every one of those things concerning astrology that its adherents maintain—that something will happen one way and not another, and that the constellation under which one is born will draw him on so that he will be of such and such a kind and so that something will happen to him one way and not another—all those assertions are far from being scientific; they are stupidity. . . .

And know, my masters, that the science of the stars that is genuine science is knowledge of the form of the spheres, their number, their measure, the course they follow, each one's period of revolution, their declination to the north or to the south, their revolving to the east or to the west, and the orbit of every star and what its course is. . . .

This is an exceedingly glorious science. . . . By means of it there may be known when the moon will or will not be seen, and the reason why one day will be long and another day short. . . .

It is this calculation of astronomical cycles of which the sages said that it is wisdom and understanding in the sight of the peoples. . . .

—Maimonides, from
"Letter on Astrology"

7

WORK, WEALTH, AND PHILANTHROPY

"A rich man toils to amass a fortune; a poor man, to make a slender living"

On the value of work ✦ Balancing labor and learning ✦ Two lessons for laggards ✦ Responsibilities of employers ✦ A worker's duties ✦ Call the Sabbath a "delight" ✦ On honesty in business ✦ The ethics of the marketplace ✦ "Fraudulent and honest persuasion" ✦ A consumer's obligations ✦ On borrowing and lending ✦ Gathering wealth and possessions ✦ The rich and the poor: a "rotating wheel" ✦ Understanding the pain of poverty ✦ Helping the poor ✦ Ways of giving ✦ Weighing your needs against another's ✦ Community responsibilities

A Jewish tradition, still practiced, is for the well-to-do to invite their poorer neighbors to enjoy a free meal at a wedding or other celebration. In "A Meal for the Poor," a short story about that tradition, the Yiddish writer Mordecai Spector tells of an unheard-of incident. Invited to the wedding of the daughter of Reb Yitzchok Berkovir, the poor in the town of Lipowitz refuse to attend. It seems they have already enjoyed a hearty repast at someone else's reception and feel no urge for another feast. They announce, however, that they would be willing to appear at the wedding if paid a ruble apiece to do so.

"The nerve of them!" shouts Reb Yitzchok in a rage, and then moans, ". . . What did I do to deserve such a fate? Why shouldn't I have the pleasure of giving a free meal to the poor?"

Angrily the rabbi orders the wedding to begin without poor people, determined to call their bluff. But the poor folk are not to be intimidated. "We've no fear that Reb Yitzchok will marry off his favorite daughter without us," they tell a visitor. "Where can he get another gang of paupers on the spur of the moment?"

They are right. Reb Yitzchok relents, promises each a ruble, and holds his wedding joyfully. Reb Yitzchok "laughed and cried at the same time. . . . And all the while he kept embracing the poor. . . . 'Brothers!' he cried out to them, dancing. 'We must be merry. Let us be merry as only Jews know how to be merry.' "

This story captures the very essence of the sages' outlook on wealth and poverty. From their perspective, there exists an almost symbiotic relationship between the well-off and the poor: each profoundly needs the other. The poor turn to the rich for sustenance and care; the rich depend on the poor to give meaning to their wealth. As Rabbi Akiva once explained to a Roman official, God doesn't provide for the poor, because He prefers people to do so and be "saved through them from the punishment of Hell."

This mutual dependency and responsibility of the well-to-do and the poor, in Jewish tradition, characterize many other economic relationships as well. Work, for example, is an obligation that falls on everybody—even God is pictured in biblical narratives as working to create the world and resting after His work is completed. Because work is so highly valued, no type of labor is demeaned. "You shall not abuse a needy and destitute laborer," the book of Deuteronomy commands; and from that injunction grow numerous laws about paying workers' wages on time, treating them with respect, and providing benefits for them as custom dictates. At the same time, the rights of employers are recognized and valued. The talmudists were fond of relating incidents of sages, hired as laborers, who refused to interrupt their work even to greet a friend or answer a question because they considered that cheating their employer.

In business matters, biblical warnings against dealing "deceitfully or falsely with one another" provide the basis for rules that meticulously monitor the activities of merchants and manufacturers. Although in some ways the scholars may now seem naïve about the intricacies of the marketplace, they knew well how to protect consumers from even the subtlest forms of fraud. With fine insight into the ways of a merchant, they argued such questions as whether a shopkeeper may sift beans in a way that leaves the best ones at the top of the barrel and to what extent an item may be spruced up to attract customers. But buyers, too, have their duties to the business community. A person should not pretend interest in buying something, the Talmud says, when he or she has no intention of doing so.

The reciprocity of needs and obligations comes through most clearly in the areas of finance and philanthropy. Though they spoke time and again of God's love for the poor, the sages did not necessarily see poverty as a virtue; and while they condemned the vain accumulation of possessions and the abuse of money and power, they did not regard all rich people as evil. With a compassion rooted in the humanistic pleas of the prophets and a realism often born of personal experience, they spoke of the degradation of poverty and the humiliation of having to depend on others for one's survival. With practical regard for worldly desires, they viewed wealth as a blessing that could lead to pleasure not only for its possessors, but for many less fortunate. For the true blessing of wealth, they taught, comes from the ability it provides to share with and help others.

Charity holds a dimension in Jewish tradition far beyond giving money or gifts to the poor. In fact, even recipients of charity are expected to give some charity themselves. Charity is an attitude: it is something you do, not only something you give. If you celebrate a moment of joy, you invite the needy to your celebration. If you can help someone find a job or lend someone money, you do so before being asked. You extend yourself for those in need in a way that causes the least embarrassment to them and draws the least attention to you. "The reward of charity," the rabbis maintained, "depends entirely upon the extent of the kindness in it."

From the words of the prophets to those of the medieval moralists, one theme is heard again and again. It doesn't matter how many religious rituals a person observes if that same person cheats in business, mistreats workers, or is too greedy to help the poor. The true measure of ethical behavior is how honest and fair you are, and what your commitment is to the welfare of others.

On the value of work

The "work ethic" has held a major place in Jewish thought since biblical times. Work is essential, the tradition affirms, both because it allows us to be self-supporting and because idleness leads to corruption.

> When Rabbi Judah went to the house of learning he would carry a pitcher on his shoulders, saying, "Great is labor, for it honors the person who does it."
>
> —Babylonian Talmud, tractate *Nedarim*, page 49b

> A man should love work and not hate work. For just as the Torah was given as a covenant, so work was given as a covenant, as it is said: "Six days you shall labor and do

all your work, but the seventh day is a Sabbath of the Lord your God" (Exodus 20:9).

—*Fathers According to Rabbi Nathan*, chapter 11

Even the rich must love work, that is to say, must engage in some worthwhile occupation and not remain idle—for idleness is the cause of terrible things.

—Menahem ben Solomon ha-Meiri (1249–1316), French scholar, commentary on *Ethics of the Fathers*, chapter 10, paragraph 1

Flay carcasses in the marketplace to earn a living, and do not say, "I am a priest and a great man, and this work is beneath my dignity."

—Rav, in the Babylonian Talmud, tractate *Pesahim*, page 113a

If a person says to you, "I have worked and have not achieved," do not believe him.

If the person says, "I have not worked, but still I have achieved," do not believe him.

But if the person says, "I have worked and I have achieved," you may believe him.

—Babylonian Talmud, tractate *Megillah*, page 6a

In the book of Genesis, Adam is cursed for eating of the forbidden fruit, with these words: "Cursed be the ground because of you; in anguish shall you eat of it all the days of your life. Thorns and thistles shall it bring forth for you, and you shall feed on the grains of the field. By the sweat of your brow shall you get bread to eat, until you return to the ground . . ." (Genesis 3:17–19). The rabbis interpreted the passage in this fashion:

> When the Holy One, blessed be He, said to Adam, "Thorns and thistles shall it bring forth for you," tears flowed from Adam's eyes, and he pleaded with God: "Lord of the Universe, shall I eat out of the same manger as my donkey?"
>
> But when he heard, "By the sweat of your brow shall you get bread," he felt relieved [knowing that unlike an animal, he would not just receive grain but would have a chance to work for the food he wanted].
>
> —Babylonian Talmud, tractate *Pesahim*, page 118a

Balancing labor and learning

Even the greatest scholars, Maimonides wrote, "worked as hewers of wood, as carriers of beams, as drawers of garden water, as iron workers, and as blacksmiths rather than ask anything of the community." The story of Rabbi Simeon bar Yohai underscores the point that society cannot be sustained by scholarship alone, no matter how selfless. Simeon is punished for "destroying the world" by his criticisms of people who work. A highly respected scholar, Simeon lived in Palestine in the middle of the second century. He openly opposed Roman rule and as a result was sentenced to death. He and his son Eleazer escaped and, according to tradition, hid out in a cave for twelve years.

> [While in the cave] a miracle occurred so that a carob tree and a well of water were created for them.
>
> Rabbi Simeon and his son would strip off their clothes and sit buried up to their necks in sand. All day long they studied, and when it was time to pray they dressed, said their prayers, and then undressed again so as not to wear out their clothes.
>
> They lived this way in the cave for twelve years. Then the prophet Elijah [who supposedly appeared occasionally

to the pious] came and stood at the entrance to the cave and announced:

"Who will tell the son of Yohai that the emperor is dead, and the decree against him has been annulled?"

Hearing these words, Simeon and his son left the cave. As they walked about, they saw a man plowing and sowing his fields. "These people give up eternal life for life here on earth," they exclaimed. Whatever they looked at was immediately burned up.

Then a heavenly voice called out and said, "Have you left your cave in order to destroy My world? Go back!"

So the two men returned and lived in the cave another twelve months, saying, "Even the punishment of the wicked in Hell is limited to twelve months." At the end of that time, a heavenly voice came forth and said, "Now, you may leave your cave."

—Babylonian Talmud, tractate *Shabbat*, page 33b

Splendid is the study of Torah when combined with some worldly occupation, for toil in them both puts sin out of mind.

But study [of Torah] that is not combined with work falls into neglect in the end, and becomes the cause of sin.

—Rabban Gamaliel, in *Ethics of the Fathers*, chapter 2, paragraph 2

If a person learns two paragraphs of the Torah in the morning and two in the evening, and is occupied with his work the rest of the day, it is as though he had fulfilled the entire Torah.

—*Tanhuma*, on Exodus, portion "Beshallakh," paragraph 20

Two lessons for laggards

Go to the ant, you sluggard;
Consider her ways and be wise;
Which having no chief, no overseer or ruler,
Provides her bread in the summer
And gathers her food in the harvest.
How long will you sleep, O sluggard?
When will you arise out of your sleep?
Yet a little sleep, a little slumber,
A little folding of the hands to sleep—
So shall your poverty come as a runner,
And your want as an armed man.

—Proverbs, chapter 6,
verses 6–12

As this legend begins, the emperor Hadrian sees an old man working hard at planting fig trees and asks him whether he expects to be able to enjoy the trees' fruits. The man answers that if he doesn't live long enough to eat the fruits of the trees, his children will eat them. "If you are privileged to eat of them," the emperor tells him, "let me know."

In the course of time, the trees produced figs. The man took a basketful to the emperor, explaining, "I am the old man whom you saw planting fig trees, and these figs are the fruits of my labor."

Impressed with the man's diligence and age, the emperor ordered that he be seated on a golden chair and his basket be filled with gold pieces.

His servant objected, "Will you show so much honor to an old Jew?"

The emperor answered, "His Creator honors him; shall I not do the same?"

Now, when the man's neighbor's wife heard his story,

she said to her husband, "The emperor loves figs. Take him some, and he will give you gold."

The man followed his wife's advice and appeared at the emperor's palace with a basketful of figs that he asked to have exchanged for gold.

Told about the man, the emperor flew into a rage. "Have this man stand at the palace gate," he ordered. "And everyone who comes in or goes out shall throw a fig in his face."

At the end of the day, the man was sent home, bruised and beaten. "I will pay you back in accordance with the honor I got!" he shouted at his wife.

To which she retorted: "Go spread the good news that it was figs and not lemons that you took, and that they were ripe and not hard."

—*Leviticus Rabbah*,
chapter 25, section 5

Responsibilities of employers

In a few powerful verses, the Bible lays the foundation for protecting the rights of workers, extending those rights to poor people who had to sell themselves as indentured servants in order to subsist. Shaped by biblical concepts, talmudic rulings insist on scrupulous fairness and consideration toward all laborers. To the extent that they could, the sages gave an employee the benefit of the doubt in any dispute with an employer. The anecdote about the sage Rabbah and his careless porters has become symbolic not only of great concern for the welfare of working people, but also of the concept of taking on responsibilities beyond the strict letter of the law in order to treat people kindly.

———◆———

If your brother under you continues in straits and must give himself over to you, do not subject him to the treatment of a slave. He shall remain under you as a hired or bound laborer; he shall serve with you only until the Jubilee year. Then he and his children with him shall be free of your authority; he shall go back to his family and return to his ancestral holding.

For they are My servants, whom I freed from the land of Egypt; they may not give themselves over into servitude. You shall not rule over him ruthlessly; you shall fear your God.

—Leviticus, chapter 25,
verses 39–43

You shall not abuse a needy and destitute laborer, whether a fellow countryman or a non-citizen in your communities. You must pay him his wages on the same day, before the sun sets, for he is needy and urgently depends on it; else he will cry to the Lord against you, and you will incur guilt.

—Deuteronomy, chapter 24,
verses 14–15

Whoever withholds an employee's wages, it is as though he has taken the person's life from him.

—Babylonian Talmud, tractate
Bava Mezia, page 112a

If a person hires workmen and asks them to work in the early morning or late evening, at a place where it is not the local custom to work early or late at night, he cannot force them to do so. Where it is customary to provide food for workmen, he must do so. If it is customary to give them dessert, he must do so—it all depends on local custom.

—Mishnah, tractate *Bava Mezia*,
chapter 7, paragraph 1

Most of us depend on our fellow man to perform hundreds of actions for us, and it happens frequently that after such work is performed, disputes arise between employer and employee with regard to payment due. When they finally part from each other, each is convinced that the other robbed him. . . .

As far as Jewish law is concerned, local standard and custom, as well as the time when the work is being done, decides the proper payment. . . . Who is able to know exactly what the local custom or standard is, particularly with regard to any specific work the employer might give the employee? Of necessity, then, if the employer wishes to do what is right, he is obliged to give the workingman whatever he demands. And that, too, is very difficult.

Therefore, anyone who wishes to . . . do the right thing should settle in advance what payment the workingman should receive and thus obviate any doubt.

—Israel Meir ha-Kohen,
The Love of Kindness

Some porters carelessly dropped a barrel of wine they were carrying for Rabbah bar Hana. As a penalty, he took their coats away from them.

The men went to Rav and complained and he ordered that their coats be returned.

"Is that the law?" Rabbah asked [knowing he had the law on his side].

"It is," answered Rav, "because Scripture says: 'That you may walk in the way of good men' " (Proverbs 2:20).

After their coats were returned, the workmen said, "We are poor men who worked all day, and we are hungry. Are we not entitled to get paid?"

"Pay them!" Rav ordered.

"Is that the law?" asked Rabbah [astounded that he should be ordered to pay people who carelessly destroyed his property].

"It is," came the answer, "for it is written: 'And keep the paths of the righteous.' "

—Babylonian Talmud, tractate
Bava Mezia, page 83a

A worker's duties

As sympathetic as the rabbis were to the hard life of working people, they were strict in their insistence that employees owe their employers a day's work for a day's pay. Within the area of employer-employee relationships, they also delved into the question of guardians—when one person watches over another's property. They set down four categories of guardians: an unpaid keeper, a paid keeper, a lessee, and a borrower, carefully detailing the obligations of each. In the last selection, a medieval legalist extends the concept of the guardian to a craftsman entrusted with precious jewelry, and discusses his responsibility to his patron.

Just as the employer is enjoined not to deprive the poor worker of his wages or withhold it from him when it is due, so is the worker enjoined not to deprive the employer of the benefit of his work by idling away his time, a little here and a little there, thus wasting the whole day deceitfully. . . . Indeed, the worker must be very punctual in the matter of time.

—Maimonides, *Code*, "Laws
Concerning Hiring,"
chapter 13, section 7

A worker must not work at night at his own work and then hire himself out during the day; not plow with his cow in the evenings and hire her out in the mornings; nor should he go hungry and afflict himself in order to feed his children—for by doing so he steals labor from his employer.

—*Tosefta,* tractate *Bava Mezia,*
chapter 8, paragraph 2

Someone once asked the rabbis, "How was the earth created?"

"No one has the exact answer," they said, "but go ask Joseph the Builder because there is no one more knowledgeable about these matters."

The questioner looked for Rabbi Joseph and found him standing on some scaffolding, in the midst of work.

"I have a question to ask you," the man called to the rabbi.

"I cannot come down to answer," the rabbi said. "I was hired for the day, and my time belongs to my employer."

—*Exodus Rabbah*,
chapter 13, section 1

The following ruling by Maimonides, based on the Talmud, was used by some later authorities as a source for allowing strikes by working people. His qualification, about causing irreparable loss, has also served as a source for forbidding strikes among policemen, firemen, and other crucial service personnel.

If a laborer began to work and then changed his mind, he may stop work—even if it is in the middle of the day, for it is said: "For it is to Me that the Israelites are servants; they are My servants" (Leviticus 25:55). They are God's servants and not servants unto servants [an employee does not belong to his or her employer]. . . .

But this is applicable only when no irreparable loss is incurred. In a situation where irreparable loss may be incurred, the worker is not permitted to change his mind.

—Maimonides, *Code*, "Laws
Concerning Hiring,"
chapter 9, section 4

A jeweler lost a ring he had been given to copy for a customer. The question asked in this responsum was: Is the jeweler considered a paid keeper who is held responsible for the ring, or is he simply a craftsman who is not responsible for the loss? The answer was often referred to by later authorities as an indication of the responsibility of craftsmen, like other workers, for property in their care.

> Certainly he is responsible for the loss. The pleasure he derives from looking at the ring, copying it, and getting paid for his work makes him responsible for the ring while it is in his possession. However, if Simon [the craftsman] had said to Reuben [the owner], "Take back your ring, I have a picture of it in my mind, and I know what to do," and Reuben had insisted, "Keep the ring so that you might look at it and not err in reproducing it," then I would say that Simon would not be considered a paid keeper. In that case, he would be simply someone watching over the ring as a favor, and not responsible for it.
>
> —David ben Solomon Ibn Abi Zimra,
> *Responsa*, volume 1, number 298

Call the Sabbath a "delight"

Work is honored, but respite from work on the Sabbath day is even more hallowed. Observing the Sabbath as a day of complete rest for all people, with special emphasis on the lowliest slave, is the Fourth Commandment. The Mishnah lists thirty-nine categories of work to be avoided on the Sabbath, such as plowing, weaving, writing, and lighting a fire, and discusses many subcategories that derive from them. Over the years the Sabbath took on a meaning far broader than the stoppage of work: it became a day set apart from all others, a day of holiness, of joy, of special ceremony, and of freedom from the everyday cares of the world. By extension, the concept of the Sabbath rest was applied to the seventh, or Sabbatical, year, when agricultural work ceased and the land lay fallow. During this year, also, all debts were canceled. The seventh times seven—technically, the forty-ninth but celebrated as the fiftieth—year became a Jubilee, a time to "proclaim liberty throughout the land, unto all the inhabitants thereof," according to the book of Leviticus. During the Jubilee, lands that had been sold were supposed to be returned to ancestral ownership, and slaves were set free. The Sabbatical and Jubilee years as described in the Bible have become part of the past. But the Sabbath day, from sundown Friday until nightfall Saturday, remains a cornerstone of Jewish practice.

The heaven and the earth were finished, and all their array. And on the seventh day God finished the work which He had been doing, and He ceased on the seventh day from all the work which He had done.

And God blessed the seventh day and declared it holy, because on it God ceased from all the work of creation which He had done.

—Genesis, chapter 2,
verses 1–3

Observe the Sabbath day and keep it holy, as the Lord your God has commanded you.

Six days you shall labor and do all your work, but the seventh day is a Sabbath of the Lord your God: you shall not do any work—you, your son or your daughter, your male or female slave, your ox or your ass, or any of your cattle, or the stranger in your settlements, so that your male and female slave may rest as you do.

Remember that you were a slave in the land of Egypt, and the Lord your God freed you from there with a mighty hand and an outstretched arm; therefore the Lord your God has commanded you to observe the Sabbath day.

—Deuteronomy, chapter 5,
verses 12–15

If you refrain from trampling the Sabbath,
From pursuing your affairs on My holy day;
If you call the Sabbath "delight,"
The Lord's holy day "honored";

And if you honor it and go not your ways
Nor look to your affairs, nor strike bargains—
Then you can seek the favor of the Lord.
I will set you astride the heights of the earth,
And let you enjoy the heritage of your father Jacob—
For the mouth of the Lord has spoken.

—Isaiah, chapter 58,
verses 13–14

On the eve of the Sabbath two ministering angels accompany a man from the synagogue to his home, one a good angel, the other a bad one.

If, when he arrives, he finds the lamp lit, the table set, and the bed covered with a spread, the good angel says, "May it be this way on another Sabbath, too." And the evil angel unwillingly answers, "Amen."

But if the house is messy and gloomy, the evil angel says: "May it be this way on another Sabbath, too." And the good angel is forced to say, "Amen."

—Babylonian Talmud, tractate
Shabbat, page 119b

On the Sabbath a tabernacle of peace is spread over the world, which is thus sheltered on all sides. Even the sinners in *Gehinnom* [Hell] are protected, and all beings are at peace, both in the upper and lower spheres, and therefore we conclude our prayer this day with the words, "who spreads a tabernacle of peace over us and over all His people Israel and over Jerusalem."

—*Zohar*, volume 1, portion
"Bereshit," page 48a

The meaning of the Sabbath is to celebrate time rather than space. Six days a week we live under the tyranny of things of space; on the Sabbath we try to become attuned to *holiness in time*. It is a day when we are called upon to share in what is eternal in time, to turn from the results of creation to the mystery of creation; from the world of creation to the creation of the world.

—Abraham Joshua Heschel,
The Sabbath

I shall never forget Shabbat in my town. When I shall have forgotten everything else, my memory will still retain the atmosphere of holiday, of serenity pervading even the poorest houses; the white tablecloth, the candles, the meticulously combed little girls, the men on their way to the synagogue. When my town shall fade into the abyss of time, I will continue to remember the light and the warmth it radiated on Shabbat. The exalting prayers, the wordless songs of the Hasidim, the fire and radiance of their Masters....

The jealousies and grudges, the petty rancors between neighbors could wait. As could the debts and worries, the dangers. Everything could wait. As it enveloped the universe, the Shabbat conferred on it a dimension of peace, an aura of love.

—Elie Wiesel, contemporary
author, from "To Be a Jew,"
in *A Jew Today*

On honesty in business

The thundering anger of the prophet Amos against businesspeople who defraud the public finds a counterpoint in the gentle piety of Rabbi Simeon ben Shetah in the last story. Amos's revenge against corruption will come from God. Rabbi Simeon's reward for honesty comes from hearing God's name blessed by a non-Jew. Both selections, and the others in this series, emphasize that honesty in business is as much a religious duty as the performance of religious law or custom.

You shall not steal; you shall not deal deceitfully or falsely with one another.

You shall not swear falsely by My name, profaning the name of your God; I am the Lord.

You shall not coerce your neighbor. You shall not commit robbery....

—Leviticus, chapter 19,
verses 11–13

Listen to this, you who devour the needy, annihilating the poor of the land, saying:

"If only the new moon were over, so that we could sell grain; the Sabbath, so that we could offer wheat for sale, using an *ephah* that is too small and a *shekel* that is too big [giving short measures of grain and charging excessively], tilting a dishonest scale and selling grain refuse as grain! We will buy the poor for silver, the needy for a pair of sandals."

The Lord swears by the Pride of Jacob: "I will never forget any of their doings."

—Amos, chapter 8,
verses 4–7

How hard it is for a merchant to keep clear of wrong or for a shopkeeper to be innocent of dishonesty! ...

As a peg is held fast in the joint between stones, so dishonesty squeezes in between selling and buying.

Unless a man holds resolutely to the fear of the Lord, his house will soon be in ruins.

—Wisdom of Ben Sira,
chapter 26, verse 29;
chapter 27, verses 1–3

Our sages have written that one does not have to guard himself against a really bad man who expresses his evil openly, nor against a really pious man whom one knows well to be sincere, but one must be on guard against the person who acts as if he were righteous, who kisses the prayer book, recites psalms and prayers day and night, yet in money matters is a "crook."

People think that such a person is really pious because he worships so earnestly . . . but in most cases people like him are not to be trusted.

True piety is determined by one's attitude to money, for only he who is reliable in money matters may be considered pious.

—Zevi Hirsch Koidonover
(died in 1712), Polish
scholar, *Kav ha-Yashar*

Rabbi Safra was once saying his morning prayers when a customer came to buy his donkey. Because he refused to interrupt his prayers, Rabbi Safra did not answer. Interpreting the rabbi's silence as disapproval of the price offered, the buyer raised his price. When the rabbi still did not answer, the buyer raised his offer again.

After the rabbi finished his prayers, he said to the buyer, "I had decided to sell you my donkey at the first price you mentioned, but I did not want to interrupt my prayers to speak to you. Therefore you may have it at that price—I will not accept the higher bids."

—Aha of Shabha (680–752),
Babylonian scholar,
She'iltot, section 252

Rabbi Simeon ben Shetah once bought a donkey from an Ishmaelite. His disciples came and found a precious stone hanging round its neck.

They said to Rabbi Simeon, "Master, 'The blessing of the Lord makes a person rich'" (Proverbs 10:22).

Rabbi Simeon replied, "I have purchased a donkey, but I have not purchased a precious stone."

He went and returned the stone to the Ishmaelite. The grateful merchant exclaimed, "Blessed be the Lord God of Simeon ben Shetah!"

—*Deuteronomy Rabbah*,
chapter 3, section 3

The ethics of the marketplace

Rabban Johanan ben Zakkai worried about whether to speak openly of the dishonest tricks of merchants and farmers. "If I speak of them," he said, "knaves might learn them. But if I don't speak of them, the knaves might think that scholars don't know of their devious practices." For the most part, he and other talmudic scholars not only discussed dishonesty in the marketplace but, because of the legal authority they held in the community, were able to lay down stringent regulations to control it. For example, they forbade hoarding food during a time of shortage to prevent prices from skyrocketing; they established one-sixth over market value as the maximum profit a seller was permitted to make; and at various periods they fixed prices on essentials such as food and clothing. Basing their decisions on biblical laws, they took pains to ensure that weights and measures used in business were accurate, and to have them inspected regularly by market commissioners. When producers and sellers found ways of getting around the laws, individual rabbis, such as Rabbi Huna and Rabban Simeon ben Gamaliel, took matters into their own hands.

The sages considered competition healthy and important in business. In the last passages, the majority even permitted merchants to attract children to their stores by giving small gifts, reasoning that competition for sales could lead only to better products and lower prices.

You shall not falsify measures of length, weight, or capacity. You shall have an honest balance, honest weights, an honest *ephah*, and an honest *hin* [kinds of measures].

—Leviticus, chapter 19,
verses 35–36

You shall not have in your pouch alternate weights, larger and smaller. You shall not have in your house alternate measures, a larger and a smaller.

You must have completely honest weights and completely honest measures if you are to endure long on the soil that the Lord your God is giving you.

For everyone who does those things, everyone who deals dishonestly, is abhorrent to the Lord your God.

—Deuteronomy, chapter 25,
verses 13–16

A wholesaler must clean his measures every thirty days, and a small producer once in twelve months.

Rabban Simeon ben Gamaliel says the reverse is true [a small producer should clean his weights more often because without constant use they may become sticky and unbalanced].

In addition, a shopkeeper must clean his measures twice a week, polish his weights once a week, and clean off his scales after every weighing.

—Mishnah, tractate *Bava Batra*,
chapter 5, paragraph 10

The scholar Samuel made a practice of hoarding food when the price was low. Then when prices went up, he would sell his food cheaply to the poor.

Word came from the other sages that he should stop doing that.

What was the reason?

His act of hoarding might raise prices, and once prices have been raised, they remain up.

—Based on the Babylonian Talmud, tractate *Bava Batra*, page 90b

---

It was said of Rabbi Huna that every Friday evening before the Sabbath, he would send a servant to the market to buy up whatever produce had not been sold and throw it into the river.

Should he not have given it to the poor instead?

He feared they would come to depend on him and not try to buy their own food.

Why did he not give the vegetables to the animals?

He believed that food meant for people should not be given to animals [and in that way be degraded].

Then why did he buy the produce at all?

He feared that if the food were not purchased, the farmers would lower their supply and raise their prices in the future [creating a hardship for the poor].

—Babylonian Talmud, tractate *Ta'anit*, page 20b

During the period of the Second Temple, women were required to bring sacrifices to the Temple in Jerusalem after every birth. Because most women could not travel to the Temple regularly, they often had to offer several sacrifices when they did go during special festivals. The usual sacrifice was a pair of doves, and the demand for them increased sharply at festival time.

It once happened in Jerusalem that the price of a pair of doves rose to a golden *dinar* [about 25 silver *dinars*].

Said Rabban Simeon ben Gamaliel, "By the Temple! I will not go to sleep tonight before the cost drops to one silver *dinar*."

He went to the courthouse and taught: If a woman has five births . . . she need bring only one offering and may then eat of the sacrificial meat, and she is not obliged to bring any additional offerings.

After that, the cost of a pair of doves fell to only one-quarter of a silver *dinar*.

—Mishnah, tractate *Keritot*,
chapter 1, paragraph 7

Rabbi Judah said: A shopkeeper must not give roasted corn and nuts to children [sent by their mothers to shop] because this encourages them to come only to him [creating unfair competition].

But the sages permit it.

Nor may a shopkeeper sell below the market price.

But the sages say, if he does, he is to be remembered for good!

—Mishnah, tractate *Bava Mezia*,
chapter 4, paragraph 12

"A shopkeeper must not give roasted corn. . . ."

What is the reason the sages have for allowing it? Because this shopkeeper can say to his competitors, "I give them nuts, you can give them plums."

"Nor may a shopkeeper sell below the market price. . . ."

What is the sages' reason for permitting it? Because he helps to bring prices down.

—Babylonian Talmud, tractate
Bava Mezia, pages 60a–b

"Fraudulent and honest persuasion"

Merchants are encouraged to make their products appealing to consumers—always, however, within the strictest limits of honesty.

A poor woman, an apple vendor whose stand was near the home of the Hasidic rabbi Hayyim of Zanz, once came to him complaining:

"Rabbi, I have no money to buy what I need for the Sabbath."

"And what about your apple stand?" asked the rabbi.

"People say my apples are bad, and they won't buy."

Rabbi Hayyim immediately ran out on the street and called, "Who wants to buy good apples?"

A crowd collected around him in no time at all. They handed out coins without looking at them or counting them, and soon all the apples were sold for two or three times what they were worth.

"Now you see," he said to the woman as he turned to go. "Your apples were good; all that was wrong was that people didn't know about it."

—Tale about Rabbi
Hayyim ben Leibush
of Zanz (1793–1876)

In this passage, "sifting beans" refers to removing the bad ones from the bin in which they are sold. The sages agreed that bad beans should be removed but may not be placed at the bottom of the barrel, where a customer can't see them.

Abba Saul says that a shopkeeper may not sift crushed beans. But the sages permit it. The sages agree, however, that he should not sift the beans at the top of the bin [leaving the bad ones at the bottom], for the only purpose for doing this is to deceive the eye.

It is forbidden to paint human beings [sold as slaves, to make them look younger], animals, and utensils [to improve their appearance].

—Mishnah, tractate *Bava Mezia*,
chapter 4, paragraph 12

Our rabbis taught: An animal may not be made to look stiff [its hair should not be stiffened to make it look bigger]. Its insides should not be blown up, and the meat may not be soaked in water [in a butcher shop, the meat should not be made to look bigger and fatter than it is].

Samuel permitted fringes to be put on a cloak [to make it attractive]; Rabbi Judah permitted fine cloth to be rubbed and shined; Rabbah permitted hemp-cloths to be beaten [to look thinner and finer]; Rava permitted arrows to be painted; Rabbi Papa ben Samuel permitted baskets to be painted.

But did we not learn in the Mishnah that it is forbidden to paint utensils?

There is no contradiction. The Mishnah is referring to repainting old utensils. The rabbis here are speaking of painting new wares to make them more attractive.

—Babylonian Talmud, tractate
Bava Mezia, pages 60a–b

. . . It is evidently proper for a man to praise his wares or, by resorting to persuasion, to earn for his labor as much as he can. We say of such a man that he is ambitious and will succeed. . . . But, unless he is very careful to weigh his actions, the outcome is bound to be evil instead of good. . . .

"But," you will say, "how in the course of bargaining can we avoid trying to convince our neighbor that the article we want to sell him is worth the price we are asking?"

There is an unmistakable distinction between fraudulent and honest persuasion. It is perfectly proper to point out to the buyer any good quality which the thing for sale really possesses. Fraud consists of hiding the defects in one's wares. . . .

—Moses Hayyim Luzzatto,
The Path of the Upright

A consumer's obligations

In any kind of buying, the purchaser is expected to show courtesy and consideration to both the owner and other buyers.

Just as fraud applies to buying and selling, it can also apply to spoken words.

A person should not say, "How much does this object cost?" if he has no intention of buying it.

—Mishnah, tractate *Bava Mezia*, chapter 4, paragraph 10

A person should not pretend to be interested in making a purchase when he has no money.

This is a matter known only in one's own heart, and of everything known only in the heart it is written: "Fear your God" [though others do not know your intentions, God does].

—Babylonian Talmud, tractate *Bava Mezia*, page 58b

If one person seeks to buy or rent either land or movables and another person comes and buys it, the second person is called wicked.

—Joseph Caro, *Code of Jewish Law*, "Hoshen Mishpat," chapter 237, section 1

Rabbi Giddal was negotiating for a certain field, and Rabbi Abbah went ahead and bought it. Rabbi Giddal then complained to Rabbi Ze'eira, who, in turn, took the case to Rabbi Isaac the Smith.

"Wait until Rabbi Abbah comes to Jerusalem for the next festival," said Rabbi Isaac.

When he came, Rabbi Isaac said to him, "If a poor man is examining a cake and another comes and takes it away from him, what then?"

"Then he is called wicked," answered Rabbi Abbah.

"And you, sir, why did you act as you did?" questioned Rabbi Isaac [referring to the field].

"I didn't know he was negotiating for it," answered Rabbi Abbah.

"Then let him have it now."

"I won't sell it to him," said Rabbi Abbah, "because it is the first field I ever bought, and it is not a good omen to sell it. But if he wants it as a gift, he may have it."

Now Rabbi Giddal was too proud to accept the land as a gift, quoting the biblical verse, "He that hates gifts shall live" (Proverbs 15:27).

And Rabbi Abbah would not take possession of it now that he knew Rabbi Giddal had been negotiating for it.

So neither took the land. It became known as the "rabbis' field" and was used as a place for students to congregate.

—Babylonian Talmud, tractate *Kiddushin*, page 59a

On borrowing and lending

The Bible forbids lending money on interest to fellow Israelites, although it does permit taking interest from "foreigners," who were not part of the Hebrew culture and economy. The talmudists proved stricter, frowning upon taking interest from anyone and extending the definition of "usury" far beyond interest collected on money lent. But by the fifth and sixth centuries, as the economic life of the Jews began shifting from agriculture to trade and commerce, many of the earlier restrictions on borrowing and lending money became inappropriate. At the same time, Jews faced increasing persecutions and harassments in many of the lands to which they had been dispersed. In many Christian countries, from the Middle Ages on, and especially after the Crusades, Jews were forbidden to own land, to take up trades, even to sell food and clothing to non-Jews. One of the few areas open to them was moneylending. Church leaders forbade Christians to take interest upon threat of excommunication; but, viewing Jews as "damned" in any event, they permitted moneylending by them. Kings, businessmen, and Church leaders themselves made Jews their moneylenders, often using Jewish businessmen as conduits to lend their money to others at exorbitant rates, which they then collected. Often, too, they imposed heavy taxes on Jewish communities or simply confiscated Jewish possessions as a way of recouping the interest they had paid. Caught in the trap of having to charge high rates in order to survive, on the one hand, and being condemned for their activities on the other, Jewish moneylenders became targets of vicious hatred and anti-Semitism. The degrading stereotypes of Jewish bankers and businessmen that developed in those days were the basis for Nazi campaigns against Jews and have remained typical of anti-Semitic attacks to this day.

Leon da Modena, a highly sophisticated and educated rabbi in Venice, explained the Jewish position on moneylending in a book he wrote on Jewish life and manners for his Christian friends. Published in Italian in 1637, the book was reprinted many times and translated into several languages. It became a source for later Jewish writings on the subject.

> If you lend money to My people, to the poor who is in your power, do not act toward him as a creditor: exact no interest from him.
>
> If you take your neighbor's garment in pledge, you must return it to him before the sun sets; it is his only clothing, the sole covering for his skin. In what else shall he sleep? Therefore, if he cries out to Me, I will pay heed, for I am compassionate.
>
> —Exodus, chapter 22, verses 24–26

> You shall not deduct interest from loans to your countryman, whether in money or food or anything else that can

be deducted as interest. You may deduct interest from loans to foreigners.

—Deuteronomy, chapter 23,
verses 20–21

Rabbi Meir says: He who lends on interest, saying to the scribe, "Come and write," and to the witnesses, "Come and sign," has no share in Him who decreed against taking interest.

—*Mekhilta of Rabbi Ishmael*,
tractate "Kaspa," chapter 1

Observe how all God's creations borrow one from the other:

Day borrows from night, and night from day....

The moon borrows from the stars, and the stars from the moon....

Wisdom borrows from understanding, and understanding from wisdom....

The heavens borrow from the earth, and the earth from the heavens....

All God's creations borrow one from the other, yet make peace with one another without lawsuits.

But if a man borrows from his friend, he seeks to swallow him up with usury and robbery.

—*Exodus Rabbah*,
chapter 31, section 15

If a man lends money to his neighbor, he must not live rent-free in his court, nor at a low rent, because that constitutes usury.

—Mishnah, tractate *Bava Mezia*,
chapter 5, paragraph 2

Usury taken even from a heathen leads to the loss of one's wealth. . . .

The permission to take usury from a non-Jew is granted only as a means of earning enough money to live on when no other means of subsistence exists.

—Babylonian Talmud, tractate
Bava Mezia, pages 70b–71a

They [the Jews] are obliged . . . to be exact in their dealings, and not defraud or cheat anyone, . . . either Jew or Gentile. . . .

As for that which some have spread abroad, both in discourse and writing, that the Jews take an oath every day to cheat some Christian and reckon it a good work: it is a manifest untruth. . . . So far it is from that, that many rabbis have written . . . that it is a much greater sin to cheat one that is not a Jew than one that is, both upon the account that the thing is bad in itself and because the scandal is greater. . . .

'Tis very true that the narrowness of their circumstances which their long captivity has reduced them to; and their being almost everywhere prohibited to purchase lands or to use several sorts of merchandises, and other creditable and gainful employments, has debased their spirits. . . .

For the same reason, they have allowed themselves the liberty to take usury notwithstanding [the biblical laws against it]. . . . But because they are not suffered to use the same means of getting a living as others which are brethren by nature, they pretend they may do it lawfully.

—Leon da Modena (1571–1648),
The History of the Present Jews Throughout the World

Gathering wealth and possessions

Obsessive acquisition of money and things is seen as both decadent and futile. Bahya Ibn Paquda's *Duties of the Heart*, written around 1080, influenced all later ethical writings in its emphasis on moral and spiritual obligations. Here Bahya attacks the uselessness of devoting one's life to accumulating material things at the expense of all other interests.

A lover of money never has his fill of money, nor a lover of wealth his fill of income. That too is futile. As his substance increases, so do those who consume it; what, then, does the success of its owner amount to but feasting his eyes?

A worker's sleep is sweet, whether he has much or little to eat; but the rich man's abundance doesn't let him sleep....

Another grave evil is this: He must depart just as he came. As he came out of his mother's womb, so must he depart at last, naked as he came. He can take nothing of his wealth to carry with him.

So what is the good of his toiling for the wind? Besides, all his days he eats in darkness, with much vexation and grief and anger.

—Ecclesiastes, chapter 5,
verses 9–11 and 14–16

A person should take account with his soul when he impetuously and industriously applies himself to his worldly interests, which he seeks to further with the utmost energy and keenest planning to the limit of his power....

He will then find that his thought on worldly affairs

is the highest of his thoughts, and his hopes thereon are the loftiest of his expectations, so that none of his various kinds of possessions is sufficient for him. He is like fire, which blows more fiercely the more wood is added to it. So, too, his heart and intent draw him day and night to his worldly interest. . . .

He looks forward to the seasons when merchandise should be accumulated and to the seasons when it should be sold. He studies market conditions, investigates cheapness or dearness of goods, and notes whether prices are rising or falling in all parts of the world. Neither heat nor cold, neither storm on the sea nor length of journeys in the desert deters him from traveling to distant places.

He does all this in the hope of reaching an end in a matter wherein there is no end and where there is a possibility that his exertions will be in vain, yielding nothing but protracted pain, trouble, and labor. And if he attains a little of what he hopes for, possibly all that he will have of it will be the taking care of it, managing it, and carefully saving it from mishaps, until it comes into the possession of the one for whom it was decreed.

—Bahya ben Joseph Ibn Paquda (end of eleventh century), Spanish philosopher, in *Duties of the Heart,* treatise 8, chapter 3, section 12

The rich and the poor: a "rotating wheel"

The differences between them may be vast, but folk wisdom reminds us that the rich are not necessarily happy nor the poor filled with despair. And both Shalom Aleichem and the Talmud question who, in the end, has a more meaningful life.

A rich man toils to amass a fortune, and when he relaxes he enjoys every luxury.

A poor man toils to make a slender living, and when he relaxes he finds himself in need.

—Wisdom of Ben Sira,
chapter 31, verses 3–4

Kasrielevky is the mythical town in which many of Shalom Aleichem's stories take place. Its inhabitants, every one of them poor, know how to laugh at their troubles and tweak the rich at the same time. In this story, a Kasrielevkite trudges across Europe and makes his way to Paris, to the very presence of the great and wealthy Baron de Rothschild. The following exchange takes place:

"Honor and power you don't need," said the Kasrielevkite. "What is it you are lacking? Only one thing. Eternal life."

"How much will it cost me?" asked Rothschild.

"Three hundred rubles," the Kasrielevkite replied.

"That much! Won't you reconsider?"

"No, absolutely not!"

So what could Rothschild do? He paid the man 300 rubles, one by one, for the secret to eternal life.

"If you want to live forever, this is my advice," said our Jew to Rothschild. "Give up this noisy Paris, pack your things, and come with me to Kasrielevky. There you will never die. Because in our town, no rich man has ever been known to die."

—Shalom Aleichem, from "Small
People with Small Views"

There is an ever-rotating wheel in this world. He who is rich today may not be so tomorrow, and he who is poor today may not be so tomorrow.

—*Exodus Rabbah,*
chapter 31, section 3

There was once a wealthy man who had no children. "What good is my wealth," he said sadly. "For whom do I work?"

People advised him to make generous contributions to the poor with his money, but he answered, "No, I will give my money only to someone who has lost all faith and despairs of ever enjoying life."

One day he saw a poor man lying on a dunghill in torn and dirty clothes. "Surely this man has lost all hope," the rich man said to himself. He gave the man 100 *dinars*, explaining to him why he had been chosen.

"Only the dead expect nothing from the world!" exclaimed the man. "As for me, I trust in God to lift me up and help me." And he refused to take the money.

The rich man, disgusted, decided he would go to the dead and hide his money among them, in a cemetery.

With time, the rich man lost all his wealth. In great need, he went to the cemetery to dig up the money he had hidden. The police, thinking he had come to rob graves, arrested him and brought him before the governor of the city.

"Don't you recognize me?" asked the governor.

"How would I know an important man like you?" answered the prisoner.

"I am the poor man who you thought had despaired of the world. You see, God remembered me, and my fortune changed," said the governor.

The two men embraced. The governor ordered that the man be permitted to take his money from the cemetery and also be given a free meal and a gift of charity every day for the rest of his life.

—Folktale in *An Elegant Composition Concerning Relief After Adversity*, compiled by Nissim ben Jacob ben Nissim Ibn Shahin

Rabbi Joseph, the son of Rabbi Joshua ben Levi, became ill and fell into a coma.

After he recovered, his father asked him, "What did you see?"

"I saw a topsy-turvy world," he answered. "The highest on earth were the lowest there, and the lowest on earth were the highest there."

"My son," said his father, "you saw a clear world."

—Babylonian Talmud, tractate *Pesahim*, page 50a

Understanding the pain of poverty

There is nothing in the world worse than poverty—it is the most terrible of all sufferings. A person who is crushed by poverty is like one to whom all the troubles of the world cling and upon whom all the curses mentioned in the Bible come.

Our rabbis said: If all the sufferings and pain in the world were gathered on one side of a scale, and poverty was on the other side, poverty would outweigh them all.

—*Exodus Rabbah*, chapter 31, section 14

A certain pious man had inherited great wealth. On the Sabbath eve, he would begin preparing for the Sabbath hours before sundown.

One time he had to leave his home shortly before the Sabbath because of urgent business. On the way back, a poor man begged him for money to help buy provisions for the Sabbath.

The pious man angrily scolded the poor man, "How could you have waited until the last minute to buy your Sabbath fare? Nobody waits so long. You must be trying to trick me into giving you money!"

When he came home, he told his wife the story of the poor man he had met.

"I must tell you that you are wrong," his wife answered. "In your whole life you never tasted poverty and have no idea what it is like to be poor.

"I grew up in a poor home. I remember many times when it was almost dark and time for the Sabbath, and my father would still be looking for even a piece of dry bread to bring home to his family. You have sinned toward that poor man!"

When the pious man heard this, he ran about the neighborhood to find the pauper, who was still seeking Sabbath food. The rich man gave the poor man bread and fish and meat and wine for the Sabbath. Then he begged his forgiveness.

—Folktale

The daughter of the wealthy landowner Kalba Savu'a betrothed herself to Rabbi Akiva, who was just a poor shepherd at the time. When her father heard of the betrothal, he vowed never to give a cent of his money or property to her.

The couple married in the winter. They were so poor they had to sleep on straw.

"If only I could afford it," Akiva told her as he picked straw from her hair, "I would give you a golden ornament with the picture of Jerusalem on it."

One day, the prophet Elijah came to visit them, disguised as a mortal. "Give me some straw," he cried out at their door. "My wife is about to give birth, and I have nothing for her to lie on."

"You see," said Akiva to his wife. "We think we are poor. There is a man who does not even have straw."

—Babylonian Talmud, tractate *Nedarim*, page 50a

Helping the poor

People are often ashamed of their poor relatives, a rabbinic passage observes, keeping distance so as not to acknowledge them. It's just the opposite with God, "for the poor are His people. When He sees a poor man, He cleaves to him." Many of the major teachings of the Bible and of later rabbis and moralists center around imitating this attribute of God's—reaching out to help the poor in whatever way possible. The Hebrew word for charity is *zedakah*, which also means righteousness. The poor have a right to charity, the tradition emphasizes, for giving it benefits the giver as much as the receiver.

If . . . there is a needy person among you . . . do not harden your heart and shut your hand against your needy kinsman. Rather, you must open your hand and lend him sufficient for whatever he needs. . . .

Give to him readily and have no regrets when you do so, for in return the Lord your God will bless you in all your efforts and in all your undertakings. For there will never cease to be needy ones in your land, which is why I command you: open your hand to the poor and needy kinsman in your land.

—Deuteronomy, chapter 15, verses 7–11

The following verses from Isaiah are read in synagogue on the Day of Atonement. The prophet answers people who ask why God does not pay heed to their prayers and fasts.

Is such the fast I desire, a day for men to starve their bodies? Is it bowing the head like a bullrush and lying in sackcloth and ashes? Do you call that a fast, a day when the Lord is favorable?

No, this is the fast I desire:

To unlock the fetters of wickedness and untie the cords of the yoke. To let the oppressed go free; to break off every yoke.

It is to share your bread with the hungry and to take the wretched poor into your home; when you see the naked to clothe him, and not to ignore your own kin. . . .

If you banish the yoke from your midst, the menacing hand, and evil speech, and you offer your compassion to the hungry and satisfy the famished creature—

Then shall your light shine in darkness, and your gloom shall be like noonday.

—Isaiah, chapter 58,
verses 5–10

A person should be more concerned with spiritual than with material matters, but another person's material welfare is his own spiritual concern.

—Rabbi Israel Salanter

Even a poor man who lives off charity should perform acts of charity.

—Babylonian Talmud, tractate
Gittin, page 7a

Tinneius Rufus, referred to in the Talmud as Turnus Rufus, was the Roman governor of Judea in the year 132, at the time of the Bar Kokhba rebellion, which Rabbi Akiva strongly supported. Although the following discussion and others like it in the Talmud are legendary, there probably was some contact between the two men.

Turnus Rufus put this question to Rabbi Akiva:

"If your God loves the poor, why does He not provide for them?"

Akiva answered, "So that we may be saved through them [by helping them] from the punishment of Hell."

"On the contrary," said the Roman. "The very act of charity condemns you to Hell because you are interfering with God's work.

"I'll illustrate with a parable: Suppose an earthly king was angry with his servant, and imprisoned him and instructed that he was to be given no food or drink. If a man went and gave him food and drink, and the king heard, wouldn't he be angry with that man? And you are called servants of God, as it is written, 'For it is to me that the Israelites are servants' " (Leviticus 25:55).

Rabbi Akiva answered, "I will illustrate with another parable. Suppose an earthly king became angry with his son, and put him in prison and ordered that no food or drink be given to him. If someone went and gave him food and drink, and the king heard about it, wouldn't he reward that person? And we are called children of God, as it is written: 'You are children of the Lord your God' " (Deuteronomy 14:1).

—Babylonian Talmud, tractate *Bava Batra*, page 10a

A certain man had been selfish all his life. When he was dying, his family urged him to eat. "If you give me a boiled egg," he said, "I'll eat it."

As he was about to eat, a poor man appeared at his doorstep and begged, "Give me charity!" The dying man turned to his family and ordered them to give the beggar his egg.

Three days later the man died. Some time afterward, the dead man appeared to his son, who asked him, "Father, what is it like in the world to which you have gone?"

His father answered, "Make it your practice to perform charity, and you will gain a place in the world to come. Throughout my life the only act of charity I ever performed was giving that egg to the poor man. Yet, when

I died, the egg outweighed all the sins I had committed, and I was admitted to Paradise."

Of him it is said: Never refrain from doing good.

—Folktale recorded in
Exempla of the Rabbis,
edited by Moses Gaster

During a drought, Rabbi Abbahu heard a voice in a dream declare: "Let Pentakaka [a person who commits five sins a day] pray and the rain will fall and the drought will end."

Pentakaka prayed, and the rains came. Rabbi Abbahu summoned the man.

"What kind of work do you do?" he asked.

"I commit five sins a day," the man answered. "I hire prostitutes; I'm an attendant at the theater; I take the prostitutes' clothes to the bathhouse; I dance and perform before them; and I beat the drum."

"And what good deeds have you performed?"

"Once when I was cleaning the theater, a woman came and stood behind the post and wept. 'What's wrong with you?' I asked her. She answered, 'My husband is in prison. I came here to hire myself out as a prostitute to get enough money to set him free.'

"Hearing that, I sold everything I had, including my bed and bedding. I gave her the money and told her to go redeem her husband and keep herself free of sin," the man explained.

Rabbi Abbahu said, "You deserve to have your prayers for rain answered."

—Jerusalem Talmud, tractate
Ta'anit, chapter 1, paragraph 4

Ways of giving

The Bible tells the touching story of how Ruth, the young Moabite woman, refused to leave her mother-in-law, Naomi, after the death of Ruth's husband in Moab. The two women returned to Judah, and Ruth went to the fields to "glean among the ears of grain" so that they would have food to eat. As it turned out, the field belonged to Boaz, Naomi's kinsman, and he later took Ruth as his wife.

For poor people like Ruth and Naomi, gleaning was crucial, for landowners were commanded by the Bible to leave behind a certain portion of their crops for the poor to take. Sheaves of wheat or ears of corn that fell on the ground during harvest, for example, automatically belonged to the poor, as did produce that grew at the edges of a field. The point was that farmers did not hand the gleanings to the poor; those in need simply took what was considered to be theirs. The same concept of avoiding handouts and allowing the needy to maintain pride while accepting help pervades all of Jewish teaching. Maimonides's "eight degrees of charity" is the most famous description of this principle.

When you reap the harvest in your field and overlook a sheaf in the field, do not turn back to get it; it shall go to the stranger, the fatherless, and the widow. . . .

When you shake the fruit from your olive trees, do not go over them again; that shall go to the stranger, the fatherless, and the widow.

When you gather the grapes of your vineyard, do not pick it over again; that shall go to the stranger, the fatherless, and the widow.

—Deuteronomy, chapter 24,
verses 19–21

The reward of charity depends entirely upon the extent of the kindness in it.

—Babylonian Talmud, tractate
Sukkah, page 49b

There are times when lending is better than giving.

Reuben, an honest man, asked Simon to lend him some

money. Without hesitation, Simon made the loan but said, "I really give this to you as a gift."

Reuben was so shamed and embarrassed that he would never ask Simon for a loan again. Clearly, in this case, it would have been better not to have given Reuben a gift of that kind.

—Judah the Pious,
Book of the Pious,
section 1691

If you want to raise a man from mud and filth, do not think it is enough to keep standing on top and reaching down to him a helping hand.

You must go all the way down yourself, down into mud and filth. Then take hold of him with strong hands and pull him and yourself out into the light.

—Hasidic rabbi Solomon
ben Meir ha-Levi of
Karlin (1738–1798)

There are eight degrees of charity, one higher than the other. The highest degree, exceeded by none, is that of the person who assists a poor Jew by providing him with a gift or a loan or by accepting him into a business partnership or by helping him find employment—in a word, by putting him where he can dispense with other people's aid. . . .

A step below this stands the person who gives alms to the needy in such manner that the giver knows not to whom he gives and the recipient knows not from whom it is that he takes. . . . An illustration would be the Hall of Secrecy in the ancient Temple, where the righteous would place their gifts clandestinely and where poor people . . . would come and secretly help themselves to succor.

The rank next to this is of him who drops money in

the charity box. One should not drop money in the charity box unless one is sure that the person in charge is trustworthy, wise, and competent to handle the funds properly....

A step lower is that in which the poor person knows from whom he is taking but the giver knows not to whom he is giving. Examples of this were the great sages who would tie their coins in their scarves which they would fling over their shoulders so that the poor might help themselves without suffering shame.

The next degree lower is that of him who, with his own hand, bestows a gift before the poor person asks.

The next degree lower is that of him who gives only after the poor person asks.

The next degree lower is that of him who gives less than is fitting but gives with a gracious mien.

The next degree lower is that of him who gives morosely.

—Maimonides, *Code*, "Laws Concerning Gifts to the Poor," chapter 10, sections 7–14

Weighing your needs against another's

Simply stated, the sages held the view that charity begins at home. In giving alms, as in other realms of responsibility, your own needs and those of your family take precedence over the demands of others. There are limits, however. In order to be given priority, your needs must be as pressing as those of other people. If you are in a position to help someone and don't because you would rather keep your money than give it to charity, rather buy your daughter a toy than feed a hungry child, then, said the rabbis, you are no better than an idol worshipper.

In the legends below, Nahum of Gamzu is punished because he attends to his own comfort before responding to a suffering man; Rabbi Hilkiah's wife is rewarded because she provides immediate relief to the destitute. Both convey the same idea: the poor cannot be kept waiting.

It is an act of charity for a man to support his grown-up sons and daughters, whom he has no legal obligation to support, in order that his sons should study Torah and his daughters be trained to follow the right way. The same holds true for a man who gives gifts to his parents when they need them. In fact, a man should give to his children and his parents before he gives to anyone else.

A man should give to his relatives . . . before giving to anyone else. . . . The poor in a man's household come before the poor in the town in which he lives. The poor of the town in which he lives come before the poor of another town, and the poor of the land of Israel come before the poor in lands outside Israel.

—Joseph Caro, *Code of Jewish Law*, "Yoreh De'ah," chapter 251, section 3

Nahum of Gamzu was blind in both eyes, his hands and legs were amputated, and his body was covered with boils.

His disciples said to him, "Master, you're such a righteous man. Why has all this happened to you?"

He answered, "I brought it on myself. Once I was traveling to my father-in-law's house, and I had three donkeys with me. One carried food, one drink, and one all kinds of dainties.

"A poor man stopped me and asked for something to eat. I answered, 'Wait until I unload my donkey.' I had barely managed to unload something when the man died.

"I laid myself on him and exclaimed, 'May my eyes that did not pity your eyes become blind; may my hands that did not pity your hands be cut off; may my legs that did not pity your legs be amputated.' And my mind was not at rest until I added, 'May my whole body be covered with boils.' "

—Babylonian Talmud, tractate *Ta'anit*, page 21a

Abba Hilkiah was the grandson of Honi the Circle-Drawer. Whenever the world needed rain, the rabbis sent him a message and he prayed, and the rains came.

Once the people needed rain desperately, and two scholars were sent to ask him to pray for it. . . .

He said to his wife, "I know these scholars have come to ask me to pray for rain. Let us go to the roof and pray before they ask, so we don't get the credit for the rain."

They went to the roof. He stood in one corner and she in another. Clouds and rain appeared first in the corner in which she stood.

When they came down, he asked the scholars why they had come, and they answered that they had come to ask him to pray for rain. "We know," they said, "that the rain has now come on your account. . . . But why did the clouds appear first in the corner in which your wife stood, and then in your corner?"

"Because," he answered, "she stays home and gives the poor bread, which they can enjoy at once, while I give them money, which they cannot enjoy at once."

—Babylonian Talmud, tractate *Ta'anit*, pages 23a–b

Community responsibilities

"I have never seen or heard of a Jewish community that did not have a community charity," Maimonides wrote. In spite of their great emphasis on charity as an individual act of kindness, the rabbis recognized the necessity for community activities if the poor were to be adequately cared for, and they legislated a variety of rules for setting up community funds. If community care was available, they strongly disapproved of door-to-door begging. But even a beggar, the Talmud says, must never be sent away empty-handed.

The single-minded commitment to charity among the early sages, with its strong biblical roots, laid the foundation in every country in which Jews lived for widespread philanthropic activities, usually involving services not only to Jews but to all the poor who needed them.

What is the meaning of the verse, "He donned victory like a coat of mail"? (Isaiah 59:17).

It tells us that just as in a coat of mail every small scale joins with the others to form a piece of armor, so every little sum of money given to charity combines with the rest to form a large sum.

—Babylonian Talmud, tractate *Bava Batra*, page 9b

The Roman emperor Claudius entrusted the king of Judea, Agrippa II (28–92), with the care and maintenance of the Temple in Jerusalem. According to the ancient historian Josephus, when repairs were completed, the leaders of the Jewish community attempted to set up a vast public-works project to keep the temple workers employed so that they would not become needy. Although Agrippa rejected one project, he did allow an alternative.

And now it was that the Temple was finished [repairs and rebuilding of the courts around it].

So when the people saw that the workmen were unemployed, who were above 18,000, and that they, receiving no wages, were in want, because they had earned their bread by their labors about the Temple . . . they persuaded him [Agrippa II] to rebuild the eastern cloisters. . . .

But King Agrippa, who had the care of the entire Temple committed to him by Claudius Caesar, considering that it . . . would require considerable time and great sums of money . . . , denied the petitioners their request about that matter; but he did not obstruct them when they desired that the city might be paved with white stone.

—Flavius Josephus, *Jewish Antiquities*, book 20, chapter 9

If a person resides in a town 30 days, he becomes responsible for contributing to the soup kitchen; three months, to the charity box; six months, to the clothing fund; nine months, to the burial fund; and twelve months, for contributing to the repair of the town walls.

—Babylonian Talmud, tractate
Bava Batra, page 8a

If a person begs from door to door we pay no attention to him.

A certain man who used to beg from door to door came to Rabbi Papa for money, but Rabbi Papa refused him.

Rabbi Sama said to Rabbi Papa, "If you don't pay attention to him nobody will. Is he then to die of hunger?"

"But," replied Rabbi Papa, "have we not been taught that we pay no attention to a beggar?"

Rabbi Sama answered, "We do not respond to his plea for a large gift, but we do respond to his plea for a small gift."

—Babylonian Talmud, tractate
Bava Batra, page 9a

Our rabbis have taught: We support the poor of the heathen along with the poor of Israel;

and visit the sick of the heathen along with the sick of Israel;

and bury the poor of the heathen along with dead of Israel;

in the interests of peace.

—Babylonian Talmud, tractate
Gittin, page 61a

8

GOVERNMENT, LAW, AND AUTHORITY

"If you pervert justice, you shake the world"

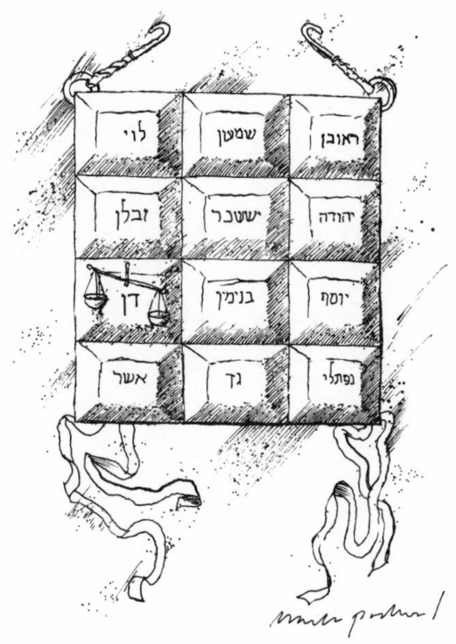

On the need for government ✦ "Beware of the ruling powers!" ✦ Moral responsibilities of officials ✦ The authority of the law ✦ "Wise men and understanding": choosing judges ✦ Pursuing justice ✦ Rights of the accused ✦ On capital punishment ✦ Responsibilities beyond the requirements of the law ✦ "For you were strangers in the land of Egypt" ✦ Assimilating into other cultures ✦ On civil disobedience and protest ✦ Rebelling against tyranny ✦ Compromise ✦ Attitudes toward war ✦ "Great is peace"

During the Babylonian Exile, more than 2,500 years ago, the elite of the land of Judah—princes, priests, and skilled craftspeople—were the first to be deported from their homeland by the Chaldean conquerors. Trying to make their way as strangers in a foreign land, the exiles received this message from the prophet Jeremiah, still in Jerusalem:

> Thus said the Lord of Hosts, the God of Israel, to the whole community which I exiled from Jerusalem to Babylon. Build houses and live in them, plant gardens and eat their fruit. Take wives and beget sons and daughters; and take wives for your sons, and give your daughters to husbands that they may bear sons and daughters. Multiply there, do not decrease.
>
> And seek the welfare of the city to which I have exiled you and pray to the Lord in its behalf; for in its prosperity you shall prosper.

These were comforting, yet in some ways shocking, words. What Jeremiah was telling the forlorn refugees was that both the Jewish people and the Jewish religion could survive outside the Land of Israel. Their beliefs could endure without a Temple and sacrifices. Their practices could continue without their own government.

Time, of course, proved the prophet right. The Babylonian exiles prospered and multiplied; and when they were permitted to return to the Land of Israel, about fifty years later, many chose to remain behind in Babylon.

Throughout the period of the Second Temple, a considerable number of Jews lived outside the Land of Israel. Their numbers grew after the destruction of the Second Temple in the year 70, and continued to increase in later years as political persecutions and hard times drove many from Palestine. Wherever Jews settled, they became part of the life of the community, and they prayed for the welfare of the government as Jeremiah had instructed long before. The guiding principle of Jewish political life became the dictum of the third-century talmudist Mar Samuel: "The law of the land is the law." In matters of taxation and government service, of civil and criminal legislation, Jews subjected themselves to the common law of the country in which they lived, for they quickly learned that their survival as individuals and as a group depended on the nature of their relationship to the government that ruled them.

However, acquiescence to the law of the land never meant denial of their own law. In many countries, Jewish communities had great autonomy in conducting their internal affairs, even convening their own courts and choosing their own judges to settle conflicts. Statements like the talmudic admonition to judges, "If the judgment you are about to give is as clear to you as the morning light, give it; if not, do not give it," grow from the practical experience of community leaders in arbitrating disputes.

Even in those areas in which jurisdiction was surrendered to government courts, the practices of Jewish law exerted strong moral pressure and raised issues of conscience. For example, long before the destruction of the Second Temple, the Romans took away the right of Jewish courts to inflict capital punishment. Yet the Talmud and later legal writings include detailed discussions on such matters as bringing a murderer to trial, cross-examining witnesses, and executing prisoners, posing serious questions about the use of the death penalty for any crime.

The moral and ethical influence of Jewish law remained—and remains—potent. Not satisfied that following the law strictly necessarily leads to justice, the sages often spoke of going beyond the requirements of the law to enforce what they felt was the spirit behind a ruling. The sage Rabbi Johanan once declared that Jerusalem had been destroyed because the people there adhered to biblical law. What other law should they have followed? he was asked. They should have gone beyond the limit of the law, he answered, moderating their judgments with mercy.

The concept of doing more than the law requires was extended to relationships with non-Jews. Persecuted and oppressed in many lands, Jews sometimes interpreted biblical distinctions among Israelites and "foreigners" as permitting discrimination against Gentiles. To counter such attitudes, Jewish leaders insisted on scrupulous honesty and fairness to all people, both as a moral imperative and as a way of sanctifying God's name.

For the most part, Jewish communities functioned well under their various legal systems, maintaining a careful balance between the precepts of their own law and the demands of the "law of the land." If conflicts arose over civil or criminal issues, talmudic law usually deferred to common law. Conflicts of conscience, however, were another matter. "Whoever disregards a royal order because he is busy with God's commandments—even the slightest commandment—is exempt," wrote Maimonides, reflecting a tradition of protest that goes back to the days when the prophets of Israel spoke out against the unjust actions of kings and priests.

At a few specific times in history, defiance led to armed rebellion. The revolt of the Maccabees, the last desperate stand of the Zealots at Masada, and the Bar Kokhba insurrection against Rome stand out as moments of great nationalism and courage. Events of our own day, such as the Warsaw Ghetto uprising, revolts at Treblinka and other concentration camps, and the State of Israel's battles for survival, fall directly in the tradition of those experiences.

Yet, while they honored the heroes of such struggles, the sages never glorified war or endorsed violence as a major means to effect change. Tradition holds that at the very moment when the Zealots were fighting their final battles in the city of Jerusalem, Rabban Johanan ben Zakkai received permission from the Roman commander Vespasian to open an academy of learning in the coastal town of Jabneh. As a result, he and the scholars who joined him are credited with sustaining Jewish institutions and teachings as we still know them.

The world rests on three things, the *Ethics of the Fathers* states: "On truth, on justice, and on peace." All three are intertwined, but the goal of the first two is to bring about the third. For Peace, said the sages, is God's name. And peace—*shalom*—is the ideal to which individuals and society must aspire.

On the need for government

Given the nature of human beings, the sages said, government is essential in any society. A special prayer for the government is generally included in Sabbath and festival services in synagogues throughout the world.

Pray for the welfare of the government, for were it not for the fear it inspires, every man would swallow his neighbor alive.

—*Ethics of the Fathers*,
chapter 3, paragraph 2

Scripture says: "You have made mankind like the fish of the sea, like creeping things that have no ruler" (Habakkuk 1:14).

Why are people compared to the fish of the sea?

Just as among the fish of the sea the larger ones swallow the smaller ones, so it is with people. If it were not for the fear of government, the stronger would swallow the weaker.

—Babylonian Talmud, tractate
Avodah Zarah, page 4a

The book of Proverbs says: "Go to the ant, you sluggard . . . which having no chief, no overseer or ruler. . . ."

Rabbi Simeon ben Halafta [known as an "experimenter"] decided to find out whether it was true that the ant has no king.

During the height of the summer he went to an ant hill and spread his coat over it. One ant came out, saw the shade, and went back and told the others that it was shady outside [ants supposedly hate the hot sun]. Immediately all the other ants came out. Then Simeon removed his coat, and the sun burned down on them.

All the ants jumped on the first one and killed it. Simeon said: "It is clear that they have no king, for if they did they could not have killed that ant without royal permission [laws would regulate their behavior toward one another]."

—Babylonian Talmud, tractate *Hullin*, page 57b

"Beware of the ruling powers!"

Not only the ruling powers but the power of ruling—and the corruption that too often accompanies it—has been a matter of concern for Jewish leaders. According to tradition, Judah ben Tabbai fled from Jerusalem when asked to become head of the Sanhedrin, the highest legislative body in Palestine. Finally persuaded to return and accept the honor, he was later asked to step aside because of an incorrect decision he gave in a case involving a capital crime. His description of the seductiveness of public office applies to many a "reluctant" politician today.

While the rabbis acknowledged the importance of government and insisted on utmost respect for authority, they took a more cynical attitude toward the officials who carry out government policy. The passages that follow reflect their fear and hatred of their Roman rulers. The story of Rabbi Eleazer ben Simeon is typical of their attitude toward informers who turned over fellow Jews to government officers. The feeling in talmudic times and throughout the centuries that followed was that the Jewish community should handle its problems internally, since it was unlikely that a Jew accused of a crime in a government court would receive a fair trial. Rabbi Eleazar made many enemies because of his cooperation with the Romans, especially since his father, Simeon bar Yohai, had been an open opponent of Rome. Tradition says that Eleazar later regretted his work and spent many years in deep penance.

Whenever someone said to me before I entered into high office, "Enter it," I had one wish: to hound him to death! Now that I have come into it, whenever someone tells me to quit it, I have one wish: to upset a kettle of boiling water on him!

For to high office it is hard to rise; and even as it is hard to rise up to it, so it is difficult to come down from it. For thus we find concerning Saul: When he was told, "Rise to kingship," he hid, as it is said, "And the Lord replied, 'He is hiding among the baggage'" (I Samuel 10:22); but when he was told, "Get down from there," he hunted after David [who was to replace him] to kill him.

—Judah ben Tabbai, in *Fathers According to Rabbi Nathan*, chapter 10

If you see in a province oppression of the poor and suppression of right and justice, don't wonder at the fact; for one high official is protected by a higher one, and both of them by still higher ones.

—Ecclesiastes, chapter 5, verse 7

Hillel said: A name made great is a name destroyed.

This teaches that one's name should not come to the attention of the government. For once a man's name comes to the attention of the government, the end is that it casts its eye upon him, slays him, and takes away all his wealth from him.

—*Fathers According to Rabbi Nathan*, chapter 12

Beware of the ruling powers! For they do not befriend a person except for their own needs: They seem like friends when it is to their own advantage, but they do not stand by a man when he is hard-pressed.

—*Ethics of the Fathers*,
chapter 2, paragraph 3

Rabbi Eleazar ben Simeon once met a Roman officer who had been sent to arrest thieves.

"How can you recognize them?" . . . he asked the officer. "Maybe you're taking the innocent and allowing the guilty to go free."

"What can I do?" replied the man. "I must carry out the king's orders."

"Here's what to do," said the rabbi. "Go into a tavern at breakfast time. If you see a man dozing with a cup of wine in his hand, ask him what he does. If he is a scholar, he probably woke up early to study [and is tired now]. If he is a day laborer, he may have risen early to do his work. If he's a person who works at night, he may have been working hard rolling out metal [by hand, so as not to disturb people who were sleeping] and is tired because of that. If he does not have any of these occupations, he is a thief. Arrest him."

Word of this conversation reached the king's court, and the rabbi was ordered to carry out his own advice.

Rabbi Eleazar immediately began to arrest thieves. Rabbi Joshua ben Karhah [Eleazar's teacher] then sent this message to him:

"Vinegar, the son of wine [evil son of a good father] how long will you continue to deliver God's people to the hangman?"

Answered Rabbi Eleazar, "I weed out thorns from the vineyard."

To which Rabbi Joshua replied, "Let the owner of the vineyard come and weed out the thorns Himself."

—Babylonian Talmud, tractate
Bava Mezia, page 83b

Moral responsibilities of officials

If the sages had few illusions about the government officials who ruled them, they did have ideals, stemming from the Bible, about what government and its leaders should be like. The book of Deuteronomy, for example, describes a dramatic ceremony in which the elders of a town clear themselves of responsibility for a murder that took place within their jurisdiction. As the Mishnah interprets the texts, the elders are held responsible because they might have had the power to prevent the crime or to protect the victim, and failed to do so. The prophet Nathan's parable, in the third selection, teaches that even kings may not hold themselves above the rules of morality. David had taken Bathsheba, wife of Uriah, for his mistress, then sent her husband to the front lines and arranged to have him killed in battle.

If, in the land that the Lord is giving you to possess, someone slain is found lying in the open, the identity of the slayer not being known, your elders and officials shall go out and measure the distances from the corpse to the nearby towns. The elders of the town nearest to the corpse shall then take a heifer which has never been worked, which has never pulled a yoke; and the elders of that town shall bring the heifer down to a watered wadi, which is not tilled or sown. There, in the wadi, they shall break the heifer's neck....

Then all the elders of the town nearest to the corpse shall wash their hands over the heifer whose neck was broken in the wadi. And they shall pronounce this declaration:

"Our hands did not shed this blood, nor did our eyes see it done. Absolve, O Lord, Your people Israel whom You redeemed, and do not let guilt for the blood of the innocent remain among Your people Israel." And they shall be absolved of bloodguilt.

—Deuteronomy, chapter 21, verses 1–8

"Our hands did not shed this blood, nor did our eyes see it done"—

But can it enter our minds that the elders of a court of justice are shedders of blood!

What they mean, however, is that the slain man did not come to us for help beforehand nor did we send him away without giving him food; nor did we allow him to leave the city without an escort.

—Mishnah, tractate *Sotah*, chapter 9, paragraph 6

But the Lord was displeased with what David had done, and the Lord sent Nathan to David. He came to him and said:

"There were two men in the same city, one rich and one poor. The rich man had very large flocks and herds, but the poor man had only one little ewe lamb that he had bought. He tended it and it grew up together with him and his children. . . . One day a traveler came to the rich man, but he was loath to take anything from his own flocks or herds to prepare a meal for the guest who had come to him; so he took the poor man's lamb and prepared it for the man who had come to him."

David flew into a rage against the man and said to Nathan, "As the Lord lives, the man who did this deserves to die! . . ."

And Nathan said to David, "That man is you! Thus said the Lord, the God of Israel:

" 'It was I who anointed you king over Israel and it

was I who rescued you from the hand of Saul. I gave you your master's house and possession of your master's wives; and I gave you the House of Israel and Judah; and if that were not enough, I would give you twice as much more. Why then have you flouted the command of the Lord and done what displeases Him? You have put Uriah the Hittite to the sword. . . . Therefore the sword shall never depart from your house—because you spurned Me by taking the wife of Uriah the Hittite and making her your wife. . . . I will take your wives and give them to another man before your very eyes and he shall sleep with your wives under this very sun. You acted in secret, but I will make this happen in the sight of all Israel and in broad daylight.' "

—II Samuel, chapter 12,
verses 1–12

The authority of the law

The selection that follows stands out as one of the great tributes to human reason and human law in talmudic literature. Among its many themes is the assertion that in legal decisions the majority rules. An individual may not bend the law at will no matter how convinced that person is that God is on his or her side.

Rabbi Eliezer ben Hyrcanus, a renowned and tragic figure in ancient Jewish life, lived during the period that spanned the destruction of the Second Temple. Although the details in this talmudic account are legendary, he did break with his colleagues on issues of law, dogmatically refusing to yield to their majority opinions. They finally excommunicated him, leaving him isolated from the center of scholarly activity at Jabneh. Yet they never denied the vastness of his knowledge. Many gathered around his deathbed to learn his last teachings; and as he died, Rabbi Akiva cried out the words that had been said of the prophet Elijah as he rose to heaven: "Oh, father, father! Israel's chariots and horsemen!"

The argument that escalates into an all-out struggle in this story revolves around a technical and relatively minor matter: the ritual purity of an oven, known as the Akhnai oven. Rabbi Eliezer insists that such an oven, which had been cut into sections separated by sand, could not become unclean, while his colleagues maintain that it could.

We learned: If an oven is cut into sections, and sand strewn between the sections, Rabbi Eliezer declares it clean, the sages that it is unclean. Such was the oven of Akhnai....

It has been taught: On that day Rabbi Eliezer brought forth every argument in the world, but the sages refused to accept them.

Then he said to them, "If I am right, this carob tree will prove it." The carob tree moved a hundred cubits from its place in the ground; some say it moved four hundred cubits.

They said to him, "No proof can be brought from a carob tree."

Then he said to them, "If I am right, this stream of water will prove it." And the stream of water began to flow backward.

But they said to him, "No proof can be brought from a stream of water."

Again he argued, "If I am right, the walls of the house of study will prove it." The walls of the house of study began to cave in.

Then Rabbi Joshua shouted at the walls, "If scholars argue with one another about matters of law, what right have you to interfere?" So the walls did not cave in entirely, out of respect for Rabbi Joshua, but neither did they straighten out, as a sign of respect for Rabbi Eliezer, and to this day they stand in an inclined position.

Rabbi Eliezer then said to them, "If I am right, heaven itself will prove it." Whereupon, a heavenly voice cried out, "What do you want of Rabbi Eliezer? The law always agrees with his views."

Rabbi Joshua rose to his feet and cried, "It is not in heaven."

What did Rabbi Joshua mean?

Rabbi Jeremiah said, "What he meant was that once the Torah was given on Mount Sinai, no attention need to be paid to a heavenly voice in matters of law. For it was written in the Torah, 'After the majority must one incline.' "

Rabbi Nathan met Elijah the prophet and asked him, "What did the Holy One, blessed be He, do at that time?"

Elijah replied, "He laughed with joy, saying, 'My sons have prevailed over Me. My sons have prevailed.' "

—Babylonian Talmud, tractate
Bava Mezia, page 59b

"Wise men and understanding": choosing judges

In ancient Judea, the court system was headed by a supreme court, called the great Sanhedrin, made up of seventy-one members whose head was the *nasi*, or president. Lower courts, known as small Sanhedrin, consisted of twenty-three members; and in small communities, courts of three judges were convened to handle many civil matters. There was no jury system, so judges carried great burdens of responsibility. Standards for choosing judges grew out of biblical teachings. Moses's father-in-law, for example, suggested that he get help in settling conflicts among the people, advising, "Seek out from among all the people capable men who fear God, trustworthy men who spurn ill-gotten gain."

The final talmudic passage tells of the deterioration of Jewish society before the fall of the Second Temple, implying that when judges become corrupt, the corruption eats away at all segments of the community.

Only those are eligible to serve as members of the Sanhedrin—whether the great or small Sanhedrin—who are wise men and understanding, that is, who are experts in the Torah and versed in many other branches of learning; who possess some knowledge of the general sciences such as medicine, mathematics, the calculation of cycles, and constellations; and are somewhat acquainted with astrology, the arts of the diviners, soothsayers, sorcerers, the superstitious practices of idolaters, and similar matters, so that they be competent to deal with cases requiring such knowledge. . . .

Neither a very aged man nor a eunuch is appointed to any Sanhedrin, since these are apt to be wanting in tenderness; nor is one who is childless appointed, because a member of the Sanhedrin must be a person who is sympathetic. . . .

Every conceivable effort should be made to the end that all the members of that tribunal be of mature age, imposing stature, good appearance, that they be able to express their views in clear and well-chosen words, and be conversant with most of the spoken languages, in order that the Sanhedrin may dispense with the services of an interpreter.

In the case of a court of three, all the above-mentioned requirements are not insisted upon. Nevertheless, it is essential that every one of the members thereof possess the following seven qualifications: wisdom, humility, fear of God, disdain of gain, love of truth, love of his fellow men, and a good reputation. . . .

And just as Moses our Teacher was humble, so every judge should be humble.

—Maimonides, *Code*, "Laws Concerning the Sanhedrin," chapter 2, sections 1, 3, 6, and 7

Every judge who judges truthfully, even for a single hour, is credited as though he had become a partner with God in the creation of the world.

—Babylonian Talmud, tractate *Shabbat*, page 10a

A judge should always think of himself as though he had a sword hanging over his head, and Hell gaping below him.

—Babylonian Talmud, tractate
Sanhedrin, page 7a

A man should not act as a judge either for someone he loves or for someone he hates. For no man can see the guilt of someone he loves or the good qualities in someone he hates.

—Babylonian Talmud, tractate
Ketubbot, page 105b

When those who displayed partiality in judgment multiplied . . . people threw off the yoke of heaven and placed upon themselves the yoke of human beings.

When those who engaged in whisperings in judgment multiplied [influencing judges to take sides] . . the *Shekhinah* [Divine Presence] departed. . . .

When there multiplied judges who said, "I accept your favor" or "I appreciate your favor," there was an increase of "Every man did as he pleased" (Judges 17:6). Commonpeople were raised to high offices and great people were brought low, and the kingdom of Israel deteriorated more and more.

—Babylonian Talmud, tractate
Sotah, page 47b

Pursuing justice

The basic tenets of justice are clearly spelled out in the Bible: a judge, a law court, a government leader, must be absolutely fair in judgment, avoiding the slightest tinge of partiality and even suppressing the inclination to favor a poor person over a rich one. But the talmudic sages were divided on how far compromise should be worked into the legal system. Some maintained, for example, that litigants could settle their disputes by compromise and arbitration rather than according to the laws governing their specific case. Others held that arbitration was a distortion of the strict justice that should be adhered to. The Talmud never resolved the issue, although later legal codes left it to the litigants to decide beforehand whether they wanted their dispute judged according to law or resolved by compromise and arbitration. The tension between strict justice and compromise in the Jewish tradition is often personified in the contrast between Moses, the stern lawgiver, and his brother Aaron, who sometimes bent the truth to settle conflicts.

Do not make a mockery of justice, for it is one of the three pillars of the world.

Why?

Because our sages taught: "On three things the world stands: on justice, on truth, and on peace." Know, then, that if you pervert justice, you shake the world, for justice is one of its pillars.

—Rabban Simeon ben Gamaliel,
in *Deuteronomy Rabbah*,
chapter 5, section 1

Hear out your fellow men and decide justly between any man and a fellow Israelite or a stranger.

You shall not be partial in judgment: hear out low and high alike. Fear no man, for judgment is God's. . . .

—Deuteronomy, chapter 1,
verses 16–17

"Hear out your fellow men and decide justly"—Rabbi Hanina said this is a warning to the judge not to listen to the claims of one litigant before his opponent arrives, and to the litigant not to try to explain his case to the judge before his opponent arrives. . . .

"You shall not be partial in judgment"—Rabbi Judah said this means that you shall not favor anyone and Rabbi Eleazar said it means you shall not be biased against anyone. . . .

"Hear out low and high alike"—Resh Lakish said that this verse shows that a lawsuit involving a small sum of money must be considered just as important as one involving a large sum.

Why is this stated? It is self-evident that every case must be given equal consideration.

Rather, the verse shows the need to give proper priority to even the most minor case—if it is first in order, it should be taken first.

—Babylonian Talmud, tractate *Sanhedrin*, pages 7b–8a

You shall not render an unfair decision: do not favor the poor or show deference to the rich; judge your neighbor fairly.

—Leviticus, chapter 19, verse 15

"Do not favor the poor"—Do not say, "This is a poor man, and in any event the rich man has to support him. I will judge in his favor and in that way he will receive some support in a respectable fashion."

"Or show deference to the rich"—Do not say, "This is a rich man, of noble descent, how can I possibly shame him and witness his shame?"

—Rashi, commentary on Leviticus, chapter 19, verse 15

If two people come to court, and one is dressed in rags and the other in fine clothes worth a hundred *manehs*, the court should say to the well-dressed person: "Either you dress like him, or dress him like yourself."

When litigants would come before Rabbah bar Huna, he would say to them, "Remove your fine shoes, and come for your case."

—Babylonian Talmud, tractate *Shevu'ot*, page 31a

Justice, justice shall you pursue, that you may thrive and occupy the land that the Lord your God is giving you.

—Deuteronomy, chapter 16, verse 20

It has been taught: The first use of the word "justice" refers to a decision based on strict law; the second to a compromise.

How so?

For example, two boats meet on a river. If both try to pass at the same time, they will collide and both will sink. But if one makes way for the other, both can go through without accident.

In the same way, two camels meet on the road up to Beth Haran. If they both keep climbing the road at the same time, both may fall down into the valley below. But if one goes first and the other afterward, they can both go up safely.

How should they decide who goes first? If one camel is laden with goods and the other is unladen, the unladen should give way to the laden. If one is closer to the destination than the other, the one that is farther away should step aside for the other.

But if both are equal distance from their destination, they should compromise, with the one who goes first compensating the other for giving way.

—Babylonian Talmud, tractate *Sanhedrin*, page 32b

Moses' motto was: Let the law cut through the mountain.

But Aaron loved peace and pursued peace and made peace between man and man.

—Babylonian Talmud, tractate *Sanhedrin*, page 6b

Rights of the accused

Jewish law attached so many conditions to proving a person guilty, especially in criminal cases, that conviction was generally much harder to achieve than in Roman law. In any crime, two witnesses had to testify not only that they saw the person commit the crime but also that they warned the person against violating the law. Even in civil cases, witnesses were thoroughly examined. Although in monetary matters admissions of guilt were accepted, in criminal cases the accused was not permitted to testify against himself or herself, which ruled out the possible use of torture to extract a confession.

The rabbis took great pains to ensure that if someone was convicted, punishment was administered in the most humane way possible. For example, when a person was flogged—a common punishment in ancient and medieval times—a doctor had to be present to check that the strain on the prisoner did not become too great.

How are witnesses to be examined? They are brought into a room and instilled with awe. Then all are sent out except for the chief witness.

The judges say to him, "Tell us, how do you know that so-and-so owes money to so-and-so?"

If he answers, "He told me, 'I owe him the money,' or so-and-so told me that he owes him money," his statement is worthless. He must be able to declare, "In our presence, he acknowledged to the other person that he owes him 200 *zuz*."

After that the second witness is admitted and examined. If their testimonies agree, the judges discuss the case.

—Mishnah, tractate *Sanhedrin*,
chapter 3, paragraph 6

A man is his own relative, and consequently no man may declare himself wicked.

—Babylonian Talmud, tractate
Yevamot, page 25b

It is a scriptural decree that the court shall not put a man to death or flog him on his own admission [of guilt]. This is done only on the evidence of two witnesses. . . .

For it is possible that he was confused in mind when he made the confession. Perhaps he was one of those who are in misery, bitter in soul, who long for death, thrust the sword in their bellies, or cast themselves down from the roofs. Perhaps this was the reason that prompted him to confess to a crime he had not committed, in order that he might be put to death.

To sum up the matter, the principle that no man is to be declared guilty on his own admission is a divine decree.

—Maimonides, *Code*, "Laws
Concerning Judges,"
chapter 18, section 6

When there is a dispute between men and they go to the law, and a decision is rendered declaring the one in the right and the other in the wrong; if the guilty one is to be flogged, the magistrate shall have him lie down and be given lashes in his presence, by count, as his guilt warrants.

He may be given up to forty lashes, but not more, lest being flogged further, to excess, your brother be degraded before your eyes.

—Deuteronomy, chapter 25,
verses 1–3

On capital punishment

In the law codes of the Hittites, the Assyrians, the Babylonians, and other early peoples, the penalty for murder varied, often depending on the power and wealth of the murderer. A murderer might be executed; or, if the family of the slain person agreed, the murderer might pay a fine or offer substitutes to be killed—a wife, a child, a slave, or several persons whose combined worth was considered equal to the worth of the murdered person. Only biblical law, of all ancient Near Eastern codes, insists that a murderer give up his or her life for taking the life of another person. No substitutes are allowed; no monetary compensations are accepted. Underlying this unbending biblical rule lies a fundamental belief in the value of human life. The life of a person cannot be measured in terms of money nor can it be weighed against other lives, says the Bible. The murderer—and only the murderer—must die because he or she bears responsibility for snuffing out an infinitely precious life.

Paradoxically, the Bible's very insistence on the value of life led many later sages and teachers to an abhorrence of the death penalty. Because it was biblical law, they could not simply abolish it. Nor were they any more willing than the Bible to substitute monetary payments for the worth of a human life. Instead, they treated capital punishment as an existing law but set up so many provisions to be met before a person could be executed for murder that they made the law almost unenforceable.

The discussions that follow may have been largely academic, since under Roman rule Jewish courts did not have the right to sentence a person to death. They do, however, reveal the extreme caution with which the talmudic sages approached the death penalty. Even on the way to execution, the Mishnah tells us, a person was given another chance—and then another—to be cleared. The dispute between Rabbi Tarfon and Rabbi Akiva on the one hand and Rabban Simeon ben Gamaliel on the other raises the eternal question: Is capital punishment a deterrent to crime?

What are the differences between civil and capital cases?

Civil cases are tried by three judges and capital cases by twenty-three. . . . Civil cases may be decided by a majority of one, either for acquittal or condemnation; capital cases may be decided by a majority of one for acquittal but by a majority of at least two for conviction.

In civil cases, a decision may be reversed from acquittal to conviction or conviction to acquittal. But in capital cases, the verdict may be reversed only from conviction to acquittal.

In civil cases, everyone [including students who attend the court sessions] may argue for or against the defendant; in capital cases, everyone may argue for acquittal but not for conviction.

In civil cases, a judge who argued for conviction may reverse himself and argue for acquittal, and vice versa. In capital cases, a judge who argued for conviction may subsequently argue for acquittal, but a judge who argued for acquittal may not reverse himself. . . .

Civil cases may be concluded on the same day, whether for acquittal or conviction. Capital cases may be concluded on the same day for acquittal, but a verdict of conviction may be given only on the next day.

—Mishnah, tractate *Sanhedrin*,
chapter 4, paragraph 1

How were witnesses in capital cases inspired with awe? They would bring them before the court and admonish them in this way:

"Perhaps what you say is based on circumstantial evidence, or hearsay, or second-hand information, even from a reliable source. Perhaps you do not realize that we will cross-examine you and scrutinize your evidence.

"Bear in mind that capital cases are not like monetary ones. In civil suits, a man can make monetary restitution [to the injured party] and be forgiven. In capital cases, he is held responsible for the blood of the wronged and of his descendants to the end of time. For so we find in the case of Cain, who killed his brother, Scripture says: 'Your brother's bloods cry out to Me' (Genesis 4:10). Not 'blood' but 'bloods,' meaning his blood and the blood of his descendants. . . ."

—Mishnah, tractate *Sanhedrin*,
chapter 4, paragraph 5

Witnesses were told that unless they saw a murder committed, circumstantial evidence was not admissible in court no matter how damaging it was. The extreme case that follows was used as an example of evidence that was inadmissible because the murder itself had not been witnessed.

What is meant by "based on circumstantial evidence"?

The judge says to the witness: "Perhaps you saw a man pursuing his fellow into a ruin. You followed him and found him sword in hand with blood dripping from it, while the murdered man lay writhing in pain. If this is what you saw, you saw nothing."

—Babylonian Talmud, tractate
Sanhedrin, page 37b

When a trial is ended the prisoner is taken out to be stoned. . . .

One man stood at the door of the courthouse with a flag in his hand and another, on a horse, was stationed at a distance from him, yet within sight. Then, if one of the judges said, "I have something to add in favor of the prisoner," the man at the door waved his flag, and the rider rushed off to stop the execution.

Even if the prisoner himself says, "I have something to plead on my own behalf," he is taken back to the court even four or five times, provided there is some substance in his words.

If then he is found innocent, he is set free. If not, he goes forth to be stoned and a herald precedes him, announcing, "So-and-so is going forth to be stoned because he committed such-and-such a crime. The witnesses against him were so-and-so. Let whoever knows anything in his favor come and state it."

—Mishnah, tractate *Sanhedrin*, chapter 6, paragraph 1

When a person is led to execution, he is given a goblet of wine that contains a grain of frankincense to drink in order to numb his senses.

—Babylonian Talmud, tractate *Sanhedrin*, page 43a

A court that orders an execution once in seven years is branded a murderous court. Rabbi Eleazar ben Azariah says: Or even once in seventy years.

Rabbi Tarfon and Rabbi Akiva said: Had we been members of the Sanhedrin, no person would ever have been put to death.

Rabban Simeon ben Gamaliel said: If so, they [Rabbi Tarfon and Rabbi Akiva] would also have multiplied the murderers in Israel.

—Mishnah, tractate *Makkot*, chapter 1, paragraph 10

Responsibilities beyond the requirements of the law

Although Jewish law makes many moral demands, the sages often spoke of going "beyond the limit of the law"—*li-fenim mi-shurat ha-din*—to take on moral responsibilities that might help someone else, even to your detriment. Over the years, Jewish philosophers have argued about whether doing more than the law requires is an obligation incumbent on everyone or a higher standard of morality to be assumed by those who aspire to especially pious lives. In either case, "beyond the limit" is an ethical ideal held up for the consideration of all, even if it can be achieved, perhaps, by only a few.

In the second selection, doing more than the law requires becomes part of the judicial process, as a judge interprets the spirit rather than the letter of the law to help the weaker of two brothers.

"Do what is right and good in the sight of the Lord" (Deuteronomy 6:18)—Our rabbis have a fine interpretation of this. They said, "This refers to compromise and going beyond the limit of the law." The intent is that initially God had said that you should observe the laws and statutes which He had commanded you. Now He says that with respect to what He has not commanded, you should likewise take heed to do the good and the right in His eyes....

And this is a great matter. For it is impossible to mention in the Torah all of a person's actions toward his neighbors and acquaintances, all of his commercial activity, and all social and political institutions. So, after He had mentioned many of them, such as, "You shall not go about as a talebearer," "You shall not take vengeance or bear a grudge," "Do not profit by the blood of your neighbor," "You shall not insult the deaf," "You shall rise before the aged," and the like, He resumes to say generally that one should do the good and the right in all matters. . . .

—Nahmanides, commentary on Deuteronomy, chapter 6, verse 18

The brother of Mari ben Isak came from Be Hozai [in ancient Persia], and said, "Divide my father's estate with me."

"I don't even know you," said Mari [who had not seen his brother for many years].

So they went before Rabbi Hisda. "Mari speaks truthfully," he said. "He may not know you, just as Joseph recognized his brothers but they did not recognize him because he had gone away without a beard and returned with a beard. Go and bring witnesses that you are his brother."

"I have witnesses," said the brother, "but they are afraid of him because he is a powerful man."

Said Rabbi Hisda to Mari, "You go and bring witnesses that he is not your brother."

"Is that justice?" cried Mari. "According to law, the burden of proof lies with the claimant."

"This is my judgment in your case," answered Rabbi Hisda, "and for all powerful men like you."

—Babylonian Talmud, tractate *Bava Mezia*, page 39b

"For you were strangers in the land of Egypt"

Going beyond what the law requires of you may mean applying the same standards of justice and consideration to outsiders as you do to your inner circle of friends and relatives. One of the most sensitive of biblical teachings urges the Israelites to treat strangers who lived in their land with kindness, for they must not forget that they, too, had been strangers in a land not their own. This teaching served as the cornerstone for the attitudes of later sages toward non-Jews, and most especially toward converts to Judaism.

Although talmudic scholars often spoke with contempt of pagan practices and with bitterness of Christians who aligned themselves with the Romans to persecute Jews, they firmly believed that the righteous among all people merited the honor and respect accorded virtuous Jews. As a standard for judging the behavior of non-Jews, they formulated a universal code of morality, known as the seven laws of the Sons of Noah, or the Noachide laws, which they regarded as binding on people everywhere. Like Adam, Noah was not considered specifically a Jew but a progenitor of all humanity.

Another aspect of the rabbis' stance toward non-Jews reflects their conviction that the Torah was God's instrument for spreading ethical teachings to all people. Through exemplary behavior toward non-Jews, they felt they enhanced the Torah and God's name in the eyes of the world. Thus the story of Abba Hosea emphasizes that returning lost property is a major precept in Judaism. To do so, when not even required, glorifies God. Conversely, unethical behavior toward non-Jews profanes God's name and disgraces the entire Jewish community.

Although many people believe that Judaism never wanted or encouraged converts, the fact is that in the days of the Second Temple, Jewish missionaries sought out and converted thousands of Greeks, Romans, Syrians, and others, including members of royal families. Ironically, their activity paved the way for early Christian missionaries, who found a ready audience for their teachings. Later, persecution of Jews made conversion to Judaism dangerous, and all missionary activity ceased. Today, though Jews do not actively seek proselytes, they accept those who sincerely want to convert.

The sages sometimes spoke angrily of converts who turned against Judaism in times of persecution. For the most part, however, they welcomed proselytes with exuberance. In his letter—one of several to Obadiah the Proselyte—Maimonides expresses anger at a teacher who insulted the convert because of his Moslem background.

> When a stranger resides with you in your land, you shall not wrong him. The stranger who resides with you shall

be to you as one of your citizens; you shall love him as yourself, for you were strangers in the land of Egypt; I the Lord am your God.

—Leviticus, chapter 19, verse 34

Our rabbis taught: The sons of Noah were given seven commandments:

To establish a legal system, and to refrain from blasphemy, idolatry, sexual immorality, bloodshed, theft, and eating flesh from a living animal.

—Babylonian Talmud, tractate *Sanhedrin*, page 56a

I bring heaven and earth to witness that the Divine Spirit rests upon a non-Jew as well as upon a Jew, upon a woman as well as upon a man, upon a maidservant as well as a manservant. All depends on the deeds of the particular individual.

—*Yalkut Shimoni*, on Judges, section 42

How do we know that even a non-Jew who occupies himself with the study of Torah is equal in God's eyes to a high priest?

We find it stated in Scripture: "You shall keep my laws and my norms, by the pursuit of which man shall live" (Leviticus, 18:5).

It does not say "priests, Levites, and Israelites," but it says "man." From this we learn that even a non-Jew who occupies himself with the study of Torah is equal to a high priest.

—Rabbi Meir, in the Babylonian Talmud, tractate *Bava Kamma*, page 38a

Know that the Lord desires the heart, and the intention of the heart is the measure of all things. That is why our sages say, the pious among the Gentiles have a share in the world to come. . . .

There is no doubt that every man who ennobles his soul with excellent morals and wisdom based on faith in God certainly belongs to the men of the world to come.

—Maimonides, from a letter to Hasdai ha-Levi, last quarter of twelfth century

Abba Hosea of Traya was a wool washer. Once a Roman princess came to his laundry and lost some jewelry there.

When Abba Hosea returned them to her, she said, "Keep them. They are of no use to me. I have many that are more precious."

Abba replied, "Our Torah orders us to return lost property."

Whereupon, the princess exclaimed, "Praised be the God of the Jews."

—Jerusalem Talmud, tractate *Bava Mezia*, chapter 2, paragraph 5

The Holy One, blessed be He, loves converts greatly.

To what may this be compared? To a king who had a flock which went out into the field every day and returned in the evening. One day a stag entered the flock, joined the goats, and grazed with them. When the flock came into the sheepfold, it came with them. When they went out to pasture, it went with them.

The king was told about the stag, and he felt great affection for it.

When the stag went out to the fields, the king would

order that it be given whatever pasture it liked, and that no one should strike it, and that everyone should treat it carefully. When it returned with the flock, the king would order, "Give it water to drink!"

The servants said to him, "My Lord, you possess so many he-goats, lambs, and kids, and you never cautioned us about them."

Said the king to them, "It is natural for the flock to graze in the field all day and to come in to sleep in the sheepfold at night. But stags sleep in the wilderness; it is not their nature to enter human settlements. Shall we not be pleased with this one who has left behind the great broad wilderness, the home of all the beasts, and has come to live in a yard?"

In the same way, should we not be grateful to the proselyte who has left behind his family, his nation, and all the other peoples of the world, and has chosen to come to us? Therefore God has given him special protection.

—*Numbers Rabbah*,
chapter 8, section 2

And how great is the duty which the Law imposes on us with regard to proselytes? Our parents we are commanded to honor and fear; to the prophets we are ordered to harken. A man may honor and fear and obey without loving. But in the case of "strangers" we are bidden to love with the whole force of our heart's affection.

And he called you fool! Astounding! A man who left father and mother, forsook his birthplace, his country and its power, and attached himself to this lowly, despised, and enslaved race. . . .

Not witless but wise has God called your name, you disciple of our father Abraham, who also left his father and his kindred and inclined Godwards. . . .

—Maimonides, from a letter to
Obadiah the Proselyte, last
quarter of twelfth century

Assimilating into other cultures

For their part, there have been Jews in every generation who converted to other religions, some out of conviction, some because they were forced to, and some who saw conversion as their passport to better careers and higher social position.

In recent times, religious conversions have posed less of a threat to the survival of the Jewish people than has assimilation. Jewish leaders have decried the merging of their people into the general cultures in which they live, to the extent that large numbers give up their identity as Jews. Many committed Jews look back with longing at early days when, largely rejected by Christian society, Jewish communities developed and enriched their own traditions within the confines of their ghettos and towns. The first selection, quoting a sermon by the sage Bar Kappara, is often cited as a classic example of resisting assimilation.

Rabbi Gerson D. Cohen, a contemporary historian and former Chancellor of the Jewish Theological Seminary, takes exception to that view. For the Jewish community—or any ethnic minority group—the best approach to the problem of assimilation, says Dr. Cohen, lies not in isolation but in meeting the challenge head-on and coping with it creatively.

For four merits were the Israelites delivered from Egypt: Because they did not change their names, and because they did not change their language, and because they did not inform against one another, and because there was no sexual immorality among them.

They did not change their names: as Reuben and Simeon they went down to Egypt, and as Reuben and Simeon they went up from it. They did not call Reuben Rufus nor did they call Simeon Luliani, nor Joseph Listis, nor Benjamin Alexander.

They did not change their language. In one place it is written, "A fugitive brought the news to Abraham the

Hebrew" and later it is written, "The God of the Hebrews has manifested Himself to us" [implying that Hebrew remained the language of the people]. . . .

—Rabbi Huna in the name of Bar Kappara, in *Song of Songs Rabbah*, chapter 4, section 12

The first shibboleth which all of us have been raised on is that Jewish survival and above all Jewish vitality in the past derived in large measure from a tenacious adherence on the part of our ancestors to all basic external traditional forms. This view has perhaps best been expressed in a renowned sermon of Bar Kappara delivered in the latter part of the second century and repeated in subsequent centuries with some minor variations. . . .

Now, whatever the merits of this sermon, or of the popular distortion of the sermon, with regard to Jacob's children, it was hardly true for Jacob's grandchildren, for even in Egypt they soon acquired very fashionable names like Aaron, Moses, Hofni, Phinehas. While to the modern these are authentically Hebrew names, they were, we know today, originally Egyptian names, which our ancestors appropriated and Hebraisized. . . .

In other words, Jews did "change their names" in accordance with the regnant fashions of their times. However, not only did they change their names; they also changed their language. . . .

In the time of the Mishnah, most Jews did not speak Hebrew. Although many apparently knew the language, few used it regularly. While many spoke Aramaic, countless others spoke Greek and no other language, so much so that even in the Holy Land, rabbis were very often forced to preach in Greek. . . .

Egyptian religion could only be expressed in ancient Egyptian forms. Babylonian religion could be expressed only in the Babylonian tongue. As a consequence, these traditions ceased to have any wide and sustained impact. By way of contrast, the Jews were willing to change their language even for religious expression. Consequently, the Jews were able to bring their message or messages to their own people, as well as to the world at large, in every language under the sun....

A frank appraisal of the periods of great Jewish creativity will indicate that not only did a certain amount of assimilation and acculturation not impede Jewish continuity and creativity, but that in a profound sense this assimilation or acculturation was even a stimulus to original thinking and expression and, consequently, a source of renewed vitality. To a considerable degree, the Jews survived as a vital group and as a pulsating culture because they changed their names, their language, their clothing and with them some of their patterns of thought and expression....

There are, of course, two ways of meeting the problem of assimilation. The first is withdrawal and fossilization. . . . However, there is and always was an alternative approach of taking the bull by the horns, as it were, and utilizing the inevitable inroads of assimilation as channels of new sources of vitality....

Assimilation properly channeled and exploited can thus become a kind of blessing, for assimilation bears within it a certain seminal power which serves as a challenge and a goad to renewed creativity.

—Gerson D. Cohen, from "The Blessing of Assimilation," a commencement address at Hebrew Teachers College, 1966

On civil disobedience and protest

Although Jews have assimilated and adapted to the cultures in which they have found themselves, there also has been a strong tradition of speaking out against wrongdoing and, when necessary, refusing to obey laws considered a violation of conscience. The right to disobey unjust orders—more accurately, a mandate to do so—is derived from a concept in Jewish law. In civil matters, a person may appoint another to serve as his or her agent. The agent then substitutes for the principal, who remains liable for the actions of the agent; as the rabbis put it: "A man's agent is as himself." In criminal matters, however, the sages ruled that "there is no agent for wrongdoing"—that is, people who commit crimes may not defend themselves on the grounds that they served as agents for others and only carried out orders.

In the selections that follow, the issue is not simply disagreeing with a law or a command but finding it immoral or unjust, and therefore unacceptable. Two midwives refuse to obey Pharaoh's orders to destroy all male children born to Hebrews, which may be the first known incident of civil disobedience in history. Rabbi Akiva explains why he must continue to study and teach Torah in spite of a Roman decree forbidding it. Akiva was later imprisoned for disobeying Roman orders and died a martyr's death. Finally, in our own time, Russian dissident Anatoly Shcharansky speaks out in a Russian court before being sentenced for treason. He was given thirteen years imprisonment, but was released after eight years on February 11, 1986.

If a man says to his agent, "Go and kill so-and-so," and he does it, the agent is guilty....

—Babylonian Talmud, tractate
Kiddushin, page 43a

Whoever disregards a royal order because he is busy with God's commandments—even the slightest commandment—is exempt [from blame]. If the master's orders conflict with the servant's, the master's take precedence.

And it goes without saying that if a king ordered a violation of God's commandments, he is not to be obeyed.

—Maimonides, *Code*, "Laws
Concerning Kings and Wars,"
chapter 3, section 9

The king of Egypt spoke to the Hebrew midwives, one of whom was named Shiphrah and the other Puah, saying, "When you deliver the Hebrew women, look at the birthstool [on which the woman delivered]; if it is a boy, kill him; if it is a girl, let her live."

The midwives, fearing God, did not do as the king of Egypt had told them; they let the boys live. So the king of Egypt summoned the midwives and said to them, "Why have you done this thing, letting the boys live?"

The midwives said to Pharaoh, "Because the Hebrew women are not like the Egyptian women; they are vigorous. Before the midwife can come to them, they have given birth."

And God dealt well with the midwives; and the people multiplied and increased greatly.

—Exodus, chapter 1, verses 15–20

Nobody is sure of the historical basis to the story of how Mordecai urged his niece and ward, Esther, to speak to her husband, the Persian King Ahasuerus, about the plans of the evil Haman to destroy all Jews in the city of Shushan. But the narrative of the Scroll of Esther, with its ultimate victory for the Jews and defeat of Haman, is central to the joyous celebration of Purim. Here, Esther has sent a message telling Mordecai that she cannot plead for her people because no one may approach the king, upon penalty of death, unless summoned by him. Mordecai replies:

"Do not imagine that you, of all the Jews, will escape with your life by being in the king's palace. On the contrary, if you keep silent in this crisis, relief and deliverance will come to the Jews from another quarter, while you and your father's house will perish. And who knows, perhaps you have attained to royal position for just such a crisis."

Then Esther sent back this answer to Mordecai: "Go, assemble all the Jews who live in Shushan, and fast in my behalf; do not eat or drink for three days, night or day. I and my maidens will observe the same fast. Then I shall go to the king, though it is contrary to the law; and if I am to perish, I shall perish!"

—Esther, chapter 4,
verses 13–16

The Roman government issued a decree forbidding Jews to read or practice the Torah. Rabbi Akiva ignored the decree, and continued to gather and teach students Torah. Pappus ben Judah asked him: "Are you not afraid of the government?"

"I will explain to you with a parable," Akiva answered.

"A fox was once walking alongside a river and he saw fishes swimming in schools from one place to another.

" 'What are you running away from?' asked the fox.

" 'From the nets men cast to catch us,' they answered.

" 'Why don't you come up to dry land' said the fox, 'so that you and I can live together the way our ancestors lived?'

"They answered, 'Are you the animal known as the cleverest of all? You are not clever, but foolish. If we're afraid in the element in which we live, how much more fearful we would be in the element in which we would die!'

"So it is with us," said Rabbi Akiva. "If this is our situation when we sit and study Torah, of which it is written: 'For that is your life and the length of your days' (Deuteronomy 30:20), how much worse off we would be if we were to go and neglect it."

—Babylonian Talmud, tractate
Berakhot, page 61b

In March and April, during interrogation, the chief investigators warned me that in the position I have taken during investigation, and held here in court, I would be threatened with execution by firing squad, or at least fifteen years. If I would agree to cooperate with the investigation for the purpose of destroying the Jewish emigration movement, they promised me early freedom and a quick reunion with my wife.

Five years ago, I submitted my application for exit to Israel. Now I'm further than ever from my dream. It would seem to be cause for regret. But it is absolutely otherwise. I am happy. I am happy that I lived honestly, in peace with my conscience. I never compromised my soul, even under the threat of death.

I am happy that I helped people. I am proud that I knew and worked with such honest, brave, and courageous people as Sakharov, Orlov, Ginzburg, who are carrying on the traditions of the Russian intelligentsia. I am fortunate to have been witness to the process of the liberation of Jews of the U.S.S.R.

I hope that the absurd accusation against me and the entire Jewish emigration movement will not hinder the liberation of my people. My near ones and friends know how I wanted to exchange activity in the emigration movement for a life with my wife, Avital, in Israel.

For more than 2,000 years the Jewish people, my people, have been dispersed. But wherever they are, wherever Jews are found, every year they have repeated, "Next year in Jerusalem." Now, when I am further than ever from my people, from Avital, facing many arduous years of imprisonment, I say, turning to my people, my Avital: Next year in Jerusalem.

Now I turn to you, the court, who were required to confirm a predetermined sentence: to you I have nothing to say.

—Anatoly B. Shcharansky,
closing words before being
sentenced in a Moscow court,
July 14, 1978

Rebelling against tyranny

In periods of great oppression, civil disobedience has sometimes turned into open violence or a complete break with authority. The first major rebellion recorded in the Bible took place about three thousand years ago, when the ten northern tribes of Israel, incensed at King Rehoboam's refusal to lighten their taxes, broke from the kingdom. They formed a separate nation under the rule of Jeroboam ben Nebat, changing forever the political makeup of the land.

In the selections that follow, Mattathias's call to arms in the year 167 B.C.E. marked the beginning of the uprising against the Hellenization of Palestine by the Greek Seleucid King Antiochus IV Epiphanes. After Mattathias's death, his son Judah Maccabee led the people to victory against the Seleucids, and his triumph forms the theme for the festival of Hanukkah.

The historian Josephus presents the speech of the Zealot commander Eleazar ben Jair in the besieged fortress of Masada. The Zealots had been leaders in the war against Rome that began in 66. Early in the war, Eleazar and his troops seized the fortress and held out against the Romans even after the destruction of the Second Temple in 70. By 73, all hope for victory was gone, and the fighters agreed to follow Eleazar's plan to kill their families and themselves as their final act of defiance against Rome. Josephus, who had defected to the Roman side and wrote historical works under the patronage of the emperor Vespasian, generally spoke with contempt of the Zealots. His description of the last hours of Eleazar and his people, however, reflects admiration and awe.

The last selection, an appeal to Polish resisters to help Warsaw Ghetto underground fighters, was written shortly before the destruction of the Ghetto in May 1943. The manifesto was among the documents hidden by Emanuel Ringelblum, Warsaw Ghetto historian and fighter.

At this time a certain Mattathias, son of John, son of Simeon, appeared on the scene. He was a priest . . . who had settled at Modin. . . .

The king's officers who were enforcing apostasy came to the town of Modin to see that sacrifice was offered, and many Israelites went over to them. Mattathias and his sons stood in a group. The king's officers spoke to Mattathias: "You are a leader here," they said . . . "You be the first now to come forward and carry out the king's order. All the nations have done so. . . ."

To this Mattathias replied in a ringing voice: "Though all the nations within the king's dominions obey him and forsake their ancestral worship, though they have chosen to submit to his commands, yet I and my sons and brothers will follow the covenant of our fathers. Heaven forbid we should ever abandon the law and its statutes. We will not obey the command of the king, nor will we deviate one step from our form of worship."

As soon as he had finished, a Jew stepped forward in full view of all to offer sacrifice on the pagan altar at Modin, in obedience to the royal command. The sight stirred Mattathias to indignation; he shook with passion, and in a fury of righteous anger rushed forward and slaughtered the traitor at the very altar. At the same time he killed the officer sent by the king to enforce sacrifice, and pulled the pagan altar down. . . .

"Follow me," he shouted through the town, "every one of you who is zealous for the law and strives to maintain the covenant."

He and his sons took to the hills, leaving all their belongings behind in the town.

—I Maccabees, chapter 2,
verses 1 and 15–28

"Since we, long ago, my generous friends, resolved never to be servants to the Romans, nor to any other than to God himself, who alone is the true and just Lord of mankind, the time is now come that obliges us to make that resolution true in practice. And let us not at this time bring a reproach upon ourselves for self-contradiction, while we formerly would not undergo slavery, though it were then without danger, but must now, together with slavery, choose such punishments also, as are intolerable: I mean this upon the supposition that the Romans once reduce us under their power while we are alive. We were the very first that revolted from them, and we are the last that fight against them; and I cannot but esteem it as a favor that God has granted us that it is still in our power to die bravely, and in a state of freedom, which has not been the case of others, who were conquered unexpectedly.

"It is very plain that we shall be taken within a day's time, but it is still an eligible thing to die after a glorious manner, together with our dearest friends. This is what our enemies themselves cannot by any means hinder, although they be very desirous to take us alive. Nor can we propose to ourselves any more to fight them, and beat them....

"To be sure we weakly hoped to have preserved ourselves, and ourselves alone, still in a state of freedom, as if we had been guilty of no sins ourselves against God, nor been partners with those of others: we also taught other men to preserve their liberty. Wherefore, consider how God has convinced us that our hopes were in vain, by bringing such distress upon us in the desperate state we are now in, and which is beyond all our expectations; for the nature of this fortress, which was in itself unconquerable, has not proved a means of our deliverance....

"Let our wives die before they are abused, and our children before they have tasted of slavery; and after we have slain them, let us bestow that glorious benefit upon one another mutually, and preserve ourselves in freedom, as an excellent funeral monument for us. But first let us destroy our money and the fortress by fire; for I am well assured that this would be a great grief to the Romans, that they shall not be able to seize upon our bodies, and shall fail of our wealth also: and let us spare nothing but our provisions; for they will be a testimonial when we are dead, that we were not subdued for want of necessaries, but that, according to our original resolution, we have preferred death before slavery."

—Josephus Flavius, *The Jewish War*, book 7, chapter 8

Poles, citizens, soldiers of Freedom! Through the din of German cannons destroying the homes of our mothers, wives, and children; through the noise of their machine guns, seized by us in the fight against the cowardly German police and SS men; through the smoke of the Ghetto that was set on fire, and the blood of its mercilessly murdered defenders, we, the slaves of the Ghetto, convey heart-felt greetings to you. We are well aware that you have been witnessing breathlessly, with broken hearts, with tears of compassion, with horror and enthusiasm, the war that we have been waging against the brutal occupier these past few days.

Every doorstep in the Ghetto has become a stronghold and shall remain a fortress until the end. All of us will probably perish in the fight, but we shall never surrender. We, as well as you, are burning with the desire to punish the enemy for all his crimes, and with a desire for vengeance. It is a fight for our freedom, as well as yours; for our human dignity and national honor, as well as yours. We shall avenge the gory deeds of Auschwitz, Treblinka, Belzec, and Majdanek!

Long live the fraternity of blood and weapons in a fighting Poland!

Long live Freedom!

Death to the hangman and the killers!

We must continue our mutual struggle against the occupier until the very end!

—Manifesto of Jewish Fighting Organization in the Warsaw Ghetto to the Polish Underground, April 23, 1943

Compromise

Judah Maccabee, Eleazar ben Jair, and other heroes hold a special place in Jewish history as symbols of strength and pride. Yet some of their actions were questioned both in their own and later times. For example, was the mass suicide of 960 men, women, and children at Masada really warranted? In view of the great emphasis on the preservation of life in the Jewish tradition, some have asked whether the defenders of Masada should not, rather, have done everything in their power to stay alive, even if that meant surrender to Rome.

If at all possible, the rabbis preferred compromise to confrontation. Given the precariousness of Jewish existence, they sought ways that would allow the people freedom to pursue their laws and learning even when they lacked political freedom. That is not to say that they tolerated betraying one's principles—the list of scholars and teachers who died for their beliefs through the centuries is long and awesome—but if violence could be avoided, if a way round could be found before differences became fixed and irreversible, they grasped at it.

The story of Kamza and Bar Kamza is an example of this attitude in its implied criticism of all the people who might have been flexible but were not. Although legendary, the story has a thread of fact in it. Rabbi Zechariah was a member of the Zealot party; and, according to Josephus, the revolt against Rome began when Zealots refused to allow sacrifices for the emperor to be offered at the altar of the Temple.

Rabbi Joshua ben Hananiah was a disciple of Rabban Johanan ben Zakkai and, like him, sought moderation. His parable—based on Aesop—helped cool the tempers of the crowds who had gathered to protest when the emperor Hadrian rescinded a promise to rebuild the Temple. Shortly after his death, rebellion erupted again, in the year 132, this time led by Bar Kokhba with the support of Rabbi Akiva. After initial victories, it ended disastrously, with thousands of Jews massacred and sold into slavery.

A certain man had a friend named Kamza and an enemy named Bar Kamza. He once gave a party and ordered his servant to invite Kamza. The man went and brought Bar Kamza instead.

"What are you doing here?" the man said.

Said Bar Kamza, "Since I'm here, let me stay, and I'll pay for what I eat and drink."

"No," replied the man.

"Then let me pay half the cost of the party."

"No."

"Then let me pay for the entire party!"

"No, again."

And the man took Bar Kamza by the hand and threw him out.

Said Bar Kamza, "Since the rabbis were all at the party and did not stop him, they must have agreed with him. I will go and inform against them to the government."

He went to the emperor and said, "The Jews are planning a revolt against you."

"How can I tell?" asked the emperor.

"Send them an offering for sacrifice at their Temple," said Bar Kamza, "and see whether they will use it on their altar."

So the emperor gave him a fine calf to deliver to the Jews. While on the way, he made a blemish on its mouth—or some say on its eye—in a place that would make it unfit for Jews to use on their altar.

The rabbis were inclined to sacrifice it anyway so as not to offend the government.

But Rabbi Zechariah ben Avkilus said to them, "People will say that we offer blemished animals on our altar."

Then it was proposed to kill Bar Kamza so he would not inform the emperor that his offering had been refused.

But again Rabbi Zechariah ben Avkilus interfered.

"Are we to condemn a man to death for making a blemish on an animal meant for sacrifice?" he argued.

As a result of this incident, Rabbi Johanan said, "Through the scrupulousness of Rabbi Zechariah ben Avkilus our house has been destroyed, our Temple burned, and our people exiled from their land."

—Babylonian Talmud, tractate *Gittin*, pages 55b–56a

Now the community of Israel had gathered in the plain of Bet Rimmon. When royal messengers arrived [to say that the Temple would not be rebuilt], the people burst out crying and wanted to revolt against the Romans.

Thereupon the sages decided: Let Rabbi Joshua ben Hananiah go and pacify the people.

So he went and he said to them:

"A wild lion once killed an animal, and a bone stuck in its throat. He announced: 'I will reward anyone who removes it.'

"An Egyptian heron, which has a long beak, came and pulled it out, and demanded his reward.

" 'Go,' answered the lion. 'You will be able to boast that you entered a lion's mouth in peace and came out in peace.'

"Even so," said Rabbi Joshua, "let us be happy that we entered into dealings with these people in peace and still have emerged in peace."

—*Genesis Rabbah*, chapter 64, section 10

Attitudes toward war

Golda Meir once said: "A leader who doesn't stutter before he sends his nation into battle is not fit to be a leader." The sages would have approved of that comment. Like their approach to rebellion, their attitude toward war was mixed. They found war distasteful, even shameful; yet they accepted the idea that there are times when it is necessary. Using biblical accounts of battles fought by the Israelites, they divided wars into two broad categories: mandatory and optional. Mandatory wars are wars of self-defense or of clear-cut moral necessity. Optional wars are wars fought for expansion, or preventively, to stop an enemy who is preparing for attack. Said the scholars: "The wars waged by Joshua to conquer Canaan were mandatory in the opinion of all [because commanded by God]; the wars waged by the House of David for territorial expansion were optional in the opinion of all." Most wars, they felt, were optional, and they ruled that such wars could not be declared by a king without the approval of the Sanhedrin. These wars, also, were subject to many restrictions.

Deep reservations about war are revealed in the selections that follow. In the last of these, the Bible set down categories of people who may be exempt from serving in a war, and the rabbis expanded on them. Some contemporary scholars have interpreted these passages as a prime source in Jewish tradition for permitting conscientious objection to serving in the armed forces during wartime. Others interpret them literally, as referring only to people who are weak and frightened rather than people who may object to a war on moral grounds.

> David said to Solomon, "My son, as for me, it was in my heart to build a house unto the name of the Lord my God [the First Temple]. But the word of the Lord came to me, saying, 'You have shed blood abundantly and have made great wars; you shall not build a house unto My

name, because you have shed much blood upon the earth in my sight.' "

—I Chronicles, chapter 22,
verses 7–8

A man must not carry a sword, bow, shield, lance, or spike on the Sabbath. . . . Rabbi Eliezer said, "But they are adornments" [which are worn rather than carried].

The sages said: "They are merely shameful, for it is said:

" 'And they shall beat their swords into plowshares
" 'And their spears into pruning hooks;
" 'Nation shall not take up
" 'Sword against nation;
" 'They shall never again know war' " (Isaiah 2:4).

—Mishnah, tractate *Shabbat*,
chapter 6, paragraph 4

"Now when Amraphel king of Shinar, Arioch king of Ellasar, Chedorlaomer king of Elam, and Tidal king of Goiim made war . . ." (Genesis 14:1).

Before their time there had been no war in the world, and it was they who came and introduced the sword and started to wage war. God said, "You wicked ones, you have introduced the sword, let the sword enter your own heart."

—*Tanhuma* (edited by Solomon Buber), portion "Lech L'cha," page 32b

---

When siege is laid to a city for the purpose of capture, it may not be surrounded on all four sides but only on three sides in order to give an opportunity for escape to those who would flee to save their lives. . . .

It has been learned by tradition that that was the instruction given to Moses.

—Maimonides, *Code*, "Laws Concerning Kings and Wars," chapter 6, section 7

Before you engage in battle . . . the officials should address the troops, as follows:

"Is there anyone among you who has built a new house but has not dedicated it? Let him go back to his house lest he die in battle and another dedicate it.

"Is there anyone who has planted a vineyard but has never harvested it? Let him go back to his home, lest he die in battle and another initiate it.

"Is there anyone who has spoken for a woman in marriage but who has not yet married her? Let him go back to his home, lest he die in battle and another marry her."

The officials shall go on addressing the troops and say, "Is there anyone afraid and disheartened? Let him go back to his house, lest the courage of his comrades flag like his."

—Deuteronomy, chapter 20, verses 5–8

Rabbi Akiva said: "Afraid" and "disheartened" are to be understood literally. That is, he is unable to stand in the battle ranks and see a drawn sword. . . .

—Mishnah, tractate *Sotah*, chapter 8, paragraph 6

Why are both terms "afraid" and "disheartened" used? To indicate that even the most physically powerful and courageous, if he is compassionate, should be exempted.

—Addition to Rabbi Akiva's comments in *tosafot* to tractate *Sotah*, chapter 8, paragraph 6

"Great is peace"

The meaning of "peace" goes far beyond politics here. Peace is a state of being, for individuals, for nations, for the world.

The first selection interprets biblical commands that the stones on the altar of the Temple were to be unhewn: no iron tools were to be used on them. The rabbis explained the prohibition against iron by saying that weapons are forged of iron, and "iron is made to shorten the years of man," while the "altar is made to prolong the years of man." Rabban Johanan ben Zakkai, the man of peace, explained further:

They are to be stones that establish peace. Now, we can reason: The stones of the altar do not see or hear or speak. Yet because they serve to establish peace between Israel and their Father in heaven, the Holy One, blessed be He, said: "Do not wield an iron tool over them." How much the more then should he who establishes peace between man and his fellow man, between husband and wife, between city and city, between nation and nation, between family and family, between government and government, be protected so that no harm should come to him?

—*Mekhilta of Rabbi Ishmael*, tractate "Bahodesh," chapter 11

Great is peace, for the prophets have taught all people to care for nothing so much as peace. . . .

Great is peace, for it was given to the meek; as it says: "But the lowly shall inherit the land, and delight themselves in abundance of peace" (Psalms 37:11).

Great is peace, for it outweighs everything. We say in the morning prayers: "He makes peace and creates everything." Without peace, there is nothing.

Even if Israel serves idols and peace reigns among them, the Holy One, blessed be He, as it were, says: "Satan shall not touch them." . . .

Peace is a grand thing and quarrelsomeness is hateful. Peace is a great thing, for even during war peace is necessary; as it says: "When you approach a town to attack it, you shall offer it terms of peace" (Deuteronomy 20:10). . . .

Great is peace, for even the dying need peace; as it says: "You shall go to your fathers in peace" (Genesis 15:15), and it says: "You shall die in peace" (Jeremiah 34:5). . . .

Great is peace, for the Holy One has created no finer attribute than peace, and it has been given to the righteous. When a righteous man departs from the world three groups of ministering angels welcome him, each with a greeting of peace. The first says: "Yet he shall come in peace"; the second: "He shall have rest on his couch"; and the third, "So it is for each one who walked straightforward" (Isaiah 57:2). . . .

Great is peace, for God is called Peace, as it says: "And he called the altar 'The Lord is Peace'" (Judges 6:24).

Great is peace, for even the angels in heaven need peace, as it says: "He makes peace in his high places" (Job 25:2). Now, can we not reason from the less important to the more important? If peace is necessary in heaven, a place where there is no hatred or enmity, how much more so is it necessary on earth, where so many conflicts are found!

—*Numbers Rabbah*,
chapter 11, section 7

Three days before the Messiah arrives, Elijah will come and stand upon the mountains. . . . Elijah's voice will be heard from world's end to world's end. And then he will say: "Peace has come to the world."

—*Pesikta Rabbati*,
Piska 35

In that day, there shall be a highway from Egypt to Assyria. The Assyrians shall join with the Egyptians and Egyptians with Assyrians, and then the Egyptians together with the Assyrians shall serve [the Lord].

In that day, Israel shall be a third partner with Egypt and Assyria as a blessing on earth; for the Lord of Hosts will bless them, saying, "Blessed be My people Egypt, My handiwork Assyria, and My very own Israel."

—Isaiah, chapter 19,
verses 23–25

9

FAITH AND FREEDOM

"In the image of God"

On the nature of God ✦ Our relationship to God ✦ "What is man that You have been mindful of him?" ✦ Are we free? ✦ "Seek good and not evil" ✦ Ascetics and "foolish pietists" ✦ Rewards and punishments ✦ On changing one's ways ✦ Why do the good suffer? ✦ The meaning of faith ✦ Can there be faith after Auschwitz? ✦ The many ways of prayer ✦ "And though he tarry, I will wait"

A dialogue often repeated after the horrors of the Holocaust was:

"At Auschwitz, where was God?"

And the answer given: "Where was man?"

Man—and woman—and God are inextricably intertwined in Jewish thought. We need and depend on God; He needs and cares for us. The talmudic sages spoke of God and humans as partners in the creation of the world, and later mystics extended the idea to mean that creation was never completed. Men and women participate in the ongoing act of creation, and the things we do and the way we behave influence the nature of the world.

Of all the creatures on earth, the scholars taught, only humans were singled out to be formed in the image of God. If that was not proof enough of God's love, He demonstrated His love even more fully by telling us of our uniqueness. To be human, then, means not only embodying the divine image but bearing the responsibility for living up to that image because we know we are special.

Some of the most profound lessons taught by the prophets and sages center around this exceptional relationship of men and women to God. Although later philosophers grappled with questions of God's existence, the biblical teachers and talmudic masters rarely dealt with such matters. Belief in God was assumed. The issue, rather, was understanding the nature of God and striving to imitate Him in our dealings with one another. "Just as He is gracious and merciful, so be you gracious and merciful," the sages taught.

The God we are told to worship and imitate has many attributes. He is described as just and righteous, all-powerful and all-knowing, infinite and unknowable. He is the King and Creator of the universe. And, yet, He is also seen as a father, as merciful as He is just, as patient as He is powerful, as close-by as He is eternal.

Threaded through the teachings of scholars and rabbis of every generation is a sense of nearness to God, a kinship that allows even the humblest person to pour out longings and sorrows, or to chastise Him without fear of reprisal. He is a God with whom one can reason. In one rabbinic anecdote, Moses pleads for the Israelites after they have sinned by building the golden calf:

> "The people have made an assistant for You, yet You are angry," says Moses. "Why, You will cause the sun to rise, and the golden calf will cause the moon to rise; You will see to the stars, and it will watch over the constellations; You will make the dew fall, and it will make the winds blow. . . ."
>
> "Moses," God answers, "you are making the same mistake the people made. The calf isn't real."
>
> "If that is so," replies Moses, "why are You so angry with Your children?"

The many ways of approaching God in the Jewish tradition allow also for a variety of interpretations of religious doctrine. The sages fixed no catechism, no system of dogmas that had to be accepted by all adherents. There are, of course, basic premises of belief—that there is a God; that He is one; that He guides the world with justice and love. But beyond these and other fundamental principles lies much room for diversity of thought. How people act, rather than what they believe, is of prime importance. We are free to choose our own paths in life, said the sages. Although God knows all, His knowledge does not determine our moral behavior. Responsibility for what we do rests squarely on us, and we are judged, both by God and by other people, by the choices we make. By the same token, people do not fall permanently from grace. We're always given a chance to change and, through our actions, to find our way back.

Yet, the very moral freedom we have in our relationship to God raises the most disturbing questions: If God is just, why does He allow so many people to suffer? If He judges our actions, why do so many bad people seem to go unpunished? "How long shall the wicked, O Lord, how long shall the wicked exult!" cried the psalmist. And the anguish of the pious Job stands as a rebuke to a God who promised to reward the good.

Like scholars and philosophers of many faiths, Jewish thinkers struggled to reconcile their belief in God's providence—His care and concern for the world and its inhabitants—with the existence of suffering and misery. They suggested a variety of possible solutions. Sometimes suffering was justified as punishment for some wrongdoing the person may not have been aware of; sometimes it was seen as a way of testing the righteous and raising them to an even higher spiritual level. Often good and evil were interpreted in terms of the world to come, where the virtuous would be rewarded and the wicked punished. Ultimately, the sages said, the ways of God cannot be fathomed by human beings, and we must accept on faith things that defy our reason.

But even if we cannot explain the existence of evil and suffering in this world, that does not mean we have to be resigned to them as an inevitable, unchanging aspect of our lives. The rabbis sometimes pictured God as suffering along with people, suffering not only because of the torments of the oppressed but because of the depravity of the oppressor, who had also been created with the potential for living in the divine image. As Jewish teachers explained it, the essence of free will is having the choice of opposing evil when we see it and of alleviating suffering wherever we find it.

At Auschwitz, where was God? That is a question no one can answer.

Where was man? That is a question, the sages might have said, we must struggle to answer, again and again.

On the nature of God

At the base of traditional Jewish thinking about God is the belief that He revealed himself to the Israelites at Mount Sinai and continues to reveal Himself through the events of history and the experiences of life. The first verse of the Ten Commandments is a statement of God's presence at the Exodus from Egypt and an implied promise of His participation in all that happens to humans. In describing God, the Bible and the Talmud often used concrete images to portray God's mercy or justice or power. Mystical writers, on the other hand, chose more abstract forms of description, portraying God as unknowable by any other beings. Medieval philosophers, influenced by Aristotle and embarrassed by the human-like traits often assigned to God by earlier sages, denied any attributes to God at all. Among the first to state this view was Saadiah Gaon, leader of the Jewish community in Babylonia and the greatest Jewish scholar of the early Middle Ages. Underlying the many divergent descriptions of God lies a fundamental belief in His absolute unity of being.

I am the Lord your God, who brought you out of the land of Egypt, out of the house of bondage.

—Exodus, chapter 20, verse 2

Hear O Israel, the Lord our God, the Lord is one.

—Deuteronomy, chapter 6, verse 4

The first book of Kings relates that the prophet Elijah, fleeing from King Ahab, spent the night in a cave. There he heard a voice command him, "Come out and stand on the mountain before the Lord." The narrative continues:

And lo, the Lord passed by. There was a great and mighty wind, splitting mountains and shattering rocks by the power of the Lord; but the Lord was not in the wind.

After the wind—an earthquake; but the Lord was not in the earthquake. After the earthquake—fire; but the Lord was not in the fire.

And after the fire—a soft murmuring sound. When Elijah heard it, he wrapped his mantle about his face and went out and stood at the entrance of the cave. Then a voice addressed him: "Why are you here, Elijah?"

—I Kings, chapter 19, verses 11–14

Do you not know?
Have you not heard?
Have you not been told
From the very first?
Have you not discerned
How the earth was founded?
It is He who is enthroned above the vault of the earth,
So that its inhabitants seem as grasshoppers;
Who spread out the skies like gauze,
Stretched them out like a tent to dwell in.
He brings potentates to naught,
Makes rulers of the earth as nothing.
Hardly are they planted,
Hardly are they sown,
Hardly has their stem
Taken root in earth,
When he blows upon them and they dry up,
And the storm bears them off like straw.
To whom, then, can you liken Me,
To whom can I be compared?

—says the Holy One.

Lift high your eyes and see:
Who created these?
He who sends out their host by count,
Who calls them each by name:
Because of His great might and vast power,
Not one fails to appear.
Why do you say, O Jacob,
Why declare, O Israel,
"My way is hid from the Lord,
My cause is ignored by my God"?
Do you not know?
Have you not heard?
The Lord is God from of old,
Creator of the earth from end to end,

He never grows faint or weary,
His wisdom cannot be fathomed.

—Isaiah, chapter 40,
verses 21–28

When God gave the Torah, no bird sang and no fowl flew, no ox bellowed, no angel stirred a wing. The Seraphim did not say, "Holy, Holy," the sea did not roar and no creature spoke.

The whole world stood hushed into breathless silence, and the voice went forth and proclaimed, "I am the Lord your God."

—*Exodus Rabbah*,
chapter 29, section 9

God said to Israel, "My children, I have created everything in the universe in pairs: heaven and earth are a pair, the sun and the moon are a pair; Adam and Eve are a pair; this world and the world to come are a pair. But my glory is one and unique in the world."

How do we know this?

For Scripture says: "Hear O Israel, the Lord our God, the Lord is one."

—*Deuteronomy Rabbah*,
chapter 2, section 31

The emperor Hadrian once said to Rabbi Joshua ben Hananiah, "I want to see your God."

"You cannot see Him," answered the rabbi.

The emperor insisted. So the rabbi had him face the sun during its height and said to him, "Look up at it."

"I cannot," he answered.

"If you cannot even look at the sun, which is just one of God's attendants," said Rabbi Joshua, "how do you presume to be able to look at the divine presence?"

—Babylonian Talmud, tractate *Hullin*, pages 59b–60a

The Holy One, blessed be He, is transcendent in His glory, He is hidden and removed far beyond all ken; there is no one in the world, nor has there ever been one, whom His wisdom and essence do not elude. . . .

The creatures of the earth think of Him as being on high, declaring, "His glory is above the heavens," while the heavenly beings think of Him as being below, declaring, "His glory is all over the earth," until they both, in heaven and on earth, concur in declaring, "Blessed be the glory of the Lord from His place," because He is unknowable and no one can truly understand Him.

—*Zohar*, volume 1, portion "Bereshit," page 103a

I found that the conception of God as Creator . . . implies the attributes of Life, Power, and Wisdom. . . .

Let nobody assume that the Eternal, blessed be He, contains a plurality of attributes. For all the attributes which we assign to Him are implied in the one attribute of Creator, and it is merely deficiency of our language which makes it necessary for us to express our notion of God in three different words, since there exists no word in our vocabulary which covers all three aspects. . . .

If someone imagines that these attributes imply a diversity within God, that is, some difference between the various attributes, I will show him his mistake by pointing out the real truth of the matter, that is, that diversity and change can take place in bodies and their accidents only, but the Creator of all bodies and accidents is above diversity and change.

—Saadiah Gaon (881–942),
Book of Doctrines and Beliefs,
chapter 2, section 2

Our relationship to God

Extending from the concept of being created in God's image is the instruction to imitate God, and the passages that follow move back and forth between praising God's qualities and urging us to follow in His ways. In the last two selections, both Franz Rosenzweig and Martin Buber compare our relationship to God to the relationships we have with men and women in our lives. In Buber's system of thought, an "I-It" relationship exists when one person has no personal involvement with another. An "I-Thou" relationship exists when people interact, communicating and sharing ideas with one another. God, said Buber, is the "Eternal Thou," who exists behind every specific "Thou" in our lives. When we truly relate to one another and take part in life, we encounter God.

And God said, "I will make man in My image, after My likeness. They shall rule the fish of the sea, the birds of the sky, the cattle, the whole earth, and all the creeping things that creep on earth."

And God created man in His image, in the image of God He created him; male and female He created them.

—Genesis, chapter 1,
verses 26–27

What is the meaning of the verse, "Follow none but the Lord your God?" (Deuteronomy 13:15). Is it possible for a human being actually to follow the ways of God?

What it means is that we should imitate the attributes of God.

As God clothed the naked—as it is written: "And the Lord God made for Adam and his wife garments of skin, and He clothed them"—so you should clothe the naked.

As He visited the sick—as it is written: "The Lord appeared to Abraham by the terebinths of Mamre" [after Abraham's circumcision]—so you should visit the sick.

As God comforted mourners—as it is written: "After the death of Abraham, God blessed his son Isaac"—so you should comfort mourners.

As God buried the dead—as it is written: "He buried him [Moses] in the valley"—so also you should bury the dead.

—Babylonian Talmud, tractate *Sotah*, page 14a

You shall be holy, for I, the Lord your God, am holy.

—Leviticus, chapter 19, verse 2

The Lord is compassionate and gracious,
slow to anger, abounding in steadfast love.
He will not contend forever,
or nurse His anger for all time.
He has not dealt with us according to our sins,
nor has He requited us according to our iniquities.
For as the heavens are high above the earth,
so great is His steadfast love toward those who fear Him.
As east is far from west,
so far has He removed our sins from us.
As a father has compassion for his children,
so the Lord has compassion for those who fear Him.
For He knows how we are formed;
He is mindful that we are dust.

—Psalms, psalm 103, verses 8–14

He has told you, O man, what is good,
And what the Lord requires of you:
Only to do justice
And to love goodness,
And to walk humbly with your God.

—Micah, chapter 6,
verse 8

The sages ascribed meanings to the different terms used for God in the Bible. They felt that "Lord" refers to His attribute of mercy, and "God" to His attribute of justice.

"When the Lord God made earth and heaven" (Genesis 2:4):

Why is the expression "Lord God" used?

This may be compared to a king who had some empty glasses. He said, "If I pour hot water into them, they will burst from the heat; if cold, they will snap." What did he do? He mixed hot and cold water together, and poured it into them, and so they remained.

Even so, God said, "If I create the world on the basis of mercy alone, its sins will be great; on the basis of justice alone, the world cannot exist. Therefore, I will create it with a combination of mercy and justice, and may it then stand."

—*Genesis Rabbah*,
chapter 12, section 15

After giving the Israelites the Ten Commandments, Moses charged them to "love the Lord your God with all your heart and with all your soul and with all your might," words that are recited in the daily prayer service. Franz Rosenzweig discusses the implications of loving God:

It is difficult to love, even to love God. Indeed, the latter is the most difficult kind of love. For the share of unhappy love that is in all love, even the happiest, and that arises from the tension between wanting to, having to love infinitely, and being able to love only finitely, is here increased *ad infinitum*. To love God always spells happy and unhappy love simultaneously, the very happiest and the very unhappiest. He comes close to man, most close—and then again withdraws to the most distant distance. He is at once the most longed for, and the hardest to bear. His hand protects eternally, but no one can behold his eternal face and remain among the living. Thus the love he returns to his lover, who must entreat it, is always something that must be asked for. . . . The solution of these difficulties and antitheses, like the solution of all the difficulties and antitheses of love, lies with the lover, with his strength to face "notwithstandingness," to bear notwithstanding, to let himself be borne notwithstanding. Here it lies with man and the strength he can put into his entreaty that God love him in return.

—Franz Rosenzweig, "The Love of God," a note on a poem by Judah Halevi

---

Entering into the pure relationship does not involve ignoring everything but seeing everything in the You, not renouncing the world but placing it upon its proper ground. Looking away from the world is no help toward God; staring at the world is no help either; but whoever beholds the world in Him stands in His presence. . . .

That you need God more than anything, you know at all times in your heart. But don't you know also that God needs you—in the fullness of his eternity, you? How would man exist if God did not need him, and how would you exist? You need God in order to be, and God needs you—for that is the meaning of your life. . . . The world is not divine play, it is divine fate. That there are world, man, the human person, you and I, has divine meaning.

Creation—happens to us, burns into us, changes us, we tremble and swoon, we submit. Creation—we participate in it, we encounter the creator, offer ourselves to him, helpers and companions.

—Martin Buber (1878–1965),
philosopher and theologian,
I and Thou

"What is man that You have been mindful of him?"

A Hasidic rabbi once suggested that every person carry two cards at all times, one in each side pocket. On one card should be written the words, "For my sake was the world created"; the other one should say, "The Lord God formed man from the dust of the earth." These constant reminders of our peculiar combination of heavenly and earthly qualities, said the rabbi, should help us keep a balanced view of ourselves.

The sages never ceased to be awed and fascinated by the human condition. Some of the most symbolic and beautiful passages in rabbinic literature revolve around the miracle of creation and the nature of human beings.

The Bible says: "The Lord God formed man from the dust of the earth, and He blew into his nostrils the breath of life; and man became a living being."

God gathered the dust from the entire earth—from its four corners, indicating that wherever he might die, it would receive him for burial.

Another explanation of "from the dust of the earth." He took the dust from that spot that He had set aside at the very beginning of civilization as the place where, in the future, the holy Temple with its altar would be built.

—Rashi, commentary on Genesis,
chapter 2, verse 7

When I behold Your heavens, the work of Your fingers,
The moon and stars that You set in place:
What is man that You have been mindful of him,
Mortal man that You have taken note of him,
That You have made him little less than divine,
And adorned him with glory and majesty;
You have made him master over Your handiwork,
Laying the world at his feet,
Sheep and oxen, all of them,
And wild beasts, too,
The birds of the heavens, the fish of the sea,
Whatever travels the paths of the seas.

—Psalms, psalm 8,
verses 4–9

Man was created as a single individual to teach us that anyone who destroys a single life is as though he destroyed an entire world; and anyone who preserves a single life is as though he preserved an entire world.

And also for the sake of peace among mankind, that no person should say to another, "My father was greater than your father." . . .

Again, a single man was created to show the greatness of God, for a man stamps many coins from a single die, and they are all alike, but the King of Kings has stamped every man with the die of Adam, yet not one of them is like his fellow.

Therefore, every person is obliged to say, "For my sake was the world created."

—Mishnah, tractate *Sanhedrin*,
chapter 4, paragraph 5

When God came to create Adam, the ministering angels divided themselves into groups and parties. Some of them said, "Let him be created," while others urged, "Let him not be created." . . .

Love said, "Let him be created because he will carry out acts of love."

Truth said, "Let him not be created because he will be filled with falsehood."

Righteousness said, "Let him be created because he will do good deeds."

Peace said, "Let him not be created because he will be filled with controversy."

What did the Lord do? He took Truth and threw it to the ground. Said the angels, "King of the Universe, why do you despise your seal [Truth traditionally being called the seal of God]? Let Truth arise from the earth!" . . .

While the angels were arguing and fighting with one another, the Holy One, blessed he He, created man. He said to the angels, "What can you do? Man has already been made."

—*Genesis Rabbah*,
chapter 8, section 5

God created man with four qualities of the angels and four qualities of the lower animals.

Like the animals, he eats, drinks, reproduces, and dies.

Like the angels, he stands erect, speaks, understands, and sees [from the sides as well as the front].

Rabbi Tifdai said, "The angels were created in the image of God and do not reproduce, while the earthly creatures reproduce but were not created in His image. Said God, 'I will create man in my image and likeness and in that way he will be like the angels. But he will also reproduce, like the animals.' "

Rabbi Tifdai also said, "The Lord reasoned: 'If I create him like the angels, he will live forever and not die; if I create him like the animals, he will die and not live forever. Therefore, I will create him as a combination of the upper and lower elements. If he sins he will die, and if he dies, he will live' [in the world to come]."

—*Genesis Rabbah*,
chapter 14, section 3

Why was Adam created on the sixth day, after all the other creatures?

So that should a person become arrogant, he may be reminded that the gnats preceded him in the order of creation.

—Babylonian Talmud, tractate
Sanhedrin, page 38a

For two and a half years the School of Shammai and the School of Hillel had a controversy, the former arguing that it would have been better for man not to have been created than to have been created, and the latter maintaining that it was better to have been created than not to have been created.

Finally, they voted and decided that it would have been better had man not been created. But since he had been created, let him scrutinize his past deeds. Others say, let him consider his future actions.

—Babylonian Talmud, tractate
Eruvin, page 13b

The implications of Rava's statement is that in striving to imitate God's goodness, humans may someday attain His creativity. But even Rava was not yet free of all sin and therefore was not capable of creating a real human being. Rava's creation was the forerunner of all later medieval and modern stories of a golem created by humans to carry out their orders.

Rava said, "If the righteous wished, they could create a world, for it is written: 'but your iniquities have been a barrier'" (Isaiah 59:2).

Rava created a man and sent him to Rabbi Zera. Rabbi Zera spoke to him, but received no answer. He said, "You are a creature of the magicians. Return to your dust."

—Babylonian Talmud, tractate *Sanhedrin*, page 65b

Are we free?

Jewish thought embodies a basic contradiction on the question of free will. On the one hand, it maintains that God not only knows but decrees all events on earth. On the other hand, it insists that each of us is free to act as we wish and that we alone are held accountable for our deeds. Medieval philosophers expressed the problem this way: Is God perfect? If so, He must be omniscient and omnipotent. But if He is omniscient, then He is unjust, for He foresees our wrongdoings yet lets us sin. Why, then, should people be punished for their actions? If He is omnipotent, why does He let people sin?

Although the contradiction has never been resolved, the doctrines of free will and individual responsibility remain fundamental to Jewish belief. Among the passages below, the discussion by Rabbi Hai ben Sherira, the last great *gaon*, or head, of the academy of learning at Pumbedita in Babylonia, attempts to solve the contradiction by emphasizing that our moral freedom does not detract from God's foreknowledge. And the selection from Maimonides maintains that God's prescience does not in any way free us of responsibility for our actions.

Rabbi Hanina said: No man injures his finger here on earth unless it was decreed for him in heaven.

—Babylonian Talmud, tractate *Hullin*, page 7b

Everything is foreseen, yet freedom of choice is granted;
in mercy is the world judged; and everything is according to the preponderance of works [good deeds].

—Rabbi Akiva, in
Ethics of the Fathers,
chapter 3, paragraph 19

The angel in charge of conception is called "Night." He takes a drop of seminal fluid and places it before the Holy One, blessed be He.

"What shall be the fate of this drop?" he asks. "Shall it produce a strong person or a weak one, wise or foolish, rich or poor?"

But he does not ask whether it will be wicked or righteous.

For, as Rabbi Hanina said, "Everything is in the hands of heaven—except the fear of heaven."

—Babylonian Talmud, tractate
Niddah, page 16b

Once the Ba'al Shem Tov and one of his students traveled to a barren area with no water. The student became very thirsty and complained to the rabbi, who said nothing. Later the student became frightened for his life. "Rabbi," he cried, "I'm so thirsty, I feel I am in grave danger."

"Do you believe," asked the Ba'al Shem Tov, "that when God created the world, he foresaw this predicament of yours and prepared water for you?"

"I believe in truth," the student answered. "And I have faith that the Holy One watches over the universe at all times."

"Wait, then," the master answered.

A short time later, they saw a man carrying two buckets of water from his shoulders. When they reached him, they gave him some money and he gave them water to drink. Then the Ba'al Shem Tov asked him, "Why are you carrying water to this isolated place?"

The man answered, "My employer has gone crazy. He sent me to get water from a special spring, and I've been carrying this water for miles without knowing why."

The rabbi turned to the student. "Just look how far God's providence has been extended for your sake," he said.

—Tale about Rabbi Israel ben Eliezer Ba'al Shem Tov

We consider it a very important article of belief that God knows that an event will occur if something is to take place in this way, or that it will not occur if that thing is to take place in another way. This, however, does not mean that God is in doubt about a thing, but that He knows how an event that did not occur would have occurred. . . .

And all conditional promises follow this principle, that God knows that, if the conditions on which God made a promise dependent have been fulfilled, the promise comes true, and that, if they have not been fulfilled, the promise does not come true. It is in the same way that the promises and threats concerning the world to come are fulfilled: if man obeys, he is rewarded; if he does not obey, he is punished, but God knows exactly what will happen. . . .

But a question arises about a person whom an enemy attacks and kills. Shall we say that if the murderer had not killed, the man would nevertheless have died, or would he have continued to live? The answer is that we do not know it, but the Lord knows it.

—Hai ben Sherira (939–1038), from a responsum on the question of free will

---

> Free will is bestowed on every human being. If one desires to turn toward the good way and be righteous, he has the power to do so. If one wishes to turn toward the evil way and be wicked, he is at liberty to do so. . . .
>
> If God had decreed that a person should be either righteous or wicked, or if there were some force inherent in his nature which irresistibly drew him to a particular course, or to a special branch of knowledge, to special views or activities, as the foolish astrologers out of their own fancy pretend, how could the Almighty have charged us through our prophets, "Do this and do not do that, improve your ways, do not follow your wicked impulses," when, from the beginning of his existence his destiny had already been decreed . . . ? What room would there be for the whole of the Torah? By what right or justice could God punish the wicked or reward the righteous? "Shall not the judge of all the earth deal justly?"
>
> —Maimonides, *Code*, "Laws Concerning Repentence," chapter 5, sections 1 and 4

"Seek good and not evil"

The book of Genesis relates that after the Flood, when the world had been destroyed and the only survivors were Noah, his family, and the animals he had saved, God said to Himself: "Never again will I doom the world because of man, since the devisings of man's mind are evil from his youth." This recognition, that evil exists in all people, was further developed in talmudic and later writings. The sages spoke of the Evil Impulse and the Good Impulse as two inclinations that vie with each other in every person. Sometimes the sages equated the Evil Impulse with uncontrolled sex drives, sometimes with more general passions. They concluded that the Evil Impulse was indispensable to life—without it, they said, "no man would build a house, marry a wife, or beget children." But it must be kept in check so that we maintain control over our lives.

The discussion between Rabbi Judah the Prince and the Roman emperor Antoninus is one of several such dialogues in talmudic literature, but the identity of the Antoninus referred to is not known.

For there is not one good man on earth who does what is best, and does not err.

—Ecclesiastes,
chapter 7, verse 20

Seek good and not evil
That you may live
And that the Lord, the God of Hosts,
May truly be with you,
As you think.
Hate evil and love good
And establish justice in the gate....

—Amos, chapter 5,
verses 14–15

The implication here is that people are not born tainted with sin but are exposed to evil as they emerge into the world.

Antoninus asked Rabbi, "When does the Evil Impulse begin to influence man—from the time the embryo is formed or from the time the baby comes into the world?"

"From the time of formation," answered Rabbi.

"If that is so," objected Antoninus, "the baby would begin to rebel in its mother's womb. It must be from the time it emerges from the womb."

After that, Rabbi said, "This lesson Antoninus taught me and Scripture supports his argument, for it is said: 'Sin is the demon at the door, whose urge is toward you' " (Genesis 4:7).

—Babylonian Talmud, tractate
Sanhedrin, page 91b

At first the Evil Impulse is like a passer-by, then he is called a guest, and finally he becomes master of the house.

—Babylonian Talmud, tractate *Sukkah*, page 52b

The difference between the wicked and the righteous is that the wicked are controlled by their hearts and the righteous have their hearts under their control.

—*Genesis Rabbah*, chapter 34, section 10

There are six parts of the body that serve a person; three are under his control and three are not under his control.

The eye, the ear, and the nose are not under a person's control: he sees what he doesn't want to see, hears what he doesn't want to hear, and smells what he doesn't want to smell.

The mouth, the hand, and the foot are under a person's control; if he wants, he can use his mouth to study Torah, or if he wants he can use it to speak gossip and blasphemy; if he wishes, he can use his hand to distribute charity, or if he wishes, he can use it to steal and kill; if he chooses to, he can use his feet to walk to synagogues or houses of study, or if he chooses to, he can walk to houses of bawdy entertainment or immorality.

—*Genesis Rabbah*, chapter 67, section 3

Who is a mighty man?

He who subdues his Evil Impulse.

—Simeon ben Zoma, in *Ethics of the Fathers*, chapter 4, paragraph 1

Ascetics and "foolish pietists"

Controlling one's impulses does not mean substituting piety for common sense or renouncing all pleasures in life. Although there have been ascetic leanings during various periods of Jewish history and among individual scholars, the main tendency has always been to avoid all extreme states. Because the rabbis considered our bodies sacred, they regarded self-imposed bodily affliction for the sake of piety a sin. During the biblical and talmudic periods, there were individuals, known as Nazirites, who took special vows of holiness that included abstaining from wine and from cutting their hair. Nazirites were required to bring a sacrifice to the Temple as a sin offering, and some scholars interpreted this to mean that even their self-deprivation bordered on the sinful. In part, the opposition to asceticism stemmed from a strong conviction that since the teachings of the elders were meant for everyone, imposing standards most people could not meet would both diminish the lessons and lead to transgressions.

The Mishnah says: "A foolish pietist brings destruction upon the world."

What is a foolish pietist?

If someone sees a child sinking in a river and says, "When I finish my prayers I will save it," and by the time he finishes his prayers the child is dead. Or, a man sees a woman drowning and says, "It is not proper for me to look at her and save her"—that is a foolish pietist.

—Babylonian Talmud, tractate *Sotah*, page 21b

A person will be called to account on judgment day for every permissible thing that he might have enjoyed but did not.

—Jerusalem Talmud, tractate *Kiddushin*, chapter 4, paragraph 12

Are not the things that the Torah has forbidden enough for you, that you wish to add more to them?

—Jerusalem Talmud, tractate *Nedarim*, chapter 9, paragraph 1

A Nazirite is considered a sinner. . . . This is so because he afflicted himself by abstaining from wine.

Now does this not present an argument from the minor to the major? If a person who abstained only from wine is called a sinner, how much more so is the person who ascetically refrains from all enjoyment? Therefore, a person who fasts unnecessarily is called a sinner.

—Babylonian Talmud, tractate *Nedarim*, page 10a

When the Temple was destroyed for the second time, many people in Israel became ascetics, vowing neither to eat meat nor to drink wine.

Rabbi Joshua ben Hananiah spoke with them and said, "My sons, why do you not eat meat nor drink wine?"

They replied, "Shall we eat flesh which used to be brought as an offering on the altar now that we have no altar? Shall we drink wine that used to be poured as a libation on the altar but is no longer done so?"

He said to them, "If that is so, we should not eat bread either, because the meal offerings have ceased."

They said, "Yes, we can manage with fruit."

"We should not eat fruit, either," he said, because we no longer have an offering of first fruits."

"Then we can manage with other fruits," they said.

"But," he replied, "we should also not drink water, because we no longer have the ceremony of pouring water."

They could find no answer to this.

He said to them, "My sons, come and listen to me. Not

to mourn is impossible, because the blow has fallen. To mourn excessively is also impossible, because we do not impose on the community a hardship which the majority cannot endure."

Therefore, the sages have ruled: A man may stucco his house, but he should leave a little bare. . . . A man may prepare a full-course dinner, but he should omit an item or two. . . . A woman may wear jewelry but leave off one or two items.

—Babylonian Talmud, tractate
Bava Batra, page 60b

The divine law imposes no asceticism on us. It rather desires that we should keep the balance and grant every mental and physical faculty its due, without overburdening one faculty at the expense of another: if a person gives preponderance to desires, he blunts his mental faculty, and vice versa. . . . Long fasting, therefore, is no form of worship for a person whose desires are checked and whose body is weak; for him feasting is a religious duty and victory over self. . . . Your contrition on a fast day does no more to bring you nearer to God than your joy on the Sabbath and holy days, if the latter is the outcome of devotion. . . .

The servant of God does not withdraw himself from secular contact lest he be a burden to the world and the world to him; he does not hate life, which is one of God's bounties granted to him. . . . On the contrary, he loves this world and a long life, because they afford him opportunities of deserving the world to come: the more good he does, the greater is his claim on the world to come.

—Judah Halevi, *Kuzari*,
book 2, section 50;
book 3, section 1

Rewards and punishments

A corollary to the concept of freedom of will is the idea that ultimately we must accept the consequences of our actions. Although the book of Exodus portrays God as "visiting the iniquity of fathers upon children and children's children," the prophet Ezekiel insisted that people are punished only for their own sins, and that view was maintained by most later scholars. The rabbis often used concrete images to portray the judgment of our conduct: a hand writing in a book, a shopkeeper attending to his ledger. Although they taught that people literally are rewarded or punished by God, "measure for measure," they also taught that, on the highest level, what we do should not be motivated by the desire for reward but simply by the doing itself.

> ... If a man is righteous and does what is just and right: ... if he has not wronged anyone; if he has returned the debtor's pledge to him and has taken nothing by robbery; if he has given bread to the hungry and clothed the naked; if he has not lent at advance interest or exacted accrued interest; if he has abstained from wrongdoing and executed true justice between man and man; if he has followed My laws and kept My rules and acted honestly—he is righteous. Such a man shall live—declares the Lord God....
>
> The person who sins, he alone shall die. A son shall not share the burden of a father's guilt, nor shall a father share the burden of a son's guilt; the righteousness of the righteous shall be accounted to him alone, and the wickedness of the wicked shall be accounted to him alone.
>
> —Ezekiel, chapter 18,
> verses 5–9 and 20

Mark well three things and you will not fall into the clutches of sin: Know what is above you—an eye that sees, an ear that hears, and all your actions recorded in the book.

—Judah the Prince, in
Ethics of the Fathers,
chapter 2, paragraph 1

In this enigmatic metaphor, the world is compared to a shop and God to a shopkeeper who extends life on credit but keeps a ledger of people's deeds. The "net is cast" so that nobody can escape—perhaps this means escape death—the "shop is open," with people free to conduct themselves as they wish; and in the end "everything is prepared for the feast," a reward for the pious, or those who have repented, in the world to come.

Everything is given against a pledge, and a net is cast over all the living;

the shop is open, the shopkeeper extends credit, the ledger lies open, the hand writes, and whoever wishes to borrow may come and borrow;

and the collectors make the rounds continually, every day, and exact payment of man with his consent or without it.

They have what to base their claims on. And the judgment is a judgment of truth.

And everything is prepared for the feast.

—Rabbi Akiva, in
Ethics of the Fathers,
chapter 3, paragraph 20

Hillel saw a skull floating on top of the water. He said to it: Because you drowned others, you were drowned; and in the end, they who drowned you will be drowned.

—*Ethics of the Fathers*,
chapter 2, paragraph 7

Antoninus said to Rabbi, "Both the body and the soul can free themselves from judgment. The body can plead, 'the soul has sinned,' and the soul can say, 'the body has sinned.' "

Rabbi answered, "I will tell you a parable. To what may this be compared? To a human king who owned a beautiful orchard which had excellent figs. Now, he appointed two watchmen over the orchard, one lame and the other blind.

"One day the lame man said to the blind man, 'I see beautiful figs in this orchard. Put me on your shoulders so that we may pick them and eat them.'

"So the lame man climbed on the blind man's shoulders, picked the figs, and they both ate. When the owner of the orchard came and asked about the figs, the lame man said, 'Have I feet to climb with?' And the blind man said, 'Have I eyes to see with?'

"What did he do? He placed the lame man upon the blind man and judged them together. So will God bring the soul, place it in the body, and judge them together."

—Babylonian Talmud, tractate
Sanhedrin, pages 91a–b

Be not like slaves who serve their master for the sake of their allowance; be rather like slaves who serve their master with no thought of an allowance—and let the fear of heaven be upon you.

—Antigonus of Sokho, in
Ethics of the Fathers,
chapter 1, paragraph 3

Be quick in carrying out a minor commandment as in the case of a major one, and flee from transgression:

for one good deed leads to another good deed and one transgression leads to another transgression;

> for the reward for a good deed is another good deed
> and the reward for a transgression is another transgression.
>
> —Simeon ben Azzai, in
> *Ethics of the Fathers*,
> chapter 4, paragraph 2

On changing one's ways

If the punishment for wrongdoing is exacting, the opportunities for reforming are broad and open-ended. Among its many themes, the book of Jonah stands as a tribute to the power of repentance and a testimony to the acceptance of those who genuinely return to righteousness. Using the metaphor of a courtroom, the talmudic masters pictured the angels in heaven arguing for and against a person, with the benefit of the doubt always on the side of the person on trial. To be accepted, however, the rabbis said, a penitent must be sincere, and they held up as an example Eleazar ben Dordia, who was punished for his actions yet rewarded for the depth of his repentance.

> Moreover, if the wicked man repents of all the sins that he committed and keeps all My laws and does what is just and right, he shall live; he shall not die. None of the transgressions he committed shall be remembered against him; because of the righteousness he has practiced, he shall live.
>
> Is it My desire that a wicked man shall die?—says the Lord God. It is rather that he shall turn back from his ways and live.
>
> —Ezekiel, chapter 18,
> verses 21–23

Jonah is sent by God to tell the people of Nineveh that they will be destroyed for their immoral ways. He tries to escape his mission but finally completes it, only to find that the people repent and God rescinds His decree against them. Jonah is angry at God's actions.

This displeased Jonah greatly, and he was grieved. He prayed to the Lord, saying, "Oh Lord! Isn't this just what I said when I was still in my own country? That is why I fled beforehand to Tarshish. For I know that You are a compassionate and gracious God, slow to anger, abounding in kindness, renouncing punishment. Please, Lord, take my life, for I would rather die than live." The Lord replied: "Are you that deeply grieved?"

Now Jonah had left the city and found a place east of the city. He made a booth there and sat under it in the shade, until he should see what happened to the city. The Lord God provided a ricinus plant, which grew up over Jonah, to provide shade for his head and save him from discomfort. Jonah was very happy about the plant.

But the next day at dawn God provided a worm, which attacked the plant so that it withered. And when the sun rose, God provided a sultry east wind; the sun beat down on Jonah's head, and he became faint. He begged for death, saying, "I would rather die than live."

Then God said to Jonah, "Are you so deeply grieved about the plant?" "Yes," he replied, "so deeply that I want to die."

Then the Lord said, "You cared about the plant, which you did not work for and which you did not grow, which appeared overnight and perished overnight. And should I not care about Nineveh, that great city, in which there are more than a hundred and twenty thousand persons who do not yet know their right hand from their left, and many beasts as well!"

—Jonah, chapter 4,
verses 1–11

Whoever climbs the scaffold to be punished, if he has great advocates, he is saved, but if not he is not saved. And these are men's advocates: repentance and good deeds.

And even if nine hundred and ninety-nine angels

argue that a person is guilty, and one argues in his favor, the person is saved. . . .

Rabbi Eliezer ben Yose ha-Gelili said: Even if nine hundred and ninety-nine parts of that angel are against him, and one part is on his side, he is saved.

—Babylonian Talmud, tractate *Shabbat*, page 32a

Rabbi Eliezer said: "Repent one day before your death."

His disciples asked: "Does anyone know on what day he will die?"

"All the more reason to repent today," answered Rabbi Eliezer, "in case you die tomorrow, and thus a person's whole life should be spent in repentance."

—Babylonian Talmud, tractate *Shabbat*, page 153a

In the place where penitents stand, even the wholly righteous cannot stand.

—Rabbi Abbahu, in the Babylonian Talmud, tractate *Berakhot*, page 34b

---

It was said of Eleazar ben Dordia that there was not a prostitute in the world he had not come to.

Once, when he heard that a prostitute who lived near the sea would take a purse of *dinars* for her services, he took a purse and crossed seven rivers to reach her.

When he was with her, she blew out her breath and said to him: "Just as the air I blew will never return to its place, so Eleazar ben Dordia will never be forgiven for his sins."

He went and sat between two hills and mountains, and cried out, "O ye hills and mountains, plead mercy for me."

"How can we pray for you?" they answered. "We stand in need of mercy ourselves, for it is said: 'For the mountains may move and the hills be shaken' " (Isaiah 54:10).

"Heaven and earth," he cried, "you plead mercy for me."

"How shall we pray for you?" they answered. "We stand in need of mercy ourselves, as it is said: 'The heavens shall melt away like smoke, and the earth wear out like a garment' " (Isaiah 51:6).

"Sun and moon," he called out, "you plead for me."

"How can we pray for you?" they answered. "We stand in need of mercy ourselves, as it is said: 'Then the moon shall be ashamed and the sun shall be abashed' " (Isaiah 24:23).

"O stars and constellations," called Eleazar in despair, "you plead for me."

"How can we pray for you?" they, too, answered. "We also need mercy for ourselves, as it is written: 'All the hosts of heaven shall molder' " (Isaiah 34:4).

"Then," said he, "this matter depends on me alone."

He put his head between his knees and wept out loud until his soul departed.

Just then a heavenly voice was heard proclaiming, "Rabbi Eleazar ben Dordai is destined for the life of the world to come."

. . . When Rabbi heard this story, he wept and said, "Some people attain eternal life after many years, and some in just an hour!" He also said, "Repentants are not only accepted, they are even called 'Rabbi'!"

—Babylonian Talmud, tractate
Avodah Zarah, page 17a

Why do the good suffer?

The selections below fall into two categories: first, the cries of victims of illnesses, plagues, persecutions, and terrors through the centuries; second, responses to their accusations. The book of Job incorporates both categories, expressing the anguish and anger of the sufferer while teaching that, ultimately, the question of why people suffer must remain unanswered.

Elisha ben Avuyah, a tragic figure of the talmudic period, gave up Judaism after seeing a man unjustly punished. The Crusade chronicle here is one of many records of the misery caused by crusaders of the eleventh, twelfth, and thirteenth centuries, as they swept away one Jewish community after another.

You will win, O Lord, if I make claim against You,
Yet I shall present charges against You:
Why does the way of the wicked prosper?
Why are the workers of treachery at ease?
You have planted them, and they have taken root,
They spread, they even bear fruit.
You are present in their mouths,
But far from their thoughts.

—Jeremiah, chapter 12,
verses 1–2

God of vengeance, Lord,
God of vengeance, appear!
Rise up, judge of the earth,
Give the arrogant their deserts!
How long shall the wicked, O Lord,
How long shall the wicked exult,
Shall they utter insolent speech,
Shall all evildoers vaunt themselves?
They crush Your people, O Lord,
They afflict Your very own;
They kill the widow and the stranger;
They murder the fatherless,
Thinking, "The Lord does not see it,
The God of Jacob does not pay heed."

—Psalms, psalm 94,
verses 1–7

And here is another frustration: the fact that the sentence imposed for evil deeds is not executed swiftly, which is why men are emboldened to do evil—the fact that a sinner may do evil a hundred times and his [punishment] still be delayed.

For although I am aware that "It will be well with those who revere God since they revere Him, and it will not be well with the scoundrel, and he will not live long, because he does not revere God"—here is a frustration that occurs in the world: Sometimes an upright man is requited according to the conduct of the scoundrel; and sometimes the scoundrel is requited according to the conduct of the upright. I say, all that is frustration.

—Ecclesiastes, chapter 8,
verses 10–14

If I called Him, would He answer me?
I cannot believe that He would hear my voice.
For He crushes me for a trifle,
and increases my wounds without cause.
He does not let me catch my breath,
but fills me with bitterness.
If it be a matter of power, here He is!
But if of justice, who will arraign Him?
Though I am in the right, my mouth would condemn me;
though I am blameless, it would prove me perverse.
I am blameless—I am beside myself—I loathe my life.
It is all one—I say—
the blameless and the wicked He destroys alike.
When disaster brings sudden death
He mocks the plea of the innocent.
The land is given over to the hand of the evildoer
who is able to bribe the judges.
If not He, who then is guilty? . . .
If I sin, You stand guard over me;
You do not let me escape my guilt.

If I sin, woe betide me,
yet if I am righteous, I cannot
raise my head, being filled with shame and sated with misery.
For You take pride in hunting me like a lion,
time and again You show Your wonders against me.

—Job, chapter 9, verses 16–24;
chapter 10, verses 14–16

Elisha ben Avuyah's break with Judaism is related, according to legend, to a command in the book of Deuteronomy that a person must send a mother bird away before taking her young from their nest.

What is it that happened with Elisha ben Avuyah?

It is said that once he was sitting and studying in the plain of Kinneret when he saw a man climb to the top of a date-palm tree, take a mother bird with her young, and descend safely.

After the Sabbath he saw another man climb a tree, free the mother bird, and take only the young, as the Torah instructs. But when the man came down, a snake bit him, and he died.

Elisha said, "It is written: 'Let the mother go and take only the young in order that you may fare well and have a long life' (Deuteronomy 22:7). Where is the goodness and where is the long life for this man?"

—*Ruth Rabbah*,
chapter 6, section 4

The heart of the people of our God grew faint and their spirit flagged, for many sore injuries had been inflicted upon them and they had been smitten repeatedly. They now came supplicating to God and fasting, and their hearts melted within them. But the Lord did as He declared, for we had sinned before Him. . . . His wrath was kindled and He drew the sword against them, until they remained as the flagstaff upon the mountaintop and as the ensign on the hill, and He gave over His nation into captivity and trampled them underfoot.

See, O Lord, and consider to whom Thou has done thus: to Israel, a nation despised and pillaged. Your chosen portion! Why have You uplifted the shield of its enemies, and why have they gained in strength? Let all hear, for I cry out in anguish; the ears of all that hear me shall be seared: How has the staff of might been broken, the rod of glory—the sainted community comparable to fine gold, the community of Mainz!

—From the *Chronicle of Solomon bar Simson* (c. 1140), describing the First Crusade as it swept through the city of Mainz in 1096

There is no death without sin, nor suffering without transgression.

—Rabbi Ammi, in the Babylonian Talmud, tractate *Shabbat*, page 55a

---

If a man sees that painful sufferings come to him, let him examine his works. . . .

If he examines his works and finds nothing, let him seek the cause in the neglect of Torah. . . .

If he still finds that this is not the cause, he may be sure these are sufferings of love, as it is written: "For whom the Lord loves, He corrects" (Proverbs 3:12).

If the Holy One, blessed be He, loves a man, he crushes him with painful sufferings.

—Rava, in the Babylonian Talmud, tractate *Berakhot*, page 5a

---

God is strict with both the righteous and the wicked. He calls the righteous to account in this world for the few wrongs they have committed in order to reward them lavishly in the world to come.

He brings peace and ease to the wicked in this world, rewarding them for their few good deeds, in order to punish them in the future world.

—Rabbi Akiva, in *Genesis Rabbah*,
chapter 33, section 1

Within our reach is neither the tranquility of the wicked nor even the suffering of the righteous.

—Rabbi Yannai, in
Ethics of the Fathers,
chapter 4, paragraph 19

Legend says that when Moses rose to heaven, God showed him the future achievements of Rabbi Akiva, who later died as a martyr.

Moses said, "Lord of the Universe, You have shown me his Torah, now show me his reward."

"Turn yourself around," said God.

Moses turned around, saw Rabbi Akiva dying a cruel death, and merchants weighing out his flesh in the marketplace.

"Lord of the Universe," cried Moses. "So much Torah, and this is his reward?"

"Be silent," replied God, "for such is My decree."

—Babylonian Talmud, tractate
Menahot, page 29b

Then the Lord answered Job out of the whirlwind, saying,
Who is this that darkens My plan by words without
knowledge?

Gird up your loins like a man;
  I will question you, and you may inform Me.
Where were you when I laid the foundations of the earth?
Tell me if you have any understanding.
  Who marked out its measure, if you know it,
Who stretched the plumb line upon it?
Upon what were the earth's pillars sunk;
  who laid down its cornerstone,
When the morning stars sang together
  and all the sons of God shouted for joy? . . .
Is it by your wisdom that the hawk goes soaring
  and spreads his wings toward the south?
Is it at your command that the eagle mounts
  and makes his nest on high?
On the rock he makes his home, on the steep crag and
  fortress.
Thence he searches for food, his eyes ranging afar.
His young ones suck up blood, and where the slain are,
  there is he.
(The Lord answered Job, saying,)
Can he who argues with the Almighty instruct Him?
Can he who reproves God answer all this?
Job answered the Lord, saying,
Behold, I am of small account; how can I answer You?
  I lay my hand to my mouth.
I have spoken once, and I will not reply again; twice, but
  I will proceed no further.

—Job, chapter 38, verses 1–7;
chapter 39, verses 26–30;
chapter 40, verses 1–5

The meaning of faith

"Faith," said the Hasidic rabbi Menahem Mendel of Kotsk, "is clearer than sight." Though human vision may not be sharp enough to penetrate universal mysteries, the rabbis believed that faith makes it possible to accept whatever happens in life with the knowledge that the God who orders the universe is good and just. They had great contempt—and pity—for a person like Elisha ben Avuyah whose faith did not stretch far enough. They labeled such a person an "Apikoros," from the Greek philosopher Epicurus, and defined him as one who declares: "There is neither judge nor judgment."

In his commentary to the Mishnah, Maimonides formulated what he considered the thirteen fundamental principles of Jewish faith. Although not accepted as binding dogma, and criticized by some scholars as too limiting and by others as too broad, Maimonides's principles have been incorporated in the daily prayer book, where they are stated as a personal declaration of faith. Perhaps most eloquent, because of its simplicity, is the faith expressed by a survivor of the Spanish expulsion of the Jews in 1492. His story was recorded by Solomon Ibn Verga during the sixteenth century in a compendium of Jewish persecutions from the destruction of the Second Temple onward.

Six hundred and thirteen commandments were given to Moses: 365 negative commandments corresponding to the number of days in the year and 248 positive commandments corresponding to the number of organs in the human body.

David came and reduced them to eleven principles, which are given in Psalm 15.

Isaiah came and reduced them to six, as it is written: "He who walks in righteousness, speaks uprightly, spurns profit from fraudulent dealings, waves away a bribe instead of grasping it, stops his ears against listening to infamy, shuts his eyes against looking at evil" (Isaiah 33:15).

Micah came and reduced them to three, as it is written: "What the Lord requires of you: only to do justice, and to love goodness, and to walk humbly with your God" (Micah 6:8).

Isaiah then reduced them to two principles, as it is written: "Thus said the Lord: observe what is right and do what is just" (Isaiah 56:1).

Finally came Habakkuk and reduced them all to one

principle, as it is written: "The righteous shall live by his faith" (Habakkuk 2:4).

—Rabbi Simlai, in the
Babylonian Talmud, tractate
Makkot, pages 23b–24a

It once happened that Hillel the Elder was returning from a trip when he heard screams coming from the city.

"I am sure they do not come from my home," he said.

Of him Scripture says: "He is not afraid of evil tidings; his heart is firm, he trusts in the Lord" (Psalms 112:7).

—Babylonian Talmud, tractate
Berakhot, page 60a

The identities of the two witnesses in the verse cited from the book of Isaiah are unclear, and Rabbi Akiva offers his own interpretation in order to lead into his message of consolation and faith.

Long ago, Rabban Gamaliel, Rabbi Eleazar ben Azariah, Rabbi Joshua, and Rabbi Akiva were coming up to Jerusalem together, and as they approached the area where the Temple had stood, they saw a fox running out of the ruins. The other sages began to weep, but Rabbi Akiva seemed cheerful.

"Why are you cheerful?" they asked him.

"Why are you weeping?" he responded.

They said, "The place that was once our Holy of Holies has now become the haunt of foxes, and should we not weep?"

He said, "And that is why I am cheerful. For Scripture says: 'And call reliable witnesses, the priest Uriah and Zechariah son of Jeberechiah' (Isaiah 8:2). Now, what connection has the priest Uriah with Zechariah? Uriah lived during the period of the First Temple, and Zechariah lived during the time of the Second Temple. But holy Scripture has linked the later prophecy of Zechariah with the earlier prophecy of Uriah.

"In the early prophecy, from the days of Uriah [the words actually are ascribed to Micah] it is written, 'Zion shall be plowed as a field'; in the book of Zechariah it is written, 'There shall yet be old men and women in the squares of Jerusalem.'

"As long as Uriah's prophecy of destruction had not been fulfilled, I was concerned lest Zechariah's prophecy might not be fulfilled. Now that Uriah's prophecy has literally come about, it is quite certain that Zechariah's prophecy also will be carried out."

"Akiva," they said to him, "you have comforted us. Akiva, you have comforted us."

—Babylonian Talmud, tractate
Makkot, pages 24a–b

I believe with perfect faith that the Creator, blessed be His Name, is the Author and Guide of everything that has been created, and that He alone has made, does make, and will make all things.

I believe with perfect faith that the Creator, blessed be His Name, is a Unity, and that there is no unity in any way like His, and that He alone is our God, who was, is, and will be.

I believe with perfect faith that the Creator, praised be His Name, is not a body, and that He is free from all the properties of a body, and that He has no form whatever.

I believe with perfect faith that the Creator, blessed be His Name, is the first and the last.

I believe with perfect faith that to the Creator, praised be His Name, and to Him alone, it is proper to pray, and it is not proper to pray to any besides Him.

I believe with perfect faith that all the words of the prophets are true.

I believe with perfect faith that the prophecy of Moses our teacher, peace be unto him, was true, and that he was the father of all prophets, both those who preceded and those who followed him.

I believe with perfect faith that the entire Torah, now in our possession, is the same that was given to Moses our teacher, peace be unto him.

I believe with perfect faith that this Torah will not be changed, and that there will never be any other Torah from the Creator, blessed be His Name.

I believe with perfect faith that the Creator, blessed be His Name, knows every deed of human beings, and all their thoughts, as it is said: "He who fashions the hearts of them all, who discerns all their doings" (Psalms 33:15).

I believe with perfect faith that the Creator, blessed be His Name, rewards those who keep His commandments, and punishes those who transgress His commandments.

I believe with perfect faith in the coming of the Messiah; and though he tarry, I will wait daily for his coming.

I believe with perfect faith that there will be a revival of the dead at the time when it shall please the Creator, blessed be His Name, and exalted be His fame for ever and ever.

—Adapted from Maimonides's commentary to the Mishnah, tractate *Sanhedrin,* chapter 10, paragraph 1

I heard from some old people who left Spain that one boat was besieged by the plague, and the captain of the boat threw the passengers ashore at an uninhabited place. And there most of them died from starvation. Those few who remained gathered all their strength to walk until they could find a settled area.

One Jew who was there with his wife and two sons

tried to walk. But the woman fainted and died because she was not accustomed to so much hard walking. The man carried his sons until all three of them fainted from hunger. When the man regained consciousness, he found his two sons dead. From the depths of his sorrow, he rose to his feet and said:

"God in heaven, You have done a great deal to make me lose my faith, but know that in spite of the efforts of all the heavenly hosts, a Jew I am and a Jew I shall remain, and all that You have brought and will bring upon me will not avail you."

And he gathered earth and leaves and covered his sons, and walked on to find a settlement.

—Solomon Ibn Verga (c. 1500–1550),
Shevet Yehudah, section 52

Can there be faith after Auschwitz?

"In the beginning there was the Holocaust," Elie Wiesel once said. As nothing else in Jewish history ever did, that catastrophe has brought about discussion and reevaluation of traditional Jewish beliefs and attitudes toward God.

Historians have observed that in the past it has often taken the Jewish community a full generation—as much as thirty years—to absorb and deal with tragedies that occurred to them as a people. Certainly this was true of the Holocaust. During the years after World War II, not many thinkers wrestled with the religious or philosophic implications of the Holocaust. Among the few who did were Martin Buber and Elie Wiesel: Buber, in his work the *Eclipse of God*, published in 1952; Wiesel, in his novels published during the late fifties and early sixties. By the mid-sixties, as the vastness of the calamity sank deeper into the Jewish consciousness, scholars and philosophers began to debate the issue at symposiums and in their writings. Theologian Richard Rubenstein threw down the gauntlet in his book *After Auschwitz*, declaring that it was no longer possible for a Jew to believe in the God of history who cares for and watches over people. Among those who opposed him were the liberal theologian Emile Fackenheim and the Orthodox scholar Eliezer Berkovits.

The debate continues. But among the writings of the Holocaust are two declarations of faith that have little to do with philosophy. The first is by an American writer imagining the thoughts of a fictional Warsaw Ghetto Jew called Yossel Rakover. This stark, powerful excerpt, which echoes the words of the Spanish Jew who had been exiled from his home more than four hundred years earlier, has often been mistaken for an authentic document rather than a piece of fiction. The second, by Anne Frank, is a well-known proclamation of faith not so much in God but in people, in spite of it all.

At the concentration camp of Buna, thousands of prisoners had come together to observe the eve of the Jewish New Year. Elie Wiesel describes the scene:

> At the place of assembly, surrounded by the electrified barbed wire, thousands of silent Jews gathered, their faces stricken.
>
> Night was falling. Other prisoners continued to crowd in, from every block, able suddenly to conquer time and space and submit both to their will.
>
> "What are you, my God," I thought angrily, "compared to this afflicted crowd, proclaiming to You their faith, their anger, their revolt? What does Your greatness mean, Lord of the Universe, in the face of all this weakness, this decomposition, and this decay? Why do You still trouble their sick minds, their crippled bodies?" . . .
>
> "Blessed be the Name of the Eternal!"
>
> Why, but why should I bless Him? In every fibre I rebelled. Because He had had thousands of children burned in His pits? Because He kept six crematories working night and day, on Sundays and feast days? Because in His great might He had created Auschwitz, Birkenau, Buna, and so many factories of death? How could I say to Him: "Blessed art Thou, Eternal Master of the Universe, Who chose us from among the races to

be tortured day and night, to see our fathers, our mothers, our brothers, end in the crematory? Praised be Thy Holy Name, Thou Who hast chosen us to be butchered on Thine altar?" . . .

Once, New Year's Day had dominated my life. I knew that my sins grieved the Eternal; I implored his forgiveness. Once, I had believed profoundly that upon one solitary deed of mine, one solitary prayer, depended the salvation of the world.

This day I had ceased to plead. I was no longer capable of lamentation. On the contrary, I felt very strong. I was the accuser, God the accused. My eyes were open and I was alone—terribly alone in a world without God and without man. Without love or mercy, I had ceased to be anything but ashes, yet I felt myself to be stronger than the Almighty, to whom my life had been tied for so long. I stood amid that praying congregation, observing it like a stranger.

—Elie Wiesel, *Night* (1958)

I believe the greatest single challenge to modern Judaism arises out of the question of God and the death camps. . . . How can Jews believe in an omnipotent, beneficent God after Auschwitz? Traditional Jewish theology maintains that God is the ultimate, omnipotent actor in the historical drama. It has interpreted every major catastrophe in Jewish history as God's punishment of a sinful Israel. I fail to see how this position can be maintained without regarding Hitler and the SS as instruments of God's will. The agony of European Jewry cannot be likened to the testing of Job. To see any purpose in the death camps, the traditional believer is forced to regard the most demonic, antihuman explosion in all history as a meaningful expression of God's purposes. The idea is simply too obscene for me to accept. . . .

Though I believe that a void stands where once we

experienced God's presence, I do not think Judaism has lost its meaning or its power. I do not believe that a theistic God is necessary for Jewish religious life. . . . We no longer believe in the God who has the power to annul the tragic necessities of existence; the need religiously to share that existence remains.

—Richard L. Rubenstein, Distinguished Professor in the Department of Religion, Florida State University, from a symposium, "The State of Jewish Belief," in *Commentary* (August 1966)

What does the Voice of Auschwitz command?

Jews are forbidden to hand Hitler posthumous victories. They are commanded to survive as Jews, lest the Jewish people perish. They are commanded to remember the victims of Auschwitz, lest their memory perish. They are forbidden to despair of man and his world, and to escape into either cynicism or otherworldliness, lest they cooperate in delivering the world over to the forces of Auschwitz. Finally, they are forbidden to despair of the God of Israel, lest Judaism perish. A secularist Jew cannot make himself believe by a mere act of will, nor can he be commanded to do so. . . . And a religious Jew who has stayed with his God may be forced into new, possibly revolutionary relationships with Him. One possibility, however, is wholly unthinkable. A Jew may not respond to Hitler's attempt to destroy Judaism by himself cooperating in its destruction. In ancient times, the unthinkable Jewish sin was idolatry. Today, it is to respond to Hitler by doing his work.

—Emile L. Fackenheim, *God's Presence in History* (1970)

God is responsible for having created a world in which man is free to make history. There must be a dimension beyond history in which all suffering finds its redemption through God. This is essential to the faith of a Jew. The Jew does not doubt God's presence, though he is unable to set limits to the duration and intensity of His absence. This is no justification for the ways of providence, but its acceptance. It is not a willingness to forgive the unheard cries of millions, but a trust that in God the tragedy of man may find its transformation.

—Eliezer Berkovits, *Faith After the Holocaust* (1973)

God. You have done everything to make me stop believing in You. Now, lest it seem to You that You will succeed by these tribulations in driving me from the right path, I notify You, God, and God of my fathers, that it will not avail You in the least. You may insult me. You may castigate me. You may take from me all that I cherish and hold dear in the world. You may torture me to death, but I will always love You and these are my last words to You, my wrathful God: . . . I die exactly as I have lived, crying, "Eternally praised be the God of the dead, the God of vengeance, of truth, of love, who will soon show His face to the world again . . ."

—Zvi Kolitz, "Yossel Rakover Speaks to God," 1946

In spite of everything I still believe that people are really good at heart. I simply can't build up my hopes on a foundation consisting of confusion, misery, and death. I see the world gradually being turned into a wilderness, I hear the ever-approaching thunder, which will destroy us too. I can feel the sufferings of millions and yet, if I look up into the heavens, I think that it will all come right, that this cruelty too will end, and that peace and tranquility will return again.

In the meantime, I must uphold my ideals, for perhaps the time will come when I shall be able to carry them out.

—Anne Frank, *Diary of a Young Girl*, entry for Saturday, July 15, 1944

The many ways of prayer

Praying in the Jewish tradition provides a bridge between each person and God. It's an affirmation of love and faith; it's also a way of conveying anger and protest. Many prayers praise God, but too much praise is considered hypocritical. Prayers are formalized, but they are also personal and emotional. And prayer is for everyone—even God.

The Hasidic masters especially stressed feelings rather than form in praying. Among the greatest of the Hasidim, Rabbi Levi Isaac ben Meir of Berdichev became known for his homey "conversations" with God, which he often sang in Yiddish before the congregation. In his famous *Kaddish* prayer, he reprimanded God for not redeeming Israel and returning the Jewish people to their homeland. Rabbi Levi probably would have felt great kinship with the old man in the final anecdote told by Professor Abraham Joshua Heschel.

"Loving the Lord your God and serving Him with all your heart and soul" (Deuteronomy 11:13).

What is service of the heart?

This is prayer.

—Babylonian Talmud, tractate *Ta'anit*, page 2a

If a person sees shooting stars, earthquakes, thunder, storms, and lightning he should say, "Blessed be He whose strength and might fill the world."

If he sees mountains, hills, seas, rivers, and deserts, he should say, "Blessed be He who brought about creation." . . .

For rain or for good tidings, a person should say, "Blessed be He who is good and does good." For evil tidings, he should say, "Blessed be the true judge." . . .

To cry over what has passed is to utter a prayer in vain. . . . If a man returns from a journey and hears cries coming from his town and says, "May it be God's will that those do not come from my house," that is a vain prayer.

—Mishnah, tractate *Berakhot*,
chapter 9, paragraphs 2 and 3

A certain man stood before the Ark in the presence of Rabbi Hanina and said, "O God, the great, mighty, fearsome, majestic, powerful, strong, fearless, certain, and honored."

When the man had finished, Rabbi Hanina said to him, "Why are you using all those words of praise? We would not even use the three we traditionally say—the great, the mighty, and the awesome—had not Moses our teacher mentioned them in the Torah and had not our later masters inserted them into our prayers.

"It is as if an earthly king had a million gold pieces, and someone praised him for owning silver ones. Would that not be an insult to him?"

—Babylonian Talmud, tractate
Berakhot, page 33b

Even the Holy One, blessed be He, prays.

What does He pray?

"May it be My will that My mercy overcomes My anger, and that My mercy dominates all My attributes so that I may deal with My children mercifully, and for their sake not extract strict justice."

—Babylonian Talmud, tractate *Berakhot*, page 7a

A villager who prayed at the house of prayer of the Ba'al Shem Tov on the High Holidays had a son who could not learn to read even one letter. Because the boy could not pray from a prayer book, his father never took him to services during the holidays. But when the boy turned thirteen, his father decided to take him to the house of prayer for the Day of Atonement.

Now, this young boy had a little pipe on which he used to play as he sat in the fields watching over his sheep. He took the pipe with him to services, and the father didn't notice.

Hour after hour, the boy sat in the house of prayer and said nothing. When the *Mussaf*, or Additional Service, began, he asked his father if he might play on his pipe. The father angrily forbade it, and when the boy continued to plead with him, he placed his hand over the youngster's pocket so that he could not take his pipe out.

Finally, the Closing Service of the day began. Suddenly the boy snatched his pocket away from his father's hand, pulled out his little pipe, and blew into it with all his might. The congregation was startled and confused by the sound. But the Ba'al Shem Tov went on with the service. At the end of the day the rabbi declared that the little boy's pipe music had carried all the congregation's prayers up to heaven.

—Tale about Rabbi Israel ben Eliezer Ba'al Shem Tov

The refrain "Glorified and sanctified be His great name" are the introductory words to the traditional Kaddish *prayer recited during synagogue services.*

Good morning to you, Lord of the world!
I, Levi Isaac, son of Sarah of Berdichev, am coming to
 you in a legal matter concerning your people of Israel.
What do you want of Israel?
It is always: Command the children of Israel!
It is always: Speak unto the children of Israel!
Merciful Father! How many peoples are there in the
 world?
Persians, Babylonians, Edomites!
The Russians—what do they say?
 Our emperor is the emperor!
The Germans—what do they say?
 Our kingdom is the kingdom!
The English—what do they say?
 Our kingdom is the kingdom!
But I, Levi Isaac, son of Sarah of Berdichev, say:
 "Glorified and sanctified be His great name!"
And I, Levi Isaac, son of Sarah of Berdichev, say:
 I shall not go hence nor budge from my place
 until there be a finish
 until there be an end of exile—
 "Glorified and sanctified be His great name!"

—Levi Isaac ben Meir of Berdichev, "Kaddish"

Two great servants move through the ages: prayer and sacrifice. In prayer man pours himself out, dependent without reservation, knowing that, incomprehensibly, he acts on God, albeit without exacting anything from God; for when he no longer covets anything for himself, he beholds his effective activity burning in the supreme flame. And those who sacrifice? I cannot despise the honest servants of the remote past who thought that God desired the smell of their burnt sacrifices: they knew in a foolish and vigorous way that one can and should give to God; and that is also known to him who offers his little will to God and encounters Him in a great will. "Let Your will be done"—is all he says, but truth goes on to say for him: "through me whom You need."

—Martin Buber, *I and Thou*

Professor Heschel describes a trip to Poland made by a friend of his during the late 1940s. His friend, an important official, was given a large compartment on a train leaving Warsaw; and when he saw a sickly, poor Jew outside, he invited the man to share his compartment.

My friend tried to engage him in conversation, but he would not talk. When evening came, my friend, an observing Jew, recited the evening prayer, while the other fellow did not say a word of prayer. The following morning my friend took out his prayer shawl and phylacteries and said his prayer; the other fellow, who looked so wretched and somber, would not say a word and did not pray.

Finally, when the day was almost over, they started a conversation. The fellow said, "I am never going to pray any more because of what happened to us in Auschwitz. . . . How could I pray? That is why I did not pray all day."

The following morning . . . my friend noticed that the fellow suddenly opened his bundle, took out his prayer shawl and phylacteries, and started to pray. He asked the man afterward, "What made you change your mind?"

The fellow said, "It suddenly dawned upon me to think how lonely God must be; look with whom He is left. I felt sorry for Him."

—Abraham Joshua Heschel,
A Passion for Truth

"And though he tarry, I will wait"

The twelfth of Maimonides's thirteen principles of faith—"I believe with perfect faith in the coming of the Messiah, and though he tarry, I will wait daily for his coming"—became the credo of thousands of Jews in the ghettos and concentration camps of the Nazi era. The belief in a Messiah who would redeem both Israel and humankind has its roots in the prophets' visions of the "end of days," and was more fully developed by the sages of the talmudic and later periods. The coming of the Messiah was seen as the beginning of a time when all the ideals taught in the Torah would come to fruition; a time when the scattered peoples of Israel would be returned to their homeland; a time of social justice, of peace, of perfection. Views differed on just who the Messiah would be and how he would come. Some scholars saw him as King David resurrected, some as the son of David. Some spoke of a priestly Messiah, others of a king. Some envisaged him riding on a donkey, others imagined him bursting through the clouds. But whatever the differences, in one area there was general agreement. Although men and women needed to wait patiently for the Messiah to come, waiting did not free them of moral responsibility in the world as it is. By seeking good and opposing evil, by striving to live in the image of God, each person could help bring the Messiah and with him the messianic age.

But a shoot shall grow out of the stump of Jesse,
A twig shall sprout from his stock.
The spirit of the Lord shall alight upon him:
A spirit of wisdom and insight,
A spirit of counsel and valor,
A spirit of devotion and reverence for the Lord.
He shall sense the truth by his reverence for the Lord.
He shall not judge by what his eyes behold.
Nor decide by what his ears perceive.
Thus he shall judge the poor with equity

And decide with justice for the lowly of the land.
He shall strike down a land with the rod of his mouth
And slay the wicked with the breath of his lips.
Justice shall be the girdle of his loins,
And faithfulness the girdle of his waist.
The wolf shall dwell with the lamb,
The leopard lie down with the kid;
The calf, the beast of prey, and the fatling together,
With a little boy to herd them.
The cow and the bear shall graze,
Their young shall lie down together;
And the lion, like the ox, shall eat straw.
A babe shall play
Over a viper's hole,
And an infant pass his hand
Over an adder's den.
In all of My sacred mount
Nothing evil or vile shall be done;
For the land shall be filled with devotion to the Lord
As water covers the sea.

—Isaiah, chapter 11,
verses 1–19

The son of David will not come until there are no haughty men in Israel, as it is written: "For then I will remove the proud and exultant within you" (Zephanian 3:11)....

Jerusalem shall be redeemed only by righteousness, as it is written: "Zion shall be saved with judgment, her repentant ones with righteousness" (Isaiah 1:27). . . .

—Babylonian Talmud, tractate
Sanhedrin, page 98a

Rabbi Joshua ben Levi pointed out a contradiction. It is written "in due time" [will the Messiah come], while it is also written "I the Lord will speed it" (Isaiah 60:22).

It means: If they are worthy, I will speed it. If not, he will come in due time.

—Babylonian Talmud, tractate *Sanhedrin*, page 98a

Rabbi Joshua ben Levi met Elijah the prophet. . . . He asked Elijah: "When will the Messiah come?"

Elijah answered: "Go and ask him yourself."

"Where is he?"

"At the gates of the town."

"How shall I recognize him?"

"He is sitting among the poor lepers. The others unbind all the bandages of their sores at the same time and then rebind them all together. But he unbinds one sore at a time and then binds it again before treating the next one, thinking to himself, 'Perhaps I will be needed, and if so I must not delay.' "

Rabbi Joshua went to the Messiah and said, "Peace unto you, master and teacher."

The Messiah answered, "Peace unto you O son of Levi."

"When will you come, master?" asked Rabbi Joshua.

"Today," came the answer.

Rabbi Joshua returned to Elijah, who asked, "What did he tell you?" . . .

"He spoke falsely to me," said Rabbi Joshua, "for he said he would come today, but he has not come."

Elijah answered him, "This is what he told you: 'Today—if you will but hearken to His voice' " (Psalms 95:7).

—Babylonian Talmud, tractate *Sanhedrin*, page 98a

Rabban Johanan ben Zakkai's response to the many false messiahs who claimed to be the true Redeemer in ancient times was this wry comment:

If you should happen to be holding a sapling in your hand when they tell you the Messiah has arrived, first plant the sapling and then go out to greet the Messiah.

—*Fathers According to Rabbi Nathan,* version B, chapter 31

The sages and prophets did not long for the days of the Messiah that Israel might exercise dominion over the world, or rule over the heathens, or be exalted by the nations, or that it might eat and drink and rejoice. Their aspiration was that Israel be free to devote itself to the Torah and its wisdom, with no one to oppress or disturb it, and thus be worthy of life in the world to come.

In that era there will be neither famine nor war, neither jealousy nor strife. Blessings will be abundant, comforts within the reach of all. The one preoccupation of the whole world will be to know the Lord. Hence Israelites will be very wise, they will know the things that are now concealed and will attain an understanding of their Creator to the utmost capacity of the human mind.

—Maimonides, *Code,* "Laws Concerning Kings and Wars," chapter 12, sections 4 and 5

10

THE VALUE OF LIFE

"How do you know that your blood is redder than his?"

Our relation to nature ✦ "You must not destroy" ✦ Protecting the environment ✦ Showing kindness to animals ✦ Placing life above laws ✦ The question of birth control ✦ The abortion controversy ✦ Weighing your life against another's ✦ Rescuing someone ✦ Is killing ever justified? ✦ May one life be sacrificed to save many? ✦ Taking one's own life ✦ Martyrdom: for the "sanctification of God's name"

In New Jersey, in 1977, a pair of Siamese twin girls was born to an Orthodox Jewish family. Connected at their chests, the twins were kept alive by one and a half hearts. Baby B had an almost normal heart that was fused to the half-heart of Baby A. Doctors at Philadelphia's Children's Hospital, to which the twins were flown, determined that if the infants were not separated, both would die; if they were separated, Baby A surely would die, while Baby B had a slim chance for survival. A decision had to be made: Should the twins be separated with the knowledge that the surgeon had to kill one in the hope of saving the other?

The twins' parents consulted three world-famous rabbis, who disputed with one another in true talmudic style. "Two men jump out of a burning airplane," one rabbi said. "The parachute of the first man opens and he falls slowly and safely toward the earth. The parachute of the second man does not open. As he plunges past his friend, he manages to grab onto his foot and hold on. But the parachute is too small to support both of them. Now they are both plunging to their death. Is it morally justified for the first man to kick his friend away because they would both die if he didn't, and it was the second man who was designated for death, since it was his parachute that didn't open?" The analogy was clear. Baby A, with only a stump of a heart, had been "designated for death," as it were, and was dragging Baby B along with her.

But there was another way of looking at the situation. A second rabbi spoke of the case of an infant who has almost completely emerged from its mother's womb when something happens and it cannot be pulled all the way out. "Now," said the rabbi, "you have two human beings in conflict with one another, the mother and the child. You have no right to select the life of one over that of the other." Continuing this analogy, did anyone have the right to select the life of Baby B over that of Baby A?

The arguments flew back and forth, four to five hours a night, for eleven nights. Finally the rabbis agreed to the separation recommended by the surgeons. In the final analysis, they felt, every effort had to be made to save one life rather than lose two, even if that one life was tenuous. They had satisfied themselves that of the infants, Baby A, with her incomplete heart, had indeed been more clearly "designated for death."

The rabbis' painful dilemma has been faced in different ways and at different times by many other scholars and sages. At its very basis lies an unyielding insistence on the worth of every human life, an insistence that does not allow one life to be considered more or less valuable than another. "I have put before you life and death, blessing and curse," says the book of Deuteronomy. "Choose life." And these words "choose life" have become the catchwords for the Jewish attitude toward all human life.

The zeal for human life is reflected in the appreciation shown all living things. Although during ancient times conquering and subduing nature was a major concern, early teachers and sages had a deep respect for their environment. A single biblical command prohibiting the destruction of fruit trees during wartime, for example, led to a wide variety of laws forbidding any kind of wanton destruction. Biblical and talmudic rules deal with air pollution and city planning, with the care of animals and the preservation of species. The dietary laws, whose purposes and meanings, unexplained in the Bible, have been disputed for generations, have one core idea throughout. In their prohibitions against eating blood or the flesh of living animals, in their restrictions on the kinds and parts of animals that may be consumed, they set limits on human dominance over the animal world.

Yet, we do dominate. The Bible unequivocably placed men and women at the pinnacle of creation; and in the hierarchy of values, a human life takes precedence over all other forms of life. Human life is considered so important that the most sacred day of the week, the Sabbath, may be violated to save it; so important, that almost every law in the Bible may be set aside in order to preserve it.

Life is precious, and we are under orders to cherish it. Nobody may destroy another life, except in self-defense and, even then, only if a person has no other means of defending himself or herself. We may not take our own lives or hurt our bodies or subject ourselves to unnecessary risks. "A person should never stand in a place of danger and declare, 'A miracle will befall me,'" said the sages. "Perhaps a miracle will not befall him."

The obligation to preserve our lives and those of others as best we can is clear-cut. It becomes a formidable duty, however, when, like the parents of the Siamese twins, we're faced with competing demands that require choices. How, for example, can any of us choose between saving our own life and that of a friend? How do we measure the life of an unborn fetus against the life—or, more difficult, the well-being—of its potential mother? These issues have been interpreted and reinterpreted throughout history. As a result, many of the answers in the selections that follow present contradictory viewpoints.

At times, even the sacred value of life has to give way to a higher value, and staying alive becomes less important than dying for ideals and principles that may not be compromised. Martyrdom for religious beliefs is called *kiddush ha-shem* in Jewish tradition, meaning the "sanctification of God's name," and martyrs are greatly loved and venerated. Yet people are not expected or encouraged to seek martyrdom under any but the most pressing circumstances. For most situations, the talmudic interpretation of a biblical verse encompasses the attitude of the sages: "You shall keep My laws and My norms by the pursuit of which man shall live." This means, the rabbis explained, that "a person shall live by those laws, but he shall not die because of them."

L'Hayyim! To Life!

Our relation to nature

After God created Adam and Eve, the Bible states, He told them to "fill the earth and master it, and rule the fish of the sea, the birds of the sky, and all the living things that creep on earth." Ecologists have argued that the callous abuse of the world's resources over the centuries stems from that biblical view of humans as rulers of the natural world. While there's no doubt that the Jewish tradition gives men and women control over all other forms of life, the sages always interpreted our role as that of guardians entrusted with the care of God's world. Responsibility, not exploitation, is the motif of these selections.

The Creator of heaven who alone is God,
Who formed the earth and made it,
Who alone established it—
He did not create it a waste,
But formed it for habitation. . . .

—Isaiah, chapter 45, verse 18

When God created the first man, he led him round all the trees in the Garden of Eden.

God said to him, "See My works, how beautiful and praiseworthy they are. Everything I have created has been created for your sake. Think of this, and do not corrupt or destroy My world; for if you corrupt it, there will be no one to set it right after you."

—*Ecclesiastes Rabbah*, chapter 7, section 13

The world was created only for the sake of the choice and the choosing one.

Man, the master of choice, should say: The whole world has been created only for my sake. Therefore, man shall take care at every time and in every place to redeem the world and fill its want.

—Rabbi Nahman of Bratslav

One glorious chain of love, of giving and receiving, unites all creatures; none is by or for itself, but all things exist in continual reciprocal activity—the one for the all; the all for the one.

—Samson Raphael Hirsch
(1808–1888), German
theologian, *Nineteen Letters*

"You must not destroy"

The book of Chronicles relates that when Assyrian armies invaded the kingdom of Judah, King Hezekiah stopped some sources of water so that the Assyrians couldn't use them. The Talmud records that some later sages disapproved of his action because in their opinion cutting off a water supply fell under a broad category of wantonly destructive acts. The talmudists even extended the biblical concept of not cutting down fruit trees in time of war to viewing as destructive any change in the balance of nature, which they called the order of creation. In the last selection, Nahmanides interprets the unexplained biblical prohibitions against cross-breeding plants and animals as a form of preserving the order of creation.

When in your war against a city, you have to besiege it a long time in order to capture it, you must not destroy its trees, wielding the ax against them. You may eat of them, but you must not cut them down. Are trees in the field human to withdraw before you under siege?

Only trees which you know do not yield food may be destroyed; you may cut them down for constructing siege-works against the city that is waging war on you, until it has been reduced.

—Deuteronomy, chapter 20,
verses 19–20

Whoever cuts down a fruit-bearing tree is flogged. This penalty is imposed not only for cutting it down during a siege; whenever a fruit-yielding tree is cut down with destructive intent, flogging is incurred. It may be cut down, however, if it causes damage to other trees or to a field belonging to another man or if its value for other purposes is greater. The law forbids only wanton destruction....

Not only one who cuts down fruit-bearing trees, but also one who smashes household goods, tears clothes, demolishes a building, stops up a spring, or wastes food in a destructive way violates the command: "You must not destroy."

—Maimonides, *Code*, "Laws Concerning Kings and Wars," chapter 6, sections 8 and 10

While the harsh story that follows makes its point about nature, the sages looked askance at Rabbi Yose's treatment of his son. Because of this and a related incident with his daughter, one of his disciples left his classes, saying, "How could a man who showed no mercy to his son and daughter show mercy to me?"

Once Rabbi Yose of Yokrat had some day laborers working for him in his fields. When night came, and they had nothing to eat, they complained to his son that they were hungry. The men were resting under a fig tree, and the son turned to the tree and said:

"Fig tree, fig tree, bring forth your fruit so that my father's workmen might eat."

The tree produced fruit, and the men ate.

When the rabbi returned, he apologized to them: "I was late because I was on a charity errand. Please forgive me."

"May God satisfy you even as your son has satisfied us," the men answered. And they told him about the fig tree.

In anger, the rabbi turned to his son and said, "My son, you have troubled your Creator to make the fig tree produce fruit before its time. May you too be taken from this world before your time!"

—Babylonian Talmud, tractate *Ta'anit*, page 24a

There was once a man whose wife died and left behind a nursing child. He could not afford to pay a wet-nurse so a miracle was performed for him. His breasts grew to become like those of a woman, and he was able to suckle his child himself.

Rabbi Joseph said, "How great was this man that such a miracle was performed on his account."

But Abbaye said, "On the contrary, how lowly is such a man that because of him the order of creation had to be changed."

—Babylonian Talmud, tractate *Shabbat*, page 53b

Now the reason for the prohibition against "mixed kinds" is that God has created in the world various species among all living things, both plants and moving creatures, and He gave them a power of reproduction enabling them to exist forever as long, as He, blessed be He, will desire the existence of the world, and He further endowed them with a power to bring forth after their kind. . . .

This driving force in the normal mating of animals is for the sake of preserving the species, even as human beings engage in sexual activity for the sake of having children.

Thus one who combines two different species thereby changes and defies the work of Creation, as if he is thinking that the Holy One, blessed be He, has not completely perfected the world and he desires to help along in the creation of the world by adding to it new kinds of creatures.

Moreover, the mating of diverse kinds of species of animals does not produce offspring, and even in the case of those that are by nature close to each other, from which offspring are born, such as mules, their seed is cut off, for they themselves cannot produce offspring. . . . Even when diverse species of vegetation are grafted together, their fruits do not reproduce afterwards. . . .

—Nahmanides, commentary on Leviticus, chapter 19, verse 19

Protecting the environment

Along with general rules against pollution and littering, the rabbis established special regulations to maintain the cleanliness and beauty of Jerusalem, the most sacred of cities.

It is forbidden to live in a town that does not have a green garden.

—Jerusalem Talmud, tractate *Kiddushin*, chapter 4, paragraph 12

Carcasses, cemeteries, and tanneries must be kept at fifty-cubits distance from a town [because of the bad odor]. A tannery must be established only on the east side of a town [because the east wind is gentle and will not carry the stench to town].

—Mishnah, tractate *Bava Batra*, chapter 2, paragraph 9

Ten special regulations were applied to Jerusalem. [Among them] that no dunghills were to be made there; that no kilns were to be kept there; that neither gardens nor orchards were allowed to be cultivated there aside from the rose gardens that existed from the days of the early prophets; that no chickens may be raised there; and no dead persons may be kept there overnight. . . .

That no dunghills were to be made there—because of snakes [which breed in dunghills].

That no kilns could be kept there—because of the smoke.

That neither gardens nor orchards were allowed to be cultivated there—because of the bad odor from manure and rotting flowers and fruits.

—Babylonian Talmud, tractate *Bava Kamma*, page 82b

The quality of urban air compared to the air in the deserts and forests is like thick and turbulent water compared to pure and light water. And this is because in the cities with their tall buildings and narrow roads, the pollution that comes from their residents, their waste, their cadavers, and offal from their cattle, and the stench of their adulterated food, makes their entire air malodorous, turbulent, reeking, and thick, and the winds become accordingly so, although no one is aware of it.

And since there is no way out, because we grew up in cities and became used to them, we can at least choose a city with an open horizon. . . . And if you have no choice, and you cannot move out of the city, try at least to live in a suburb situated to the northeast. Let the house be tall and the court wide enough to permit the northern wind and the sun to come through, because the sun thins out the pollution of the air, and makes it light and pure.

—Maimonides, *The Preservation of Youth*

Showing kindness to animals

The rabbis often spoke of taking "pity on living things" and forbade inflicting unnecessary pain on any creature. The nineteenth-century scholar Samson Raphael Hirsch explained: "The boy who, in crude joy, finds delight in the convulsions of an injured beetle or the anxiety of a suffering animal will soon also be dumb toward human pain." Most authorities today would probably permit animal experimentation, if it was to help humans, but would insist on controlled conditions that keep animal pain to a minimum.

The Bible has a series of laws about animals that have no rational explanation, and traditionally these laws are supposed to be accepted on faith. Ignoring tradition, both Maimonides and Nahmanides offered humane reasons for some of them.

Even those things that you may hold superfluous in the world, such as fleas, gnats, and flies, even they are part of the creation of the world.

God carries out His purpose through everything, even through a snake, even through a gnat, even through a frog.

—*Genesis Rabbah*,
chapter 10, section 7

A man is forbidden to eat before he has fed his animal, for it says: "I will provide grass in the fields for your cattle," and then it says: "you shall eat your fill" (Deuteronomy 11:15).

—Babylonian Talmud, tractate
Berakhot, page 40a

If, along the road, you chance upon a bird's nest, in any tree or on the ground, with fledglings or eggs and the mother sitting over the fledglings or on the eggs, do not take the mother together with her young. Let the mother go and take only the young, in order that you may fare well and have a long life.

—Deuteronomy,
chapter 22, verse 6

"Do not take the mother together with her young"—Scripture will not permit a destructive act that will cause the extinction of a species even thought it has permitted the ritual slaughtering of that species. And he who kills mother and children in one day, or takes them while they are free to fly away, is considered as if he destroys the species.

—Nahmanides, commentary
on Deuteronomy,
chapter 22, verse 6

No animal from the herd or from the flock shall be slaughtered on the same day with its young.

—Leviticus,
chapter 22, verse 28

It is prohibited to kill an animal with its young on the same day so that people should be restrained and prevented from killing the two together in such a manner that the young is slain in the sight of the mother; for the pain of the animals under such circumstances is very great. There is no difference in this case between the pain of man and the pain of other living beings, since the love and tenderness of the mother for her young ones is not produced by reasoning, but by imagination, and this faculty exists not only in man but in most living beings. . . .

The same reason applies to the law that enjoins us to let the mother fly away when we take the young. . . . If the law provides that such grief should not be caused to cattle or birds, how much more careful must we be not to cause grief to our fellow man.

—Maimonides,
Guide of the Perplexed,
part 3, chapter 48

Rabbi [Judah the Prince] suffered from gallstones and other diseases that the scholars explained in this way:

The sufferings of Rabbi came to him because of a certain incident, and left in the same way.

What was the incident that led to his suffering?

A calf was being taken to slaughter when it broke away from the herd, hid its head under Rabbi's clothes, and bellowed in terror.

Rabbi pushed it away, saying, "Go, for this you were created."

Then they said of him in heaven, "Since he showed no pity, let us bring suffering upon him."

And how did Rabbi's sufferings depart?

One day his servant was sweeping the house and was about to sweep away some young weasels she found lying on the floor.

"Leave them alone," he said to her. "It is written: 'His mercy is upon all His works.' "

Then they said of him in heaven, "Since he has shown compassion, let us be compassionate with him."

—Babylonian Talmud, tractate
Bava Mezia, page 85a

God tested Moses through sheep.

When Moses tended the flock of his father-in-law, Jethro, one young kid ran away. Moses followed it until it reached a shaded area where it found a pool of water. There it stopped to drink.

Moses approached it and said, "I did not know you ran away because you were thirsty. Now you must be weary." So he placed the kid on his shoulders and carried it back.

Then God said, "Because you showed mercy in leading

the flock of a mortal, you will surely show mercy in tending my flock, Israel."

—*Exodus Rabbah,*
chapter 2, section 2

The Polish scholar Rabbi Ezekiel Landau was asked whether Jews are permitted to hunt for sport. His answer is often cited as the dominant view of hunting in the Jewish tradition.

But how can a Jew kill a living thing without any benefit [to anyone], and engage in hunting merely to satisfy "the enjoyable use of his time"? . . .

For there in the Talmud, it is permitted to slay them [wild animals] only when they invade the habitations of man; but to pursue after them in the woods, their own dwelling-place, when they are not accustomed to come to human habitation, there is no commandment to permit that. Such pursuit simply means following the desires of one's heart.

In the case of one who needs to do all this and whose livelihood is derived from it, of him we would not say that [hunting] is cruel, as we slaughter cattle and birds and fish for the need of man. . . . But he who has no need to make a livelihood from it, his hunting has nothing to do with his livelihood, this is cruelty.

—Ezekiel Landau, *Responsa, Noda bi-Yehudah,* "Yoreh De'ah,"
volume 2, number 10

Placing life above laws

The principle that saving your own life or that of another person preempts all but the most fundamental laws of humanity forms the foundation of the Jewish outlook on human life. The Sabbath regulations have become symbols of the many other rulings that could be broken not only when a threat to life is imminent, but even at the risk of danger.

The slaughter of Jewish rebels, described below, and the decision of Mattathias and his advisors to violate the Sabbath to fight the enemy may have influenced the thinking of later sages. The events occurred after Mattathias and his sons had disobeyed the orders of Antiochus IV Epiphanes to worship idols, about 167 B.C.E. They fled to the Judean hills, and many of their followers hid in the desert.

Word soon reached the king's officers and the forces in Jerusalem, the city of David, that men who had defied the king's order had gone down into hiding-places in the wilds. A large body of men went quickly after them, came up with them, and occupied positions opposite. They prepared to attack them on the Sabbath.

"There is still time," they shouted. "Come out, obey the king's command, and your lives will be spared."

"We will not come out," the Jews replied. "We will not obey the king's command or profane the Sabbath."

Without more ado the attack was launched; but the Israelites did nothing in reply; they neither hurled stones, nor barricaded their caves. "Let us meet death with a clear conscience," they said. . . .

So they were attacked and massacred on the Sabbath, men, women, and children, up to a thousand in all, and their cattle with them.

Great was the grief of Mattathias and his friends when they heard the news. They said to one another, "If we all do as our brothers have done, if we refuse to fight the Gentiles for our lives as well as for ours laws and customs, then they will soon wipe us off the face of the earth."

That day they decided that, if anyone came to fight against them on the Sabbath, they would fight back, rather than all die as their brothers in the caves had done.

—I Maccabees, chapter 2,
verses 31–41

We may do anything to save ourselves except for three things: idolatry, sexual immorality [including incest and adultery], and murder.

—Babylonian Talmud, tractate *Pesahim*, page 25a

The Mishnah says: "Whenever a human life is endangered, the laws of the Sabbath are suspended."

The more eagerly someone goes about saving a life, the more worthy he is of praise. . . .

If a person sees a child fall into the sea on the Sabbath, he may spread a net and rescue the child—the sooner the better—and he need not get permission from a court of law, even though in spreading the net he may also catch fish [which is forbidden on the Sabbath].

If he sees a child fall into a pit, he may break through the earth on one side and step down to pull the child up—the sooner the better—and he need not get permission from a court of law, even though in the process of rescuing the child he may be building stairs.

And if he sees a door shut on a room in which an infant is alone, he may break down the door to get the baby out—the sooner the better—and he need not get permission from a court of law, even though by breaking down the door he may knock off chips that can be used for firewood.

—Babylonian Talmud, tractate *Yoma*, page 84b

[A group of rabbis] were walking along a road. They discussed the following question:

How do we know that the duty of saving a life supersedes the Sabbath laws? . . .

Rabbi Eleazar ben Azariah, answering the question, said: "If we may disregard the Sabbath laws in order to perform a circumcision, which affects only one member of the body, how much more should we disregard those laws for the whole body when it is in danger?" . . .

Rabbi Yose ha-Gelili says: "When the Bible says, 'Nevertheless you must keep my Sabbaths,' (Exodus 31:13) the word 'nevertheless" implies a distinction. There are Sabbaths on which you must rest, and there are Sabbaths on which you should not rest."

Rabbi Simeon ben Menasya says: "Behold it says: 'You shall keep my Sabbath, for it is holy for you' (Exodus 31:14). This means, the Sabbath is given to *you*, but you are not surrendered to the Sabbath."

Rabbi Nathan says: "Behold it says: 'The Israelite people shall keep the Sabbath, observing the Sabbath throughout the generations' (Exodus 31:16). This implies that we should disregard one Sabbath for the sake of saving the life of a person so that person may be able to observe many Sabbaths."

—*Mekhilta of Rabbi Ishmael*,
tractate "Shabbata," chapter 1

Rabbi Judah said in the name of Samuel: "If I had been there I would have told them something better: 'You shall keep My Laws and My norms by the pursuit of which man shall live' (Leviticus 18:5).

"He shall live by them, but he shall not die because of them."

—Babylonian Talmud, tractate
Yoma, page 85b

The question of birth control

The celebration of human life is perhaps best summarized in the biblical command to "be fruitful and multiply." Because having children is considered both a joy and a duty, the early sages encouraged large families, but they did not rule out the possibility of birth control. The first selection, repeated in several places in the Talmud, serves as the classic springboard for all birth-control discussions. Yet it's a passage engulfed in ambiguities. Authorities in every period have been divided on whether the three women described *may* use a contraceptive or *must* use one; whether Rabbi Meir and the other sages disagree only on the use of a contraceptive by a child bride or by all three women; whether the contraceptive was permitted during intercourse or only afterward. Nevertheless, the passage does set a precedent for the use of birth-control methods. Another precedent is established in the second selection. Although neither rabbis nor scientists today know what the "sterilizing potion" mentioned was, on the basis of this text and other legal sources, Orthodox authorities have favored the use of oral contraceptives over other kinds.

Generally, Orthodox rabbis have strictly interpreted texts and discussions by commentators over the centuries, and thus limit the use of contraceptives to situations in which pregnancy might cause a hazard to a woman's health. Their attitude toward oral contraceptives is presented by Immanuel Jacobovits, chief rabbi of Great Britain. Reform and Conservative authorities use broader interpretations of the sources. As early as 1927, the Reform scholar Jacob Z. Lauterbach expanded on the reasons for permitting contraception, and in later years the Reform movement officially sanctioned the dissemination of birth-control information.

Conservative rabbi Robert Gordis raises another issue that has troubled leaders of all branches of Judaism: the decreasing numbers of Jews, as a result of the slaughter of so many during the Holocaust, a drop in the birth rate, and an increase in intermarriages. The problem has been considered so pressing that several national organizations have been formed to combat it. Expressing an opposing, minority point of view is Shirley Frank, writing in the Jewish feminist magazine *Lilith*. Many feminists have also objected to the traditional Orthodox interpretation that, technically, the command to "be fruitful and multiply" applies only to men, so that women may use contraceptive devices but men may not.

Three types of women use an absorbent [called a *mokh*]: a minor, a pregnant woman, and a nursing mother.

The minor, lest she become pregnant and die; a pregnant woman, lest she cause her fetus to become a *sandal* [a flat, fish-shaped fetus]; and a nursing mother, lest she wean her child too soon and it die.

And what is a minor? From the age of eleven years and a day to the age of twelve years and a day. One who is below or above this age carries on her marital intercourse in the usual manner. So says Rabbi Meir. But the sages say: The one as well as the other [both from eleven to twelve years as well as below or above that age] carries on her marital intercourse in the usual manner, and mercy will come from heaven, as it is said: "The Lord protects the simple" (Psalms 116:6).

—Babylonian Talmud, tractate
Yevamot, page 12b

Judah and Hezekiah were twins. One was completely developed at the end of nine months, and the other at the beginning of the seventh month [the implication is that they were born three months apart].

Their mother, Judith, wife of Rabbi Hiyya, suffered agonizing pains during childbirth. When she recovered, she disguised herself and appeared before Rabbi Hiyya.

"Is a woman commanded to propagate the race?" she asked.

"No," he answered.

As a result of that conversation, she drank a sterilizing potion so she would have no more children.

—Babylonian Talmud, tractate
Yevamot, page 65b

Oral contraceptives are, of course, frequently mentioned in the Talmud and all subsequent rabbinic works over the past two thousand years in one of the most remarkable antecedents to a modern discovery. . . .

Nevertheless the . . . rather more restrictive attitude today [among Orthodox authorities] is no doubt due, above all, to the patent difference between the "potion" mentioned in the Talmud and the modern "pill." . . . The ancient drink, as the sources indicate, was clearly used only in rare individual cases. It was certainly not mass-produced nor could it have been a very reliable agent, whether for contraceptive or sterilization purposes. Whatever the similarities in a technical sense, therefore, the "pill" as used today would obviously have vastly different social and moral ramifications. For instance, nothing could have been further from the minds of the talmudic sages who permitted the "potion" than to sanction any contraceptive, oral or otherwise, in order to facilitate extra- or premarital sexual relations, or routinely to reduce families to an average of less than two children for reasons of social convenience or economic comfort. . . .

Thus, all recent [Orthodox] responsa agree on considering a sanction only on some sound medical grounds. . . . But they also agree that oral contraceptives, since they involve no direct interference with the generative act or organs, represent by far the least objectionable method of birth control.

—Immanuel Jacobovits,
Jewish Medical Ethics
(1975)

As Jews, we take pride in our historic emphasis upon the values of family life. We believe that it is the sacred duty of married couples to "be fruitful and multiply," unless child-bearing is likely to impair the health of the mother or the offspring. . . . We believe, moreover, that a righteous God does not require the unlimited birth of children who may, by unfavorable social and economic circumstances, be denied a chance for a decent and wholesome life. Therefore, we declare that parents have the right to determine the number, and to space the births of their children in accordance with what they believe to be the best interests of their families. We hold, moreover, that apart from its procreative function, the sex relation in marriage serves positive spiritual values. Contraceptive information and devices should be legally and inexpensively available to married persons.

—Commission on Justice and Peace
of the Central Conference of
American Rabbis, from a report
printed in the *Yearbook* (1960)

As in any system, the law can be construed narrowly or broadly. It seems reasonable that the health of a mother or a child cannot properly be limited to surviving acute disease or total hunger. A human being has other needs inseparable from his human status. Chronic malnutrition or inadequate housing, a lack of educational opportunities or of recreation—all these constitute a genuine threat to the health of a child. Moreover, health must include mental health. If a mother or her child is deprived of these essentials of human existence, or is perpetually worried about them, the psychological trauma induced in the mother is a palpable health hazard. . . .

Traditional Judaism would have no sympathy for men and women who are physically and economically capable of rearing a family and refuse to do so because of selfishness or indolence. But it would also not ignore the contention that it is better for reluctant parents not to bring unwanted children into the world. . . .

In our day, however, two new factors of overriding importance have entered into the situation. One is the worldwide population explosion. . . .

On a smaller scale, but equally perilous for those concerned, is the opposite threat facing the Jewish people—not overpopulation but genocide from within and without....

[Jewish] parents should be encouraged to bring a larger number of children into the world within their capacity and the scope of their desires. Though the cost of raising a child in modern society is high, modern Jewish couples should increase their family size as a matter of Jewish loyalty and social policy, if they are at all able to afford it economically, physically, and culturally.

—Robert Gordis, *Love & Sex: A Modern Jewish Perspective* (1978)

The fact remains that we cannot replace the Holocaust victims, and any attempt to equate the unborn with Jews who were murdered is an insult to the martyrs' memories—for surely we define those six million Jewish lives in terms more significant than their numbers alone. . . .

If, on the other hand, we really seek to perpetuate the memory of the Holocaust victims and to render their lives and perhaps even their deaths somehow meaningful, it may well be that a person who studies Jewish history, researches *shtetl* life, or teaches Yiddish is doing more to effect these goals than a person who stays home producing a large number of babies....

Ultimately it is not appealing to be told that one must raise additional numbers of children, not only to make sure there are enough of us left after any possible future disaster, but to make sure there are enough of us left after taking into consideration those who intermarry, convert to various other religions and cults, or are hopelessly lost through assimilation. To assert that our major problem is now our low birth rate does not make these other problems go away; nor does it make them less severe. There is still a desperate need to ensure Jewish survival by making Judaism and Jewish life clearly meaningful and necessary.

—Shirley Frank, from "The Population Panic," in *Lilith* (Fall/Winter 1977–1978)

The abortion controversy

The one clear-cut fact that emerges from the following selections is that there is no single Jewish attitude toward abortion. As on the birth-control issue, many viewpoints vie with one another, and many sources are put forward to support the differing arguments.

A few generalizations can be made, however. First, in Jewish law, a fetus does not have the status of a human being. Second, if a choice has to be made between saving the life of a fetus and that of its mother, the mother's life always takes precedence.

The sources for the first generalization are the Bible and the Mishnah. The book of Exodus indicates that the penalty for killing a fetus is payment of a fine rather than execution as it would be if a person were killed. The Mishnah orders the fetus of a pregnant woman about to be executed destroyed along with her, implying that it is not a separate person but merely part of the mother. The source for the second generalization again is the Mishnah. Rabbi David Feldman, author of *Marital Relations, Birth Control, and Abortion in Jewish Law,* explains the application of this ruling to life today.

Most Orthodox authorities interpret these points in a more restrictive way, limiting the right of abortion to those who need it for medical reasons, which might include severe mental anguish. Dr. Fred Rosner, a physician and talmudic scholar, lists the reasons in traditional sources for not permitting abortion. Reform and Conservative rabbis generally take a more lenient position.

When men fight, and one of them pushes a pregnant woman and a miscarriage results, but no other misfortune ensues, the one responsible shall be fined according to what the woman's husband may exact from him, the payment to be based on reckoning.

But if other misfortune ensues [the woman dies], the penalty shall be life for life....

—Exodus, chapter 21,
verses 22–23

If a pregnant woman is taken out to be executed, one does not wait for her to give birth; but if she has already sat on the birthstool, one waits until she gives birth. . . .

—Mishnah, tractate *Arakhin*,
chapter 1, paragraph 4

If a woman is having difficulty giving birth, the fetus within her womb may be cut up and brought out limb by limb, because her life takes precedence over its life.

But if the greater part has already been born, it may not be touched, for we do not set aside one person's life for that of another.

—Mishnah, tractate *Oholot*,
chapter 7, paragraph 6

Abortion in Jewish law and morality is primarily for the mother's physical or mental welfare.

In speaking of the mother's welfare one could make a rough generalization about Jewish law. . . . If a woman were to come before the rabbi and say, "I took thalidomide or I had rubella during pregnancy. There is a fifty-fifty chance my child is going to be deformed. What kind of life is that for a person? Therefore I want an abortion," the rabbi would say no. However, if the same woman in the same circumstances came to the same rabbi . . . and formulated the question differently, saying, "I took thalidomide or I had German measles. There is a fifty-fifty chance that the child is going to be deformed, and that *possibility* is driving me to distraction and grave mental anguish," then the rabbi would say, "Well, go have an abortion, you poor woman."

The difference is clear. In the first formulation the woman is speaking about the fetus and what *might* be. . . . In the second formulation, however, she is not talking about the potential, about the fetus, and what *might* be. She is talking about the *actual*, namely, the mother, and when you talk about the actual and you talk about a person, especially a woman, then the entire burden of Jewish law in all these areas—birth control, abortion, sterilization, marital sex, and so on—is weighed in favor of the woman.

—David M. Feldman, from
"Abortion and Ethics," in
Conservative Judaism
(Summer 1975)

If the unborn child is not considered a *nefesh* [person], why should its destruction not be allowed under all circumstances? Why is only a threat to the mother's life or health an acceptable reason for therapeutic abortion?

One answer is given by Rabbi Ya'ir Bacharach, who, contrary to the Mishnah . . . states that one waits for a condemned pregnant woman to give birth because a potential human being can arise from each drop of human seed. Interference with this pregnancy would constitute expulsion of semen for naught, . . . strictly prohibited by Jewish law. . . .

A second reason . . . is that the unborn fetus, although not a person, does have some status . . . as a "partial person."

A third reason . . . is that one is not permitted to wound oneself, and thus a woman undergoing vaginal abortion by manipulative means is considered as intentionally wounding herself. . . .

A fourth reason . . . is asserted by at least one rabbi who states that the operative intervention entails danger. . . .

A final reason for prohibiting abortion on demand in Jewish law is suggested by the present chief rabbi of the British Commonwealth, Immanuel Jakobovits, and Belgian Rabbi Moshe Yonah Zweig among others. They point to the Mishnah . . . which permits abortion prior to birth of the child only when the mother's life is endangered. The implication is that when the mother's life is not at stake, it would be prohibited to kill the unborn fetus.

—Fred Rosner, from "The Jewish Attitude Toward Abortion," in *Tradition* (Winter 1968)

My religious tradition is one that has revered and sanctified human life for nearly four thousand years. . . . It is precisely because of this regard for that sanctity that we see as most desirable the right of any couple to be free to produce only that number of children whom they felt they could feed and clothe and educate properly. . . .

It is that regard for the sanctity of human life which prompts us to support legislation enabling women to be free from the whims of biological roulette and free mostly from the oppressive crushing weight of anachronistic ideologies and theologies which, for reasons that escape my ken, continue to insist that in a world already groaning to death with overpopulation, with hate and with poverty, that there is still some noble merit or purpose to indiscriminate reproduction.

—Balfour Brickner, Reform rabbi, from testimony before Senator Birch Bayh's Subcommittee on Constitutional Amendments, March 7, 1974

The law on abortion is and should be liberal, to meet genuine cases of hardship and misery that are not soluble in any other way. But society has an obligation to educate its members to ethical standards that rise above the level of abortion on demand. In other words, abortion should be legally available but ethically restricted, to be practiced only for very good reasons. Men and women must be persuaded that though the abortion of a fetus is not equivalent to taking an actual life, it does represent the destruction of potential life and must not be undertaken lightly or flippantly.

—Robert Gordis, *Love & Sex: A Modern Jewish Perspective*

Weighing your life against another's

The teaching that "we do not set aside one person's life for that of another" applies to your own life as well as to the lives of others, and is the basis for Rabbi Akiva's ruling in the passage below. The cryptic puzzle of the two men in the desert has been the subject of heated debate for centuries. The weight of tradition is on the side of Rabbi Akiva, the greater of the two authorities; and in the selections here he is defended by the early-twentieth-century essayist Ahad Ha-Am. Contemporary British rabbi and scholar Louis Jacobs challenges Ahad Ha-Am's argument.

The controversy between Ben Petura and Rabbi Akiva developed as a commentary on the biblical phrase "That your brother may live with you" (Leviticus 25:36).

Two men are traveling through the desert, and one of them has a flask of water. If both of them drink, they will die. But if one drinks, he will be able to reach civilization.

Ben Petura taught that they should both drink and die, rather than have one witness the death of his companion.

Until Rabbi Akiva came and taught: "It is written: 'That your brother may live *with you.*' This means that your life comes before the life of your fellow man."

—Babylonian Talmud, tractate *Bava Mezia*, page 62a

We do not know who Ben Petura was; but we do know Akiva, and we may be sure that his is the authentic voice of Judaism. Ben Petura, the altruist, does not value human life for its own sake; for him it is better that two lives should perish, where death demands no more than one, so long as the altruistic sentiment prevails. But Jewish morality looks at the question objectively. Every action that leads to loss of life is evil, even if it springs from the purest sentiments of love and compassion, and even if the victim is himself the agent. In the case before us, where it is possible to save one of the two lives, it is a moral duty to overcome the feeling of compassion, and to save what can be saved. But to save whom? Justice answers: let him who has the power save himself. Every man's life is entrusted to his keeping, and to preserve your own charge is a nearer duty than to preserve your neighbour's.

—Ahad Ha-Am (Asher Hirsch Ginsberg; 1856–1927), from "Between Two Opinions"

Even if Akiva's view is adopted, this means no more than that there is no obligation for *both* to die, if one can drink the water and survive. In the ordinary way, this would mean that the one who has the water in his possession will drink, but this is not as Ahad Ha-Am says it is: because "to preserve your own charge is a nearer duty than to preserve your neighbour's" but simply because there cannot be any *obligation* for one to hand over the water to the other, seeing that the other one would have the same obligation to hand it back again! Akiva would agree, however, that if the man holding the water wanted to give it to his neighbor, his would be a special act of piety. . . . Ben Petura, too, would of course not object to one of the two allowing his friend to drink the water and survive. The debate between Akiva and Ben Petura concerns only the case where both want to drink; here, Akiva argues that it would be wrong for *both* to die, if one can live. . . .

But the rare individual, who in a moment of tremendous crisis, can rise to the heights of giving his life for his friend . . . is a saint and would be recognized as such by Judaism. Jewish history has not lacked such "Fools of God."

—Louis Jacobs, from "Greater Love Hath No Man . . . The Jewish Point of View of Self-Sacrifice," in *Judaism* (Winter 1957)

Rescuing someone

While no person is obliged to sacrifice his or her life for another, we are all obliged to do everything in our power to save a person whose life is endangered. According to Joseph Caro, the sixteenth-century codifier of Jewish law, the obligation extends even to endangering our own lives because "the victim faces certain danger whereas the rescuer faces only a doubtful risk." Not all authorities go as far as Caro, but all would agree with Maimonides that while no legal punishment can be enforced for "standing idly by the blood of your neighbor," the responsibility to help a person in trouble is a binding ethical imperative.

If one person is able to save another and does not save him, he transgresses the commandment, "Neither shall you stand idly by the blood of your neighbor" (Leviticus 19:16).

> Similarly, if one person sees another drowning in the sea, or being attacked by bandits, or being attacked by wild animals, and, although able to rescue him either alone or by hiring others, does not rescue him; or if one hears heathens or informers plotting evil against another or laying a trap for him and does not call it to the other's attention and let him know; or if one knows that a heathen or a violent person is going to attack another and although able to appease him on behalf of the other and make him change his mind, he does not do so; or if one acts in any similar way—he transgresses in each case the injunction "Neither shall you stand idly by the blood of your neighbor."
>
> Although there is no flogging for these prohibitions, because breach of them involves no legal action, the offense is most serious, for if one destroys the life of a single Israelite, it is regarded as though he destroyed the whole world, and if one preserves the life of a single Israelite, it is regarded as though he preserved the whole world.
>
> —Maimonides, *Code*, "Laws Concerning Murder and the Preservation of Life," chapter 1, sections 14 and 16

Is killing ever justified?

There's a vast difference between giving priority to your own life, in Rabbi Akiva's framework, and taking someone else's life in order to save your own. The Bible and Talmud did justify killing in self-defense, but even then the sages placed many conditions on it and expressed reservations about it, as the description of Jacob waiting to meet his brother, Esau, reveals.

The scholar Rava's statement on the "redness" of each person's blood has become a shorthand slogan symbolizing the equality of all life. The problem posed to him became a poignantly pressing one in the Nazi death camps, when people desperately sought ways to save themselves and their families. In the last selection, a rabbi's refusal to give a ruling on the question asked by an inmate at

Auschwitz seems almost a cruel shirking of duty. There's no doubt that the rabbi, a learned scholar, knew the many prohibitions against sacrificing one life to preserve another, but rather than make a clear-cut decision in such a heart-rending situation, he kept silent, allowing his silence to stand as a statement in itself.

If a thief is seized while tunneling [breaking in], and he is beaten to death, there is no bloodguilt in this case. If the sun his risen on him, there is bloodguilt in that case.

—Exodus, chapter 22,
verses 1 and 2

What is the reason for the law of breaking in?

Because . . . the thief must have reasoned, "If I go there, the owner will try to stop me, but if he does, I'll kill him." So the Torah states: If he has come to kill you, forestall him by killing him! . . .

But if it is as clear to you as the sun that his intentions are peaceable, do not kill him.

—Babylonian Talmud, tractate
Sanhedrin, page 72a

The following must be saved from sinning, even at the cost of their lives: a person who pursues his fellow to kill him; a man who pursues another man for homosexual purposes; and a man who pursues a betrothed maiden in order to dishonor her.

—Mishnah, tractate *Sanhedrin*,
chapter 8, paragraph 7

It has been taught: If a person was pursuing his fellow in order to kill him, and the pursued could have saved himself by maiming the limb of the pursuer, but instead killed his pursuer, the pursued is subject to execution on that account.

—Babylonian Talmud, tractate
Sanhedrin, page 74a

When Jacob was waiting for Esau, who was on his way to Jacob's camp with four hundred men, the Bible says he "was greatly frightened and was distressed." (Genesis 32:8)

Rabbi Judah bar Ilai said: Are not fear and distress the same thing?

The meaning, however, is that he was afraid that he might be killed, and he was distressed that he might kill.

For he thought: "If he defeats me, will he not kill me? While if I win over him, will I not kill him?"

—*Genesis Rabbah*,
chapter 76, section 2

A man came to Rava and said to him, "The governor of my town has ordered me to kill a certain man. And if I don't do as he says, he will have me killed. What shall I do?"

Rava answered him, "Let him kill you rather than commit murder yourself.

"How do you know that your blood is redder than his? Perhaps his blood is redder."

—Babylonian Talmud, tractate
Sanhedrin, page 74a

At Auschwitz, on the eve of the Jewish New Year in the early 1940s, about fourteen hundred teenage boys were rounded up and locked into a cell. Plans were made to destroy them in the crematorium the next evening. All during the day, parents and friends of the boys sealed in the cell bargained with the kapos, *the Jewish guards who watched over the camps, to release the boys. Those people who had managed to smuggle in diamonds and money bribed the* kapos *to set their boys free. Because the* kapos *were held responsible for the number of boys locked up, every time they released one child they seized another in his place. The people in the camp knew that each time they saved one youngster, they condemned another to death. A rabbi in the camp at the time later wrote this account:*

A simple Jew from Oberland approached me and said:

"Rabbi, my only son, who is dearer to me than the pupil of my eye, is among the boys destined to be burned. I have the wherewithal to redeem him, but I know without doubt that the *kapos* would take another in his place. I ask you, Rabbi, to give me a ruling, according to the Torah: Am I permitted to redeem my son? Whatever you tell me I will do."

When I heard the question I began to tremble and I answered him:

"My dear man, how can I give you a clear ruling on such a question? Even in the days when the Temple was standing, questions such as this one that dealt with life and death would be brought before the Sanhedrin. And here I am in Auschwitz, without a single book on Jewish law, with no other rabbis, and without peace of mind because of the terrible troubles and tragedies here."

If the system of the *kapos* had been first to free one boy and then substitute another for him I might have had room to maneuver a bit. I might have been able to reason that it was not certain that each boy released was replaced by another. The *kapos* were, after all, Jewish, and Jewish law so strongly forbids taking one life in order to save another. Perhaps, I might have argued, at the last moment their Jewish consciousness might be awakened, and they would not violate this important law. . . .

Unfortunately, I knew with certainty that the method of the *kapos* was always to seize a replacement first and then to release a redeemed child. In that way, they protected themselves and kept the number constant. So I had no way to get around the situation.

The man who approached me kept after me.

"Rabbi, you must make a decision for me," he insisted. And again I pleaded with him: "My dear man, leave me with this question because I cannot give you an answer or even half an answer without studying a single book and in a matter as terrible as this." . . .

Finally, when he saw that I would not decide the issue for him, the man said to me with great emotion: "Rabbi, I have done what the Torah commanded me. I have asked my rabbi for a decision, and there is no other rabbi whom I can consult. If you cannot give me an answer about whether I may redeem my son, that's a sign to me that according to the law you were not able to permit it, for if it were permitted, you would certainly have told me so. I take it for granted, then, that according to Jewish law I must not do it. That's enough for me. My only child will be burned in fulfillment of the Torah. I accept this decision with love and joy. . . ."

—Zevi Hirsch Meisels, *Responsa, Mekadeshe Hashem*, volume 1, "Sha'ar Mahmadim," number 3

May one life be sacrificed to save many?

The incident below, not unusual in the ancient world, has a counterpart in terrorist activities today. The assertion that no single life may be destroyed to save two or ten or a thousand others is clear. Disagreements set in around the question of whether a person designated for death by terrorists or attackers may be turned over to save others. The discussion revolves around Sheba ben Bichri, who rebelled against King David and then fled to the city of Abel. As told in the second book of Samuel, David's commander Joab surrounded the city and threatened to destroy it, until a "wise woman" convinced her townspeople to cut off Sheba's head and throw it to Joab, and in that way save the city.

Tradition generally follows the reasoning of Rabbi Johanan that any person who specifically has been named may be handed over to save others even if that person is not under indictment as Sheba ben Bichri was. The justification is that the person has not been chosen at random to be murdered but that forces outside the control of the endangered group led to his or her selection. But then . . . the second story raises new doubts. Shouldn't people who aspire to true piety go beyond the letter of the law when faced with such a dilemma?

> A group of people are walking along a road when they are stopped by heathens who say to them, "Give us one of you and we will kill him. If not, we will kill all of you."
>
> Let all of them be killed, and let them not surrender one soul from Israel. But if the heathens single out one person, as was the case with Sheba ben Bichri, that person may be surrendered to them, so that the others may be saved.
>
> Rabbi Simeon ben Lakish said: Only someone who is under sentence of death, the way Sheba ben Bichri was, may be turned over. But Rabbi Johanan said: Even someone who is not under sentence of death like Sheba ben Bichri [but has been specified, may be turned over].
>
> —Jerusalem Talmud, tractate *Terumot*, chapter 8, paragraph 12

Along with its other themes, this story indicates the strong feelings against informers in early Jewish communities.

> Ulla bar Kosheb was sought by the government. He ran away and hid in Lydda at the home of Rabbi Joshua ben Levi. The government laid siege to the town and informed its inhabitants that their city would be destroyed if they did not turn over the fugitive.

Rabbi Joshua went up to Ulla and convinced him to give himself up, and then turned him over to the authorities. The prophet Elijah, of blessed memory, had been accustomed to reveal himself to Rabbi Joshua ben Levi, but from that moment on he stopped appearing.

The rabbi fasted for several days, and finally Elijah reappeared. The prophet said to Rabbi Joshua, "Should I reveal myself to informers?" [implying that he had stayed away because Rabbi Joshua had informed on Ulla].

"But I acted according to the teachings of the Mishnah," answered Rabbi Joshua.

Said Elijah: "And is this a teaching for pious people?"

—Jerusalem Talmud, tractate
Terumot, chapter 8, paragraph 12

Taking one's own life

Although very few injunctions against suicide appear in the Bible or Talmud, the strong condemnation of it in the minor tractate *Mourning* became the basis of all later Jewish law on the subject. The tractate probably dates from the early Middle Ages, but it claims to quote sages of the first and second centuries. In the Talmud itself perhaps no image portrays the sages' attitude toward self-destruction as well as that of Rabbi Hananiah ben Teradyon, who suffered the agonies of a martyr's death yet refused to allow his life to be shortened. Paradoxically, the Talmud records with approval the suicide of Rabbi Hananiah's executioner, who jumped into the flames with the dying rabbi. That suicide, however, was regarded as one of atonement, related to martyrdom and far removed from the useless destruction of one's life.

Scripture says: "For your lifeblood too I will require a reckoning" (Genesis 9:5).

Rabbi Eleazar taught that this means, "I will require a reckoning from you for your *own* lifeblood."

—Babylonian Talmud, tractate
Bava Kamma, page 91b

Rabbi Hananiah ben Teradyon was found by the Romans studying Torah, publicly holding gatherings of pupils, and keeping a scroll of the Torah next to his heart.

They wrapped him in the scroll, placed bundles of branches round him, and set them on fire. Then they brought tufts of wool that had been soaked in water and placed them near his heart so that he should not die quickly....

His disciples called to him, "Rabbi, what do you see?"

He answered, "The parchments are being burned, but the letters are soaring on high."

"Open your mouth, so that the fire will penetrate you," they said.

He answered, "Let Him who gave me my soul take it away, but no one should injure oneself."

—Babylonian Talmud, tractate
Avodah Zarah, page 18a

For a suicide no rites whatsoever should be observed. Rabbi Ishmael said, "He may be lamented. Alas, misguided fool! Alas, misguided fool!"

Whereupon Rabbi Akiva said to him, "Leave him to his oblivion: Neither bless him nor curse him!"

There may be no rending of clothes, no baring of shoulders, and no eulogizing for him. But people should line up for him and the mourner's blessing should be recited over him, out of respect for the living. The general rule is: The public should participate in whatever is done out of respect for the living; it should not participate in whatever is done out of respect for the dead.

Who is to be accounted a suicide?

Not one who climbs to the top of a tree or to the top of a roof and falls to his death. Rather it is one who says, "Behold, I am going to climb to the top of the tree" or "to the top of the roof, and then throw myself down to my death," and thereupon others see him climb to the top of the tree or to the top of the roof and fall to his death. Such a one is presumed to be a suicide, and for such a person no rites whatsoever should be observed.

If a person is found strangled hanging from a tree, or slain impaled upon a sword, he is presumed to have taken his own life unwittingly; to such a person no rites whatsoever may be denied.

It happened that the son of Gorgos ran away from school. His father threatened to box his ears. In terror of his father, the boy went off and cast himself into a cistern. The incident was brought before Rabbi Tarfon, who ruled: "No rites whatsoever are to be denied him."

—Tractate *Mourning*,
chapter 2, paragraphs 1–4

Martyrdom: for the "sanctification of God's name"

While taking one's own life is regarded as the most heinous of all crimes, sacrificing oneself for one's beliefs stands out as among the noblest of all deeds. Yet, the sages, who valued life so highly, warned against seeking martyrdom unnecessarily. One point they stressed was that a Jew may violate religious laws to save his or her life if forced to do so in private, but in public such a violation "profaned the name of God." Maimonides codified the talmudic regulations, but he was vehemently criticized by some commentators for his own assertion that people who martyr themselves when martyrdom can be avoided are no better than suicides. Germanic scholars, especially, took exception to his stance and praised martyrdom even in situations when it was not required by Jewish law.

Throughout the Middle Ages and in the centuries that followed, the tradition of maryrdom had a powerful hold in Germanic countries and may have been part of a general cultural attitude that later influenced Holocaust victims. Entire Jewish communities died fighting for their beliefs or took their own lives for the "sanctification of God's name" as a way of resisting forced conversion and the corruption of their religious tenets. Their models were Rabbi Akiva and Hannah and her seven sons, whose martyrdom during the Maccabean rebellion had a strong influence on early Christian martyrs. A different perspective prevailed in Spanish countries, where many Jews converted to Christianity and practiced Judaism in secret rather than give up their lives for their religion. Maimonides's rulings somewhat reflect that tradition.

The Holocaust made martyrs of hundreds of thousands of Jews. One of them, Samuel Zygelbojm, killed himself in 1943 as a way of calling the world's attention to the plight of Jews trapped under Nazi terror in Europe. His proclamation of death is also a testimony to life and to the responsibility we all have to preserve not only our own lives but those of others.

The words "Those who love Me and keep My commandments" (Exodus 20:6) refer to those who dwell in the land of Israel and risk their lives for the sake of the commandments.

"Why are you being led to be decapitated?"

"Because I circumcised my son to be an Israelite."

"Why are you being led out to be burned?"

"Because I read the Torah."

"Why are you being led out to be crucified?"

"Because I ate the unleavened bread" [on Passover].

"Why are you getting a hundred lashes?"

"Because I performed the ceremony of the Lulav" [part of the festival of Sukkot]....

These wounds caused me to be beloved of my Father in heaven.

—*Mekhilta of Rabbi Ishmael*,
tractate "Bahodesh," chapter 6

Should an idolater arise and coerce an Israelite to violate any one of the commandments mentioned in the Torah under the threat that otherwise he would be put to death, the Israelite is to commit the transgression rather than suffer death....

This rule applies to all the commandments except the prohibitions of idolatry, inchastity, and murder. With regard to these: if an Israelite should be told, "Transgress one of them or else you will be put to death," he should suffer death rather than transgress. The above distinction holds good only if the idolater's motive is personal advantage, for example, if he forces an Israelite to build him a house or cook for him on the Sabbath, or forces a Jewess to cohabit with him, and so on; but if his purpose is to compel the Israelite to violate the ordinances of his religion, then if this took place privately and ten fellow Israelites were not present, he should commit the transgression rather than suffer death. But if the attempt to coerce the Israelite to transgress was made in the presence of ten Israelites, he should suffer death and not transgress....

All the foregoing applies to a time free from religious persecution. But at a period when there is such persecution, such as when a wicked king arises . . . and issues decrees against Israel, with the purpose of abolishing their religion or one of their precepts, then it is the Israelite's duty to suffer death and not violate any one, even of the remaining commandments, whether the coercion takes place in the presence of ten Israelites or in the presence of idolators.

When one is enjoined to transgress rather than be slain, and suffers death rather than transgresses, he is to blame for his death.

When one is enjoined to die rather than transgress, and suffers death so as not to transgress, he sanctifies the name of God....

Where one is enjoined to suffer death rather than transgress, and commits a transgression and so escapes death, he has profaned the name of God. . . . Still, as the transgression was committed under duress, he is not punished with flogging, and, needless to add, he is not sentenced by a court to be put to death, even if, under duress, he committed murder. For the penalty of death or flogging is only inflicted on one who transgresses of his own free will, in the presence of witnesses and after due warning.

—Maimonides, *Code*, "Laws Concerning Basic Principles of the Torah," chapter 5, sections 1–4

. . . Seven brothers with their mother had been arrested, and were being tortured by the king with whips and thongs to force them to eat pork, when one of them, speaking for all, said, "What do you expect to learn by interrogating us? We are ready to die rather than break the laws of our fathers."

The king was enraged and ordered great pans and cauldrons to be heated up, and this was done at once. Then he gave orders that the spokesman's tongue should be cut out and that he should be scalped and mutilated before the eyes of his mother and his six brothers. This wreck of a man the king ordered to be taken, still breathing, to the fire and roasted in one of the pans. As the smoke from it steamed out far and wide, the mother and her sons encouraged each other to die nobly. "The Lord God is watching," they said, "and without doubt has compassion on us." . . .

After the first brother had died in this way, the second was subjected to the same brutality. . . . After him the third was tortured. . . . When he too was dead, they tortured the fourth in the same cruel way. . . . Then the fifth was dragged forward for torture. . . . Next the sixth was brought in. . . .

The mother was the most remarkable of all and deserves to be remembered with special honor. She watched her seven sons all die in the space of a single day, yet she bore it bravely because she put her trust in the Lord. She encouraged each in turn in her native language. . . .

The youngest brother was still left, and the king, not

content with appealing to him, even assured him on oath that the moment he abandoned his ancestral customs he would make him rich....

Since the young man paid no attention to him, the king summoned the mother and urged her to advise the lad to save his life....

She leaned toward him, and flouting the cruel tyrant, she said in their native language, "My son, take pity on me. I carried you nine months in the womb, suckled you three years, reared you and brought you up to your present age. I beg you, child, look at the sky and the earth; see all that is in them and realize that God made them out of nothing, and that man comes into being in the same way. Do not be afraid of this butcher; accept death and prove yourself worthy of your brothers, so that by God's mercy I may receive you back again along with them."

She had barely finished when the young man spoke out, "What are you all waiting for? I will not submit to the king's command; I obey the command of the law given by Moses to our ancestors. . . ."

The king, exasperated by these scornful words, was beside himself with rage. So he treated him worse than the others, and the young man died. . . .

Then, finally, after her sons, the mother died.

—II Maccabees, chapter 7

When Rabbi Akiva was taken out for execution, it was the time for saying the *Shema* [the prayer declaring God's unity].

While they were combing his flesh with iron combs, he recited the prayer. His disciples said to him, "Our teacher, even at this point?"

He said to them, "All my days I have been troubled by the verse, 'You shall love God with all your soul,' which [I interpreted to mean] even if he takes your soul.

I asked myself when I shall have the opportunity to fulfill this. Now that I have the opportunity, shall I not fulfill it?"

—Babylonian Talmud, tractate *Berakhot*, page 61b

Samuel Zygelbojm, a leader of the Bund, *the Jewish labor organization in Poland, had escaped to London, where he served as a representative of the Polish Jews in the Polish Government-in-Exile. His suicide letter was sent to the Polish Government-in-Exile, which then forwarded it to the British and American governments.*

With these, my last words, I address myself to you, the Polish Government, the Polish people, the Allied Governments and their peoples, and the conscience of the world.

News recently received from Poland informs us that the Germans are exterminating with unheard-of savagery the remaining Jews in that country. Behind the walls of the ghetto is taking place today the last act of a tragedy which has no parallel in the history of the human race. The responsibility for this crime—the assassination of the Jewish population in Poland—rests above all on the murderers themselves, but falls indirectly upon the whole human race, on the Allies and their governments, who so far have taken no firm steps to put a stop to these crimes. By their indifference to the killing of millions of hapless men, to the massacre of women and children, these countries have become accomplices of the assassins. . . .

Let my death be an energetic cry of protest against the indifference of the world which witnesses the extermination of the Jewish people without taking any steps to prevent it. In our day and age, human life is of little value; having failed to achieve success in my life, I hope that my death may jolt the indifference of those who, perhaps even in this extreme moment, could save the Jews who are still alive in Poland.

My life belongs to my people in Poland and that is why I am sacrificing it for them. May the handful of people who will survive out of the millions of Polish Jews achieve liberation in a world of liberty and socialist justice together with the Polish people. . . .

—Samuel Zygelbojm, from his
suicide note, May 12, 1943

11

DEATH AND THE WORLD TO COME

"Be prepared . . ."

A time for dying ✦ Confronting the inevitable ✦ Defining death ✦ A "flickering lamp" ✦ Mourning as catharsis ✦ Grief and consolation ✦ "Can I bring him back again?" ✦ Attaining eternal life

Not long ago, death and dying were taboo subjects in our society. People spoke guardedly of how a mother "passed away" or a father "was laid to rest," denying by their choice of words the terrible finality of death. Today some of that old attitude has been overcome, and people have felt freer to explore the processes of dying and the stages of mourning. This freedom has led to ardent debates on such subjects as euthanasia and a patient's "right to die" with dignity and grace.

The sages could not have anticipated the development of complex machines that keep people technically alive long after their brains have functionally died. Nor could they have foreseen an era when the transplantation of organs from one human to another would become commonplace, while the definition of death would be open to dispute. The insights the early sources offer us come from a different perspective. Yet, the realism that marks the rabbis' approach to the subject of death has special application to the new openness with which we, too, have come to confront it. Their anecdotes and laws, their sudden jolts of humor, provide a solid framework within which we can respond both to the challenges of new technology and to the everyday—yet overwhelming—fact of our mortality.

Their attitude toward death is reflected in a legend that surrounds the final hours of Moses, the great teacher and lawgiver of Israel. When God told Moses that his life was drawing to a close, Moses would not accept the verdict. With one hour of life left, he pleaded, "Lord of the Universe, let me become like the beasts of the field that eat grass and drink water, let me live and see the world." But God refused. Again he prayed, "If not, then let me become like a bird that flies in every direction, gathers its food every day, and returns to its nest every evening." Once more, God refused.

Seeing that he could not be saved through prayer, Moses sat down and occupied himself by writing God's name on a scroll. When Samael, the angel of death, approached and saw Moses writing, his face radiant with holiness, the angel withdrew in fear. God sent Samael back again, however, and this time, Moses fought with him until he blinded the bearer of death with his staff. Then a heavenly voice declared, "Enough, Moses, the time of your death has come."

Now Moses obeyed God's command. He lay down, closed his eyes, and folded his hands across his chest, resigned to his fate. But in one final burst of rebellion, his soul refused to leave his body. Then, the legend concludes: "God kissed Moses and took away his soul with a kiss of the mouth. And God wept."

Like the Moses they depicted, the rabbis believed in holding tightly on to life, doggedly struggling to stay alive against all odds. A person in the last anguished moments of life is still a person, they said, and every life, even as it ebbs, is to be revered. But like Moses, when they saw that no hope for life remained, they accepted death as a reality. And for those left behind, they devised forms and rituals that brought home the reality of the event. In traditional Jewish practice, the body of a deceased is washed and covered with a shroud but never altered with cosmetics or dressed in elaborate clothes that give the appearance of life. During a funeral, the coffin is kept shut, as if to reinforce our understanding that the person is no longer part of our world. At the cemetery, family members themselves often shovel some earth onto the coffin after it has been lowered into the grave, another concrete symbol of the irrevocability of death.

Finally, just as they portrayed God weeping for Moses, the sages recognized the need people have to express their grief openly. The ritual of *shiva*, instituted in talmudic times and continued in practice today, sets aside the first seven days after burial as a period of intense mourning, when the bereaved give themselves up to their sorrow, staying home, abstaining from the normal activities of life, and accepting callers who come to offer consolation.

Mourning continues in modified form for thirty days—or for a year after the death of a parent—though during that time the focus of attention slowly shifts back to the living. The rabbis discouraged people from mourning excessively, as if, they said, the mourner wanted to show greater compassion for the dead than God Himself. Life, not death, they never ceased to remind us, is the great adventure of human existence.

But the adventure doesn't end with the termination of life. One of the few beliefs that became fixed as firm dogma during the talmudic period was the belief in the resurrection of the dead and, with it, eternal life in the world to come. It is a belief that affirms God's power of creation, and holds out hope for salvation and for the ultimate vindication of suffering here on earth. It never became a consistently organized belief, and one theory vies with another as to when and where and how resurrection and eternal life will come about. But one thing is made clear. The world to come as each individual experiences it is a direct result of that person's life and works in the world as we know it. Moses Hayyim Luzzatto stated it this way: "Whoever fails to take account of his deeds in this world will not have time to take account of them in the next world. Whoever has not acquired wisdom in this world will not acquire it in the grave."

A time for dying

In the book of Genesis, death comes into the world as Adam's punishment for eating of the forbidden fruit, and later sages often spoke of death as the consequence of sin. Since nobody is free of sin, they said, even the righteous must die. But another, more dominant attitude, accepts death as a natural ending to life, part of the cycle of all living things. The Bible epitomizes this outlook in its unadorned description of the death of the patriarch Jacob. After recording his last words to each of his sons, the book of Genesis says: "Then he instructed them, saying to them, 'I am about to be gathered to my kin. Bury me with my fathers. . . .' When Jacob finished his instructions to his sons, he drew his feet into the bed and, breathing his last, he was gathered to his people."

At five years of age the study of Scripture;
At ten, the study of Mishnah;

At thirteen, subject to the commandments;
At fifteen, the study of Talmud;
At eighteen, marriage;
At twenty, the pursuit [of a livelihood];
At thirty, the peak of strength;
At forty, wisdom;
At fifty, able to give counsel;
At sixty, old age creeping on;
At seventy, fullness of years;
At eighty, the age of "strength";
At ninety, body bent;
At a hundred, as good as dead and gone completely out of the world.

—Rabbi Judah ben Tema, in
Ethics of the Fathers,
chapter 5, paragraph 24

Whoever dies before he is fifty has been cut down before his time.
At the age of fifty-two: this is the death of the prophet Samuel the Ramathite.
At the age of sixty: this is the death of which Scripture speaks, for it is said: "You will come to your grave in ripe old age, like a shock of grain to the threshing floor in its season" (Job 5:26).
At the age of seventy: this is the death of divine love, for it is said: "The span of our life is seventy years" (Psalms 90:10).
At the age of eighty: this is the death of "strength," for it is said: "Or given the strength, eighty years" (Psalms 90:10)....
After this, life is anguish.

—Tractate *Mourning*,
chapter 3, paragraph 8

If a person has reached the "age of strength" [eighty years old], a sudden death is like dying from a kiss.

—Babylonian Talmud, tractate *Mo'ed Katan*, page 28a

As a man enters the world, so he departs.

He enters the world with a cry, and departs with a cry.

He enters the world weeping, and leaves it weeping.

He enters the world with love, and leaves it with love.

He enters the world with a sigh, and leaves it with a sigh.

He enters the world devoid of knowledge, and leaves it devoid of knowledge.

It has been taught in the name of Rabbi Meir:

When a person enters the world his hands are clenched as though to say, "The whole world is mine. I shall inherit it."

But when he leaves, his hands are spread open as though to say, "I have taken nothing from the world."

—*Ecclesiastes Rabbah*, chapter 5, section 14

When a man is about to depart from life, Adam, the first man, appears to him and asks him why and in what state he leaves the world.

The man says, "Woe to you that because of you I have to die."

To which Adam replies, "My son, I transgressed one commandment and was punished for so doing; see how many commandments of Your Master, negative and positive, you have transgressed. . . ."

Adam appears to every man at the moment of his departure from life to testify that the man is dying on account of his own sins and not the sin of Adam.

—*Zohar*, volume 1, portion "Bereshit," page 57b

If God didn't conceal from each person the day of his death, no one would build a house, and no one would plant a vineyard because each person would say, "Tomorrow I will die, why should I work for others?"

Therefore, God concealed the day of a person's death, so that he will build and plant. If he merits [a long life], he will enjoy the fruits of his labor. If he doesn't, others will benefit from his work.

—*Yalkut Shimoni*, on Ecclesiastes, section 968

Confronting the inevitable

Rabbi Meir perceived death as an integral part of the creation of the world. Drawing on that tradition, Franz Rosenzweig, in the last selection, speaks of the binding, unbreakable kinship of life and death.

"And God saw all that He had made, and behold it was very good" (Genesis 1:31).

Rabbi Meir said: "Behold it was very good"—this refers to death.

—*Genesis Rabbah*, chapter 9, section 5

While seated at the bedside of Rabbi Nahman, Rava saw him slipping into death.

Said Rabbi Nahman to Rava, "Tell the angel of death not to torture me."

To which Rava replied, "You're a man of great honor, you may speak directly to him."

Answered Nahman, "Who is honored, who is distinguished, who is singled out before the angel of death?"

As Nahman was dying, Rava said, "Do show yourself to me [after you die]."

Nahman did show himself to Rava in a dream, and Rava asked, "Did you suffer much pain?"

Rabbi Nahman answered, "It was as easy as taking a hair from a pitcher of milk. But were God to say to me, 'Go back to the world as you were before,' I would not want to go. For the fear of death is so great there."

—Babylonian Talmud, tractate *Mo'ed Katan*, page 28a

Rabbi Eleazar ben Pedat was supposedly so poor that he lived in a windowless room. Rabbi Johanan ben Nappaha was supposedly so beautiful that light shone from his body. But Rabbi Johanan also suffered the tragedy of having ten sons die in their youth.

Rabbi Eleazar became sick and Rabbi Johanan went to visit him. He noticed that Rabbi Eleazar was lying in a dark room, and he bared his arm so that light radiated from it.

Rabbi Eleazar began to cry, and Rabbi Johanan asked him, "Why are you crying? Is it because you have not studied enough Torah? After all, we have learned, it does not matter whether a person sacrifices much or little, as long as he directs his heart toward heaven.

"Or is it because you are so poor? Not everybody has the privilege of enjoying two tables [learning and wealth].

"Is it because you have no children? Look, here, this is the tooth of my tenth son [who died]."

Rabbi Eleazar replied, "I'm weeping because of your beauty, which will wither in the earth."

He said to him, "You are right to cry over that."

And they both wept.

—Babylonian Talmud, tractate *Berakhot*, page 5b

When Rabbi Bunem lay dying, his wife burst into tears.

He said, "What are you crying for? My whole life was only that I might learn how to die."

—Tale about Hasidic rabbi
Simhah Bunem of Przysucha
(1765–1827)

It is so difficult to know that all verification lies ahead, to know that only death will verify. That it is the ultimate proving ground of life. And that being able to live means being compelled to die. He who withdraws himself from life may think that he has withdrawn himself from death, but he has actually withdrawn only from life, and death, which he meant to elude, now surrounds him on all sides....

There is no cure for death. Not even health. But the healthy man has the strength to walk alive to his grave. The sick man invokes Death, and lets himself be carried on his back, half-dead from fear of him. Health experiences even Death only "at the right time." It is good friends with him, and knows that when he comes he will remove the rigid mask and take the flickering torch from the hands of his frightened, weary, disappointed brother, Life. He'll dash it on the ground and extinguish it, and only then under the skies that flame up for the first time when the torch has been extinguished, he'll enfold the swooning one in his arms and only then, when Life has closed its eloquent lips, he'll open his eternally silent mouth and say: "Do you recognize me? I am your brother."

—Franz Rosenzweig,
A Treatise on Healthy and Unhealthy Thinking

Defining death

Increasingly, in our society, the encounter with death has been made even more difficult by disputes about how, actually, to define it. Advances in medical science have made it possible to keep a patient's heart beating or breath coming with the use of mechanical devices for some time after the person might be considered dead by all other standards. The question "When is a person dead?" is especially crucial in transplant operations, in which, to be useful, a donor's organs need to be removed instantly after death, preferably while blood still circulates through them. Traditionally, in common law and Jewish law, death has been defined as the cessation of breathing or heartbeat, or both. These criteria in Jewish law are derived from the selections below, in which the nose and heart represent the vital functions of living (with somewhat more emphasis given to the nose, which provides the "breath of life"). Conservative rabbi Seymour Siegel, chairman of the Rabbinical Assembly's Committee on Law and Standards, argues that because of the changes in modern medicine, Jewish leaders need to accept "brain death" as a new criterion along lines suggested by medical groups and adopted by some states. Rabbi J. David Bleich, an Orthodox talmudic scholar, insists that Jewish law allows no latitude for so changing the standards of determining death.

> If debris falls on someone, and it is doubtful whether he is under it, or whether he is alive or dead . . . the heap of debris should be opened for his sake [even on the Sabbath]. If he is alive, the debris should be removed, and if he is dead, he should be left there [until the Sabbath ends].
>
> —Mishnah, tractate *Yoma*,
> chapter 8, paragraphs 6 and 7

"If he is alive the debris should be removed"—But isn't it self-evident that the debris should be removed if the person is found alive?

The statement is made to teach that even if he has a short time to live the debris should be removed. . . .

Until what point does one search [to see whether the person is alive]?

Until his nose [to see whether he is breathing].

There are some who say until his heart [to see whether it is beating]. . . .

Rabbi Papa said: The dispute arises only if one is looking from below upward [if the person has his feet up and his head down it would be necessary to reach his heart and listen for a beat] but if from above downward [his head is up and his feet down], it is not necessary to search any further than the nose, as it is said: "In whose nostrils was the merest breath of life" (Genesis 7:22).

—Babylonian Talmud, tractate *Yoma*, page 85a

The basic talmudic definition is that death occurs when respiration ceases. The cessation of heartbeat was also taken into consideration. There are many today who believe that a better definition of death should be based on the cessation of brain activity as evidenced by the absence of EEG's [brain waves]. When the brain waves stop, spontaneous breathing and heartbeat are impossible, and therefore the patient can be said to be dead even though his systems may be moving by means of machines.

It is felt that when the rabbis defined death by referring to the circulation and breathing, they were reflecting the best scientific information available in their day, but now that we have means to measure the activity of the brain, the organ which is the central mechanism for the support of life, new criteria of death should be adopted.

—Seymour Siegel, from "The Ethical Dilemmas of Modern Medicine," in *United Synagogue Review* (Fall 1976)

It must be emphasized that in all these questions involving the very heart of a physician's obligations with regard to the preservation of human life, *halakhic* [legal] Judaism demands of him that he govern himself by the norms of Jewish law whether or not these determinations coincide with the mores of contemporary society. Brain death and irreversible coma are not acceptable definitions of death insofar as *halakha* is concerned. The sole criterion of death accepted by *halakha* is total cessation of both cardiac and respiratory activity. Even when these indications are present, there is a definite obligation to resuscitate the patient, if at all feasible. Jewish law recognizes the malformed, the crippled, the terminally ill and the mentally retarded as human beings in the full sense of the term. Hence the physician's obligation with regard to medical treatment and resuscitation is in no way diminished by the fact that the resuscitated patient may be a victim of brain damage or other debilitating injury.

—J. David Bleich, from "Establishing Criteria of Death," in *Contemporary Halakhic Problems* (1977)

A "flickering lamp"

The many controversies surrounding the problem of defining death spill over with even greater force to the question of whether terminally ill patients in the final hours of life should be allowed to die without being given artificial means to sustain them. Motivated by the traditional reverence for life, almost all contemporary rabbis have forbidden any form of active euthanasia to hasten death, such as providing an overdose of pills or injecting a lethal serum into a patient's veins. Many, however, have agreed with Reform leader Solomon Freehof that "if the patient is a hopelessly dying patient, the physician has no duty to keep him alive a little longer. He is entitled to die." That viewpoint permits a physician to refrain from intervening with heroic measures—electrical stimulation of a terminal patient's heart, for example—when no hope for life remains and machines would only prolong the agony of patient and family.

The biblical story of King Saul's death serves as a precedent for opposition to actively ending an ebbing life even when the patient pleads for death. Rabbi Moses ben Israel Isserles's permission to remove an "obstacle" that prevents death and the story of the clever servant who prevented prayer from interfering with the death of Rabbi Judah the Prince suggest that it is in the spirit of Jewish law to allow a hopelessly ill person to die a natural death.

In the first selection, a young Amalekite comes to David's camp at Ziklag and tells him that King Saul and his son Jonathan are both dead.

"How do you know," David asked the young man who brought him the news, "that Saul and his son Jonathan are dead?"

The young man who brought the news answered, "I happened to be at Mount Gilboa, and I saw Saul leaning on his spear, and the chariots and horsemen closing in on him. He looked around and saw me, and he called to me. When I responded, 'At your service,' he asked me, 'Who are you?' And I told him that I was an Amalekite.

"Then he said to me, 'Stand over me and finish me off, for I am in agony and am barely alive.' So I stood over him and finished him off, for I knew that he would never rise from where he was lying. Then I took the crown from his head and the armlet from his arm, and I have brought them here to my lord." . . .

David said to the young man who had brought him the news, "Where are you from?" He replied, "I am the son of a resident alien, an Amalekite."

"How did you dare," David said to him, "to lift your hand and kill the Lord's anointed?"

Thereupon David called one of the attendants and said to him, "Come over and strike him!" He struck him down and he died. And David said to him, "Your blood be on your own head! Your own mouth testified against you when you said, 'I put the Lord's anointed to death.'"

—II Samuel, chapter 1, verses 5–16

A dying man is considered the same as a living man in every respect. He may . . . inherit property, and he may bequeath property. If a limb is severed from his body, it is regarded as a limb severed from a living person, and if flesh, as flesh from a living person. . . .

He may not be stirred, nor may he be washed, and he should not be laid upon sand or salt, until the moment he dies.

His eyes may not be closed. Whosoever touches him or stirs him sheds blood.

Rabbi Meir used to compare a dying man to a flickering lamp: the moment one touches it he puts it out. So, too, whoever closes the eyes of a dying man is accounted as though he has snuffed out his life.

—Tractate *Mourning*, chapter 1, paragraphs 1, 3, and 4

However, if there is something that causes a delay in the departure of the soul, such as clattering noise near the patient, as if someone is pounding wood, or if there is salt on his tongue, and these delay the soul's leaving the body, then it is permitted to remove the hindrances, because there is no direct act involved but simply the removal of an obstacle that prevents death.

—Moses ben Israel Isserles,
commentary on Joseph Caro's *Code of Jewish Law*, "Yoreh De'ah," chapter 339, section 1

On the day Rabbi was dying, the rabbis announced a public fast and offered prayers for heavenly mercy. Furthermore, they decreed that whoever said that Rabbi had died would be stabbed with a sword.

Rabbi's handmaid climbed to the roof and prayed, "The angels want Rabbi to join them, and the mortals want Rabbi to remain with them; may it be God's will that the mortals overpower the angels."

However, when she saw how much he suffered, she prayed, "May it be the will of the Almighty that the angels overpower the mortals." As the rabbis continued their prayers for mercy, she picked up a pitcher and threw it down from the roof to the ground where they stood. For a moment they ceased praying, and the soul of Rabbi departed to its eternal rest.

—Babylonian Talmud, tractate
Ketubbot, page 104a

Rabbi Hayyim Palaggi, chief rabbi of Smyrna during the mid-nineteenth century, was asked whether it was permissible to pray for the death of an incurably ill woman who suffered constant, agonizing pain. He answered that ordinarily it is forbidden to pray for another person's death.

But here, where she wishes it herself and can no longer endure her pain, under these circumstances, it is possible to say that it is permitted. I came to this conclusion from what the Talmud says in *Ketubbot* 104a [the story of Judah the Prince].

Now it is made clear in this section of the Talmud that the servant-maid of Rabbi Judah saw his great pain. Furthermore, we know from the Talmud and the later scholars that they learned laws from this servant-maid [she was a learned woman]. She was full of wisdom and piety. Therefore we may learn from her this law, that it is permitted to ask mercy for a very sick person that he may die, so that his soul may come to rest. For if this action of hers were not according to the law, the Talmud would not have quoted it. Or if they had quoted it, simply because it was an incident that occurred, and they did not think that she had done well, the Talmud would have said so. As for the rabbis who continued to pray that he should live, they did not know Rabbi Judah's suffering as much as the servant-maid did. . . .

As it is said in *The Book of the Pious*, . . . that we must not cry out aloud at the time when the soul is departing, in order not to cause the soul to return and bear more pain. Why did Ecclesiastes say, "There is a time for dying?" It means that, when the time comes for a man's soul to go forth, people should not cry aloud so that his soul should return, for he can only live a short time and in that short time he must bear great pain. That is why Ecclesiastes said: "There is a time for living and a time for dying."

—Hayyim Palaggi (1788–1869),
responsum in *Hikekei Lev*,
volume 1, number 50

Mourning as catharsis

"Those who grieve," Maimonides wrote in his *Guide of the Perplexed*, "find comfort in weeping and in arousing their sorrow until the body is too tired to bear the inner emotions." The contemporary talmudic authority Rabbi Joseph B. Soloveitchik expresses a similar thought in his explanation of the open display of grief at Jewish funerals and houses of mourning. The services themselves are conducted in utmost simplicity, following practices instituted by Rabban Gamaliel II, head of the Sanhedrin in the period after the fall of the Second Temple in 70. Many additional rituals attached to burial and mourning provide a safe arena in which to release the anguish, the sorrow, and the guilt that usually accompany a death. A small thing: in a ritual reminiscent of "rending one's garments" in biblical days, mourners make a tear in the clothes they wear, and that formalized act of tearing often offers a sense of relief from the hurt they feel.

A much more important aspect of mourning is reciting the *Kaddish* prayer in memory of a parent who has died. Often thought of as a prayer for the dead, the *Kaddish* is actually a tribute that honors and glorifies God, with no mention at all of death. One of the oldest prayers in the prayer book, the *Kaddish* is still recited in Aramaic, the popular language of Jews in ancient times. Although not originally a prayer for mourners, through the ages it has become an emotional symbol of grief and acceptance, shared by all people who have suffered a close loss. The obligation to say *Kaddish* after the death of a parent rests on men only, but many women, like the learned philanthropist Henrietta Szold, have insisted on reciting it also.

> Formerly, they used to bring food to the house of mourning, rich people in baskets of silver and gold, poor people in baskets of willow twigs; and the poor felt ashamed. Therefore, a law was passed that everybody should use baskets of willow twigs, out of deference to the poor. . . .
>
> Formerly, they used to serve drinks in a house of mourning, the rich serving in white glasses and the poor in colored glasses [which were much less expensive]; and the poor felt ashamed. Therefore, a law was passed that everybody should serve drinks in colored glasses in deference to the poor. . . .
>
> Formerly, they used to bring out the deceased for burial, the rich on a tall bed, ornamented with rich covers,

the poor on a plain box; and the poor felt ashamed. Therefore, a law was passed that all should be brought out on a plain box, in deference to the poor. . . .

Formerly, the expense of burying the dead was harder for a family to bear than the death itself, so that sometimes family members fled to escape the expense. This was so until Rabban Gamaliel ordered that he be buried in a plain linen shroud instead of expensive garments. And since then people have buried their dead in simple shrouds. . . .

—Babylonian Talmud, tractate
Mo'ed Katan, pages 27a–27b

The *hesped* [funeral oration], an ancient Biblical institution, . . . seeks, first of all, to make people weep. "*Agra de-hespeda daluye*—the merit of a funeral oration is in raising the voice." The *halakhah* did not like to see the dead interred in silent indifference. It wanted to hear the shriek of despair and to see the hot tear washing away human cruelty and toughness. "And Abraham came to mourn for Sarah and to weep for her." To mourn, to feel a great sorrow, to be of a distressed mind when confronted with death is, according to the *halakhah*, a cathartic experience. It reminds proud, vain and egotistical man of a frightening reality which we all like to forget —namely, the reality of death. It is true, of course, that Judaism has never been death-centered, that it never tried to motivate the religious activity of man by having him encounter death. In fact, the reverse is the case. . . . Nevertheless, to have man recall what he has been trying hard to forget is redeeming and cleansing; the whole *halakhic* structure of *avelut* [mourning] rests upon this assumption.

—Joseph B. Soloveitchik, from a
eulogy delivered for the Talne
Rebbitzen Rebecca Twersky,
January 30, 1977

Mourners recite the Kaddish *at the burial and for eleven months after the death of a parent at daily, Sabbath, and festival services.*

Glorified and sanctified be God's great name throughout the world which He has created according to His will. May He establish His kingdom in your lifetime and during your days, and within the life of the entire house of Israel, speedily and soon; and say, Amen.

May His great name be blessed forever and to all eternity.

Blessed and praised, glorified and exalted, extolled and honored, adored and lauded be the name of the Holy One, blessed be He, whose glory is beyond all the blessings and hymns, praises and consolations that are ever spoken in the world; and say, Amen.

May there be abundant peace from heaven and life, for us and for all Israel; and say, Amen.

He who creates peace in His high places, may He create peace for us and for all Israel; and say, Amen.

—*Kaddish*

It is impossible for me to find words in which to tell you how deeply I was touched by your offer to act as "*Kaddish*" for my dear mother. I cannot even thank you—it is something that goes beyond thanks. It is beautiful, what you have offered to do—I shall never forget it.

You will wonder, then, that I cannot accept your offer. Perhaps it would be best for me not to try to explain to you in writing, but to wait until I see you to tell you why it is so. I know well, and appreciate what you say about, the Jewish custom; and Jewish custom is very dear and sacred to me. And yet I cannot ask you to say *Kaddish* after my mother. The *Kaddish* means to me that the survivor publicly and markedly manifests his wish and intention to assume the relation to the Jewish community

About eight years have since passed, but I am still mourning and unable to accept consolation. And how should I console myself? He grew up on my knees, he was my brother, he was my student; he traded on the markets, and earned, and I could safely sit at home. He was well versed in the Talmud and the Bible, and knew [Hebrew] grammar well, and my joy in life was to look at him. Now, all joy has gone. He has passed away and left me disturbed in my mind in a foreign country. Whenever I see his handwriting or one of his letters, my heart turns upside down and my grief awakens again. In short, "I shall go down to the nether world to my son in mourning" [Jacob's words in Genesis 37:35].

—Maimonides, from a letter to
Japhet ben Eliahu of Acco, 1176

It seems to me that the duty of comforting mourners takes precedence over the duty of visiting the sick, because comforting mourners is an act of benevolence toward the living and the dead.

—Maimonides, *Code*, "Laws
Concerning Mourning,"
chapter 14, section 7

When Rabban Johanan ben Zakkai's son died, his disciples came to comfort him. Rabbi Eliezer entered, sat down before him, and said to him, "Master, by your leave, may I say something to you?"

"Speak," he answered.

Rabbi Eliezer said, "Adam had a son who died, yet he allowed himself to be comforted concerning him. And how do we know that he allowed himself to be comforted concerning him? For it is said: 'Adam knew his wife again' (Genesis 4:25). You, too, should be comforted."

Said Rabban Johanan to him, "Is it not enough that I grieve over my own that you remind me of Adam's grief?"

Rabbi Joshua entered and said to him, "By your leave, may I say something to you?"

"Speak," he answered.

Rabbi Joshua said, "Job had sons and daughters, all of whom died in one day, and he allowed himself to be comforted for them. You, too, should be comforted. And how do we know that Job was comforted? For it is said: 'The Lord gave and the Lord has taken away; Blessed be the name of the Lord' " (Job 1:21).

Said Rabban Johanan to him, "Is it not enough that I grieve over my own that you remind me of the grief of Job?"

Rabbi Yose entered and sat down before him. He said to him, "Master, by your leave, may I say something to you?"

"Speak," he answered.

Rabbi Yose said, "Aaron had two grown sons, and both died on the same day, yet he allowed himself to be comforted for them, as it is said: 'And Aaron was silent' (Leviticus 10:3). Silence is no other than consolation. Therefore, you, too, should be comforted."

Said Rabban Johanan to him, "Is it not enough that I grieve over my own that you remind me of the grief of Aaron?" . . .

Rabbi Eleazar ben Arakh entered. As soon as Rabban Johanan saw him, he said to his servant, "Take my clothing and follow me to the bathhouse [a sign that his mourning was over], for he is a great man and I shall be unable to resist him."

Rabbi Eleazar entered, sat down before him, and said to him, "I will tell you a parable. To what may this be likened? To a man with whom the king deposited some object. Every single day the man would weep and cry out, saying, 'Woe is me. When shall I be quit of this trust in peace?'

"You, too, master, had a son: he studied the Torah, the Prophets, the Holy Writings; he studied Mishnah, Halakhah, and Aggadah; and he departed from this world without sin. And you should be comforted for having returned your trust unimpaired."

Said Rabban Johanan to him, "Rabbi Eleazar, my son, you have comforted me the way men should give comfort."

—*Fathers According to Rabbi Nathan*, chapter 14

This parable was written as a commentary on the verse "A good name is better than fragrant oil, and the day of death than the day of birth" (Ecclesiastes 7:1). According to tradition, King Solomon was the author of the book of Ecclesiastes, but biblical criticism dates its composition to a much later period.

When a person is born, everybody celebrates; when the person dies, everybody cries. But it should not be this way. When a person is born, there should be no rejoicing over him because nobody knows what will befall him and which way he'll turn—will he be a pious man or a wicked one; will he be good or evil?

When a person dies there is cause to rejoice if he departs with a good name and leaves the world in peace.

A parable can be drawn to two ships that sailed on a great sea, one leaving the harbor and the other entering it. Everybody cheered the ship that sailed out of the harbor, but nobody rejoiced over the ship that entered.

A shrewd man was there, and he said: "My view is just the opposite of yours. There is no reason to rejoice over the ship that is leaving the harbor because nobody knows what will be its fate, what seas and storms it may encounter. But everyone should cheer the ship that is entering the harbor because it left the seas peacefully and returned to the harbor safely."

And that is what Solomon meant when he said, "And the day of death [is better] than the day of birth."

—*Ecclesiastes Rabbah*, chapter 7, section 4

"Can I bring him back again?"

The general rule laid down for mourning was "three days for weeping, seven days for lamenting, and thirty days to refrain from cutting the hair and donning pressed clothes." Beyond that—although allowing a year of modified formal mourning for parents—the rabbis opposed obsessive mourning as dangerous to one's own health and that of other members of the family who may be neglected. King David set an example in his acceptance of the death of the son born to his beloved Bathsheba. The prophet Nathan had announced to David that the boy would die as punishment for David's having had Bathsheba's husband Uriah killed in battle.

Nathan went home, and the Lord afflicted the child that Uriah's wife had borne to David, and it became critically ill. David entreated God for the boy; David fasted, and he went in and spent the night lying on the ground.

The senior servants in his household tried to induce him to get up from the ground; but he refused, nor would he partake of food with them. On the seventh day the child died.

David's servants were afraid to tell David that the child was dead; for they said, "We spoke to him when the child was alive and he wouldn't listen to us! How can we tell him that the child is dead? He might do something terrible." When David saw his servants talking in whispers, David understood that the child was dead; David asked his servants, "Is the child dead?" "Yes," they replied.

Thereupon David rose from the ground; he bathed

and anointed himself, and he changed his clothes. He went into the House of the Lord and prostrated himself. Then he went home and asked for food, which they set before him and he ate.

His courtiers asked him, "Why have you acted in this manner? While the child was alive, you fasted and wept; but now that the child is dead, you rise and take food!" He replied, "While the child was still alive, I fasted and wept because I thought: 'Who knows? The Lord may have pity on me, and the child may live.' But now that he is dead, why should I fast? Can I bring him back again? I shall go to him, but he will never come back to me."

—II Samuel, chapter 12,
verses 15–23

Mourn for a few days, as propriety demands, and then take comfort for your grief.

For grief may lead to death, and a sorrowful heart saps the strength....

Do not abandon yourself to grief; put it from you and think of your own end.

Never forget, there is no return; you cannot help him and can only injure yourself.

Remember that his fate will also be yours: "Mine today and yours tomorrow."

When the dead is at rest, let his memory rest too; take comfort as soon as he has breathed his last.

—Wisdom of Ben Sira,
chapter 38, verses 17–18
and 20–23

A person who meets a mourner after a year and speaks words of consolation to him then, to what can he be compared?

To a physician who meets a person whose leg had been broken and healed, and says to him, "Let me break your leg again, and reset it, to convince you that my treatment was good."

—Rabbi Meir, in the Babylonian
Talmud, *Mo'ed Katan*, page 21b

Attaining eternal life

Although Jewish sages and philosophers speculated through the ages on the nature of eternal life after death, that belief never became systematized. Some theories held that after death, the soul hovers near the body for a while, and then is judged and sent off to be rewarded in heaven or purged in hell, which comprise the world to come. At some future time, the soul and body are reunited and resurrected into a life of eternal bliss. Others believed that the soul sleeps, waiting until the final judgment will occur in the messianic era, and then the resurrected body and soul will be ushered into the glories of the world to come. For some scholars, like Maimonides, the world to come is a world of pure spirit, where the soul, freed from the body, lives on eternally. In all the theories, the rewards of immortal life are not the material pleasures of life on earth but the spiritual joys of dwelling forever in the presence of God. And though some descriptions of the horrors of Hell can be found in medieval Jewish literature, most scholars viewed being deprived of the divine presence as punishment enough for the wicked.

What does a person have to do to merit life in the world to come? Everything depends on life here on earth. "Some people attain eternal life after many years, and some people in just an hour," Rabbi Judah the Prince was fond of saying. The future world of goodness is not only for saints but for all who, in some way, try to direct their lives toward it.

And many of those who sleep in the dusty earth shall awake, some to everlasting life, others to everlasting reproach and contempt. Then the knowledgeable shall shine like the brightness of the sky; those who justified the many, like the stars, forever and ever.

—Daniel, chapter 12,
verses 2–3

Oh, let Your dead revive!
Let corpses arise!
Awake and shout for joy,
You who dwell in the dust!—
For Your dew is like the dew on fresh growth;
You make the land of the shades come to life.

—Isaiah, chapter 26,
verse 19

Men cannot see God when they are alive, but they can see Him at their death.

—*Numbers Rabbah*,
chapter 14, section 22

The ones who were born are to die and the ones who have lived are to be brought to life again, and the ones who are brought to life are to be summoned to judgment....

For against your will are you formed, against your will are you born, against your will do you live, against your will die, and against your will shall you give account and reckoning before the King of King of Kings, the Holy One, blessed be He.

—Rabbi Eleazar ha-Kappar, in
Ethics of the Fathers,
chapter 4, paragraph 29

This world is like a foyer leading to the world to come. Prepare yourself in the foyer, so that you may enter into the inner chamber.

—Rabbi Jacob, in
Ethics of the Fathers,
chapter 4, paragraph 21

Richer is one hour of repentance and good works in this world than all of life of the world to come; and richer is one hour's calm of spirit in the world to come than all of life of this world.

—Rabbi Jacob, in
Ethics of the Fathers,
chapter 4, paragraph 22

When Rabban Johanan ben Zakkai was ill, his disciples visited him. When he saw them, he began to cry.

"Lamp of Israel, right-hand pillar, mighty hammer," they said to him. "Why do you weep?"

He answered, "If I were being led today before a human king, whose anger, if he were angry with me, would not be everlasting; whose prison, if he imprisoned me, would not hold me forever; who, if he sentenced me to death, would not sentence me to eternal death; and whom I can persuade with words and bribe with money, even so I would weep.

"And now I am being led before the King of Kings, the Holy One, blessed be He, who lives and endures forever and ever. If He is angry with me, His anger is everlasting. If He imprisons me, His prison will hold me forever. If He sentences me to death, it is to eternal death. And I cannot persuade Him with words nor bribe Him with money. And furthermore, two paths lie before me, one to the Garden of Eden and one to Gehinnom [Hell], and I do not know to which I will be taken.

"Should I then not weep?"

—Babylonian Talmud, tractate *Berakhot*, page 28b

In the world to come, there is neither eating nor drinking nor procreation nor business dealings nor jealousy nor hate nor competition.

But righteous men sit with their crowns on their heads and they enjoy the splendor of the Divine Presence.

—Rav, in the Babylonian Talmud, tractate *Berakhot*, page 17a

---

Maimonides elaborates on Rav's theory:

In the world to come, there are no bodies, but only the souls of the righteous alone, without bodies, like the angels. . . . Nothing occurs in the world to come which would involve bodies, such as sitting and standing, sleep and death, sadness and laughter. . . .

And what is the meaning of the sages' statement "they enjoy the splendor of the Divine Presence"? This means that the righteous attain to a knowledge and realization of the truth concerning God which they did not know in this world, while they were confined by a murky and lowly body.

—Maimonides, *Code*, "Laws Concerning Repentance," chapter 8, section 2

Afterlife is felt to be a reunion and all of life a preparation for it. The Talmud compares this world to a wedding. Said Rabbi Bunem, "If a man makes every preparation for a wedding feast but forgets to purchase a wedding ring, the marriage cannot take place." Similarly, a man may labor all his life, but if he forgets to acquire the means—to acquire the ring—the instrument of sanctifying himself to God, he will not be able to enter the life eternal.

Death may be the beginning of exaltation, an ultimate celebration, a reunion of the divine image with the divine source of being.

Dust returns to dust, while the image, the divine stake in man, is returned to the bundle of life.

Death is not sensed as a defeat but as a summation, an arrival, a conclusion.

—Abraham Joshuah Heschel, from "Reflections on Death," in *Conservative Judaism* (Fall 1973)

The Hasidic rabbi Elimelech of Lyzhansk said:

When I die and stand in the court of justice, they will ask me if I had been as just as I should have.

I will answer no.

Then they will ask me if I had been as charitable as I should have.

I will answer no.

Did I study as much as I should have?

Again, I will answer no.

Did I pray as much as I should have?

And this time, too, I will have to give the same answer.

Then the Supreme Judge will smile and say:

"Elimelech, you spoke the truth. For this alone you have a share in the world to come."

—Tale about Elimelech of Lyzhansk (1717–1787)

Bibliography

This bibliography includes ancient and modern sources from which passages in the book were taken. The early sources are listed by title and presented in chronological order. When a translation of a work has been used, it is indicated; otherwise, the places and publication dates given refer to Hebrew editions. Generally, English titles are used for works that have been translated into English or have become known by those titles. In most cases, when an English title is given, the Hebrew title appears in parentheses. Modern sources are presented in alphabetical order according to author. The listing includes both works cited in this book and sources for further reading and study.

Throughout the book, transliterations of names from Hebrew to English are based on the system followed by the *Encyclopaedia Judaica.*

Sources from ancient times through the nineteenth century

Hebrew Bible. Most of the biblical translations in this work are taken from translations in modern English published in Philadelphia by the Jewish Publication Society of America. These include *The Torah: The Five Books of Moses* (1962); *The Prophets: Nevi'im* (1978); *The Book of Psalms* (1972); and *The Five Megilloth and Jonah* (1969). When the text of the new translation was not appropriate to the context of a passage, the translation was taken from the Jewish Publication Society's classic translation, *The Holy Scriptures According to the Masoretic Text* (1917). Translations from the book of Job come from Robert Gordis, *The Book of God and Man: A Study of Job* (Chicago: The University of Chicago Press, 1965). Major commentaries on the Bible are found in Hebrew in *Mikra'ot Gedolot* (New York: Pardes Publishing House, 1951).

The Wisdom of Ben Sira or *Ecclesiasticus.* Translated in *The New English Bible with Apocrypha.* New York: Oxford University Press and Cambridge University Press, 1970. One of the books of the Apocrypha—collections of writings excluded from the canon of the Hebrew Bible—Ben Sira is made up of aphorisms, maxims, and poetic teachings. Its author, Simeon ben Jesus ben Sira, probably lived during the second century B.C.E.

Maccabees. Book I and *Book II.* Translated in *The New English Bible with Apocrypha.* New York: Oxford University Press and Cambridge University Press, 1970. Part of the Apocrypha, both books describe the revolt of Mattathias and his sons against Seleucid Greek rule in Palestine and the subsequent reign of the Hasmoneans, providing the origins for the story of Hanukkah.

Complete Works of Flavius Josephus. Translated by William Whiston. Grand Rapids: Kregel, 1970. The writings of Josephus, who lived during the first century, are a major source for the history of the Jews during the period of the Second Temple, and especially for knowledge about the last stand of the Zealots at Masada.

Mishnah. 6 vols. Jerusalem: Mosad Bialik; Tel Aviv: Dvir, 1958. First major codification of the oral law, edited by Rabbi Judah the Prince about 200 C.E. It is divided into six orders, or divisions, and these are subdivided into tractates. References are to tractate, chapter, and paragraph. The translations in this book are either original or adapted from a variety of sources. A standard modern translation is by Herbert Danby (Oxford: Clarendon Press, 1933).

Tosefta. Edited by Moses Samuel Zuckermandel. 3d ed. Jerusalem: Wahrmann, 1963. A collection of materials similar to those in the Mishnah that were not included in the codification of the Mishnah but still carry great authority. Arranged according to the order of the Mishnah, it is referred to by tractate, chapter, and paragraph.

Ethics of the Fathers (Pirke Avot). Part of the Mishnah, it is included toward the end of the fourth order, *Nezikin*, but has been reprinted often as a separate treatise. The English translations of most of the selections in this book come from Judah Goldin, *The Living Talmud: Wisdom of the Fathers* (New York: New American Library, 1957).

Jerusalem Talmud. 7 vols. Vilna: Romm, 1922. Compiled around the year 400, a hundred or so years before the completion of the Babylonian Talmud, it is smaller and less authoritative than the Babylonian. In spite of its name, the work was not compiled in Jerusalem but probably in Tiberias and Caesarea. It is often called the Palestinian Talmud. References to it are generally by tractate, chapter, and paragraph.

Babylonian Talmud. 20 vols. Vilna: Romm, 1895. Consists of the Mishnah and Gemara—expositions and interpretations of the Mishnah—and follows the order of the Mishnah. Because pagination is standardized in all editions of the Talmud, references are to tractate, page number, and side of page: "a" is the first side, "b" the second side. Translations of the Talmud in this volume are either original or adapted from the monumental Soncino translation prepared under the editorship of Isidore Epstein (London: The Soncino Press Limited, 1935-1950). The translations, especially of nonlegal discussions, legends, and anecdotes, have been written for clarity and understanding rather than as a literal word-for-word definition. A modern, critical edition of the Talmud in Hebrew with vocalized and punctuated texts, edited by Adin Steinsaltz, began publication in Israel in 1969. It is from this edition that the story of Jesus in Chapter Six is taken. Direct references to Jesus traditionally have been censored in many standard editions of the Talmud.

Minor Tractates of the Talmud: Derekh Erez Rabbah, Derekh Erez Zuta, and *Mourning (Semahot).* Although appended to the fourth order of the Talmud, *Nezikin,* in standard editions, these and other small tractates were compiled at a later period—probably between the seventh and ninth centuries. But they contain much material from talmudic times. *Derekh Erez Rabbah* and *Zuta* deal with matters of deportment and correct conduct; the tractate *Mourning* is concerned with laws relating to death, burial, and mourning. Translations of selections from that tractate in this book were taken from Dov Zlotnick, *The Tractate Mourning* (New Haven: Yale University Press, 1966).

The Fathers According to Rabbi Nathan (Avot de-Rabbi Nathan). Translated by Judah Goldin. New Haven: Yale University Press, 1955. Considered one of the minor tractates of the Talmud, it is a commentary on the *Ethics of the Fathers.* The work has come down to us in two versions: the one referred to here and most often quoted in the book is version A; the other, version B, has been translated by Anthony Saldarini (Leiden: E. J. Brill, 1975).

Mekhilta de-Rabbi Ishmael. 3 vols. Translated by Jacob Z. Lauterbach. Philadelphia: Jewish Publication Society, 1933. A *midrash*—interpretations and expositions—on the book of Exodus, much of it dating from the time of the *tannaim* in the first and second centuries. The work is divided into tractates according to subject matter. References are to tractates and chapters.

Sifra de-Vei Rav. Edited by Isaac Hirsch Weiss. Vienna: J. Schlossberg, 1862. A *halakhic* (legalistic) *midrash,* interpreting the book of Leviticus and containing much material from the time of the *tannaim.* Explanations and interpretations follow the format of Leviticus, chapter by chapter and verse by verse, and references in this book are to the chapter and verse interpreted.

Sifrei. A *halakhic midrash* interpreting the books of Numbers and Deuteronomy. Selections from the Sifrei on Deuteronomy are based on Louis Finkelstein and H. S. Horovitz, *Sifrei de-Vei Rav* (Berlin: 1939; reprinted, New York: Jewish Theological Seminary, 1969).

Midrash Rabbah. Vilna: Romm, 1921. Collections of homilies, sayings, and other *aggadic* (nonlegal) interpretations of the Pentateuch and the Five Scrolls (The Song of Songs, Ruth, Lamentations, Ecclesiastes, and Esther). Some of these works were probably edited in Palestine during the fifth and sixth centuries; others, during the eighth to tenth centuries. The translations in this book were either original or adapted from the Soncino translation prepared under the editorship of H. Freedman and M. Simon. 10 vols. (London: The Soncino Press Limited, 1948).

Tanhuma. A compilation of classical rabbinic homilies on the Pentateuch. Two editions are drawn on in the text: a standard one (Berlin: Horeb, 1927) and a different version edited by Solomon Buber in 1885 (Jerusalem, 1963–1964). References to the standard edition cite the book of the Bible interpreted, the portion, and the paragraph number. References to the Buber edition cite book, portion, and page number.

Pesikta Rabbati. 2 vols. Translated by William G. Braude. New Haven: Yale University Press, 1968. A collection of rabbinic sermons and homilies for festivals and special Sabbaths. References in this volume identify selections as part of a *Piska,* or section, as they are given by Braude, rather than using the more traditional identification by page number in the Hebrew edition published by Meir Friedmann (Vienna, 1880).

Midrash Samuel (Midrash Shemu'el). Edited by Solomon Buber. Cracow: Joseph Fischer, 1893. Expositions and interpretations of the prophetic book of Samuel.

Pirkei de-Rabbi Eliezer. Warsaw, 1852. Narratives built around stories in the Bible. Probably written in Palestine in the eighth century.

Yalkut Shimoni. Jerusalem, 1951. An anthology of rabbinic homilies and interpretations on the entire Bible.

She'iltot de Rav Ahai Gaon. Jerusalem: Mosad ha-Rav Kook, 1975. A collection of discourses and themes for sermons by Rabbi Aha (also known as Ahai) of Shabha, a leading scholar of the eighth century. It is the first book after the close of the Talmud to be attributed to an author.

Book of Doctrines and Beliefs. Saadiah Gaon. Abridged edition translated by Alexander Altmann. In *Three Jewish Philosophers*. Cleveland and New York: The World Publishing Company, 1960. Major philosophic work by one of the first great Jewish philosophers, written in 933.

An Elegant Composition Concerning Relief After Adversity. (Hibbur Yafeh min ha-Yeshu'ah). Nissim ben Jacob ben Nissim Ibn Shahin. Jerusalem: Mosad ha-Rav Kook, 1969. Folktales and stories collectd by Rabbi Nissim, an influential North African scholar of the first half of the eleventh century. An English translation was published by Yale University Press (New Haven, 1977).

Duties of the Heart. Bahya ben Joseph Ibn Paquda. 2 vols. Translated by Moses Hyamson. Jerusalem: Boy's Town, 1968. Highly influential ethical treatise by a Spanish moral philosopher of the eleventh century.

Commentary on the Torah. Rashi (Rabbi Solomon ben Isaac). In *Mikra'ot Gedolot*. New York: Pardes Publishing House, 1951. The best known and among the greatest of all commentaries. It has been translated into English by M. Rosenbaum and A. M. Silvermann, *Pentateuch with Targum Onkelos, Haftoroth, and Rashi's Commentary*. 5 vols. (New York: Hebrew Publishing Company, 1935). Rashi's commentary on the Talmud is printed in all editions of the Talmud.

Kuzari. Judah Halevi. Translated by H. Hirschfeld. Abridged edition with introduction by Isaac Heinemann. In *Three Jewish Philosophers*. Cleveland and New York: The World Publishing Company, 1960. Written in the first half of the twelfth century, this polemical philosophical work takes the form of a dialogue between a Jewish scholar and the king of the Khazars, in which the scholar explains the basic teachings of Judaism.

Chronicle of Solomon bar Simson. Translated by Shlomo Eidelberg. In *The Jews and the Crusaders: The Hebrew Chronicles of the First and Second Crusades*. Madison: The University of Wisconsin Press, 1977. A portrayal of the devastation of Jewish communities by the First Crusade, written about 1140.

The Code of Maimonides (Mishneh Torah). Book I, translated by Moses Hyamson. Jerusalem: Boy's Town, 1965. Books IV and V and XI through XIV, translated as part of the Yale Judaica series. New Haven: Yale University Press, 1949–1972. Each book of Maimonides's monumental code includes groups of laws pertaining to different subjects. The laws referred to in this anthology appear in the following books: Book I, *Book of Knowledge*: "Moral Dispositions and Ethical Conduct," "Basic Principles of the Torah," "The Study of Torah," and "Repentance." Book IV, *Book of Women*: "Marriage," "Divorce," and the "Wayward Woman." Book V, *Book of Holiness*: "Forbidden Intercourse." Book VII, *Book of Seeds*: "Gifts to the Poor." Book XI, *Book of Torts*: "Robbery and Lost Property" and "Murder and Preservation of Life." Book XII, *Book of Acquisitions*: "Neighbors." Book XIII, *Book of Civil Laws*: "Hiring." Book XIV, *Book of Judges*: "Sanhedrin," "Rebels," and "Kings and Wars."

Guide of the Perplexed. Moses Maimonides. Translation from the Arabic by Michael Friedlander. New York: Pardes Publishing House, 1946. Maimonides's great philosophic work, compiled around 1190.

The Preservation of Youth. Moses Maimonides. Translated from the Arabic by Hirsch L. Gordon. New York: Philosophical Library, 1958. Also known as the *Guide to Good Health*, this medical treatise was composed in 1198 for the sultan of Egypt, who suffered from bouts of depression.

"Thirteen Principles of the Faith." Moses Maimonides. Adapted from Maimonides's commentary to the Mishnah, this personal declaration of faith appears in most daily prayer books. The translation here comes from *The Authorized Daily Prayerbook*. Edited by Joseph H. Hertz (New York: Bloch Publishing Company, 1975).

Letters of Maimonides. The following letters are included in this volume: "Letter on Astrology." Translated by Ralph Lerner. In Ralph Lerner and Mahdi Muhsin, *Medieval Political Philosophy*. Glencoe, Ill.: The Free Press, 1963; "Letter to Samuel Ibn Tibbon." Translated by H. Adler. In *Miscellany of Hebrew Literature*. London, 1872; "Letter to Japhet ben Eliahu." In S. D. Goitein, *Letters of Medieval Jewish Traders*. Princeton, New Jersey: Princeton University Press, 1973; "Letter to Hasdai ha-Levi" and "Letter to Obadiah the Proselyte." In Franz Kobler, ed., *Letters of Jews Through the Ages*. vol. 1, 2d ed. New York: Hebrew Publishing Company, 1978.

Book of the Pious (Sefer Hasidim). Edited by Jehudah Wistinetzki. Frankfurt A.-M., 1924. Moralistic teachings of Germanic Jews of the twelfth and thirteenth centuries. Much of its contents has been attributed to Judah the Pious of Regensburg. Two versions of the book have come down to us: one based on an early edition printed in Bologna, and the other on a manuscript found in Parma. The numbering of sections used in this anthology follows the Parma version.

Fox Fables. Berechiah ben Natronai ha-Nakdan. Translated by Moses Hadas. In *Fables of a Jewish Aesop*. New York: Columbia University Press, 1967. Hebrew fables by the leading fabulist of the late twelfth and early thirteenth centuries.

The Holy Letter (Iggeret ha-Kodesh). Translated by Seymour J. Cohen. New York: Ktav Publishing House, 1976. Thirteenth-century treatise on marital sex usually attributed to Nahmanides (Rabbi Moses ben Nahman).

Commentary on the Torah. Nahmanides. In *Mikra'ot Gedolot.* New York: Pardes Publishing House, 1951. One of the major commentaries on the Bible. It has been translated by Charles B. Chavel. 5 vols. (New York: Shilo Publishing House, 1971–1976).

Sha'arei Teshuvah. Jonah ben Abraham Gerondi. Jerusalem, 1961. Both this and the following entry are classic moralistic works by a leading thirteenth-century Spanish rabbi.

Iggeret Teshuvah. Jonah ben Abraham Gerondi. Jerusalem, 1971.

Zohar. 3 vols. Vilna, 1894. The pivotal work of Jewish mysticism. Written mostly in Aramaic, it was probably composed by Moses de Leon at the end of the thirteenth century. References follow a standardized format of volume, weekly Torah reading portions, and page numbers based on the edition printed in Mantua, 1558–1560. Several of the translations in this book were taken from Harry Sperling and Maurice Simon, *The Zohar.* 5 vols. (London: The Soncino Press Limited, 1931–1934).

Tosafot. Collections of comments and interpretations of the Talmud, first written in France and Germany during the twelfth to the fourteenth centuries, many by students and descendants of Rashi. Comments of the tosafists are included in all standard editions of the Talmud.

Responsa. Legalistic questions and responses to them by rabbinic authorities in many lands. Following are the major responsa quoted in this book with the editions or translations used:

A Responsum of Rabbi Hai ben Sherira Gaon. In Franz Kobler, ed. *Letters of Jews Through the Ages.* vol. 1, 2d ed. New York: Hebrew Publishing Company, 1978.

Responsa of Rabbi Meir ben Baruch of Rothenburg. Translated by Irving Agus. In *Rabbi Meir of Rothenburg.* Philadelphia: Dropsie College for Hebrew and Cognate Learning, 1947.

Responsa of Rabbi Asher ben Jehiel. Zalkva, 1803.

Responsa of Rabbi Moses ben Isaac Alashkar. Jerusalem, 1959.

Responsa of Rabbi David ben Solomon Ibn Abi Zimra. Warsaw, 1882.

Responsa of Rabbi Solomon ben Jehiel Luria. Jerusalem, 1969.

Shevut Yaakov. Responsa of Rabbi Jacob ben Joseph Reischer. Lemberg, 1860–1861.

Noda bi-Yehudah. Responsa of Rabbi Ezekiel ben Judah Landau of Prague. New York, 1965–1966. The translation of the responsum on hunting comes from Solomon Freehof, *A Treasury of Responsa* (Philadelphia: Jewish Publication Society, 1963).

Hikekei Lev. Responsa of Rabbi Hayyim Palaggi. The translation of the responsum quoted is taken from *A Treasury of Responsa.*

Testaments and ethical wills. Medieval moralistic letters of instruction by fathers to their heirs. All the excerpts of ethical wills in this book come from Israel Abrahams, *Hebrew Ethical Wills* (Philadelphia: Jewish Publication Society, 1926).

Menorat ha-Maor. Israel ben Joseph Al-Nakawa. Edited by H.G. Enelow. New York: Bloch Publishing Company, 1932. A fourteenth-century compilation of moralistic and ethical teachings.

Shevet Yehudah. Solomon Ibn Verga. Jerusalem: Mosad Bialik, 1946–1947. Descriptions of sufferings and persecutions of Jews through the ages, compiled in the first half of the sixteenth century.

Code of Jewish Law (Shulhan Arukh). 10 vols. Joseph Caro. Vilna: Romm, 1911. Published in 1564, it still serves as the authoritative code for observant Jews throughout the world. Much of it is based on Maimonides's *Code* and other earlier works. The code is divided into four main sections: "Orah Hayyim," "Yoreh De'ah," "Even ha-Ezer," and "Hoshen Mishpat." All editions include glosses, or notes, by the Polish rabbi Moses Isserles.

The History of the Present Jews Throughout the World. Leon da Modena. Translated from the Italian by Simon Ockley. London, 1707. A description of Jewish customs and beliefs written about 1616.

Memoirs of Glueckel of Hameln. Translated by Marvin Lowenthal. New York: Harper and Brothers, 1932. Lively, insightful autobiography of a seventeenth-century German businesswoman and mother of twelve.

The Path of the Upright (Mesillat Yesharim). Moses Hayyim Luzzatto. Translated by Mordecai M. Kaplan. Philadelphia: Jewish Publication Society, 1948. Powerful eighteenth-century ethical work in the best tradition of the medieval moralists.

Kav ha-Yashar. Zevi Hirsch Koidonover. Vilna: Romm, 1888. An ethical work published in 1705, emphasizing the rewards of good and the punishments of evil.

An Autobiography. Solomon Maimon. New York: Schocken Books, 1947. First published in 1792–1793, and translated into English in 1888, it records the unorthodox views of this brilliant Polish-born philosopher.

The Nineteen Letters. Samson Raphael Hirsch. Jerusalem and New York: Feldheim Publishers, 1969. A defense of traditional Judaism, first published in 1836.

Condensed Code of Jewish Law (Kizzur Shulhan Arukh). Solomon Ganzfried. Translated by Hyman E. Goldin. New York: Hebrew Publishing Company, 1927. A popular handbook of religious laws based on the *Code* of Joseph Caro. First published in 1864.

Modern sources

Abrahams, Israel. *Jewish Life in the Middle Ages.* New York: Atheneum, 1973.

Ahad ha-Am (Asher Hirsch Ginsberg). *Essays, Letters, Memoirs.* Translated from the Hebrew and edited by Leon Simon. Oxford: East and West Library, 1946. Includes the essay "Between Two Opinions" quoted in Chapter Ten.

Bamberger, Bernard. *Proselytism in the Talmudic Period.* New York: Ktav Publishing House, 1968.

Baron, Salo W. *A Social and Religious History of the Jews.* 16 vols. New York: Columbia University Press, 1952 on.

Belkin, Samuel. *In His Image: The Jewish Philosophy of Man as Expressed in Rabbinic Tradition.* New York: Abelard-Schuman, 1960.

Berkovits, Eliezer. *Faith After the Holocaust.* New York: Ktav Publishing House, 1973.

Bialik, Hayyim Nahman; and Rawnitzki, Yehoshua Hana. *Sefer ha-Aggadah.* Tel Aviv: Dvir, 1934. Classic, highly useful anthology in Hebrew of rabbinic legends and homilies.

Bin Gorion, Emanuel, ed. *Mimekor Yisroel: Classical Jewish Folktales Collected by Micha Joseph Bin Gorion.* 3 vols. Bloomington, Ind.: Indiana University Press, 1976.

Bleich, J. David. *Contemporary Halakhic Problems.* New York: Ktav Publishing House, 1977. Much of the material here is based on articles by the author that appeared in the Orthodox journal *Tradition.*

Blidstein, Gerald. *Honor Thy Father and Mother.* New York: Ktav Publishing House, 1975.

Buber, Martin. *Eclipse of God: Studies in the Relation Between Religion and Philosophy.* New York: Harper & Row, 1952.

———. *I and Thou.* Translated by Walter Kaufmann. New York: Charles Scribner's Sons, 1970.

———. *Tales of the Hasidim: Early Masters.* New York: Schocken Books, 1947.

———. *Tales of the Hasidim: Later Masters.* New York: Schocken Books, 1948.

———. *Tales of Rabbi Nachman.* New York: Avon Books, 1970.

Cohen, Gerson D. "The Blessings of Assimilation in Jewish History." A commencement address at Hebrew Teachers College, 1966.

———. *Messianic Postures of Ashkenazim and Sephardim.* New York: Leo Baeck Institute, 1967.

———. "The Song of Songs and the Jewish Religious Mentality." In *The Canon and Masoreh of the Hebrew Bible*, edited by Sid Z. Lerman. New York: Ktav Publishing House, 1974.

Cohen, Jack S. "Halakhic Parameters of Truth." *Tradition* 16, no. 3 (Spring 1977): 83–97.

Cohen, Seymour S. "Judaism and the Worlds of Business and Labor." *Proceedings of the Rabbinical Assembly* 25 (1961): 17–44.

Cronbach, Abraham. "Social Thinking in the Sefer Hasidim." *Hebrew Union College Annual* 22 (1949): 1–147.

Daube, David. *Collaboration with Tyranny in Rabbinic Law.* New York: Oxford University Press, 1965.

Dimitrovsky, Haim, ed. *Exploring the Talmud. Vol. 1: Education.* New York: Ktav Publishing House, 1976.

Drake, Donald. "The Twins Decision." *Philadelphia Inquirer*, October 16, 1977. Story of Siamese twins given in Chapter Ten.

Elon, Menachem, ed. *The Principles of Jewish Law.* Jerusalem: Keter Publishing House, 1975.

Encyclopaedia Judaica. 16 vols. Jerusalem: Keter Publishing House, 1971. Modern comprehensive reference work with important scholarly articles.

Encyclopedia of Bioethics. 4 vols. Glencoe, Ill.: The Free Press, 1978. Viewpoints of various religious groups on such bioethical issues as abortion and euthanasia.

Epstein, Louis. *Sex Laws and Customs in Judaism*. New York: Ktav Publishing House, 1948.

Fackenheim, Emil L. *God's Presence in History*. New York: New York University Press, 1970.

Feinstein, Moses. *Igrot Moshe*. 2 vols. New York: Balshon, 1959.

Feldman, David. "Abortion and Ethics: The Rabbinic Viewpoint." *Conservative Judaism* 29, no. 4 (Summer 1975): 31–38.

———. *Marital Relations, Birth Control, and Abortion in Jewish Law*. New York: Schocken Books, 1974.

———. "The Scope of Tradition and Its Application." In *The Second Jewish Catalog*. Philadelphia: Jewish Publication Society, 1976.

Finkelstein, Louis. *Jewish Self-Government in the Middle Ages*. New York: Jewish Theological Seminary, 1924.

———, *The Pharisees*. 2 vols. 3d ed. Philadelphia: Jewish Publication Society, 1962. Basic to an understanding of talmudic teachings.

———, ed. *The Jews: Their History, Culture, and Religion*. 2 vols. 3d ed. New York: Harper & Row, 1960.

Fox, Marvin. *Modern Jewish Ethics*. Columbus, Ohio: Ohio State University Press, 1975.

Frank, Anne. *The Diary of a Young Girl*. New York: Pocket Books, 1972.

Frank, Shirley. "The Population Panic—Why Jewish Leaders Want Jewish Women To Be Fruitful and Multiply." *Lilith* 1, no. 4 (Fall/Winter 1977–1978): 12–17.

Freehof, Solomon B. *Reform Responsa for Our Time*. Cincinnati: Hebrew Union College Press, 1977.

———. *A Treasury of Responsa*. Philadelphia: Jewish Publication Society, 1963.

Freudenstein, Eric G. "Ecology and the Jewish Tradition." *Judaism* 19 (1970): 406–414.

Friedenwald, Harry. *The Jews in Medicine*. 2 vols. Baltimore: Johns Hopkins University Press, 1944. Basic source materials on Jewish physicians. Includes "Oath" of Amatus Lusitanus quoted in Chapter Five.

Gaster, Moses. *Ma'aseh Book*. 2 vols. Philadelphia: Jewish Publication Society, 1934. Collection of early legends and folktales.

Gendler, Everett E. "War and the Jewish Tradition." In *A Conflict of Loyalties,* edited by James Finn. Indianapolis: Bobbs-Merrill Company, 1968.

Ginzberg, Louis. *The Legends of the Jews*. 7 vols. Philadelphia: Jewish Publication Society, 1968. Classic translation of talmudic legends centered on the Bible.

———. *On Jewish Lore and Law*. Philadelphia: Jewish Publication Society, 1955.

Glatstein, Jacob; Knox, Israel; and Margoshes, Samuel. *Anthology of Holocaust Literature*. Philadelphia: Jewish Publication Society, 1973. Includes suicide letter of Samuel Zygelbojm quoted in Chapter Ten.

Glatzer, Nathan. *Franz Rosenzweig: His Life and Thought*. New York: Schocken Books, 1961.

Goldin, Judah, ed. *The Jewish Expression*. New York: Bantam Books, 1970.

Gordis, Robert. *Love & Sex: A Modern Jewish Perspective.* New York: Farrar, Straus & Giroux, 1978.

———. *Poets, Prophets, and Sages: Essays in Biblical Interpretation.* Bloomington, Ind.: Indiana University Press, 1971. Includes an excellent essay on the "wisdom" writers.

Green, Arthur. "A Contemporary Approach to Jewish Sexuality." In *The Second Jewish Catalog.* Philadelphia: Jewish Publication Society, 1976.

Greenberg, Moshe. "Some Postulates of Biblical Criminal Law." In *The Jewish Expression*, edited by Judah Goldin. New York: Bantam Books, 1970. Important essay on the differences between biblical law and other ancient law codes.

———. "Rabbinic Reflections on Defying Illegal Orders: Amasa, Abner, and Joab." *Judaism* 19 (1970): 30–37.

Greenberg, Simon. "And He Writes Her a Bill of Divorcement." *Conservative Judaism* 24, no. 3 (Spring 1970): 75–141.

Hauptman, Judith. "Women's Liberation in the Talmudic Period." *Conservative Judaism* 26, no. 4 (Summer 1972): 22–28.

Helfand, Jonathan I. "Ecology and the Jewish Tradition: A Postscript." *Judaism* 20 (1971): 330–335.

Herberg, Will. *Judaism and Modern Man.* Philadelphia: Jewish Publication Society, 1951.

Heschel, Abraham Joshua. *The Insecurity of Freedom.* New York: Farrar, Straus & Giroux, 1966. Includes the essays "To Grow in Wisdom" and "The Patient as a Person," which are quoted in this book.

———. *A Passion for Truth.* New York: Farrar, Straus & Giroux, 1973.

———. "Reflections on Death." *Conservative Judaism* 28, no. 1 (Fall 1973): 3–9.

———. *The Sabbath.* New York: Farrar, Straus & Giroux, 1951.

Horowitz, George. *The Spirit of Jewish Law.* New York: Central Book Company, 1953.

Hyman, Paula E. "The Other Half: Women in the Jewish Tradition." *Conservative Judaism* 26, no. 4 (Summer 1972): 14–21.

Israel Meir ha-Kohen. *Hafez Hayyim.* Jerusalem, 1972.

———. *Likutei Halakhot.* Piotrkow, 1909.

———. *The Love of Kindness (Ahavat Hesed).* Translated by Leonard Oschry. Jerusalem and New York: Feldheim Publishers, 1976.

Jacobs, Louis. "Greater Love Hath No Man . . . The Jewish Point of View of Self-Sacrifice." *Judaism* 6 (1957): 41–47.

———. *Jewish Law.* New York: Behrman House, 1968.

Jakobovits, Immanuel. *Jewish Medical Ethics.* New York: Bloch Publishing House, 1975.

The Jewish Encyclopedia. New York: Funk & Wagnalls Company, 1901–1907. The classic encyclopedia with many learned and still useful articles.

"Jewish Values in the Post-Holocaust Future: A Symposium." *Judaism* 16 (1967): 266–299.

The Jewish Woman: An Anthology. Special issue of *Response*, no. 18 (Summer 1973).

Kadushin, Max. *The Rabbinic Mind*. New York: Jewish Theological Seminary, 1938.

Kaplan, Mordecai M. *Judaism as a Civilization: Toward a Reconstruction of American Jewish Life*. New York: Reconstructionist Press, 1967.

Katz, Jacob. *Exclusiveness and Tolerance: Jewish-Gentile Relations in Medieval and Modern Times*. New York: Oxford University Press, 1961.

Kaufman, Yehezkel. *The Religion of Israel: From Its Beginnings to the Babylonian Exile*. Chicago: University of Chicago Press, 1960.

Kellner, Menachem Marc. *Contemporary Jewish Ethics*. New York: Sanhedrin Press, 1978.

Kimmelman, Reuven. "Non-Violence in the Talmud." *Judaism* 17 (1968): 316–334.

———. "The Rabbinic Ethics of Protest." *Judaism* 19 (1970): 38–58.

Klein, Isaac. *A Guide to Jewish Religious Practice*. New York: Jewish Theological Seminary, 1979.

———. *Responsa and Halakhic Studies*. New York: Ktav, 1975.

Kolitz, Zvi. "Yossel Rakover Speaks to God." In *The Tiger Beneath the Skin*. New York: Creative Age Press, 1947.

Lamm, Norman. "The Fifth Amendment and Its Equivalent in the Halakhah." *Judaism* 5 (1956): 53–59.

———. "The Fourth Amendment and Its Equivalent in the Halakhah." *Judaism* 16 (1967): 300–312.

———. "Judaism and the Modern Attitude Toward Homosexuality." In *Encyclopaedia Judaica Yearbook*. Jerusalem: Keter, 1974.

Lamm, Maurice. "After the War: Another Look at Pacifism and SCO." *Judaism* 20 (1971): 416–430.

———. *The Jewish Way in Death and Mourning*. New York: Jonathan David Publishers, 1969.

Lauterbach, Jacob Z. "Birth Control—A Responsum." *Central Conference of American Rabbis Yearbook* 37 (1927): 369–384.

———. *Rabbinic Essays*. Cincinnati: Hebrew Union College Press, 1957.

Lieberman, Sarah Roth. "When Justice Demands, Tradition Changes." *Sh'ma* 9, no. 164 (December 22, 1978): 29–30.

Lieberman, Saul. *Hellenism in Jewish Palestine*. New York: Jewish Theological Seminary, 1950.

Marcus, Jacob R. *The Jew in the Medieval World*. New York: Meridian Books, 1960.

Matt, Hershel J. "Sin, Crime, Sickness or Alternative Life Style? A Jewish Approach to Homosexuality." *Judaism* 27 (1978): 13–24.

Meisels, Zevi Hirsch. *Responsa M'kadeshe Hashem*. vol. 1 (in Hebrew). Chicago, 1955.

Mendele Mocher Seforim (Shalom Jacob Abramowitsch). "Matchmaking at a Fair." In *Fishke the Lame*, translated by Angelo S. Rappaport. London: Stanley Paul & Company, 1928.

Metzker, Isaac, ed. *A Bintel Brief*. New York: Ballantine Books, 1971.

Mintz, Jerome. *Legends of the Hasidim: An Introduction to Hasidic Culture and Oral Tradition in the New World*. Chicago: University of Chicago Press, 1968.

Neusner, Jacob, ed. *Understanding Rabbinic Judaism: From Talmudic to Modern Times*. New York: Ktav Publishing House, 1974.

Newman, Louis I., ed. *The Hasidic Anthology*. New York: Schocken Books, 1972.

Ozick, Cynthia. "The Jewish Half-Genius." A lecture given at the Institute for Judaism and Contemporary Jewish Thought at Bar-Ilan University. Printed in the *Jerusalem Post*, July 7, 1978.

Rackman, Emanuel. *One Man's Judaism*. New York: Philosophical Library, 1970.

———. "Violence and the Value of Life: The Halakhic View." In *Violence and Defense in the Jewish Experience*, edited by Salo W. Baron and George S. Wise. Philadelphia: Jewish Publication Society, 1977.

Reines, Chaim W. "The Self and the Other in Rabbinic Ethics." *Judaism* 2 (1953): 123–132.

Riemer, Jack, ed. *Jewish Reflections on Death*. New York: Schocken Books, 1974.

Rosner, Fred. *Modern Medicine and Jewish Law*. New York: Yeshiva University, 1972.

Roth, Sol. "The Morality of Revolution: A Jewish View." *Judaism* 20 (1971): 431–442.

Rubenstein, Richard L. *After Auschwitz*. Indianapolis: Bobbs-Merrill Company, 1966.

Samuel, Maurice. *The World of Sholom Aleichem*. New York: Alfred A. Knopf, 1943.

Schechter, Solomon. *Studies in Judaism*. 2d ser. Philadelphia: Jewish Publication Society, 1908.

Scholem, Gershom. *Major Trends in Jewish Mysticism*. New York: Schocken Books, 1954.

Schwartz, Leo W. *Great Ages and Ideas of the Jewish People*. New York: Random House, 1956. Analytic surveys of major periods in Jewish history.

Schwartzchild, Steven S. "The Question of Jewish Ethics Today." *Sh'ma* 7, no. 124 (December 24, 1976). This article aroused a great deal of discussion, which continued into many issues of the journal.

Sholom Aleichem (Shalom Rabinovitz). *The Old Country*. Translated by Julius and Frances Butwin. New York: Crown Publishers Inc., 1946. Collection of his stories, including "I'm Lucky—I'm an Orphan."

———. *Some Laughter, Some Tears*. Translated by Curt Leviant. New York: G.P. Putnam's Sons, 1968. Includes story "Boaz the Teacher."

Siegel, Seymour. *Conservative Judaism and Jewish Law*. New York: Rabbinical Assembly, 1977.

———. "Ethics and the Halakhah." *Conservative Judaism* 25, no. 3 (Spring 1971): 33–40.

Silberg, Moshe. *Talmudic Law and the Modern State*. Translated by Ben Zion Bokser; edited by Marvin S. Wiener. New York: Burning Bush Press, 1973.

Silver, Abba Hillel. *Where Judaism Differed*. New York: Macmillan Publishing Company, 1972.

Soloveitchik, Joseph B. "A Tribute to the Rebbitzen of Talne." *Tradition* 17, no. 2 (Spring 1978): 73–83. Eulogy for Rebecca Twersky delivered January 30, 1977.

Steinberg, Milton. *Basic Judaism*. New York: Harcourt, Brace & World, 1947.

Trachtenberg, Joshua. *Jewish Magic and Superstition*. Cleveland and New York: World Publishing Company, 1961.

Twersky, Isidore. "Some Aspects of the Jewish Attitude Toward the Welfare State." *Tradition* 5, no. 2 (Spring 1963): 137–158. Important essay on Jewish view of charity.

Vorspan, Albert. *Jewish Values and Social Crisis: A Casebook for Social Action*. New York: Union of American Hebrew Congregations, 1974.

Wiesel, Elie. *A Jew Today*. Translated from the French by Marion Wiesel. New York: Random House, 1978.

———. *Night*. Translated from the French by Stella Rodway. New York: Avon Books, 1969.

———. *Souls on Fire*. Translated from the French by Marion Wiesel. New York: Random House, 1972.

Zimmels, Hirsch J. *Magicians, Theologians, and Doctors*. New York: Feldheim Publishers, 1952.

Zimmerman, Sheldon. "Confronting the Halakhah on Military Service." *Judaism* 20 (1971): 204–212.

Index

About the Author

Francine Klagsbrun has written more than a dozen books for both adults and young people, among them *Married People: Staying Together in the Age of Divorce* and *Too Young To Die: Youth and Suicide*, and was the editor of the bestselling *Free To Be . . . You and Me.* Her articles have appeared in many national magazines, including *The New York Times Book Review, Newsweek*, and *Ms.*, and she lectures widely on family and social issues. She began her Jewish education in a Hebrew day school and continued at the Jewish Theological Seminary, where she was awarded a Bachelor of Hebrew Literature degree.

She is a member of the Publication Committee of the Jewish Publication Society and the Board of Governors of the Melton Research Center for Jewish Education and serves on the Professional Advisory Committee of the National Jewish Family Center of the American Jewish Committee. She lives in New York City with her husband and daughter.